Life and works of Sir Christopher Wren. From the Parentalia; or memoirs - Primary Source Edition

Christopher Wren, E H. 1871-1931.
illus New, Ernest J. Enthoven

LIFE AND WORKS OF SIR CHRISTOPHER WREN. FROM THE PARENTALIA OR MEMOIRS BY HIS SON CHRISTOPHER.

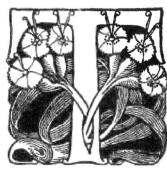HE EDITOR'S ACKNOWLEDGMENTS ARE DUE TO MESSRS. PHILIP NORMAN, F.S.A., AND G. H. BIRCH, F.S.A., FOR KIND ASSISTANCE TO MR. NEW IN THE PREPARATION OF HIS DRAWINGS. ALSO TO MR. WILLIAM NIVEN, F.S.A., FOR PERMISSION TO MAKE USE OF THE DRAWING OF ALLHALLOWS, BREAD STREET, IN HIS WORK ON WREN'S CHURCHES. (THIS CHURCH WAS DESTROYED MANY YEARS AGO.) THE DRAWING OF THE INTERIOR OF ST. STEPHEN'S, WALBROOK, SHOWS IT BEFORE THE RECENT RESTORATION.

THE EDITOR IS ALSO INDEBTED TO MESSRS. MACMILLAN & CO. AND MESSRS. R. AND R. CLARK OF EDINBURGH, FOR PERMISSION TO MAKE USE OF THEIR GREEK TYPE DESIGNED BY MR. SELWYN IMAGE.

PART I. SECTION I.
OF THE WORKS IN MATHE-MATICKS OF SIR CHRISTOPHER WREN.

SIR CHRISTOPHER WREN, the only son of Dr. Christopher Wren, Dean of Windsor, was born at East-Knoyle in Wiltshire, on the 20th day of October in the Year of our Lord 1632. His Mother was Mary Daughter and Heir of Mr. Robert Cox of Founthill in the same County.

His first Education in Classick Learning was (by reason of a tender Health) committed to the Care of a Domestick Tutor, the Rev. William Shepheard, M.A. excepting that for some short Time before his Admission in the University, he was placed under Dr. Busby at Westminster School.

In the Principles of Mathematicks, upon the early Appearance of an uncommon Genius, he was initiated by Dr. William Holder, before-mention'd; some Time Sub-Dean of the Royal Chapel; Canon-Residentiary of St. Paul's and Ely, &c. (This Gentleman was a great Virtuoso and a Person of many Accomplishments, fam'd for his wonderful Art, in making a young Gentleman named Alexander Popham, who was born deaf and dumb to speak: He wrote an ingenious Discourse of the Elements of Speech 1669: had good Skill in the Theoretick and Practical Parts of Musick; and published a Treatise of the 'Natural Grounds and Principles of Harmony,' 1694; and of the ancient Greek Musick. Also a Discourse concerning Time, 1712, with Application of the Natural Day, Lunar Month, and Solar Year, as Natural; & of such as are derived from them: as Artificial Parts of Time, for Measures in Civil and Common Use, for the better Understanding of the Julian Year and Calendar.) *Edit 3.*

At the Age of Thirteen, this young Mathematician had invented a new Astronomical Iustrument, of general Use, which (together with an Exercise in Physicis, De Ortu Fluminum, founded on some Hints, & Principles suggested by his Father,) he dedicated in this Manner,

REVERENDO PATRI DOMINO CHRISTOPHERO WREN, S.T.D. & D.W. CHRISTOPHERUS FILIUS HOC SUUM PAN-ORGANUM ASTRONOMICUM D.D. XIIIᵒ· Calend: Novem. Anᵒ· 1645.

Si licet, & cessent rerum (pater alme) tuarum
Pondera, devotæ respice prolis opus.

Hic ego sidereos tentavi pingere motus,
Coelicaque in modulos conciliare breves.
Quo (prolapsa diù) renoventur tempora gyro,
Seculaque, & menses, imparilesque dies.
Quomodo sol abeat, redeatque, & temperet annum,
Et (raptum contrà) grande perennet iter.
Cur nascens gracili, pleno orbe refulget adulta,
Cur gerat extinctas menstrua luna faces.
His ego numinibus dùm lito, atque ardua mundi
Scrutor, & arcanas conor inire vias,
Adsis O ! faveasque pater, succurre volanti
Suspensum implumis dirige prolis iter,
Nè malè, præcipiti, nimiùm prae viribus audax
(Sorte sub Icareâ) lapsus ab axe ruam:
Te duce, fert animus, studiis sublimibus hisce
Pasci, dùm superas detur adire domos.

Dedicatio, ad Patrem, *Tractatûs* De Ortu Fluminum.

Jurè accepta Tibi *refero mea* Flumina; *pulchrè*
Derivata suum respicit Unda *caput.*

About the same Time, he invented a Pneumatick Engine; the Description of which, with the Schemes, he thus introduced to his Father ;

Permitte mihi obsecro (Reverende Pater) prolusiones meas tuae semper paternitati vovere; & si arrideant quae olim in Physicis, De Ortu Fluminum: quaeque nuper in Opticis, nova tentavi; solitâ nunc etiam indulgentiâ, Pneumaticum Hoc (quod antè inter otia excogitavi, jamque ad incudem reduxi) excipias rogo.

He contrived also a peculiar Instrument of Use in Gnomonicks, which He explained in a Treatise, intitled Scioteri con Catholicum: the Use & propos'd End of which, was the Solution of this Problem, viz. "On a "known Plane, in a known Elevation, to describe such Lines with the "expedite turning of Rundles to certain Divisions, as by the Shadow of "the Style may shew the equal Hours of the Day."
In the Year 1646, and Fourteenth of his Age, Mr. Wren was admitted a Gentleman-Commoner at Wadham College, in the University of Oxford; where he soon attracted the Friendship, & Esteem of the two most celebrated Virtuosi, and Mathematicians of their Time, Dr. John Wilkins, Warden of Wadham, (afterwards Bishop of Chester) and Dr. Seth Ward, Savilian Professor of Astronomy, (afterwards Bishop of Sarum ;) which continued with Intimacy and Affection during their Lives. By the Means of Dr. Wilkins, who was Chaplain to his Royal Highness

Charles Elector Palatine, while resident in England, he had the Honour to be introduced to the Acquaintance and Favour of that Prince, a great Lover and Encourager of Mathematicks, and useful Experiments.
There is extant an Epistle to his Royal Highness, introductive of a Present to Him on those Subjects, which is here inserted from the first rough Draught.

To his Most Illustrious Highness CHARLES, *Prince Elector Palatine of the Rhine, &c.*

Most Illustrious Prince,
When of old a Votive-Table was hung up to some Deity or Hero, a few small Characters, modestly obscuring themselves in some shady Corner of the Piece (as yet the modern Custom is) were never prohibited from revealing the poor Artist, and rendering him somewhat a Sharer in the Devotion: Indeed I was almost prompted to such a Presumption, out of my own Zeal to a Prince, so much *mercurialium custos virorum*, but the learned Votary who consecrates these Tables to your Highness (being one who suffers me to be a most addicted Client of his) civilly obstetricated my Affection to your Highness, by adding his Commands to me to tender this Oblation: And had not my too indulgent Patron by undeservedly thinking them not unfit for his own presenting, (tho' exceedingly beneath your Highness's Acceptance) robb'd me of my Humility, and taken away the extreme low Thoughts I should otherwise have had of them, I must needs have called the first Device, but a rustick Thing concerning Agriculture only,* and therefore an illiberal Art, tending only to the saving of Corn, improper in that glorious prodigal Soil of your's where every Shower of Hail must necessarily press from the Hills even Torrents of Wine. The other Conceipt I must have deplor'd as a tardy Invention, impertinently now coming into the World, after the Divine German Art of Printing. Of the third Paper I cannot say any Thing too little, 'tis Extenuation enough to say that they are two Mites, two living Nothings, nay, but painted Nothings, the Shadow of Nothing; and this Shadow rarified too, even to forty thousand Times its former Extension; if it presents you with any Thing in Nature, 'tis but with a pair of Atoms. Now if it be possible for your Highness to force your self to accept such extreme Littlenesses as these, you will therein imitate the Divinity, which shews it self *maxime in minimis*, and preserve that Devotion towards your Highness, which I conceived while yet a Child,

Suppos'd Dr. Wilkins

* *A Planting-Instrument, which being drawn by a Horse over a Land ready plow'd and harrow'd shall plant Corn equally without Want and without Waste.*

b 2

3

when you was pleased to honour my Father's House by your Presence, for some Weeks,* who therefore must eternally retain a Sense of being

Your Highness's most humble and
most devoted Servant,

CHRISTOPHER WREN.

Of his Tract above mentioned, intitled 'Sciotericon,' and other Inventions, and Experiments, at the Age of Sixteen, relating to Gnomonicks, is a memorable complimental Account from an eminent Mathematician of that Time, as follows:

Spectatissime Juvenis,
Sciotericon tuum ΑΚΡΙΒΩΣ concinnatum, cursusque heliaci fidelem interpretem accepi equidem, & summâ lustravi cum voluptate; caeterum haereo, utrum artificis ingenium, an authoris munus magis congratuler; utrumque stupens demiror, deosculor; ubi Solis diurna conversio, atque accessu, decessuque annuo intra solstitiales terminos dimetitur; quin & ipsa coeli facies, & variegatae plagae uno intuitu contemplandae exponuntur. ΟΡΓΑΝΟΝ ΟΡΓΑΝΩΝ non alio delectu gaudens quam proprio, & si magneticae acus invento minus aequale, certè magis infallibile, quòd illud alienum superbiens ductum tuo subdis dictamini, & sine istius adminiculo veraci concilias concordiâ, jubesque (tuâ manu dimotâ) ad institutum tuum subsistere. Insuper non infra hujus solarii circulum tua admiranda compinguntur. In paternis aedibus solertiae tuae specimina, & limatae Philosophiae ΑΕΙΨΑΝΑ omnibus aulaeis anteferenda appenduntur; & pro re natâ, in cameris, in tricliniis, & per quascunque fenestras sol radios immittit, eos gnomonicorum subjicis regulis. Neque coelestis motus contrario dispositu (qualis inter analemma, & horologium solet dirigi) sed (retorti luminis beneficio) ipsissimi solaris circuitus projectione aemulâ. Ut sol de sphaerâ suâ deductus tanquam sponsus procedens de thalamo exultat ut gigas ad currendum viam. O te faelicem! qui ipsum Phoebum ante conspectum provehis. Quantam messem spondent haec tenuioris aetatis semina? Nec malè auguror te id genus studiorum ΤΑΜΕΙΑ, & Eleusinia ingressum, ad illorum delicias provehendas natum, terrasque adhuc in hoc globo incognitas tuâ disquisitionis clave adaperiendas; adeo in id nervos intendis tuos. Quodque vortat tibi faeliciter summoperè adprecor. Vale Mathematicorum ocelle, & ama

tui observantissimum,
THOMAS AYLESBURY.

De salutiferae passionis,
  10 April, 1649.

* *The Deanry-House at Windsor, which his Highness occasionally made use of for Retirement, and Benefit of the Air.*

At the Age of Sixteen, he contrived, and modelled on Pasteboard, illustrated with curious Astronomical Delineations in proper Colours, a new Hypothesis, entitled, 'Hypotyposis Prosthaphaereseⲱn Lunae, in quâ Circulationes ejus secundum Rationes Tyconianas, novâ hac Hypothesi exactè demonstrantur.' *Extat penes collectorem*

About the same Age, he translated into Latin, a Tract of Mr. Oughtred's Clavis Mathematicae, (clavis verè aurea) viz. of Geometrical Dialling; which that eminent and learned Mathematician published with his other Works, inserting this memorable Remark in his Preface.

Partem autem illam quae geometricam horologiorum sciotericorum rationem tradit, ex Anglico idiomate in Latinum vertit Dominus Christophorus Wren, Collegii Wadhamensis commensalis generosus, admirando prorsus ingenio juvenis, qui nondum sexdecim annos natus, Astronomiam, Gnomonicam, Staticam, Mechanicam, praeclaris inventis auxit; ab eoque tempore continuò augere pergit; & reverà is est a quo magna possum, neque frustrà prope diem expectare. *Oughtred Clavis Math. Praefatio. Oxoniae 1652. Edit. 3*

An Essay of his Skill in Gnomonicks, at that Age, was a very curious Reflecting-Dial, designed on the Cieling of a Room, with this Inscription embellished with divers Devises, particularly two Figures representing Astronomy, and Geometry, and their Attributes, artfully drawn with his Pen, viz.: *Extat penes collectorem*

Chr. Wren.
Angustis satagens his laquearibus
Ad coeli methodum tempora pingere
A Phoebo obtinuit luminis ut sui
Idaeam, speculo, linqueret aemulam,
Quae coelum hoc peragret luce vicariâ,
Cursusque effigiem fingeret annui;
Post annos Epochae——

VIrgIneo qVIbVs
Vere faCtVs hoMo est eX Vtero DeVs,
etatIsqVe sVae nVperae. *Scil. 1648 Ætat. suae, 16*

An early Proficiency in Learning and Mathematicks, may be further discerned by the following Specimens of some few of his Juvenile Studies, the 'Dawnings of a bright Day,' viz. An Epistle to his Father, informing him of the Friendship he had obtained of Dr. Scarborough, (afterwards Sir Charles Scarborough, a celebrated Physician, and Mathematician:) of his Invention of a Weather-Clock; and an Instrument to write in the Dark: Of a Treatise of Spherical Trigonometry, in a new Method; with an Epitome of the same, engraved on a small circular Brass Plate. Of his Proposal to translate Part of Mr. Oughtred's 'Clavis Mathema- *Æthero-criticon. See the poetical Description*

b 3

5

ticae of Geometrical Dialling,' and his epistle to the Reverend Author upon that Occasion.—To which are added some poetical Essays; one, particularly, to reform the Fables of the Zodiack.

Anno 1647. aetat. suae 15.

[Scil. Caroli Scarborough, M.D.]

DOctoris Clarissimi consortio (Reverende Pater,) suprà modum mihi amicissimi utor; nec dedignatur affabilis & humillimus vir, plurima quae in mathematicis multo cum plausu egit, meae (non dicam judicio) sed phantasiae ineptae subjicere, & quid sentiam lenissimâ aure attendere; saepè etiam imparibus meis ratiociniis inniti, dum ipse vicissim quicquid in Organicis, Mechanicisve pulchrum inveni, aut a te accepi, magnâ cum illius delectatione profero; quorum aliqua, ut ex aere, sibi suis fabrefieri impensis curarem, heri à me impetravit; Ætherocriticon scilicet; & Memoriale Cylindrum, cujus ope, noctu & in tenebris scribitur.

Extat in M.S.

Composui nuper Trigonometriae Tractatum, qui methodo novâ, totam, puto, Trigonometriae Sphaericae Theoriam, paucis quibusdam regulis brevissimè complectitur: *Cujus epitomen ipse rursus in rotulâ aeneâ,

Desideratur

Jacobi circiter Aurei magnitudine, descripsi; multumque in eâ, propriâ manu, arrepto artificis stylo sculpsi: Hâc visâ a doctore rotulâ, non acquievit donec sibi similem acquisierit. Extare nôsti in linguâ vernaculâ laudatissimum Oughtredi de Horologiographiâ Geometricâ tractatum, quem ut linguâ Romanâ vestiret, Doctorem [Scarborough] saepissimè (senio fatigatus) author rogaverat; Ille verò majoribus implicatus negotiis, in me laborem transtulit, Cui jam penè finem imposui: Epistolam quoque authori additurus, ut hoc modo, in magnum mei commodum, (talia promittente Doctore) Senis conciliem favorem simulque totius studiosorum in Mathesi chori, qui Oughtredum, quasi patrem & magistrum agnoscunt.

The Epistle abovementioned to the Rev. Mr. Oughtred, was in this Form.

Scil. Mathematicae

Venerabili Authori
CLAVIS verè Aureae;
Saeculi sui
(Si quis unquam ab Apollonio & Diophanto
Heroibus)
Magno Geometrae,
Æterno Oramento. S.

Tam appositè hoc nostrô aevô (vir ornatissime) effulsit, e mathematicarum artium sphaerâ, Clavis Tua, ut illam vel ipsi peritiores cynosuram fidelem agnoverint; nec immeritò, quum jam, tê duce, turbidum latumque algebrae oceanum, certô, tutôque remigiô exercent, ut reliqua illa Matheseos adhuc incognita paulatim detegant. Sed erant e trivio, lippi

6

quidam, qui Stellam Hanc Eximiam, tanquam obscuram & nebulosam culpabant, veluti scintillulas illas in coelo minores, quae licèt verè immensae sint & fulgidae, nec magnitudine nostro huic cedunt globo, imò nec caeteris forsan ejusdem chori, cum tamen vastissimâ sphaerae abysso lateant, nimiâ sublimitate suam adimunt gloriam, & vulgarem omnem effugiunt aciem. Optimè igitur auctiori operis tui splendori consulens, tam nostro quam Romano horizonti (in secundis editionibus) conspicuum magis efficisti Hoc pulcherrimum sidus: At tamen in Romano hemisphaerio, à faculâ illâ incomitatum apparuit, quae horologiographicam artem tam eleganter illustravit. Quocircà ut in digniori quoque linguâ clavi tuae (ut gemmae margarita pensilis) annexa prodeat, huic me rei, tenues conatus adhibere jussit clarissimus Doctor Scarborough; vir, cujus non ità tibi aliena est amicitia, non ità literatis ignotus est ingenii splendor, ut mihi necesse sit, Illum non minùs in medicinâ, & penitioribus harum artium adytis, quam omnimodâ ferè politiori literaturâ versatissimum dicere; cujus humanitati, & apertissimo genio, non minimum e tenui (si quem habeo) Matheseωs gustu debeo; imò cujus & arti vitam ipsam dum nuper morbo languescerem, quasi ΘΕΟΥ ΧΕΙΡΙ debeo. Parce igitur, vir optime, quod ex illius obsequio tantis nominibus sacro, in vestram peccarem gravitatem, dum pueri stylum tuis aptare scriptis connatus sum, quae verborum lenocinia non ambiunt, sed propriâ magis brevitate conspicua renident, brevitate, inquam, illa tam saturâ, sensuque ad apices usque literarum refertâ: merito enim in Clavi Tuâ, usitatum mortalibus, sed mysteriis ineptum, ratiocinium rejecisti, & symbolis, notisque, sine perplexâ verborum farragine, legentium animis uno ferè intuitu mirandos conceptus tuos inseris. Ardua sanè methodus, sed eò magis divina; hoc enim, ut mihi videtur, est caelites imitari, qui locutionis humanae morâ non impediti, reserando tantum animum mysteria invicem pandunt. Religiose igitur in hâc Horologiographiâ Tuâ verbum ferè verbô reddere connatus sum; (licet hanc fortasse quùm ad praxin magis pertineat, laxiùs uti decebat, aliquantò scripsisti) nempè verebar, ne inscitiâ meâ vel unus istius scientiae pereat apex, cujus ego me vel tyronem esse satis docilem, plurimum gloriae duco, & hoc summè ambio, ut (licèt adhuc ignotum) annumeres inter cultores tui observantissimos.

CHRISTOPHORUM WREN.

This famous Mathematician, Mr. William Oughtred, in his Preface abovenoted, to his 'Clavis Mathematicæ' where he had given a just Character of Mr. Christopher Wren, makes this Encomium on the incomparable Anatomist, Physician & Mathematician, Dr. Charles Scarborough, before-mentioned, viz.: Accessit & alter *hortator vehemens, dominus Carolus Scarborough, doctor mediciniae, suavissimis moribus,

Dr. Seth Ward

perspicatissimoque ingenio vir, cujus tanta est in mathesi solertia, & suprà fidem foelix tenaxque memoria, ut omnes Euclidis, Archimedis, aliorumque nonnullorum ex antiquis propositiones & demonstrationes recitare ordine, & in usum proferre potis sit.

Mr. Christopher Wren was an Assistant to the said Dr. Scarborough, in anatomical Preparations and Experiments, especially upon the Muscles of human Bodies, during their Studies at Oxford and elsewhere; and particularly he explained by Models formed on Pasteboards, the Anatomical Administration of all the Muscles of an human Body, as they naturally rise in Dissection, &c. for the Use of Dr. Scarborough's celebrated Lectures in the publick Theatre in Surgeon's-Hall. — These Models, by credible Report, were deposited in the said Theatre, and destroyed at the Fire of London. Hence came the first Introduction of Geometrical and Mechanical Speculations into Anatomy.

Zodiacus Reformatus.

Atria multiplici radiantia lumine coeli
Stellarumque sacros usus, quoscunque, vetusti
Vana superstitio foedè detorserat aevi,
Pangere fert animus. Tu, quem purissima vestit
Gloria circumdans, oculis impervia nostris,
Qui solo in numeros cogis vaga sidera nutu,
Mundi magne parens, regni coelestis origo,
Annue conanti, devotumque accipe carmen:
Nil mihi Castalio sapiunt de fonte liquores,
Nil mihi Pierides, & inania nomina Musae
Dulce sonant, tu solus ades, placidèque faveto,
Dùm tua facta canam, vastumque ingentis Olympi
Dùm populo modulabor opus, gens nescia veri
Ut fatuum, longâque animum caligine mersum
Attollat coelo, & flammantia lumina mundi
Dum stupet, authori solùm tibi ponat honores,
Codicis & sacri varios conformet ad usus.

  Hos ergò aethereos ignes sub nocte micantes,
Indigenas coeli, numerosumque agmen Olympi,
Nominibus, numerisque suis distinguere primi
Coepère Assyrii, studiis gens dedita sacris;
Hi solis, lunaeque vices, metasque vagantum
Stellarum, liquidasque vias inquirere docti
(Ne nimiùm confusa forent, quaerentibus astra,
Aut forsan coelo sua ne mensura deesset)
In species varias animantûm, & nomina certa
Disposuère; novis ornantes astra figuris.

8

Faelices animae! (primò ratione sagaci
Quae detexistis coeli secreta; docentes
Terrarum populos, in coeli limina certos
Ferre gradus; primasque suas agnoscere sedes;)
Non vos incuso (coeli prosapia!) quorum,
Nec caeca ambitio, nec lucri insana libido,
Fictorumque unquam veneratio stulta deorum,
Sublimes animos formis pellexerit istis,
Fallere mortales miseros; sed degener orbis,
Et fictis ludens, vatum fanatica turba,
Falsidici vates, temerant qui carmine verum,
(Spurca superstitio postquam possederat urbes
Niliacas, mentesque leves) inventa Parentûm
In nugas torsere suas, coeloque pudenda
Monstra intrusèrunt; nam quae non horreat auris
Pasiphaen Tauro junctam? Vaccaeque Tonantem?
Incestoque toros infandaque crimina divum,
Quaeque Thyestaeas absolvant fercula mensas?*   *Saturni
At licèt aeternae gens legis nescia, veri   scil. filios
Contemtrixque Dei, stolidè erravère poctae,   suos devo-
Haeccine adhuc decuit servari nomina stellis   rantis
Christicolas inter? Patriae coelestis alumnos
His decuit sedem maculis foedare futuram?
Cur nos alterius coelestia regna patere
Quam Veri Artificis, tacitè pateremur honori?
Cumque sub astrorum formis, celebrare poetae
Divorum soleant, praeclaraque gesta virorum,
Cur non fas nobis potius dispersa per orbem
Inclyta facta Dei canere, & miracula dextrae?
Immensam & quoties aulam stellantis Olympi
Suspicimus, sancto Scripturae à fonte petitis
Historiis, veteres astrorum aptare figuras.

Aries ♈

Hic mihi Zodiaci princeps, & janitor anni
(Quà secat Aequatrix obliquam linea zonam,
Et monet aequales cum lucibus esse tenebras,)
Dux gregis occurrit stellato vellere fulgens.
Hunc, quià Phryxum olim vexit, Phryxique sororem,
Trans mare, cum fugerent iram fraudemque novercae,
Jupiter in coelo (sic mendax fama) locavit:
At quonam hoc merito? Pecori debebat honores,
(Quòd profugi vector) tantos, ut ad aethera tollat?

9

Vah steriles nugae! quid enim haec deliria tanti?
Sed tu, quàm melius, fulgentia lumina coeli
Christicola aspiciens, feriis Paschalibus ortum
Cum Phoebo, Domini Paschalem dixeris Agnum?

*Gen. xxii.*13

  Ceu fuit ille Aries, Patriarchâ sacra parante,
Obtulit Isaaco qui se (vadis instar) ad aras;
Dignus ob hoc coeli nitidas augere figuras,
Quòd Christo, Christique typo se praestitit arrham.
Ipse (Rubo quasi adhuc latitans) vix cernitur illic
Ter sex exiguis ubi ducit sidera stellis:
Et, licet occiduum rapiatur pronus in orbem,
Flectit in ortivum remeantia lumina solem.

Taurus

Proxima Lanigero, roseum conversus ad ortum,
Lucida, procumbens, jactat sua sidera Taurus;
Sive sit Europae Cretaeas vector ad oras,
Infamisve tuô scelerato Taurus amore
Pasiphàe; nostrum non est aspergere tantis
Criminibus sacrum (multò minùs aethera) carmen.
Aut si peccantûm populorum crimina coelo
Inscribi fas sit, cur non hic jure legendus,

* Exod.
xxxii. 4

Aureus iste fuit vitulus,* cui turba rebellis
Isacidûm quondam (divino foedere rupto)
Montibus Horebi stolidos celebrabat honores:
At nunc subvectus coelo (memorabile signum
Foedifragae gentis) medio spectatur in orbe,
Ter denis de nocte micans, stellisque duabus;
Quarum quae dextro nitidissima splendet ocello

† Act. vii.
43

Stella dei Remphan Pharii† est, in cujus inanem
Descivit foedè cultum sine mente popellus,
Flevit & exilium meritò Babylonis in oris.
Apparent Hyades per frontem & cornua sparsae,
Et quae collustrant septenâ lampade dorsum;
Isacidûm lachrymae, scelerisque piacula tanti;
Jamque rigare solent effusis imbribus orbem,
Cùm primum madido Phoebum comitantur ab ortu,

‡ Hyades ab
'ναιυ *pluere*

Indicioque docent quâ sint ab origine natae,
Hactenus imbrifero Graüs cognomine dictae.‡

Gemini

Succedunt Tauro, Geminorum sidera, (Phoebi
Exurit Lybicas ubi scandens currus arenas;

10

Quaque novas secat aestates à vere Colurus;)
Haec erat (ut veterum commenta est fabula vatum)
Laedae progenies, & Cygni furta Tonantis,
Quorum promeruit, vitâque & morte vicissim
Divisâ, pietas coelum, aethereasque choreas:
Scilicet ex istis Pollux Jovis agnita proles,
Interitusque expers, mortali semine cretum
Alternàtim ornat, partito numine fratrem.
Nobile par fratrum; nisi nobis pagina foetam
Nobiliore pari, memorasset sacra Rebeccam;*   *Gen. xxv.
E quibus, Aeterno selectus Judice, Jacob,   21
Pro Polluce magis, pro Castore convenit Esau.
Votigenae fratres, dubiae discordia matris.
Pondera, primatumque ipso captantia partu;
(Dum pater Isaacus senior, sterilisque stupescit
Conjux, dividuo turgentia viscera foetu)
Nunc quoque sidereâ nudi spectantur arenâ,
Arcto stringentes luctantia pectora nexu;
Implicitumque jubar ter seno lumine vibrant.

Cancer

Fallor? An aequorci jam nactus brachia Cancri
Cynthius, assiduis nostrum fervoribus orbem
Torret, nocturnas vix admissurus habenas.
Hunc pede (non alio merito, vel origine) pressum
Alciden referunt coelo posuisse, quod illi
Forcipibus calcem, missus Junone, momordit;
Quin potius terrâ sineret periisse sepultum,
Quam coelo inscribi, quem vivum senserat hostem.
Siccine coelorum splendentia regna patere
Futilibus nugis patietur dia poesis?
At mihi priscorum ratio non displicet illa,
Qui Cancri speciem stellis donasse videntur,
Rursus in humentes, quià sol cùm pervenit illuc
Cancri more means retro, delabitur austros:
Visurus nunquam flammis propioribus arcton:
Cur non & nobis parili sub imagine, vates†   †I. Regum
Devius, & similis Cancro, dicatut ‡ Iadon?   XIII. 22
Quem jussi immemorem, (nimiùm dum credulus ori   ‡Joseph
Mendaci auscultans, tulerat vestigia retrò)   hoc nomine
A Domino immissi leto dedit ira leonis: appellatur
Hinc trux illa ferae propè stat frendentis imago,

Quà tribus atque decem (non multi luminis) ardet
Sideribus Cancer, (delusi emblema prophetae)
Ne tamen hic Geminos nimimum mireris Asellos,*
Quos mediâ Cancri cernis considere testa;
Hic deceptoris vector, vectorque prophetae
Alter decepti, juncto augent lumine sidus.

*Duae stel-
lae in signo
cancri sic
denominatae

Leo 🦁

Nè mirere trucem pecudes comitare Leonem,
Indomitamque feram veteres posuisse furores;
Pacificum, variâ sphaerae testudine, coelum
Ingeminare melos agnosce, modosque potentes,
Harmonicoque choros ducentia sidera gyro;
Attamen ingenitae nondum satis immemor irae,
Spirat adhuc ignes, & pectore flagrat anhelo,
Praecipuè tunc, cùm rabientem Syrius urget.
Hunc, sylvis olim Nemeaeis, vulnere clavae
Herculeae cecidisse ferunt, quem ad sidera Juno
Transtulit occisum, praeclara quinque minores
Praeter ter denas, accendens lampade flammas.
Quid tanti, haec? Majora cano (nec ficta) Leonem
Herculae plusquam prostratum robore dextrae;

†Judicum
xiv. 5, 6, 8

Scilicet hunc, imberbis adhuc quem† Sampsonis ira
Faucibus elisis, vasti nec vulnere trunci,
Sed manibus solùm jugulavit inermibus, Hyblae
Florileges aptam prebens cultoribus alvum.

‡Daniel vi.
16, 22, 23

Seu fuit ex illis unus, quorum ora‡ prophetes
Clausa specu medio intrepidus mulcebat, atroces
Quem stupuère ferae, nec jam discerpere pectus
Angelicis totidem plenum virtutibus ausae.

||Apocal.
v. 5.

Sitve emblema|| Leo sceptrum-gestantis Jüdae,
Quem fore Messiae stirpem, sobolisque futurum
Salviscae proavum, sancti cecinere prophetae.

Virgo 🌾

Quod si virgineis mansuescere velle leones
Sub manibus constet, praegressum Virgo Leonem
Non inconcinnè sequitur; quam supplice voto
Jam Vertumnus adit, gravidis oneratus aristis,
Frugibus ut benè sit, satagens, dum Virginis astra
Spiciferae refugum excipiunt Hyperionis axin.
Seu fuit illa Ceres, quae latè prospicit arvis

12

Frugiferis, avidi fortunans vota coloni:
Sive Isis totum furiis agitata per orbem,
De bove, jam Pharium numen: seu candida, sedem
Vendicet hanc potius, terras, Astraea, relinquens,
Ter denis ubi cincta micat, stellisque duabus.
　　At mihi, prae reliquis, placet, haec illustria coeli,
Virginis eximias consignent, sidera, laudes
Jepthiadis; * castae primo quam flore juventae,
Intentam choreis, temerè devovit ad aras
Infaelix genitor, vittis nec tempora virgo
Funestis cingi, patriâ victrice, recusat.
Gloria foeminei sexus miranda; minorem
Ni faculam, multò majori lumine, obumbres
Tu genetrix, tu sponsa Dei, tu palmitis illa
Divini radix, virgo intemerata Maria;
Numinis afflatu solo, maris inscia, cujus
Sancta salutifero tumuerunt viscera foetu,
Illaesoque Deum peperisti virgine flore;
Tu sine pulchra tuae haec splendescant sidera laudi,
Et tremulis, prae se, vibrent tua nomina flammis,

* *Judicum*
xi. 30,
31, 34.

Libra ♎

At jam signiferi medio sub tramite circi,
Libra pari, lucis mensurans tempora, lance,
Cum tenebris, rigido nimios cum frigore soles,
Occurrens jactat bis quatuor astra novemque.
　　Virginis Astraeœ trutina est (sic fama poetis)
Quâ terrestris adhuc hominum discernere facta
Consuevit parili lancis libramine Virgo;
Jamque polo dominae pedibus subjecta (colurus
Signifero in partes quà sese dividit aequas)
Autumni à calido confinia seperat aestu;
Aetnaeumque deum, siculis qui praesidet antris,
Artificem agnoscit, puro nam cuderat auro,
Fabrilisque sui monumentum insigne laboris
Sideribus Libram inseruit: Tu loripes astra
Splendida conflasti squallens? credamne, Cyclopûm
Fumosis coeli partem radiare favillis?
　　His consignetur potiùs sapientia stellis
Summa Creatoris, magnaeque potentia dextrae,
Quae regit immensum justo moderamine mundum,
Noctivagasque faces, quae dat sua lumina soli;

13

Aere quae medio libratam sistere molem
Telluris, pelagique jubet; vastumque capaci
Continet oceanum palmâ; spatiosaque coeli
Atria circumdat manibus; parilique supinos
Pondere suspendit montes, quae nubila fraenat;
Irrigat optatis sitientes imbribus agros;
Temperat & prudens structurae cuncta biformis,
Non secus ac justo pendens libramine lancis.

Scorpio ♏

Quae nova jam coeli facies? Quisve horridus annum
Declivem Boreas contristat, & asperat auras?
Scilicet auratas Phoebi jam tardat habenas
Scorpius, atque hebetes radios, gelidoque veneno
Lethiferi tinctos stimuli, vix sustinet ultrò
Extendi effaetis marcentia lumina terris.
Monstrum ingens late protendit brachia, caudae
Nigraque circuitu sinuat curvamina longo;
Undique bis denis, trinisque aspersa favillis;
Quas fertur posuisse Jovem, memorabile victi
Orionis signum; nam cum sua robora jactans
Omnia derisit, terraeque animalia sprevit;
Hoc monstrum objecit tellus irata, superbam
Saevo urinigenae domuit quod cuspide linguam.
    Si documenta viris temerè deducat ab astris
Vana superstitio, meliori emblemate nobis
Hoc placet inventum; mundi fabricator, olympo
Sidus hoc inferuit, discant ut ad aethera duros,
Difficilesque aditus, & vix penetrabile, sedes
Ad superas quod ducit iter; per monstra ferarum,
Scorpium & horrendum, dirâ qui cuspide caudae
Vulnerat in venas, subitum insinuatque venenum:
Haud aliter justos tenebrosi tortor averni
Subdolus infestat, sidum, Christique ministrum,
Undique inexpleto quaerit, quem devoret ore.
    Ite procul timidi, sacrâque absistite sede,
Queis fixus stat corde pavor, procul ite fugaces:
At vos heroes! Vos sancta in bella, piorum
Fortunata phalanx, Christo auctorata magistro;
Pergite magnanimi, fidoque umbone salutis
Muniti, sanctique armati flaminis ense.
Horrida inaccessum per monstra, per ardua, coelo
14

Quaerite iter; mundi transite obstacula; tandem
Eveniet tempus, quandò haec super astra dabuntur
Aeternae sedes, requies & certa laborum;
Quâ sanctas, nec telum hostile, neve aspidis ira,
Sollicitent animas, nec mortis causa, metusve,
Nec Satanae rabies; tuti gradiemini in atrum
Scorpium, & ardentes Erebi calcabitis angues,
Gaudentes Christi aeternos celebrare triumphos,
Altitonans postquam descenderit aethere Judex,
Carne triumphali victricia signa reportans:
Tunc mortem absorptam, tunc caeco carcere clausum
Luciferum, eniti frustrà cernetis, averni
Sulfureos nigris spumantem faucibus ignes.

Sagittarius ♐

Aspice ut intentus cursu venatur anhelo,
Stelliferasque plagas vasti perlustrat olympi
Arcitenens jaculis, in coeli monstra minaci
Missurus nervo volucrem, diramque Sagittam,
Et certo letum tibi, Scorpio, destinat ictu;
Jam pede sanato, jam saevâ tabe sagittae,
Herculeae lacerum miseratus Jupiter, astris
Chironem inseruit, dum morbo fractus atroci,
Et vitae impatiens miserae, crudelia saepè
Fata vocat, Parcas surdas, nimiumque morantes;
Jussus at Autumni humiferam jam claudere metam,
Sidere triceno decoratus splendet, & uno.
    Tantos Centaurus, pedibusque citatus equinis
Saturni incesti spurius meruisset honores,
Dedecus! impuro coelum ut contaminet Astro?
Planius & melius (nisi me sententia fallit)
*Ipse est aurato diademate tempora cinctus,   *Apocal.
Et niveo portatus equo, fortemque sagittis   vi. 2
Armatus dextram, (sic visio sacra) Johanni
Spectandum qui se dederat dilapsus Olympo.

Capricornus ♑

Jamque Magellanicas linquens Australibus oras
Flammis, auricomus nostrum meditatur ad orbem
Scandere paulatim Phoebus, tardeque morantem,
Lucibus extentis, cogit decrescere noctem,

Aegocerota intrans:

Pan deus, Arcadiae qui currere gaudet in altis
Montibus, hunc coelo ascivit, quòd fortè gigantes
Immanes fugiens, variis cùm quisque deorum
(Terrore anguipedum) formis laturère ferarum,
Ipse sub hirsuti velatus tegmine capri
Illusit rabidas hâc fraude Typhòeos iras,
Imposuitque sui stellis monumenta pericli.

Sunt quoque qui Capram, puerum quae lacte tonantem
. . . . Desunt caetera.

Alia tentamina poetica, stylo variato.
In Domini Natalem.

En qui supremâ luce prognatus, patris
Splendor coruscus gloriae; qui sydera
Fraenis cöercet, quem decemplex machina
Coeli pavescit, & tremunt fundamina
Mundi loquelis quassa fulminantibus;
In exoletâ nascitur jam infans casâ;
Hospes jumentis; brumae adustus frigore;
Dum mandra cunas praebet, & membris sacri
Culmus puelli gaudet agrestis premi;
Circumque floccis purae ab insolentibus
Nives tenelli provocantur pectoris;
An natus isto viliùs quis principe?
At ecce pennata hinc epheborum cohors
(Pompâ superbi major omni Caesaris)
Tantis ministrat sedula in natalibus;
Et non nocivo gloriae dum fulgure
Squallentis antri dissipat caliginem,
Dat nesciente splendidissimam diem
Sole, exuitque noctis obscurae peplum:
Nascentis illinc solis a cubilibus
Ducit sabaeos stella natalis sophos,
Qui purpurato provoluti poplite,
Illustri fulvi e ponderosis offerunt
Gazis metalli munus, & quicquid tulit
(Phoebi renascentis jubar fragantius
Experta) tellus, thuris & myrrhae ferax.
An natus isto ditius quis Paupere?
Cum Bethlemiacis, nato, in praesepibus, agnos
Offerrent agno rustica turba Dei.
16

Eximıı cepit species Corydona puelli,
Et qui divino fulsit in ore decor:
Arripuitque leves, (queis vincere suetus) avenas,
Talibus & laudes caepit ınire modis.
O nix! O niveo candor qui fronte relucet!
O niveo aspersum vellere molle caput!
O mitis tenero residet quae pectore bruma!
O manus! O purâ roscida colla nive!
Audiit hunc pendens, nivibus gravis, aere nubes,
Candoresne, inquit, neperit iste meos?
Nec plura, ıllimes dıffundit credula floccos
Coelo multiforae qua patuêre casae:
Sistıte cui Corydon, crudeles sistite plumae,
Membra nec audaci laedite sacra gelu;
Non vestri hic candor generis, nix ista calescit,
Nempe empyraeâ de regione venit.

De Pomo-Punico immenso, quod, strenae loco, Jani kalendis exhibuit
optimo viro amico suo charissimo E. F. Christophorus Regulus; cujus
in cortice erat fissura, ut solet, per quam grana apparuerunt, & circa cor-
ticem scriptus erat hic versiculus, literis aureis—

Natum est in titulos crescere rite tuos.

Accipe quae mitto (num dicam Punica?) dona;
Nescio quid falsı Punica dona sonent.
At nihil hic falsi, nil fucı; ni male forsan
Gentilem sapiant Punica Poma fidem.
Candidus hic amor est, & amici pectoris ardor,
Votaque ab officio scripta, dicata, pio.
Tot tibi faelices concedat Jupiter annos,
Tot tibi Nestoreos mitia fata dies;
Candida tot facılı surgant tibi sidera cursu
Grana quot extremo cortice tecta latent.
*Grana jacent intus positi velut ordine dentes,   *Scil. per
Sic oris speciem Punica Poma gerunt: fissuram
Os istud tibi, si gustes, mea vota loquetur,
Nempe potest proprio dulcius ore loqui.

Extract of a Letter written, as it seems, in the Year 1649, & 17th of his Age.

To my Reverend Father Doctor Wren.

Reverende Pater,

HUmanissimo summorum amicorum hospitio receptus ferias hasce pas-
catis transegi, & quantâ cum jucunditate, ex hoc brevissimo loci elogio
conjicere licet: Domus praeclara (vel potius palatium principe non in-
dignum, sive amplitudinem, seu fabricae pulchritudinem, seu supellec-
tilis splendorem (respicias summo paenè montis altissimi clivo insidet;
horti circumjacent amaenissimi, innumeris ambulacris referti, tam sab-
ulo quam cespite montano stratis: Nec desunt piscinae ingentes, nec luci
altissimi, quorum summitates, clamosissimae cornicum respublicae, ni-
dorum suorum pagis, seu potius civitatibus integris onerant: Vivarium
quoque adjacet satis amplum & amaenum; foris sane paradisum esse ter-
restrem, intus autem coelum ipsum dixeris, (& quidem verius quam de

Martial

Caesaris palatio poeta, " par coelo domus est at melior dominus.")
Quid ni enim beatissimum hunc locum. Coelum vocem? In quo prisca
pietas & religio terris fugatae sceleratis, latibulum hic tandem invenisse
dicantur, in quo virtutes omnes, non ut alibi saepe, degunt, sed hic inco-
lere amant; gratiaeque tergeminae (divinae scilicet) hunc sibi locum,
quasi Parnassum suum aut Pindum evangelicum elegerunt; Quo denique
matres sanctae, & virgines, cantica divina psallendo, aut orationum thura
castissima offerendo, aut sacra legendo, meditando, confabulando, diem
fere integram in beatissimo dei & angelorum consortio absumunt. Inter
tot delicias, tibi quod benè valeam scribere, quid erit nisi ΤΑΤΤΟΛΟΓΕΙΝ ?
Tantae faelicitati meae vix certè quicquam amplius desiderari potest,
modo valeas ipse, & benedicas

Filio tuo obsequentissimo,

CHRISTOPH. WREN.

5 Cal. April.

*Anony-
mous

Vide notas
MS. ad

At the Age of Nineteen he compos'd a short Algebraic Tract, relating
to the Julian Period, of great Use in Chronology; which was *inserted in
the Fifth Edition of Helvicus's 'Theatrum Historicum Chronologicum;'
after the Prolegomena. Printed at Oxford, Ann. 1651.
Opus hoc ΠΟΛΥΧΡΗΣΤΟΝ, dilucidum, & rebus chronologicis appositiss-
imum, (quo annus periodi Julianae è datis cyclis indagari, & erui docetur) editioni quinta Helvici assutum, ab Authore aegrè efflagitavit Ty-

18

pographus, utpote quod egregius ille juvenis annorum novendecim haud adeò dignum Helvici Theatro spectaculum verecundè censebat.—De quà re insuper hanc notam Pater ejus Reverendus memoriae tradidit.— "Deniqui Filio meo modesté renitenti incentivum adhibui, ut tractatu- "lum illum algebraicum Julianae periodi (è cyclis in historia datis) ex- "piscandae, accommodatissimum, sudante hoc praelo Oxoniensi, prefigi "sineret."

Helvici Theatrum Chrono- logicum, per Decanum Chr. Wren

In 1650 he proceeded Bachelor of Arts at Wadham College; in 1653, Master of Arts; and in the same Year was elected into a Fellowship of All Souls.
In 1657, he was chosen Professor of Astronomy in Gresham College in London; and in 1660, Savilian Professor of Astronomy in the University of Oxon, (upon the Resignation of Dr. Seth Ward, afterwards Bishop of Sarum). In 1661, he took his Degree of Doctor of Civil Law at Oxon; and was some Time after admitted to the same Degree at Cambridge. In 1680, he was elected President of the Royal Society.

[Christophorus Wren, A.M. collegii omnium animarum socius electus erat in professorem Astronomiae Savilianum in Academiâ Oxon. Feb. 5 1660, admissus 15 Maii sequentis. Doctoratum posteà in jure civili sus- cepit; & regiae majestati rei architectonicae procurator supremus, sive generalis, meritissimus audit.]

Hist. & Antiq. Univer. Oxon. Lib. II. p. 42

"Some Space after the Conclusion of the Civil Wars, Dr. Wilkins's "Lodging at Wadham-College in Oxford, was made the Place of Resort "for virtuous and learned Men, of Philosophical Minds, where the first "Meetings were held which laid the Foundation of the Royal Society "for improving of natural Knowledge: The principal and most constant "at the Assemblies were Dr. Seth Ward, the Bishop of Exeter, Mr. "Boyle, Dr. Wilkins, Dr. Wallis, Dr. Willis, Sir William Petty, Mr. "Matthew Wren*, Dr. Godard, Dr. Bathurst, Dr. Christopher Wren, "and Mr. Rook.
"Here they continued without any great Intermissions, till about the "Year 1658; but then being called away to several Parts of the Nation, "and the greatest Number of them coming to London, they usually "met at Gresham College, at the Wednesday's and Thursday's Lectures "of Dr. Wren (Professor of Astronomy) and Mr. Rook, (Professor of "Geometry). This Custom was observed once if not twice a Week, in "Term-Time; 'till they were scattered by the miserable Distractions of "that fatal Year, when the Continuance of their Meetings there might "have made them run the Hazard of the Fate of Archimedes: For then

Dr. Sprat's Hist. of the Royal Society

Eldest Son of Mat. Bishop of Ely

"the Place of their Meeting was made a Quarter for Soldiers. But upon
"the Restoration of the King, Philosophy had its Share in the Benefits
"of that glorious Action: For the Royal Society had its Beginning in
"the wonderful pacifick Year 1660, and as it began in that Time, when
"the Kingdom was freed from Confusion and Slavery; so in its Progress,
"its chief Aim hath been to redeem the Minds of Men from Obscurity,
"Uncertainty, and Bondage."

Preamble of a Charter to incorporate the Royal Society, [from a first
Essay, and rough Draught, by Mr. Christopher Wren.]

CHARLES, &c.

WHEREAS amongst our regal hereditary Titles (to which by divine
Providence, and the Loyalty of our good Subjects, We are now happily
restored) nothing appears to Us more august, or more suitable to our
pious Disposition, than that of Father of our Country, a Name of Indul-
gence as well as Dominion; wherein we would imitate the Benignity of
Heaven, which in the same Shower yields Thunder and Violets, and no
sooner shakes the Cedars, but dissolving the Clouds, drops Fatness. We
therefore, out of a paternal Care of our People, resolve, together with
those Laws which tend to the well Administration of Government, and
the People's Allegiance to us, inseparably to join the supreme Law of
Salus Populi, that Obedience may be manifestly not only the publick but
private Felicity of every Subject, and the great Concern of his Satisfac-
tions & Enjoyments in this Life.—The Way to so happy a Government,
we are sensible is in no Manner more facilitated than by the promoting
of useful Arts and Sciences, which, upon mature Inspection, are found to
be the Basis of civil Communities and free Governments, and which
gather Multitudes, by an Orphean Charm, into Cities, and connect them
in Companies; that so, by laying in a Stock, as it were, of several Arts, and
Methods of Industry, the whole Body may be supplied by a mutual
Commerce of each others peculiar Faculties; and consequently that the
various Miseries, and Toils of this frail Life, may, by as many various
Expedients, ready at Hand, be remedied, or alleviated; and Wealth and
Plenty diffused in just Proportion to every one's Industry, that is, to
every one's Deserts.
And there is no Question but the same Policy that founds a City, doth
nourish and increase it; since these mentioned Allurements to a Desire
of Cohabitation, do not only occasion Populosity of a Country, but render it more potent and wealthy than a more populous, but more barbar-

ous Nation; it being the same Thing, to add more Hands, or by the Assistance of Art to facilitate Labour, and bring it within the Power of the few.

Wherefore our Reason hath suggested to us, and our own Experience in our Travels in foreign Kingdoms and States, hath abundantly confirmed, that we prosecute effectually the Advancement of Natural Experimental Philosophy, especially those Parts of it which concern the Encrease of Commerce, by the Addition of useful Inventions tending to the Ease, Profit, or Health of our Subjects; which will best be accomplished, by a Company of ingenious and learned Persons, well qualified for this sort of Knowledge, to make it their principal Care and Study, and to be constituted a regular Society for this Purpose, endowed with all proper Privileges and Immunities.

Not that herein, we would withdraw the least Ray of our Influence from the present established Nurseries of good Literature, and Education, founded by the Piety of our Royal Ancestors, and others, to be the perpetual Fountains of Religion, and Laws; that Religion, and those Laws, which, as we are obliged to defend, so the holy Blood of our martyr'd Father hath inseparably endear'd to us; but, that we purpose to make further Provision for this Branch of Knowledge likewise, Natural Experimental Philosophy; which comprehends all that is required towards those Intentions we have recited; taking care in the first Place for Religion, so next, for the Riches and Ornament of our Kingdoms; as we wear an Imperial Crown, in which Flowers are alternately intermixed with the Ensigns of Christianity.

And whereas we are well informed, that a competent Number of Persons of eminent Learning, Ingenuity, and Honour, concording in their Inclinations and Studies towards this Employment, have for some Time, accustomed themselves to meet weekly, and orderly to confer about the hidden Causes of Things; with a Design to establish certain, and correct uncertain Theories in Philosophy; and by their Labours in the Disquisition of Nature, to approve themselves real Benefactors to Mankind: And, that they have already made a considerable Progress, by divers useful and remarkable Discoveries, Inventions, and Experiments, in the Improvement of Mathematicks, Mechanicks, Astronomy, Navigation, Physick, and Chymistry; we have determin'd to grant our Royal Favour, Patronage, and all due Encouragement, to this illustrious Assembly, and so beneficial and laudable an Enterprise. —Know therefore, &c.

A Catalogue of New Theories, Inventions, Experiments, & Mechanick Improvements, exhibited by Mr. Wren, at the first Assemblies at Wadham-College in Oxford, for Advancement of Natural and Experimental Knowledge, called then the New Philosophy: Some of which, on the Return of the publick Tranquillity, were improved and perfected, and with other useful Discoveries, communicated to the Royal-Society.

Ex autograph

Picture of the Pleiades.
Hypothesis of ♄ in Solid.
Hypothesis of the Moon's Libration, in Solid.
Illumination of the ☾ and Planets, in a dark Room.
A New Projection Goniscope.
New facile exact Ways of Observation.
To find whether the Earth moves.
The Weather-Wheel.
The Libra Expansionis Aeris.
Weather-Clock.
Perpetual Motion, or Weather-Wheel & Weather-Clock compounded.
The Ballance, to weigh without Weights.
Strainer of the Breath, to make the same Air serve in Respiration.
Artificial Eye, with the Humours truly and dioptically made.
The like Eye made with one Humour only.
To write in the Dark.
To write double by an Instrument.
A Scenographical Instrument, to survey at one Station.
A Perspective Box, to survey with it.
Several new Ways of graving and etching.
Many curious and new Ways of turning.
To weave many Ribbons at once with only turning a Wheel.

*See Museum of the R. S. Dr. Grew p. 371

Divers Improvements in the Art of Husbandry.*
Divers new Engines for raising of Water.
A Pavement harder, fairer, and cheaper than Marble.
To grind Glasses.
A Way of Imbroidery for Beds, Hangings, cheap and fair.
New Ways of Printing.
Pneumatick Engines.
New Designs tending to Strength, Convenience, & Beauty in Building.
Many new Designs in Sciography.
Divers new Musical Instruments.
A Speaking Organ, articulating Sounds.
New Ways of Sailing.

22

The best Ways for reckoning Time, Way, Longitude, and observing at
    Sea.
Probable Ways for making fresh Water at Sea.
Fabrick for a Vessel for War.
To build in the Sea, Forts, Moles, &c.
Inventions for better making and fortifying Havens, for clearing Sands,
    and to found at Sea.
To stay long under Water.
Ways of submarine Navigation.
Easier Ways of Whale-fishing.
New offensive, and defensive Engines.
Secure and speedier Ways of attacking Forts than by Approaches and
    Galleries.
New Ways of Intelligence, new Cyphers.
Some Inventions in Fortification.
To pierce a Rock in Mineing.
To purge or vomit, or alter the Mass by Injection into the Blood, by
    Plaisters, by various dressing a Fontanell.
Some Anatomical Experiments.
To Measure the Basis and Height of a Mountain, only by journeying
    over it.
To Measure the straight Distance, by travelling the winding Way.
A Compass to play in a Coach, or the Hand of the Rider.
To perfect Coaches for Ease, Strength and Lightness, &c.

§ In Automaton ΑΙΘΕΡΟΚΡΙΤΙΚΟΝ,

Chordâ Musicâ animatum,

Authore & Inventore Chr. Wren.

Grandior, Italici solito modulamine plectri,
Quae tremuit nuper, pollice tacta fides.*
Cum coelo tacitum servat nunc foedus, & ausu
Indicat aethereos, nobiliore, modos:
Quicquid vis gelidae regionis, in aëra nostrum
Imprimit, oblatâ machina fronte refert;
Sive leoninum,✝ rabies canis augeat, aestum;
Quo gravis exhaustum fervor hiulcat humum;
Sive sub hydrophoro situlum vertente, procellas
Depluat imbriferi roscida barba noti:

§ Cujus est
mentio suprà
in epistolâ
ad patrem
suum
* The great
Base Springs
of Viols
call'd Cat-
lings, be-
cause made
of Cats-
Guts
✝ Diebus
caniculari-
bus sole

Aërios quocunque modo, vaga sydera, tractus
Nutibus officiant, nocte, dieve, suis;
Sphaerarum studiosa fides discernit, & index
Impiger in scripto protinus orbe notat·
Tantane vis nervo est? Despectae viscera felis
Concinere aethereis sic potuisse choris?
An quae vis felis vivae [predicere nimbos‡]
Extinctae servant viscera sicca parem?
Quis neget harmonicis volvi coelestia gyris,
Ludere qui fidibus sydera & ipsa videt?

Mr. Henry Oldenburg, the first Secretary to the Royal Society, with Disingenuity, and Breach of Trust, communicated, and clandestinely convey'd into foreign Parts, particularly Germany and France, divers of the Inventions, and original Experiments of the Author; which were afterwards unfairly claim'd by others, as the true Inventors, and published abroad under other Names.

As the first Ideas and Essays of ingenious Minds, have their peculiar Weight, with the candid and judicious Virtuosi; the following Papers are here inserted, appearing to be the original Sketch, in an English Dress, of an Inauguration Speech, deliver'd by Mr Wren in Latin, at Gresham-College, from the Astronomy-Chair, upon his Election to that Professorship.‖ The Oration is extant, and may have a Place among his compleater Works: However the Extract subjoin'd, containing some Particulars omitted in his publick Speech, also divers Variations from it, and some Things (it may be) explanatory thereof, is of further Use or Entertainment to the Curious.

The Speech.

Looking with respectful Awe on this great and eminent Auditory, while here, I spy some of the politer Genii of our Age; here, some of our Patricians; there many choicely learned in the Mathematical Sciences, & everywhere, those that are more Judges than Auditors; I cannot, but with Juvenile Blushes, betray that which I must apologize for. And indeed I must seriously fear, lest I should appear immaturely covetous of Reputation, in daring to ascend the Chair of Astronomy, and to usurp that big Word of Demonstration, *Dico*, with which (while the humble Orator insinuates only) the imperious Mathematician commands Assent: When it would better have suited the Bashfulness of my Years, to have worn out more Lustra in a Pythagorean Silence.

I must confess I had never design'd any Thing further, than to exercise my Radius in private Dust, unless those had inveigh'd against my Sloth

24

and Remissness, with continual but friendly Exhortations, whom I may account the great Ornaments of Learning and our Nation, whom to obey is with me sacred, and who, with the Suffrages of the worthy Senators of this honourable City, had thrust me into the publick Sand. That according to my slender Abilities, I might explain what hath been delivr'd to us by Ancients, concerning the Motions and Appearances of the Celestial Bodies, and likewise what hath been found out of new by the Moderns; for we have no barren Age; and now in this Place, I could point to Inventors; Inventors, a Title so venerable of old, that it was Merit enough to confer on Men Patents of Divinity, and perpetual Adoration.

Nor need I therefore to so knowing an Auditory, relate to what End, or praise Hercules (as they say) by troubling you with a tedious Encomium of Astronomy: We shall leave this to the Dutch Writers, whose swelling Title-Pages proclaim that their Books are useful to Theologians, Philosophers, Philologers, Mathematicians, Grammarians, and who not? —It were frivolous to tell you, how much Astronomy elevates herself above other Sciences, in as much as her Subject, the beauteous Heavens (infinite in Extension, pure and subtile, and sempiternal in Matter, glorious in their starry Ornaments, of which every one affords various Cause of Admiration, most rapid, yet most regular, most harmonious in their Motions, in every Thing, to a wise Considerer, dreadful and majestick) doth precede either the low or the uncertain Subjects of other Sciences: It were pedantick, to tell you of the Affinity of our Souls to Heaven, of our erected Countenances, given us on purpose for Astronomical Speculations; or to acquaint you, that Plato commended it to his Commonwealth's-Men, while he says, "Ex ejusmodi disciplinis, instrumentum "quoddam animi expurgatur, reviviscitque, quod anteà ex aliis studiis "infectum, occaecatumque fuerat, solo enim hoc inspicitur veritas:" Tho' truly elsewhere he gives us this great Truth—"Animadvertisti eos, qui "naturâ mathematici sunt, ad omnes ferè disciplinas acutiores apparere; "qui autem ingenio hebetiores sunt, si in hoc erudiantur, etiamsi nihil "amplius utilitatis assequantur, seipsis tamen ingeniosiores effici solere." I might be too verbose should I instance this particularly in shewing how much the Mathematical Wits of this Age have excell'd the Ancients, (who pierc'd but to the Bark and Outside of Things) in handling particular Disquisitions of Nature, in clearing up History, and fixing Chronology: For, Mathematical Demonstrations being built upon the impregnable Foundations of Geometry and Arithmetick, are the only Truths, that can sink into the Mind of Man, void of all Uncertainty; & all other Discourses participate more or less of Truth, according as their Subjects are more or less capable of Mathematical Demonstration. Therefore, this rather than Logick is the great Organ Organon of all infallible Science; altho' I will not exclude Logick from being an Instrument of Reasoning, but rather include it in Geometry; for, the technical, & most useful Part of it, concerning Syllogism, and the Art of Reasoning, is but a geometrical Ordering the *data per media proportionalia* to determine the *quesitum*. It would be endless to run through the whole Encyclopaedy, & shew you in every Part the great Use of Astronomy; even Queen Theology hath been much beholding to the trusty Service of this *ancilla*, in settling the sacred History by the Help of Chronology, which as it is a Part of Astronomy, is built chiefly upon the unerring Chronicles of the *gesta superûm & coelorum*, Observations of Eclipses, great Conjunctions, and the like Appearances; without which Indexes of Times, all sacred and profane History were but indigested Heaps, and Labyrinths, where Men are at a Loss either to begin or end. But Chronology (a Thing too much neglected by the Ancients) hath given an Ichnography of this Labyrinth, and describ'd Times, as it were in a Map, by which we may run back secure to many Chyliads of Years, conversing with those of remote Ages, and there finding new Discoveries, as by Navigation we converse with those of distant Climates.

Some, it may be, will knit the Brow, if I should say, that even Holy-Scripture itself, sometimes requires an astronomical Interpreter; who else shall give a good Account of the Hexaemeron, or decide the Controversy about the Retrocession of the Shadow upon the Dial of Ahaz? When without a Miracle that might be many Ways done by the meer Fabrick of the Dial; for it is easy to frame a Dial with such a Stile, that every Day at such a Time, the Shadow shall seem to return; but what the Dial was, we know, if we believe the Hebrew Writer, who describes it obscurely, yet so that I can easily fancy it to be the same with that which the Eastern Nations used, and which Vitruvius tells us, Berosus Chaldaeus brought into Greece—*Hemicyclium excavatum ex quadrato, ad enclimaque succisum, hoc est, ad elevationem poli.*—The Retrocession must therefore be real, either in the Sun or Shadow only; but what if it were in neither truely, but from a Parelion? the Sun returned ten Degrees by which it had gone down; might not a Parelion suddenly appear at ten Degrees distance from the Sun, the Sun being just set under the Horizon, or being hid by a Cloud? (for, Parelions are Refractions made in nitrous Vapours higher than the Clouds) so the Shadow of this Parelion would make an Appearance as if the Sun had started back; 'tis what Cadamustus, and other Describers of the East Indies say, happens often in the Island Sumatra, in the month of April; for ten or fifteen Degrees the Sun seeming to start back, and then to return again, where otherwise he would have appear'd. This may be done either by a Parelion, or a strong Refraction through a Vapour in an angular form, like a Glass Prism, passing between the Eye and Sun; for, if you gently pass a Prism of Crystal before any Objects, the Objects will appear to start out of their Places.

26

Neither need we fear to diminish a Miracle by explaining it; this Retrocession of the Sun was given as a Sign, so was the Rainbow, which had it appear'd never since, had been miraculous.

I might ask the Theologian, who shall explain to me, how our Saviour, who was buried on Friday-Night, and rose again before Day on Sunday, could be said to be three Days and three Nights in the Sepulchre, when his Stay there was but a full Day and two Nights? The World hath hitherto shifted off this Difficulty with a Synedoche, by taking in Parts of Friday and Parts of Sunday, but yet they want a third Night; neither doth Grotius, with an Acceptation sometimes of any Part of a Day or Night, for a whole Nycthemeron, in the Civil Law, much mend the Matter: Here seems to be need of an Astronomer, who thus possibly may explain it.—While there was made by the Motion of the Sun, a Day and two Nights in the Hemisphere of Judaea, at the same Time in the contrary Hemisphere was made a Night and two Days; join these together, you have three Days and three Nights; for Christ suffer'd not for Judaea alone, but for the whole World, and in Respect of all the Inhabitants of the Earth conjunctim, he rested three Days and three Nights, tho' in Respect of Judaea, or any particular Horizon, but one Day and two Nights.

Who but the Astronomer shall explain to us how many hundred Times one of the great Luminaries exceeds the other, which yet is but one of some Thousands as great as itself, or bigger? Who can better magnify the Arm that expanded the Heavens, than he who tells you, that Seven thousand Miles will fall short of the Diameter of this Earth, and yet that this Diameter repeated a thousand Times will not reach the Sun; or this Distance between the Sun and us, repeated a thousand Times, reach the nearest fix'd Star? And yet in probability some are infinitely more remote than others.—Certainly as Secretaries of Princes are they only, from whom true Histories of those Princes are to be expected; so he only can truly describe the World, whose Skill in Astronomy hath given him right to the glorious Title of Hipparchus, to be *conciliorum naturae particeps & interpres.*

But not to inlarge in extending the Dition of Astronomy to the Empyraeum; her Influence is great over sublunary Sciences; among which, should I say that even Physick hath its use of Astronomy, I might seem to patronize the ungrounded Fancies of that Sort of astrological Medicasters, who do nothing without the Favour of their Archaeus, and intitle one Planet or other to every Herb, or Drug, which they suppose invalid, unless mystically tim'd with this or that Aspect; ceremoniously numbering the critical Days, not considering that neither Time or Number hath any reality *extra intellectum humanum.* But, tho' with Contempt of these Follies, let me seriously ask the most rational philosophical Enquirer into Medicine, whether those Aphorisms, wherein Hippocrates hath marshal'd Diseases under the Seasons of the Year, and the several Winds, and the Varieties of Weathers, have not as much of the Aphorism in them, as the rest; and were not as diligently collected from the Brasen-Tables, from Experiments deriv'd in Succession from his aged Preceptors before him, and from his own unerring Industry, as the rest? But it may be objected, that these astrological Aphorisms savour much of the Chaldean & Syrian, from whom it appears the Graecians receiv'd much of their Art of healing, as they did almost all their other Learning: And indeed we find by Herodotus, that the Knowledge of Physick by way of Aphorism was proper to the Babylonians, who recorded publickly the History of the Disease, and Method of Cure of every particular Patient that recover'd, to which Records others resorted in difficult Cases, that had the like Diseases, & the great Learning of these Nations being Astrology, we may imagine that they made good Observations of epidemical Diseases from the Distempers of the Air, from the coelestial Influxes, which are now either wholly lost, or deprav'd, or useless, as not suited to our Climate: What other Subject those medicinal Books of the Friend & Contemporary of Hippocrates, Democritus ΠΕΡΙ ΑΚΑΙΡΩΝ ΚΑΙ ΣΠΙΚΑΙΡΙΩΝ, reckon'd in the Catalogue of his Works by Laertius, should contain, I know not, sure I am, that if we dissected Animals of the same Species, in various Changes of Weather, we should find great difference in the Brain, as to Dryness or Moisture, and Weight; and in the Viscera, and Mass of Blood, as to the Quantity, and Salt in it: and in the Lymphaeductus, as to their Turgency, as I have frequently tried: And if with these, we join the Experiments of the Fermenting of Wines, and other Liquors against moist Weather; the souring of them in Thunder, and dry Weathers; adding likewise the History of Pests, and epidemical Diseases, we shall find a great Deal of Reason to conclude, that there is a true Astrology to be found by the enquiring Philosopher, which would be of admirable Use to Physick, though the Astrology vulgarly receiv'd, cannot but be thought extremely unreasonable and ridiculous, as any Thing among the many Impostures that have been impos'd by Antiquity upon the credulous World to him that hath given up himself to Demonstration.

Hitherto in these greater Faculties, Theology, sacred and profane History and Physick, we have been but assisted a little by Astronomy, but if we look into the next Class of Science, we shall perceive ourselves wholly indebted to her. It is Astronomy that enlarg'd both our Understanding and Habitation; hath given Politeness, and consequently Religion and Laws to the barbarous World. He that looks upon that little Parcel of the World, which the Ancients contented themselves with, and sees now, how we furrow the great Ocean, and gather our aromatick Harvests from

28

the remotest Parts of the Globe, and can enjoy in our own Europe, whatever Thule or Aethiopia, the rising or setting Sun can produce, must needs rejoice that so much larger an Inheritance is fallen to Mankind, by the Favour of Astronomy. It was Astronomy alone, that of old undertook to guide the creeping Ships of the Ancients, whenever they would venture to leave the Land to find a neighbour Shore; tho' then she was a humoursome Guide, and often vailing the Face of Heaven with Clouds, would cruelly leave them to the giddy Protection of Fortune, and for the most Part only toss'd them up and down, and sported herself with their Ruin: But if she deign'd to shew them one Glimpse of a Star, if but of Alcor, or the least albicant Spot of Heaven, it was enough to pave a Way for them homeward, through the Horror of the Waves & Night. In this is truly perceiv'd the Influx of Heaven, when the Influx of one Cynosura can move a thousand Sail of Fraught-Ships and render the one Element as habitable, and more fruitful than the other, tho' more hazardous. Thus did the Ancients every where cultivate the Mediterranean Waters, but their Fear of venturing into the Ocean they dissembled by Religion, lest they should violate the Rites of Thetis, and the Water Deities.

At Last, Astronomy took to herself another Assistant, Magneticks, a Kind of Terrestrial Astronomy, an Art that tells us the Motions of our own Star we dwell on, whose every Fragment moving in true Sympathy with the great One, bids us, in spite of Clouds, pass the vast Ocean, & possess every Piece of our own Star: and now were the Gates of true Science open'd, and the poor Philosophers Anaximander, Anaximenes, Leucippus, Empedocles are laugh'd at, for making the Earth a Pillar, or a Table, or a Drum, or inclin'd of its own Nature. In a few Months we shake Hands with the Antipodes, and pity the supposed heretical Bishop for his unseasonable venting the Truth; & also the pious Ignorance of the Fathers, that would have the Plane-Earth fixed upon infinite long Roots. But divine Astronomy, intended to discover to Man her own yet hidden Glory, as well as those of the Terrestrial Globe, for after the prodigious Attempt of Columbus, and as it appears to me, the difficulter Voyage of Vasco de Gama, who before pursu'd the weak Beginnings of Hanno the Carthaginian, and twice scour'd the Torrid Zone, in doubling the Cape, first finding it habitable, discovering the Errors of the Ancients about Africk, and first opening a Way to the Indies by Sea. By these, and succeeding Voyages, perform'd by the Circumnavigators of our Nation, the Earth was concluded to be truly globous, and equally habitable round. This gave occasion to Copernicus to guess why this Body of Earth of so apt a Figure for Motion, might not move among other Coelestial Bodies; it seem'd to him in the Consequences probable and apt to salve the Appearances, & finding it likewise among the antiquated Opinions, he resolved

29

upon this Occasion to restore Astronomy. And now the Learned begin to be warm, the Schools ring with this Dispute; all the mathematical Men admire the Hypothesis, for saving Nature a great deal of Labour, and the Expence of so many Intelligences for every Orb, and Epicycles; yet the apparent Absurdity of a moving Earth makes the Philosophers contemn it, tho' some of them taken with the Paradox, begin to observe Nature, and to dare to suppose some old Opinions false; and now began the first happy Appearance of Liberty to Philosophy, oppress'd by the Tyranny of the Greek and Roman Monarchies.

Among the honourable Assertors of this Liberty, I must reckon Gilbert, who having found an admirable Correspondence between his Terella, and the great Magnet of the Earth, thought, this Way, to determine this great Question, and spent his Studies and Estate upon this Enquiry, by which *obiter*, he found out many admirable magnetical Experiments: This Man would I have adored, not only as the sole Inventor of Magneticks, a new Science to be added to the Bulk of Learning, but as the Father of the new Philosophy; Cartesius being but a Builder upon his Experiments. This Person I should have commended to Posterity in a Statue, that the deserv'd Marble of Harvey might not stand to future Ages, without a Marble Companion of his own Profession. He kept Correspondence with the Lyncei Academici, at Rome, especially with Franciscus Sagredus, one of the Interlocutors in the Dialogues of Gallilæus, who labour'd to prove the Motion of the Earth, negatively, by taking off Objections, but Gilbert positively; the one hath given us an exact Account of the Motion of Gravity upon the Earth; the other of the secret, and more obscure Motion of Attraction and magnetical Direction in the Earth; the one I must reverence for giving Occasion to Kepler (as he himself confesses) of introducing Magneticks into the Motions of the Heavens, and consequently of building the elliptical Astronomy; the other of his perfecting the great Invention of Telescopes, to confirm this Astronomy; so that if one be the Brutus of Liberty restor'd to Philosophy, certainly the other must be the Collatinus.

And here I should not slightly mention that great foreign Wit, Kepler, the Compiler of another new Science, Dioptricks, (in which, of the Mathematicks only, we can boast that we had not the Graecians for our Masters) but more eminent for being the Eudoxus of this Age, the Inventor of the elliptical Hypothesis; but since he was only the first Founder of these magnalia, and that the Perfection of both these are justly to be expected from Men of our own Nation at this Day living, and known to most of this Auditory, the Clarity of these latter, makes me cease from a larger Encomium of Kepler, and reserve it for Posterity to bestow upon them, when it shall be more seasonable to give them an Apotheosis among those great Inventors I have named.

And indeed, of all the Arguments which the Learned of this inquisitive Age have busy'd themselves with, the Perfection of these two, Dioptricks, and the Elliptical Astronomy, seem most worthy our Enquiry: For natural Philosophy having of late been order'd into a geometrical Way of reasoning from ocular Experiment, that it might prove a real Science of Nature, not an Hypothesis of what Nature might be, the Perfection of Telescopes, and Microscopes, by which our Sense is so infinitely advanc'd, seems to be the only Way to penetrate into the most hidden Parts of Nature, and to make the most of the Creation.

I cannot (most worthy Auditors) but very much please myself in introducing Seneca, in his Prophecy of the new World,—

> Venient annis saecula seris,
> Quibus, oceanus vincula rerum
> Laxet, & ingens pateat tellus,
> Novosque Tiphys detegat orbes,
> Nec fit terris ultima Thule.

But then I only begin to value the Advantages of this Age in Learning before the former, when I fancy him continuing his Prophecy, & imagine how much the ancient laborious Enquirers would envy us, should he have sung to them, that a Time would come, when Men should be able to stretch out their Eyes as Snails do, & extend them to fifty feet in length; by which means, they should be able to discover Two thousand Times as many Stars as we can; and find the Galaxy to be Myriads of them; and every nebulous Star appearing as if it were the Firmament of some other World, at an incomprehensible Distance, bury'd in the vast Abyss of intermundious Vacuum: That they should see Saturn, a very Proteus, changing more admirably than our Moon, by the various Turnings, and Inumbrations of his several Bodies, & accompany'd besides with a Moon of his own; that they should find Jupiter to be an oval Earth, whose Night is enlighten'd by four several Moons, moving in various Swiftnesses, and making Multitudes of Eclipses: That they should see Mars, Venus, and Mercury to wax and wain: And of the Moon herself, that they should have a Prospect, as if they were hard by, discovering the Heighths and Shape of the Mountains, and Depths of round and uniform Vallies, the Shadows of the Mountains, the Figure of the Shores, describing Pictures of her, with more Accurateness, than we can our own Globe, and therein requiting the Moon for her own Labours, who to discover our Longitudes, by eclipsing the Sun, hath painted out the Countries upon our Globe, with the point of her conical Shadow, as with a Pencil. After all this, if we should have told them, how the very fountain of Light is variegated with its Faculae and Maculae, proceeding round in regular Motions, would not any of the Astronomers of his Time have chang'd their whole Life for a few windy Days, (in which principally the Solar spots appear) or a few clear Nights of our Saeculum.

But I have lost myself upon this Subject, as endless as the Universe itself: So large a Field of Philosophy is the very Contemplation of the Phases of the coelestial Bodies, that a true Description of the Body of Saturn only, were enough for the Life of one Astronomer; how much more the various Motions of them; which I am not now to descant on, but reserve for the continual Subject of my future Discourses in this Place, a Place, in which the Magnificence of our illustrious Founder Gresham hath adorn'd this opulent City, with the Profession of the Sciences, in his own House, by a rare Example, leaving the Muses to be here his Heirs and Successors for ever; who seem to be affected with the Place, having preserv'd it in Esteem, by furnishing it hitherto with Men of most eminent Abilities, especially in mathematical Sciences; among whom the Names of Gunter, Brerewood, Gillibrand, Foster, are fresh in the Mouths of all Mathematicians, for the excellent Remains they have either left behind them in Print, or adorn'd the Tables with, in reading. Amongst which, the useful Invention of Logarithms, as it was wholy a British Art, so here especially receiv'd great Additions: and likewise, the whole Doctrine of Magneticks, as it was of English Birth, so by the Professors of this Place was augmented by the first Invention and Observation of the Mutation of the magnetical Variation; a Thing, I confess, as yet crude, yet what may prove of Consequence in Philosophy, & of so great Use, possibly to the Navigator, that thereby we may attain the Knowledge of Longitudes, than which, former Industry hath hardly left any Thing more glorious to be aim'd at in Art.

And now since the Professorship I am honour'd with, is a Benefit I enjoy from this City, I cannot conclude without a good Omen to it. I must needs celebrate it as a City particularly favour'd by the Celestial Influences, a Pandora, on which each Planet hath contributed something; Saturn hath given it Diuturnity, and to reckon an earlier *Aera ab Urbe condita* than Rome itself. Jupiter hath made it the perpetual Seat of Kings, and of Courts of Justice, and fill'd it with inexhausted Wealth. Mars has arm'd it with Power. The Sun looks most benignly on it, for, what City in the World so vastly populous, doth yet enjoy so healthy an Air, so fertile a Soil? Venus hath given it a pleasant Situation, water'd by the most *amaene* River of Europe; and beautify'd with the external Splendor of Myriads of fine Buildings. Mercury hath nourish'd it in mechanical Arts and Trade, to be equal with any City in the World; nor hath forgotten to furnish it abundantly with liberal Sciences, amongst which I must congratulate this City, that I find in it so general a Relish of Mathematicks, and the *libera philosophia,* in such a Measure, as is hardly to be found in

32

the Academies themselves. Lastly, the Moon, the Lady of the Waters seems amorously to court this Place:

> "Atque urbem magis omnibus unam
> Posthabitâ coluisse Delo."

For to what City doth she invite the Ocean so far within Land as here? Communicating by the Thames whatever the Banks of Maragnon or Indus can produce, and at the Reflux warming the frigid Zones with our Cloth; and sometimes carrying and returning safe those Carines that have encompass'd the whole Globe. And now since Navigation brings with it both Wealth, Splendor, Politeness and Learning, what greater Happiness can I wish to the Londoners? Than that they may continually deserve to be deem'd as formerly, the great Navigators of the World; that they always may be, what the Tyrians first, and then the Rhodians were call'd, "The Masters of the Sea;" and that London may be an Alexandria, the establish'd Residence of Mathematical Arts.

<table>
<tr><td>Extracts from the Conclusion of the second Part of Dr. Sprat's History of the Royal Society, &c.</td><td>Sect. XL.
p. 311.
Lond. 1667</td></tr>
</table>

"IN the whole Progress of this Narration, I have been cautious to for-
"bear commending the Labours of any private Fellows of the Society.
"For this, I need not make any Apology to them: seeing that it would
"have been an inconsiderable Honour, to be prais'd by so mean a Writer:
"But now I must break this Law, in the particular Case of Dr. Christo-
"pher Wren: for doing so, I will not alledge the Excuse of my Friend-
"ship to him; though that perhaps were sufficient; and it might well be
"allow'd me to take this Occasion of publishing it: But I only do it, on
"the meer Consideration of Justice: For in turning over the Registers of
"the Society, I perceived that many excellent Things, whose first Inven-
"tion ought to be ascrib'd to him, were as casually omitted: This moves
"me to do him Right by himself, and to give this separate Account of
"his Endeavours, in promoting the Design of the Royal Society, in the
"small Time wherein he has had the Opportunity of attending it.
"The first Instance I shall mention, to which he may lay peculiar Claim, *Laws of*
"is the Doctrine of Motion, which is the most considerable of all others, *Motion*
"for establishing the first Principles of Philosophy, by geometrical De-
"monstration. This Descartes had before begun, having taken up some
"Experiments of this kind upon Conjecture, and made them the first
"Foundation of his whole System of Nature. But some of his Conclu-
"sions seeming very questionable, because they were only dervived from
"the gross Trials of Balls meeting one another at Tennis and Billiards,
"Dr. Wren produc'd before the Society, an Instrument to represent the

d 1

" Effects of all sorts of Impulses, made between two hard globous Bodies,
" either of equal, or of different Bigness and Swiftness, following or meet-
" ing each other, or the one moving, the other at rest. From these Varie-
" ties arose many unexpected Effects; of all which he demonstrated the
" true Theories, after they had been confirm'd by many hundreds of Ex-
" periments in that Instrument. These he propos'd as the Principles of
" all Demonstrations in natural Philosophy. Nor can it seem strange, that
" these Elements should be of such universal Use; if we consider that
" Generation, Corruption, Alteration, and all the Vicissitudes of Nature,
" are nothing else but the Effects arising from the meeting of little Bodies,
" of different Figures, Magnitudes and Velocities."

NEWTONI Philosophiae Naturalis Principia Mathem.
LEGES MOTUS.

.19

SCHOLIUM.

HActenus principia tradidida mathematicis recepta & experientiâ multiplici confirmata. Per leges duas primas & corollaria duo prima, Galil-
aeus invenit descensum gravium esse in duplicata ratione temporis, &
motum projectilium fieri in parabola conspirante experientiâ, nisi quat-
enus motus illi per aeris resistentiam aliquantulam retardantur. Ab iisdem legibus & crollariis pendent demonstrata de temporibus oscillanti-
um pendulorum, suffragante horologiorum experientiâ quotidiana. Ex
his iisdem & lege tertia Christophorus Wrennus eques auratus, Johannes
Wallisius S. T. D. & Christianus Hugenius, hujus aetatis geometrarum
facile principes, regulas congressuum & reflexionum duorum corporum
seorsim invenerunt, & eodem fere tempore cum Societate Regia com-
municarunt, inter se (quoad has leges) omnino conspirantes: & primus
quidem Wallisius, deinde Wrennus & Hugenius inventum prodiderunt.
Sed & veritas comprobata est a Wrenno coram Regia Societate per ex-
perimentum pendulorum: Quod etiam clarissimus Mariottus libro in-
tegro exponere mox dignatus est.
" The second Work which he has advanced, is the ' History of Seasons:'
" which will be of admirable Benefit to Mankind, if it shall be constantly
" pursued, and deriv'd down to Posterity. His Proposal therefore was, to
" comprehend a Diary of Wind, Weather, and other Conditions of the
" Air, as to Heat, Cold, and Weight; and also a general Description of
" the Year, whether contagious or healthful to Men or Beasts; with an
" Account of Epidemical Diseases, of Blasts, Mill-Dews, and other Ac-
" cidents, belonging to Grain, Cattle, Fish, Fowl, and Insects. And be-
" cause the Difficulty of a constant Observation of the Air, by Night and
" Day, seem'd invincible, he therefore devis'd a Clock* to be annex'd to

34

"a Weather-Cock, which mov'd a Rundle cover'd with Paper, upon *Musaeum of*
"which the Clock mov'd a black Lead Pencil, so that the Observer by *the Royal*
"the Traces of the Pencil on the Paper, might certainly conclude, what *Society,*
"Winds had blown in his Absence for twelve Hours space: After a like *Dr. Grew's*
"Manner he contriv'd a Thermometer to be its own Register: And be- *Catalogue*
"cause the usual Thermometers were not found to give a true Measure *p. 357*
"of the Extension of the Air, by Reason that the accidental Gravity of
"the Liquor, as it lay higher or lower in the Glass, weigh'd unequally on
"the Air, and gave it a farther Contraction or Extension, over and above
"that which was produced by Heat and Cold; therefore he invented a
"circular Thermometer, in which the Liquor occasions no Fallacy, but
"remains always in one Height, moving the whole Instrument like a
"Wheel on its Axis."
[In an Improvement of his Invention of the Weather-Wheel, (the only
true Way to measure Expansions of the Air) he contriv'd the Instrument
to be more firmly made, by causing the circular Pipes (which cannot be
truely blown in Glass) to be form'd of Brass, by those who make Trumpets and Sack-butts, who wiredraw their Pipes through a Hole to equal
them, and then filling them with melted Lead, turn them round into
what Flexures they please: The Inside of the Pipe he varnish'd with
China Varnish, to preserve it from the Quicksilver, and the Glass fix'd to
it, with Varnish; which is the best Cement in the World, for thus the
Chinese fix Glass and Mother of Pearl in their Works.]
To his Invention of the Weather-Clock, other Motions were afterwards
added by Mr. Robert Hook, Professor of Geometry in Gresham-College.
It hath six or seven Motions, first a Pendulum-Clock, which goes with
three quarters of a 100 lb. Weight, and moves the greatest Part of the
Work with this, a Barometer, a Thermometer, a Rain-Measure; such an
one as is next describ'd; a Weather-Cock; to which subserves a Piece of
Wheel-Work analogous to a Way-Wiser; and a Hygroscope; each of
which have their Register, and the Weather-Cock hath two; one for the
Points, the other for the Strength of the Wind. All working upon a Paper
falling off a Rowler which the Clock also turns.
Mr. Hook's Proposal for augmenting the Weather-Clock, was first offer'd
by him to the Royal-Society in the Year 1664, upon the Description of *Dr. Plot's*
one made by Sir Christopher Wren. [Waller's 'Life of Hook,' page XI.] *nat. Hist.*
The Instrument call'd the Thermometer, tho' of very ancient Invention, *of Oxford,*
there having been one of them found by Robert de Fluctibus graphic- *p. 229*
ally delineated in a M.S. of five hundred Years Antiquity at least; yet it
has still receiv'd other useful Advancements from that curious Artist Sir
Ch. Wren, by the Invention of the circular Thermometer.
"He contriv'd an ‡Instrument to measure the Quantities of Rain that *‡ In the*
"falls in any Space of Time, on any Piece of Ground, as suppose on one *Musaeum of*

"Acre in one Year; this, as soon as it is full, will pour out itself, and at "the Year's End discover how much Rain has fallen on such a space of "Land, or other hard Superficies, in order to the Theory of Vapours, "Rivers, Seas, &c." [A Triangular Tin Vessel hanging in a Frame, as a Bell, with one Angle lowermost. From whence one Side rises up perpendicular, the other sloaped; whereby the Water, as it fills, spreads only on one Side from the Centre, till at length it fills & empties itself. Which being done, a leaden Poise on the other Side, immediately pulls it back to fill again.]

"He devised many subtil Ways for the easier finding the Gravity of the "Atmosphere, the Degrees of Drought and Moisture, and many of its "other Accidents. Amongst these Instruments, there are Balances, which "are useful to other Purposes, that shew the Weight of the Air by their "spontaneous Inclination.

"Amongst the new Discoveries of the Pendulum, these are to be attri- "buted to him, that the Pendulum in its Motion from rest to rest; that is, "in one Descent and Ascent, moves unequally in equal Times, according "to a Line of Sines: That it would continue to move either in circular or "eliptical Motions; and such Vibrations would have the same Periods "with those that are reciprocal; and that by a Complication of several "Pendulums depending one upon another, there might be represented "Motions like the planetary helical Motions, or more intricate· and yet "that these Pendulums would discover without Confusion (as the Plan- "ets do) three or four several Motions, acting upon one Body with differ- "ing Periods; and that there may be produced a natural Standard for "Measure from the Pendulum for vulgar Use.

"He has invented many Ways to make astronomical Observations more "accurate and easy: he has fitted and hung Quadrants, Sectants, and "Radii, more commodiously than formerly: He has made two Telescopes "to open with a Joint like a Sector, by which Observers may infallibly "take a Distance to half Minutes, and find no Difference in the same Ob- "servation reiterated several Times; nor can any warping or luxation of "the Instrument hinder the Truth of it.

"He has added many Sorts of Retes, Screws and other Devises to Tele- "scopes, for taking small Distances, and apparent Diameters to seconds. "He has made Apertures to take in more or less Light, as the Observer "pleases, by opening or shutting like the Pupil of the Eye, the better to "fit Glasses to crepusculine Observations. He has added much to the "Theory of Dioptricks, [by giving a true Account of Refraction, and of "Vision; as that the chrystalline Humor is not the principal Instrument "of Refraction in the Eye, nor essential to Vision, but merely to conven- "ient Vision.] "He had added much to the Manufacture itself of grind- "ing good Glasses. He has attempted, and not without Success, the mak-

36

"ing of Glasses of other Forms than Spherical. He has exactly measur'd
"and delineated the Spheres of the Humors in the Eye, whose Propor-
"tions one to another were only guess'd at before. This accurate Discus-
"sion produc'd the Reason, why we see Things erected, and that Reflec-
"tion conduces as much to Vision as Refraction.

[He contrived an artificial Eye, truly and dioptrically made (as large as a
Tennis-Ball) representing the Picture as Nature makes it: The Cornea,
and Crystalline were Glass, the other Humours, Water. He took an exact Survey of an Horse's Eye, measuring what the Spheres of the Crystalline and Cornea were, and what the Proportions of the Distances of
the Centers of every Sphere were upon the Axis: the Projection in triple
the Magnitude, was presented to Sir Paule Neile, and the Experiment
occasionally reiterated.]

The Model of an Eye in the Musaeum of the Royal Society, Dr. Grew p. 359

" He discoursed to the Society a natural and easy Theory of Refraction,
" which exactly answered every Experiment. He fully demonstrated all
" Dioptricks in a few Propositions, shewing not only (as in Kepler's Di-
" optricks) the common Properties of Glasses, but the Proportions by
" which the individual Rays cut the Axis, and each other; upon which
" the Charges (as they are usually called) of Telescopes, or the Propor-
" tion of the Eye-Glasses, and Apertures are demonstrably discovered.

"He has made constant Observations on Saturn; and a Theory of that
"Planet, truly answering all Observations, before the printed Discourse
"of Hugenius on that Subject appeared.

By a thirty-six Foot Glass, he drew many exact Pictures of Saturn, not
only of his Ansulae, but his Spots; and attained to a Theory of his Rota-
tion, and various Inclination of his Body. He also drew the Spots of
Mars. He made the Tube an Astronomical Instrument to observe the
Seconds; by which he took the Motions of Jupiter's Satellites, & Saturn's
Moon; and not only drew Pictures of the Moon as Hevelius had done,
but gave more exact Surveys and Maps of her, and discovered exactly
her various Inclinations, and therein Hevelius's Errors; he caused a
Needle to be made of forty Inches, in order to discover the Annual Motion of Variation in it.

"He has essay'd to make a true Selenography by Measure; the World
"having nothing yet but Pictures, rather than Surveys or Maps of the
"Moon. He has stated the Theory of the Moon's Libration, as far as his
"Observations could carry him. He has composed a Lunar Globe, re-
"presenting not only the Spots and various Degrees of Whiteness upon
"the Surface, but the Hills, Eminencies and Cavities, moulded in solid
"Work. The Globe thus fashioned into a true Model of the Moon, as
"you turn it to the Light represents all the menstrual Phases, with the
"Variety of Appearances that happen from the Shadow of the Moun-
"tains and Vallies.

1661

Ex auto-graph

To Dr. Wren at All-Souls College in Oxford.

SIR,

I AM commanded by the Royal Society to acquaint you, that his Majesty expects you should prosecute your Design of making the Representation of the Lunar Globe in Solido; and that you should proceed in drawing the Shapes of little Animals as they appear in the Microscope; and that he doth expect an Account of this from you shortly.

I am, SIR, &c.

Hen. Powle.

Extract of a Letter from Sir Robert Moray, and Sir Paul Neile, on the same Subject

To Dr. Wren Savilian Professor of Astronomy at Oxford.

Much honoured Friend.

THE King hath commanded us to lay a double Charge upon you, in his Name, to perfect a Design, wherein he is told, you have already made some Progress, to make a Globe representing accurately the Figure of the Moon, as the best Tubes represent it: and to delineate by the Help of the Microscope the Figures of all the Insects and small living Creatures you can light upon, as you have done those you presented to his Majesty. If it were needful to add any further Excitement to your Industry, we should tell you how much our whole Society is rejoiced, that his Majesty has a just Esteem of your Parts, and honours you with his Commands, which we are confident will prevail with you, and therefore we reserve all other Motives for other Things, only we expect you will signify to us your Readiness to comply with his Majesty's Pleasure; and you may be sure we will improve it as much to your Honour and Advantage, as is possible for much honoured Friend,

Your most affectionate humble Servants,

R. Moray, P. Neile.

Whitehall, 17 May, 1661.

Second Letter from Sir Robert Moray. To Dr. Wren, &c.

My worthy Friend,

SINCE my last I told the King you had finished your Lunar Globe, and desired to know what are his further Commands; and he commanded me to let you know, he would have you bring it hither to him. I have also to tell you, that in Compliance with your Desire to be eased of the further Talk of drawing the Figures of small Insects by the Help of the Microscope, we have moved his Majesty to lay his Commands on another, one Vander Diver; and we have also persuaded Mr. Hook, to undertake the same Thing. This is all the Trouble you shall now have from, my worthy Friend,

Your real humble Servant,
R. Moray.

Whitehall, 13 August,
    1661,

N.B. Sir Robert Moray, one of his Majesty's Privy Council in Scotland, was an excellent Mathematician, and well versed in Natural Philosophy and Chymistry; he was among the first who modelled, instituted, and promoted the Royal Society, and was elected the second, after the Lord Brounker, President. He was universally beloved and esteemed; of so great Piety, that in the Midst of Armies & Courts, he spent many Hours a Day in Devotion. He had an Equality of Temper in him that nothing could alter; and was in Practice a Stoick. He had a Superiority of Genius & Comprehension to most Men. He had a most diffused Love to all Mankind, & delighted in every Occasion of doing Good, which he managed with great Discretion and Zeal.—A Character so parallel in all Points, to that of Sir Christopher Wren, naturally produced a most friendly and inviolable Attachment to each other. He died suddenly at Whitehall, and being particularly in the King's Favour, was at his Majesty's own Charge, buried in Westminster-Abbey, in the Year 1673. *[Character of Sir R. Moray. See Bp. Burnet Echard, &c.]*

In Observance of the King's Commands, and Directions of the Royal Society,* the Globe of the Moon in solid Work was accurately finished, and presented to his Majesty at Whitehall, fixed on a Pedestal of Lignum Vitae, curiously turned, with this Inscription engraved on the Foot, and a Scale of Miles. ** Penes collectorem*

CAROLO SECVNDO
M. BR. FR. ET HIB. R.
CVIVS AMPLITVDINI QVIA VNVS NON
SVFFICIT
NOVVUM HVNC ORBEM SELENOSPHAERIO
EXPRESSVM
D. D. D.
CHR. WREN

His Majesty received it with particular Satisfaction, and ordered it to be placed among the Curiosities of his Cabinet.

Dr. Sprat, late Bishop of Rochester, in his Observations on Monsieur de *London 1665*

Sorbier's Voyage into England, (dedicated to Dr. Wren) has this Reflection.—"In which is Monsieur Sorbier more ridiculous, his History or
" his Policy? his History in speaking so many false Reproaches aloud,
" his Policy in whispering such Trifles with so much Caution. I beseech
" you, Sir, let us allow him the Reputation of his new Invention intire,
" tho' he did not think fit to name the famous Author of the Lunar Globe,
" which he saw in the King's Closet."

London
1665

** Bishop of
Chester*

Extract from the Preface of Mr. Hook's Micrographia.

By the Advice of that excellent Man Dr. Wilkins,* I first set upon this
Enterprize, [Micrographie, or Physiological Descriptions of minute
Bodies made by the Help of magnifying Glasses] yet still came to it with
much Reluctancy, because I was to follow the Footsteps of so eminent
a Person as Dr. Wren, who was the first that attempted any Thing of this
Nature; whose original Draughts do now make one of the Ornaments of
that great Collection of Rarities in the King's Closet. This Honour which
his first Beginnings of this Kind have received, to be admitted into the
most famous Place of the World, did not so much incourage, as the Hazard of coming after Dr. Wren did affright me; for of him I must affirm,
that since the Time of Archimedes, there scarce ever met in one Man, in
so great a Perfection, such a mechanical Hand, and so philosophical a
Mind.

*Dr. Sprat's
Hist. of
the Royal
Society*

** In the Musaeum of
the Royal
Society.
Dr. Grew,
p. 364*

" He has made Maps of the Pleiades, and other Telescopical Stars, and
" proposed Methods to determine the great Doubt of the Earth's Motion or Rest, by the small Stars about the Pole to be seen in large Telescopes
" In order to Navigation, he has carefully pursu'd many magnetical Experiments; of which this is one of the noblest & most fruitful of Speculation. A large *Terella or orbicular Loadstone about four Inches and
" a Half in Diameter, is placed in the Midst of a plain Board, with a Hole,
" into which the Terella is half immers'd, till it be like a Globe, with the
" Poles in the Horizon; together with 32 Needles upon the Margin of
" the Table, by which the different Respect of the Needle to the several
" Points of the Terella may be observ'd. Then is the Plane dusted over
" with Steel-Filings equally from a Sieve· The Dust by the magnetical
" Virtue is immediately figur'd into Furrows, that bend like a Sort of
" Helix, proceeding as it were out of one Pole, & returning into the other;
" And the whole Plane is thus figur'd like the Circles of a Planisphere.
" It being a Question among the Problems of Navigation, very well worth
" resolving, to what mechanical Powers the sailing (against the Wind
" especially) was reducible, he shewed it to be a Wedge; and he demon-
" strated how a transient Force upon an oblique Plane, would cause the

" Motion of the Plane against the first Mover: and he made an †Instru-
" ment that mechanically produced the same Effect, & shewed the Reason
" of sailing to all Winds.
" The Geometrical Mechanicks of Rowing he shewed to be a Vectis on
" a moving or cedent Fulcrum. For this End he made Instruments to find
" what the Expansion of Body was towards the Hindrance of Motion in
" a liquid Medium; and what Degree of Impediment was produced, by
" what Degree of Expansion: with other Things that are the necessary
" Elements for laying down the Geometry of Sailing, Swimming, Row-
" ing, Flying, and the Fabricks of Ships.
" He has invented a very curious and exceedingly speedy Way of Etch-
" ing. He contriv'd a peculiar *Instrument to draw Perspective with.
" He has started several Things towards the Emendation of Water-
" Works. He has made Instruments of Respiration; and for straining the
" Breath from fuliginous Vapours, to try whether the same Breath, so
" purify'd, will serve again.

†In the
Musaeum
of the Royal
Society,
Dr. Grew,
p. 364

*In the
Musaeum of
the R. S.
Dr. Grew,
p. 376

A Description of the Vessel for cooling, and percolating the Air at once,
he produc'd to the Society, and left in Mr. Boyle's Hands; by which it
appear'd, that something else in Air is requisite for Life, than that it
should be cool only, and free from the fuliginous Vapours and Moisture
it was infected with, in Expiration; for, all those were deposited in its
Circulation through the Instrument, upon a Suggestion that nitrous
Fumes might be found requisite, he contriv'd Ways to supply that too,
by placing some benign chymical Spirits, that by fuming might infect
the Air within the Vessel.

" He was the first Inventor of drawing Pictures by microscopical Glasses.
" He has found out perpetual, at least long liv'd Lamps, and Registers of
" Furnaces, and the like, for keeping a perpetual Temper, in order to va-
" rious Uses; as hatching of Eggs, Insects, Production of Plants, chym-
" ical Preparations, imitating Nature, in producing Fossils & Minerals,
" keeping the Motion of Watches equal, in order to Longitudes and as-
" tronomical Uses, and infinite other Advantages.

He made it no small Part of his Business to have a Fire frequently going
in the Elaboratory for choicer Experiments in Chymistry, well knowing
that many Parts of Philosophy are not to be pierc'd far into, without this
Help; & little to be done in the Business of Trades without it. Mechanical Philosophy only teaches us what probably may be done in Nature,
by the Motion and Figures of the little Particles of Things, but Chymistry helps to determine what is actually done by the Motions of those
invisible Parts of Liquors, Spirits and Fumes; and oftentimes gives Light
enough to contradict mechanical Hypotheses that otherwise seem well
grounded. Thus in the Body of Man, if we consider it only mechanically,
we may indeed learn the Fabrick and Action of the organical Parts, but

without Chymistry, we shall be at a Loss to know what Blood, Spirits & Humours are ; from the due Temper of which, (as of the Spring in the Barrel Wheel) the Motions of all the Part depend. With divers new and useful Experiments in this Art, he had frequent Opportunities of entertaining his Royal Highness Prince Rupert, & his Majesty King Charles the Second, who were both illustrious Spagyrists and Operators. The Prince, as a distinguishing Mark of his Esteem, was pleased to enroll him in a List of such special Friends, to whom he Yearly sent a Present of Wine, from his Appenage on the Rhine.

Life of Ant. a Wood, p. 559. Oxon. 1730

" The noted Chymist and Rosicrucian Peter Sthael, of Strasburgh, in " Royal-Prussia, was brought to Oxford by the honourable Mr. Robert " Boyle, An. 1659. Among the chiefest of his Scholars were Dr. John " Wallis, Mr. Christopher Wren, afterwards a Knight, and an eminent " Virtuoso, with others of great Names in Physick and Learning.

Dr. Plot's nat. Hist. of Oxford-shire, p. 287

He found out several new geometrical Bodies, that arise by the Application of two Cylinders, & one lenticular body fit for grinding one another; by whose mutual Attrition, will necessarily be produc'd a *conoides hyperbolicum*, and two *cylindroides hyperbolica*. The Engine whereby this may be done being represented in Sculpture in our Philosophical Transactions, and design'd for grinding hyperbolical Glasses.

Philosophical Transactions, No. 53

He first observ'd, that a plain straight edg'd Chisel set any way obliquely to a Cylinder of Wood, did necessarily turn it into a *cylindroides hyperbolicum convexo concavum*; the several Sections whereof are accurately demonstrated by Dr. Wallis. [*Wallisii mechanica, sive de motu. pars* 2 *de calculo centri gravitatis* cap. 5. prop. 32.]

Philosophical Transactions, No. 98. *p.* 6146

In the Year 1658, he first found out a straight Line equal to a cycloid, & the Parts thereof. As is clearly made appear in his Behalf by the Right Honourable and learned the Lord Viscount Brounker, Chancellor to her Majesty, and President of the Royal Society; and the Reverend & learned Dr. John Wallis.

He was the first Inventor of the Art of Graving in Mezzo-tinto; which was after prosecuted & improv'd by his Royal Highness Prince Rupert, in a Method somewhat different, upon the Suggestion (as is said) of the learned and ingenious John Evelyn, Esq. Of this Art some original Essays are extant: viz. the Head of a Moor, &c. by the Inventor: the Executioner of St. John Baptist by the Prince; on the Sword is the Mark, R. P. f. (i.e. *Rupertus Princeps fecit.*) over it, an Electoral Coronet:

Extract from Dr. Plot's Natural History of Oxfordshire, page 269. *Chap. IX. of Arts, Sect.* 140.

The erect southern declining Dial, over All-Souls-College Chapel, is a neat Piece of Work, so curiously contrived by Sir Christopher Wren; that tho' it stands high, yet by the Help of two Half Rays, & one whole one for every Hour, one may see to a Minute what it is a Clock, the Minutes being depicted on the Sides of the Rays, viz. Fifteen on each side, and divided into fives by a different Character from the rest.

He invented the Art of Double Writing, that is, of making two several Pens upon two several Papers to write one and the same Ducture of Letters, with as near as possible the same Beauty and Facility that is found in common Writing, by an Instrument call'd the Diplographical Instrument.

Ad Regem, feliciter Reducem.

Diffluit en gemino quam prodiga sepia ductu,
　Ut cadat in titulos, Carole magne, tuos.
Marte, ac consilio nam te bis scribere magnum,
　Unica si nequeat dextera, dupla valet.

Apply'd to
K. Charles
II. after his
Restoration

Uses of the Diplographical Instrument.

First, That by the Help of this Instrument only, every ordinary Penman may at all Times be suddenly fitted to write two several Copies of any Deeds & Evidences, from the shortest to the largest Length of Lines, in the very same Compass of Time, and with as much Ease and Beauty, without any dividing or ruling, as without the Help of the Instrument, he could have dispatch'd but one.

Secondly, That by this diminishing the tedious Labour of Transcriptions of the greater Sorts of Deeds, Indentures, Conveyances, Charters, and all other Duplicates, the Works of the Pen, (which in so many several Kinds, and several Offices are yearly numberless) are not only shorten'd, but the Penmen themselves both reliev'd, and recompens'd by an honest Gain, with half the wonted Toil.

Thirdly, There will be both Copies thus drawn, such an exact Likeness in the same Number, and Order of Lines, & even of Words, Letters and Stops, in all Places of both Copies; that being once sever'd, there shall hardly be discern'd any Difference between them, except such as is meerly casual, as Spots or Marks in the Parchment.

Fourthly, This Instrument will undoubtedly prevent the mischievous Craft of Corruption, Forgery and Counterfeiting of Hands and Seals, or if any such foul Practice be attempted, will effectually and manifestly discover it; for what will it avail to counterfeit a Seal, or the Hand that signs, unless a Duplicate could be made in every Line, Letter and Dot, like the twin Copy? Which without the Help of the same Instrument is impossible: so expedient might it be to all Intents and Uses of the State, in Matters of the greatest Consequence, that publick Acts be written by this Instrument, for Testimony and Assurance to all Times.

Three Years after he had brought this Invention to Maturity, it seems, other Persons at London, publickly pretended to be the Authors; which oblig'd him to assert his Right to it, in a Letter to a certain Friend, who, among others, had been a Judge of the first Experiment.*

Probably to Dr. John Wilkins

Sir,—

The Account you give me in your last Letter, that a Double-Writing Instrument hath of late been at London, pretended to by several, as a Production of their own, and so divulged to divers, hath given me Occasion of putting into your Hands (what certainly I have more Right to dispose of, than any late Pretender) that Double-Writing Instrument, of the Effect of which, about three Years ago, yourself Sir, as I remember, among other the Ingeniosi were Judges, at the same Time when accidentally it was commanded to the View of the then great, now greatest† Person in the Nation. I confess my Thoughts were then to suffer it to be made publick, & Friends spur'd me to it, apprehending it not as a meer Curiosity, but of excellent and very general Use. Moreover, to copy out in every Punctilio the exact Resemblance, or rather the very Identity of the two Copies, as if one should fancy such a Piece of Magick as should make the same Thing really two; or with drunken Eyes should see the same Thing double, is what might be thought almost impossible for the Hand of Man. But Business drew me suddenly from London, and from the Opportunity of publishing it; content that I had at least communicated it to the ingenious Few, I willingly left it: And indeed the Thing always appearing to me but of obvious (tho' useful) Invention, I was easily drawn off to neglect it all this while, by the intervening of Studies and Designs that I much more esteem'd; amongst which this took up so little a Place, that I am beholding to the Person who, by vindicating it to be his own, has put me again in Mind of it. I accuse none of Plagiary, because having shewn it to few, I think it would be more Trouble to any knowing Person, to enquire it out of others, than to invent it anew; and therefore had it been thought on by any other, about that Time I shew'd it, I should have readily imagin'd, (because of the Obviousness of the Experiment) that it might as easily have had a double Father, as have produc'd a twin Copy; but I am apt to believe from good Information, that those who now boast of it, had it from one, who having fully seen the Author's, and examin'd it carefully (as it is easy to carry away, being of no complicate Composure) describ'd it justly to his Friend, and assisted him in the making of it; and the very glorying in a Thing of so facile Composure sufficiently discovers a Narrowness of Spirit in Things of Invention, and is therefore almost Argument enough, that he was not justly so much as a second Inventor; nor hath the Author reason to take it for an Injury, that one reported a deserving Person in other Abilities, would please to own a cast-

† *Oliver Cromwell*

44

off Toy of his, but rather owes him a Civility out of Gratitude for fathering it, and saving him that Labour of Education he intended, which will
now be needless, the dispersing of divers Instruments among the Merchants, with Directions for the Use. But it may be, there are divers who
knowing such a Thing to have been talked of some Years ago, as coming
from another Hand, will be easily ready to turn all this with Advantage
upon myself: indeed tho' I care not for having a Successor in Invention,
yet it behoves me to vindicate myself from the Aspersion of having a
Predecessor.

This Draught of a Letter bears no Date, yet, by the Contents, the Time
may be nearly computed; it appears, the first Device & Experiment was
made three Years before the Protectorate, scil. 1650. The Time of his
justifying his Right, and appealing to his Judges was in 1653. When the
great Man abovemention'd was invested with the office of Protector, and
so became the greatest Person in the Nation.
It is difficult to reconcile this Account with what is recorded of Sir William Petty, "That he in 1647, had a Patent granted him by the Parlia-
" ment for seventeen Years, to teach his Art of Double Writing." [Rush-
worth's Hist. Coll. Part IV.] [Ward's Lives of Gresham Professors,
p. 218.]——It is evident, that in the Years before recited, he had no Intelligence of Petty's Art and Patent.
It is a common Saying: "Good Wits jump."
He contriv'd a Needle that would play in a Coach, as well useful to know
the Coast and Way join'd with the Waywiser, as a pleasant Diversion to
the Traveller, who might thus, as it were sail by Land. The Machine is
fram'd after this Manner. In a Sphere of Glass of two Inches Diameter,
half full of Water, cause a heavy short broad Needle fix'd to a Chart to
swim, being buoy'd up by the Chart, and both varnish'd; instead of a Cap
and Pin, let the perforated Needle play about a small Wire, or Horse-
Hair extended like a perpendicular Axis in the glass Sphere, whose Nadir being made weighty with lead, and an Horizon, as it were, cemented
to it; let it play in Circles like the Compass; then let an hemispherical
Concave, containing the Sphere in its Circles, be hung upon Springs after
this Manner. Suppose a Basis upon which are erected perpendicularly
three stiff brass Springs, from the Ends of which Springs are Strings
strain'd, forming an equilateral Triangle, the Middle of whose Sides pass
through three small Loops on the Brim of the Concave, which therefore hanging on the Strings, represent a Circle inscrib'd in a Triangle:
from the Middle of the Basis arises a Worm-Spring, fasten'd by a String
to the Nadir of the Concave, drawing it down a little, and acting against
the other three Springs. These Springs will take off at once much of both
the downright & collateral Concussions; the Circles will take off Oscilla-

45

tions, the Agitations remaining will be spent in the Water, & still'd by the Chart; for thus we see a Trencher swimming in a Bucket keeps the Water from spilling in the Carriage; & the Chinese have their Compass swimming in Water, instead of Circles. Lastly all the Bottom of the Basis is to be bristled round like a Brush, somewhat inclining, which will ease it like a hundred Springs: It should be placed in the Middle of the Floor of the Coach, where by opening a Window may be seen likewise the Way-wiser on the Pearch.

Dr. Grew's Musaeum of the Royal Society, p. 260,
The Way-Wiser for a Coach, contriv'd by Sir Christopher Wren, and given by Bishop Wilkins to the Royal Society, is very manageable. It hath five Indexes pointing to so many different Measures, sc. Perches, Furlongs, Miles, Tens of Miles, and Hundreds of Miles; & turn'd about with as many Wheels. Made to work in a Coach, thus; in the Middle of the Axletree is cut a little Box to receive the Wiser: from whence the Axletree is made hollow to the End. In this Hollow lies a Rod, loose from the Axletree, & fasten'd at one End to the Nave of the Wheel, and so turns round with it. And with a Worm it hath at the other End, at the same Time, it turns the Perch of the Wheel-Wiser, and that all the rest.

In the Musaeum of the Royal Society, Dr. Grew, p. 371
Yet by this Measure, one Yard will sometimes be lost in a hundred Yards. He contriv'd a Box-Hive, given to the Royal Society by Sir Robert Moray: the Description whereof was first publish'd by Mr. Hartlib in the Year 1652. Since then by Mr. Moses Rusden: design'd to keep them warmer, and more safe; but especially to prevent their swarming, & the better to propagate them into the Colonies.

In the Musaeum of the Royal Society
He exhibited great Variety of sciographical, scenographical, dioptrical and catoptrical Experiments, which when executed with good Painting, and geometrical Truth in the Profile, would deceive the Eye with surprizing Effects; such, for Instance, was the catoptrick Paint, given to the Royal Society by Bishop Wilkins, on the one Side the Paint appears as if it were altogether rude and irregular, so as nothing can be made of it, but a metalline Cylinder being plac'd perpendicular upon a certain Point of the Table, the Rays are in such sort incident thereon, and thence reflected to the Eye, as to represent a Variety of curious Works in Landskip and Figures &c.

Extract from the Collection of Philosophical Experiments of Dr. Hook, and others, publish'd by the Rev. Mr. Derham, London, 1726. p. 1.

Of the Invention of the Barometer, in the Year 1659.

* *Mr. Derham*
IN one of Dr. Hooke's Papers I* find this Remark, viz. the Instrument for finding the different Pressure of the Air upon the Parts of the Earth subjacent, was first observ'd by the honourable Mr. Boyle, who upon the Suggestion of Sir Christopher Wren, erecting a Tube of Glass so fill'd

with Mercury, as is now usually done in the common Barometers, in order to find out, whether the Pressure of the Moon, according to the Cartesian Hypothesis did affect the Air; instead of finding the Fluctuation which might cause the Phoenomena of the Tides, discover'd the Variation of its Pressure to proceed from different Causes, and at different Times, from what that Hypothesis would have predicted. That Property of the Air (for ought appears) was never discover'd till that Time, &c.

To this I shall add another Remark. I find in the Minutes of the Royal Society, Feb. 20, 1678-9. Upon a Discourse of some Experiments to be made with the Barometer on the Monument, it was queried, how this Experiment of the different Pressure of the Atmosphere came at first to be thought of? And it was related, that it was first propounded by Sir Christopher Wren, in order to examine Monsieur DesCartes's Hypothesis, whether the passing by of the Body of the Moon did press upon the Air, and consequently also upon the Body of the Water: and that the first Trial thereof was made at Mr. Boyle's Chamber in Oxford.

The Time when these Observations were made was about the Year 1658 or 9. At which Time, Mr. Boyle having a Barometer fix'd up for the Observing the Moon's Influence upon the Waters, happen'd to discover the Use of it in relation to the Weather, and to assure himself, that it was the Gravitation of the Atmosphere which kept up the Quicksilver to such a Height as the Learned abroad, particularly Torricelli, had suspected before.

But although this Use of the Baroscope is owing to Sir Christopher Wren and Mr. Boyle; yet to do every Man Justice, I shall give the History of this excellent Instrument, from the Extracts of a very ingenious Friend.

The first inventor of it was Torricelli at Florence, in 1643. From whence Father Mersenne brought it into France the Year following, 1644. And Monsieur Pascal being inform'd of it by Monsieur Petit the Engineer, they both tried it in 1646, at Rouen, with the same Success as it had been tried in Italy. Some Time after which, an Experiment was made with a Tube of forty-six Foot, fill'd with Water, & also with Wine; which Experiment Mons. Pascal gave an Account of, in a Piece printed in 1647, in which Year he was inform'd of Torricelli's Solution of the Phoenomenon of the Weight of the Air; and devis'd for the examining of it, the famous Experiment with two Tubes, one within the other; which he mentions in a Letter written in November, 1647, & lastly in 1648. The same Mons. Pascal made his Experiments of the Tops and Bottoms of Hills, Buildings, &c. Which last Experiments Mons. Des Cartes laid Claim to; affirming that he desir'd Mons. Pascal to make them two Years before, and predicted their Success, contrary to Mons. Pascal's Sentiments.

Mons. Azout also laid the same Claim, but it is most probable that Mons. Pascal had the best Title.

After the Torricellian Experiment had been much celebrated in divers Places, at last Otto de Guerrick Consul of Magdeburgh, was inform'd of it by Father Valerian at Ratisbone, who claim'd it as his own Invention; but this was not till the Year 1654. After which Guerrick's Experiment, (call'd the Magdeburgh Experiment) was much talked of.

From this short History of the Barometer, not only the Inventor & Improvers of it appear, but in some Measure also the excellent Uses of it: particularly the Gravitation of the incumbent Atmosphere, (one of the noblest philosophical Discoveries) the Changes of the Weather, &c.

W. Derham.

Extract from the Life of Dr. Hook, publish'd by Mr. Waller,
Lond. 1705. p. 7.

In the Year 1655 or 6, were many curious Experiments, Observations, and Inquiries made at Oxford, and Instruments for those Purposes contriv'd, as particularly the Barometer, of which he [Mr. Hook] says the first Occasion of the Invention was a Suggestion of Sir Christopher Wren, in order to find whether the Hypothesis of Mons. Des Cartes, by giving the Reason of the Tides from the Pressure of the Moon upon the Air in its Passage by the Meridian, were true or not. At this Time I † have heard Mr. Hook say, it was the first observ'd, that the Height of the Mercury in the Barometer did not conform itself to the Moon's Motion, but to that of the different Gravitation of the Air, as has been since sufficiently verified. Yet in a * French Treatise printed at Paris, 1664. Several Years after this Observation at Oxford, the Discovery of the Gravitation of the Air is attributed to Mons. Pascal, deduced from several Experiments, made about the Year 1650, at Clermont in Auvergne by Mons. Perier; at Paris by others: and at Stockholm by Messieurs Des Cartes and Chanute; which if it shall be true, as is there related, and the Inferences from that Experiment, such as are in the same Tract mention'd, 'tis strange they should not have been apply'd to the Use of so beneficial an Instrument sooner, which I do not find they were, till after this Observation at Oxford.

Mr. Hook supposes that Reita was the first that made use of convex Eye Glasses, taking in a larger Area than the concave ones used before, and that he invented the Rete or Mensurator, placed in the common Focus of the Glasses; which Sir Christopher Wren perfected; and invented the angular Instrument consisting of two Telescopes join'd at a moveable Joint, so as to take Angles by two Observers, to a Quadrant.

† Mr. Waller

* Traitez de l'Equilibre des liqueurs &c.

Philos. Exper. Derham, p. 272

48

The third Thing Mons. Cassini [in his Original and Progress of Astronomy] unjustly lays Claim to, in the Behalf of the Royal Academy of Paris, is the finding a Standard for an universal Measure by the Length of a Pendulum vibrating a certain Time. This was first invented and tried by Sir Christopher Wren, some Years before the Beginning of the Society.

Philos. Exper. Derham, p. 390

The fourth Thing Mons. Cassini instances in, as of Right to be ascrib'd to the Royal Academy of Paris, is the Improvement of Telescopes both for Length and Goodness; which was first performed here, by Sir Paul Neile, Sir Christopher Wren, and Dr. Goddard, who instructed and employed Mr. Rieves in the manual Operation; and by that Means it was carried to the Perfection of making Object-Glasses of sixty and seventy Foot long, very good, before any Mention was made of such being made in France. Some such Attempts indeed, had been made in Italy by Divini, and Campani; but upon the comparing one of the best of them, brought hither by Mons. Monconys, I found that a Telescope I had then by me of Mr. Rieves's making, of the same Length with the Italian, was full as good, if not better; which Mr. Monconys acknowledged.

In Coelestial Observations we have far exceeded all the Antients, even the Chaldeans, & Egyptians themselves; whose vast Plains, high Towers, and clear Air, did not give them so great Advantages over us, as we have over them by our Glasses. By the Help of which, they have been much out-done by the famous Galileo, Hevelius, Zulichem, and our own Countrymen, Mr. Rook, and Dr. Wren, &c.

Hook's Micrographia Preface

APPENDIX TO PART I. SECT. I.

Extract of a Letter from Mr. Hook, May 4, 1665, in Reference to the Comet, Anno 1664; and Dr. Wren's Hypothesis of Comets laid before the Royal Society.

NUMB. I.

To Dr. Wren at Oxford.

SIR,

I Hope you received the Globe and Observations which I sent you; you had had them much sooner, but in Truth I could not get the Copy of your Hypothesis, though the Amanuensis was ordered by the Society to have had it ready above a Week before. Those Observations of my own making, I have not yet had Time to adjust so well as I desired, for the Sun came upon me before I was aware, and so I must stay till the Constellation of ♌ appear in the Morning, before I can be able to rectify the Places of the Telescopical Stars, by which I observed the Comet to pass; which I hope I may do about a Fortnight hence; about which Time also I expect to see both the old or first Comet with a Telescope; & the second or last Comet with my Eye: for, if the Motion of them be regular, as I see not the least Cause to doubt, I hope to be able to design their Places among the fixed Stars, without erring much more than I am able to see at once with a Telescope; & therefore I hope it will be no difficult Matter to find either of them, unless the first may be gone so far as to disappear by reason of Distance, which is indeed the greatest Part of my Fear: for, if it continue to move those Ways I have imagined it, whether we take the Supposition of the Motion of the Earth, and imagine the Comet to be moved in a Circle, one side of which touches, or rather goes within the Orb of the Earth on one Side, and without the Orb of Saturn, or at least that of Jupiter on the other, whose Plane is inclined to that of the Ecliptick about 20 Deg. or whether we suppose the Earth to stand still, and the Comet to be moved in a great Circle whose convex Side is turned towards the Earth (which supposing no certain Parallax has been observed, may be supposed of any Bigness, keeping only the same Proportion between the nearest Distance of it from the Earth and the Radius or Diameter of that Circle) it must appear again very near the same Place about a Fortnight hence. And I am apt to think the Body of the Comet is of a Constitution that will last much longer than either a Month or a Year, nay than an Age; and if I can be so lucky to meet with it again, I hope to trace it to its second appearing.—But I weary you with my Conjectures; and I doubt not but that before this, you have perfected the Theory of Comets, so as to be able to predict much more certainly what we are to expect of these Comets for the Future; whereof if at your Leisure you will please to afford me a Word or two, you will much oblige me, &c.

In one of Mr. Hook's Discourses of Comets, containing a brief Explication of several Opinions of the Antients, and some of the Moderns, of the Nature of Comets; he takes Notice of a late Information from France of a Person, D. Anthelm, a Carthusian of Dijon, pretending to have a true Theory of Comets, and to be able to predict them; which, says he, I think, may be much more exactly done, than what Anthelm has, by the Way I have published in my Cometa, which was invented by Sir Christopher Wren; By which, from any four Observations truly made one may certainly find the Line, Distance, Motion, Inclination to the Ecliptick, its Place among the fixed Stars, the Length of its Tail, Brightness, &c. so long as it shall appear to the naked Eye; for so long that Theory will hold pretty near, &c. *Posthumous Works of Dr. Hook, p. 104 and 5*

All the considerable Astronomers who have written of Comets, since Galileo, do conclude them not to be sublunary, but far removed above the Moon, and aethereal. Such were almost all those who writ of that great and very bright Comet, which appeared to the World in the Year 1618, and such are those who have writ of Comets, that have appeared since; and more particularly of those two great ones, which appeared in the End of 1664, and in the Beginning of the Year 1665, many of which are comprised in the Theatrum Cometicum, printed in 1667.

NUMB. II.

To the Royal Society.

Mr. President,

WE begin a new Year, and therefore may pause a little, and look back on what we have done, and consider what we may do. 'Tis a great Encouragement to us, that by the Influence of his sacred Majesty, the Prudence and Diligence of yourself, the ingenious Performances of the Society, we have hitherto kept up our Meetings full, and in good Repute at home and abroad, & not without sufficient Appearance of doing something considerable; so that we need not now fear lest the World from all our Experiments, should make this one Experiment, that there is little Use of these Enquiries: and I make no question, but the Design of so many excellent Persons meeting in this Society, (besides the present Satisfaction that accrues from the Converse and Communication of every one's Thoughts in the Disquisition of Nature) carries along with it, principally a Zeal of approving themselves benefactors to Mankind, and of perfecting something, for which Posterity may be really obliged to us.

Of effecting this; there seems three Ways: By advancing, 1. Knowledge. 2. Profit. 3. Health; and Conveniences of Life.

For the first of these, the Improvement of Theories, we need be least solicitous, it is a Work will insensibly grow upon us, if we be always doing something in Experiment; and everyone is more prone to exercise Fancy in building paper Theories, than patient to first pile the unsure Foundation and hew solid Materials out of the History of Nature. This is rather our Talk, and in many Things we must be content to plant Crab-stocks for Posterity to graft on.

The second, I make no question, will be excellently effected by two Things now in Hand; the carrying on the History of Trades, & the Improvement of the Art of Navigation; which being now committed to an excellent Hand, cannot but produce something very extraordinary. Besides, there can hardly be any Thing propos'd worth our Consideration, that will not itself, or some Corollary from it, be reduceable to this Head.

For the third, the Health of Mankind, the restoring Part is properly the Work already of one whole Faculty, in which no Age or Nation affords more learned and inquisitive men than this of ours. Yet I wish we might incorporate with them so far, as to have a Fire going in the Elaboratory for choicer Experiments in Chymistry, especially since many Parts of Philosophy are not to be pierced far into, without this Help; and little is to be done in the Business of Trades without it. Mechanical Philosophy only teaches us what probably may be done in Nature by the Motion and Figures of the little Particles of Things, but Chymistry helps to determine what is actually done by the Motions of those invisible Parts of Liquors, Spirits, and Fumes; and oftentimes gives Light enough to contradict mechanical Hypotheses, that otherwise seem well grounded. Thus in the Body of a Man, if we consider it only mechanically, we may indeed learn the Fabrick and Action of the organical Parts, but without Chymistry, we shall be at a Loss to know, what Blood, Spirits and Humours are, from the due Temper of which (as of the Spring in the Barrel Wheel) the Motions of all the Parts depend.

To carry on both together, I could wish we were frequent in Dissections of Animals, of any Sort whatsoever, and that Figures be drawn, where Nature appears anomalar, as she is most in Fishes and Insects; especially in the Parts that serve for Concoction. And with this we may take in the

Experiment about Generation: The Spring should not be lost, for observing the Progress of hatching Eggs; and likewise the springing of Grain and Seeds; which in a ruder Proportion gives some Light to the Generation of Animals. Tame Rabbets may be kept purposely for Dissection, as well because they are frequently pregnant, as because of late, some Observations have been made from them, which seem to thwart those of Dr. Harvey, how truly, will be worth our Enquiry.

Besides these, there is another Part of Physiology, which concerns us as near as the Breath of our Nostrils, and I know not any Thing wherein we may more oblige Posterity, than that which I would now propose. It is not the Work of any one Person, and therefore fit for a Society, nor of a little Time, though of little Trouble, and therefore fit to be propos'd now at the Beginning of the Year, & to be carried on with other Things. The History of Seasons is this excellent Work I would recommend to you, desir'd by all modern Philosophers, though no Body hath had yet the Patience to pursue it.

It consists of two Parts: 1. A meteorological History. 2. A History of Things depending upon Alteration of the Air and Seasons.

The meteorological Parts will be compleated by five Histories.

1. A punctual Diary of the Motion of the Air, the Winds; wherein should be noted, not only the Rumb but Force of the Wind, as the Seamen have these Distinctions, if I mistake not; from a Calm they begin with a soft Wind; a fresh Wind; a stiff Gale; a Storm; and sometimes a Hurricane. These may be noted down by a Cypher, and 1, 2, 3, 4, &c. And the Rumb by Letters.

2. A punctual Diary of the Qualities of the Air, as to Heat and Cold observ'd by a Thermometer; and likewise of the Moisture of the Air observ'd by some other Instrument.

3. The Refractions should be observ'd, and the Rising of dry Vapours by the Telescope, and the Tremulation of the Air.

4. A Diary of the State of the Air, as fair, cloudy, Rain, &c.

5. A Register of other accidental Meteors, as figur'd Snows, Parelii, Coronae, unusual Colours and Shapes of Clouds, call'd Fights in the Air. Fiery Meteors in the Night, falling Stars, (in which I could give Direction for finding, if any Thing falls from them in their Extinction.)

The second Part will be compris'd in,—

1. The History of the Growth of those annual Things of Food, as Fruits and Grain. The Causes of Dearth and Plenty and Diseases. Especially the Annals of the Plough should be kept. How the Weather retarded or accelerated Seed Time, springing, flow'ring, corning, ripening and Har-

vest; with the Diseases and Enemies of that Year: as whether blighted, mildew'd, smutted, choked with this or that Weed, eaten with Rook-worms, or infected with a little blue Mite, covering the Ear while green, a Calamity which I have observ'd, but wants a Name.—Lastly, the Plenty, Scarcity, and Price of Corn. We are enough to learn this in every County of England, by enquiring or corresponding with those that are a little more curious in Country Affairs.

2. The State of Grass and Hay, and consequently of Cattle; the Plenty, Dearth, Diseases and Murrains of them.

3. Wines, which though foreign, bear a great Share in our Diet, and therefore a Note should be given of them; of their Goodness or Vices that Year. So for Coffee, Tobacco, and such like of general Use.

4. The Seasons of Fish & Fowl are retarded or accelerated by Weather: foreign Fowl are observ'd to come in great Multitudes, near the Time of their Departure, to some Coasts of England, & there to stay for a Wind, which when it happens for their Turn, in few hours there is not one to be seen in the whole Country. The Seasons of Fish depend much upon the Seasons of the Water-flies and Insects their Food; in two Rivers, parted by the same Meadow, I have known the Difference of ten Days or more. The Seasons of Insects, are of themselves very considerable. The Multi-tudes or Paucity of venemous Creatures, and of many other the like Things are very well worth registring; and all other Things found to be either Consequence, Signs, or Presages of Weather and Seasons.

5. Above all, the Physicians of our Society should be desir'd to give us a good Account of the epidemical Diseases of the Year; Histories of any new Disease that shall happen; Changes of the old; Difference of Opera-tions in Medicine according to the Weather and Seasons, both inwardly, and in Wounds: and to this should be added, a due Consideration of the weekly and annual Bills of Mortality in London.

Thus instead of the Vanity of prognosticating, I could wish we would have the Patience for some Years, of registring past Times, which is the certain Way of learning to prognosticate;—Experiment and Reason is the only Way of prophesying natural Events. And I shall not therefore need to press the Utility of this Design, since I am confident there is none here, but apprehends what excellent Speculations, what a Multitude of new ingenious Consequences will hence arise conducible to Profit, Health, Convenience, Pleasure, and Prolongation of Life. And I dare be confident, that no one Part in the whole Extent of Philosophy will afford us more delightful or more useful Speculations, or render us more con-siderable to all Posterity.

The only Thing I fear is, lest we should want Patience, and flag in the Design, since in few Years at the Beginning, it will hardly come to any visible Maturity. But as it is a long Work, so it is of no Difficulty, nor will take up more Time, than once a Year to have an Audit wherein every-one shall bring in his Account of that Part which, in this History was enjoin'd him.

The greatest Difficulty will be in keeping the Diary of the Winds and Air, because it seems to require constant Attendance; but this at first may be delegated to four or five Men, who near their Abodes have Wea-ther-Cocks in view,& have diligently taken the Position of their Houses; these may sometimes compare Notes, what have escaped the Observa-tions of one will be taken by another. So likewise for the Thermometer. Some Help may be given for the exacter Observance of the Wind, as thus: A Point being taken in a convenient Part of a Window, where a square Vane of a Weather-Cock appears, the nearer & higher above the Eye, the better; an Ellipsis may be drawn on the Glass, and the Rumbs within the Ellipsis so, that it may be a Projection upon the Plane of the Window, of an imaginary Card, placed horizontally upon the Steeple whose Center is the Axis of the Vane; therefore observing only with one Glance, how the Edge of the Vane lies amongst these Lines of the Win-dow, you have the Wind exactly given you. This Way hath been put in Execution with very good Effect, and some other useful Additions at Oxford.

But because it is convenient, that the Changes of Winds in the Night too, should not pass unobserved; such a Vane as is at Whitehall, shewing by an Index within a Room, may be very necessary for this Purpose.

But this is not yet enough, for many Changes may happen while the Ob-server is absent or asleep. I might seem to promise too much, should I say, an Engine may be fram'd, which if you visit your Chamber but one half Hour in the Day, shall tell you how many Changes of Wind have been in your Absence, though there were Twenty, and at what Hour every Change happen'd, and whether it were soft, stiff, or vehement. Neither shall the Instrument be subject to be out of Tune, or if it be, your own Hand may rectify it.

Neither shall the Thermometer need a constant Observance, for after the same Method may that be made to be its own Register. Some Errors likewise there are in the Use of the Thermometer, which should there-fore be used with some Cautions.

For the pretended Ways of discovering the two other Qualities of Drought & Moisture in the Air, they are all uncertain that I ever heard of. Tryals have been made of Lute-strings, which by their various Ten-sure move an Index, but these Strings alter in their Parts, and in the same Temper of Air will not return to the same Degrees. The Beards of Oats are more uncertain.

It is indeed an Error to think there are any Degrees of Siccity, since all

e 4

Siccity is but less or no Humidity: And therefore the Degrees of Humidity being nothing else but the Quantity of moist Vapour in the Air, it is best done by collecting the very Moisture of the Air after a peculiar Manner, which I shall be ready to produce.

Many other Things I might suggest of this Nature, which if the Design be once begun, I shall most willingly submit, upon Occasion, to the Judgment of the Society.

Extract from Dr. Grew's Musaeum Regalis Societatis P. 284.

CHRYSTAL, at least some Sorts of it, is the softest, saith Boethius, of all Gems. He should have said of all perspicuous Gems: For the Turcois is much softer. The most usual Figure of Chrystal, is sexangular: Yet Terzagi mentions a Rock of square-pointed Ones. But it is observable, That he saith, the Bed on which they grew, seem'd to be Gold-Ore: If so, it might proceed from some governing Principle in the Ore. For I have heard it noted, as I remember, by Sir Christopher Wren, that Grain-Gold is often found naturally figur'd into Cubes.

Extract of a Letter to the Right Honourable the Lord Brouncker.

[Preparative to his Majesty's Entertainment at the
Royal Society, Oxon 1661.]

My Lord,

THE Act and Noise at Oxford being over, I retir'd to myself as speedily as I could, to obey your Lordship, and contribute something to the Collection of Experiments design'd by the Society, for his Majesty's Reception. I concluded on something I thought most suitable for such an Occasion; but the Stupidity of our Artists here, makes the Apparatus so tedious, that I foresee I shall not be able to bring it to any Thing within the Time propos'd: What in the mean while to suggest to your Lordship I cannot guess; the Solemnity of the Occasion, and my Solicitude for the Honour of the Society, makes me think nothing proper, nothing remarkable enough. 'Tis not every Year will produce such a Master-experiment as the Torricellian, and so fruitful of new Experiments as that is, & therefore the Society have deservedly spent much Time upon that and its Offspring: And if you have any notable Experiment that may appear to open new Light into Principles of Philosophy, nothing would better beseem the Pretensions of the Society, though possibly such would be too jejune for this Purpose, in which there ought to be something of Pomp: On the other Side, to produce Knacks only, and Things to raise Wonder, such as Kercher, Scottus, & even Jugglers abound with, will scarce become the

56

Gravity of the Occasion: It must therefore be something between both, luciferous in Philosophy, and yet whose Use and Advantage is obvious, and without a Lecture; and besides may surprize with some unexpected Effect, and be commendable for the Ingenuity of the Contrivance. Half a Dozen of Experiments thus qualified, will be abundantly enough for an Hour's Entertainment; and I cannot believe the Society can want them, if they look back into their own Store. For myself, I must profess freely, I have not any Thing by me suitable to the Idea I have of what ought to be perform'd before such an Assembly. Geometrical Problems, and new Lines, new Bodies, new Methods, how useful soever, will be but tastless in a transient Show. New Theories, or Observations, or astronomical Instruments, either for Observation or Facilitation of the Calculus, are valuable to such Artists only who have particularly experimented the Defects that these Things pretend to supply.

Sciographical Knacks, of which yet a hundred Varieties may be given, are so easy in the Invention, that now they are cheap. Scenographical, Catoptrical, and Dioptrical Tricks, require excellent Painting, as well as Geometrical Truth in the Profile, or else they deceive not. Designs of Engines for Ease of Labour, or promoting any Thing in Agriculture, or the Trades, I have occasionally thought upon divers, but they are not intelligible without Letters and References, and often, not without something of Demonstration. Designs in Architecture, &c., the few chymical Experiments I have been acquainted with, will, I fear, be too tedious for an Entertainment. Experiments in Anatomy, tho' of the most Value for their Use, are sordid and noisom to any but those whose Desire of Knowledge, makes them digest it. Experiments for the Establishment of natural Philosophy are seldom pompous; 'tis upon Billiards, and Tennis-Balls; upon the purling of Sticks and Tops; upon a Viol of Water, or a Wedge of Glass, that the great Des Cartes hath built the most refined & accurate Theories that human Wit ever reach'd to; and certainly Nature in the best of her Works is apparent enough in obvious Things, were they but curiously observ'd; and the Key that opens Treasures, is often plain and rusty, but unless it be gilt, 'twill make no Show at Court.

If I have been conversant in philosophical Things, (as I know how idle I have been) it hath been principally in these Ways, which I have recounted to your Lordship, by which your Lordship perceives how useless I am for this Service; yet if your Lordship will still pursue me, I know not what Shift to make, but to retire back to something I have formerly produc'd.

I have pleas'd myself not a little with the Play of the Weather-wheel, (the only true Way to measure Expansions of the Air) and I imagine it must needs give others Satisfaction, if it were once firmly made, which, I suppose, may be done, if the circular Pipes (which cannot be truly blown in Glass) were made of Brass, by those who make Trumpets, and Sack-outts, (who wire-draw their Pipes thro' a Hole to equal them, and then filling them with melted Lead, turn them round into what Flexures they please) the Inside of the Pipe must be varnish'd with China-varnish to preserve it from the Quicksilver; and the Glasses fixed to it with Varnish, which I suppose will be the best Cement in the World; for thus the Chinese fix Glass and Mother of Pearl in their Works. It would be no unpleasing Spectacle to see a Man live without new Air, as long as you please. A Description of a Vessel for cooling and percolating the Air at once, I formerly show'd the Society, and left in Mr. Boyle's Hands; I suppose it worth putting in Practice; you will at least learn thus much from it, that something else in Air is requisite for Life, than that it should be cool only, and free from the fuliginous Vapours and Moisture it was infected with in Expiration; for all those will in Probability be deposited in its Circulation thro' the Instrument. If nitrous Fumes be found requisite, (as I suspect) Ways may possibly be found to supply that too, by placing some benign Chymical Spirits, that by fumeing may infect the Air within the Vessel.

If an artificial Eye were truly & dioptrically made (which I would have at least as big as a Tennis-Ball) it would represent the Picture as Nature makes it. The Cornea & Chrystalline must be Glass, the other Humours, Water. I once survey'd a Horse's Eye as exactly as I could, measuring what the Spheres of the Chrystalline & Cornea were; and what the Proportions of the Distances of the Centers of every Sphere were upon the Axis: The Ways by which I did it are too long to rehearse, but the Projection in triple the Magnitude, Sir Paul Neile may possibly find; or if your Lordship think it worth while, I shall reiterate the Experiment.

A Needle that would play in a Coach, will be as well useful to know the Coast and Way join'd with the Way-wiser as a pleasant Diversion to the Traveller; & would be an acceptable Present to his Majesty, who might thus as it were sail by Land. The Fabrick may be thus: In a Sphere of Glass of two Inches Diameter, half full of Water, cause a short heavy broad Needle fixed to a Chart to swim, being buoy'd up by the Chart, and both varnish'd; instead of a Cap and Pin, let the perforated Needle play about a small Wire, or Horse-Hair, extended like a perpendicular Axis in the Glass-Sphere, whose Nadir being made weighty with Lead, and an Horizon as it were cemented to it, let it play in Circles like the Compass; Then let a hemispherical Concave containing the Sphere in its Circles, be hung upon Springs after this Manner.

Suppose a Basis upon which are erected perpendicularly three stiff Brass-Springs, from the Ends of which Springs, are Strings strain'd, forming an equilateral Triangle, the Middle of whose Sides pass through three small Loops on the Brim of the Concave, which therefore hanging on the

58

Strings represents a Circle inscrib'd in a Triangle. From the Middle of the Basis arises a Worm-spring, fasten'd by a String to the Nadir of the Concave, drawing it down a little, and acting against the other three Springs. These Springs, I suppose, will take off at once much of both the downright and collateral Concussions; the Circles will take off Oscillations, the Agitations remaining will be spent in the Water, and still'd by the Chart; for thus we see a Trencher swimming in a Bucket keeps the Water from spilling in the Carriage: & the Chinese have their Compass swimming in Water instead of Circles.

Lastly, I would have all the Bottom of the Basis bristled round like a Brush, somewhat inclin'd, which is a cheap Addition, and will ease it like a hundred Springs: It should be placed on the Middle of the Floor of the Coach, where by opening a Window you might see likewise the Way-wiser on the Pearch. My Lord, if my first Designs had been perfect, I had not troubled your Lordship with so much Tattle, but with something perform'd and done: But I am fain, in this Letter, to do like some Chymist, who when Projection (his fugitive darling) hath left him threadbare, is forced to fall to vulgar Preparations to pay his Debts.

My Lord, I am,

Yours, &c.

CHR. WREN.

59

PART I. SECTION II.
OF ANATOMY, ETC.

R. WREN assisted Dr. Willis, in his excellent Treatise of the Anatomy of the Brain, in the Manner which the learned Author has thus testify'd in his Preface to that Work, viz.

Praeter suppetias ab hujus manu (Doctoris Lower) in dissecando peritissima allatas, celare non decet, quantas insuper acceperim a viris clarissimis Domino Tho. Millington, M.D. nec non a Domino Christophoro Wren, L.L.D. & Astronomiae professore Saviliano; qui utrique dissectionibus nostris crebrò interesse, & circà partium usus rationes conferre solebant. Porrò prior ille vir doctissimus, cui privatò observationes meas, & conjecturas, de die in diem proponebam, me animo incertum, & propriae sententiae minùs fidentem, suffragiis suis saepè confirmabat. Caeterùm alter vir insignissimus Doctor Wren, pro singulari quâ pollet humanitate plurimas cerebri & calvariae figuras, quo exactiores essent operae, eruditissimis suis manibus delineare non fuit gravatus.

Dr. Willis' Method of dissecting the Brain, (wherein he had the Assistance of the deservedly famous Sir Christopher Wren, Dr. Millington, &c.) is new, and most natural, and so exact, that there is scarce any one Part in it, but what has receiv'd considerable Advancements.

Among divers new Experiments in Anatomy, which he exhibited at the Meetings at Oxford, were Schemes of several Fishes dissected, in which the Fabrick of the Parts appear'd very often irregular, & differing much both from Brutes, and one another. Several Things he observ'd very considerable in Fowls. Some Parts of Animals he more exactly trac'd by the Help of Glasses as the Kidneys, the Plexus in the Brain, &c. The Nerves he found to have little Veins and Arteries in them. He then found the Lymphaeducts to empty themselves into the Receptacle of Chyle, from all Parts both of the Bowels and Limbs, &c.

" He was the first Author of the noble anatomical Experiment of inject-
" ing Liquors into the Veins of Animals. An Experiment now vulgarly
" known; but long since exhibited to the Meetings at Oxford, & thence
" carried by some Germans, and publish'd abroad; by this Operation, di-
" vers Creatures were immediately purg'd, vomited, intoxicated, kill'd,
" or reviv'd according to the Quality of the Liquor injected. Hence arose
" many new Experiments, and chiefly that of transfusing Blood, which

60

" the Society has prosecuted in sundry Instances, that will probably end
" in extraordinary Success.

It should seem, by the Date, and a Paragraph in a Letter to a Person of
Distinction in Ireland,* he made the first Experiment of Infusion, about
the Year 1656. After the Recital of several new Experiments in Philosophy, and Anatomy, he thus proceeds,—"The most considerable Ex-
" periment I have made of late, is this; I injected Wine and Ale into the
" Mass of Blood in a living Dog, by a Vein, in good Quantities, till I
" made him extremely drunk, but soon after he pissed it out: With two
" ounces of Infusion of Crocus Metallorum thus injected, the Dog imme-
" diately fell to vomiting, and so vomited till he died. It will be too long
" to tell you the Effects of Opium, Scammony, and other Things which I
" have try'd this Way. I am in further Pursuit of the Experiment, which I
" take to be of great Concernment, and what will give great Light to the
" Theory and Practice of Physick.

*Probably
Sir William
Petty

An Account of the Rise and Attempts of a Way to convey Liquors immediately into the Mass of Blood.

WHereas there have lately appear'd in publick some Books, printed beyond the Seas, treating of the Way of injecting Liquors into Veins: in
which Books the Original of that Invention seems to be ascrib'd to others, besides him, to whom it really belongs; it will surely not be thought
amiss if something be said, whereby the true Inventor's Right may beyond Exception be asserted and preserv'd; to which End, there will need
no more, than barely to represent the Time when, and the Place where,
and among whom it was first started, and put to trial. To join all these
Circumstances together, 'tis notorious, that at least six Years (a good
while before it was heard of, that any one did pretend to have so much as
thought of it) the learned and ingenious Doctor Christopher Wren did
propose in the University of Oxford, (where he now is the worthy Savilian Professor of Astronomy, and where very many curious Persons are
ready to attest this Relation) to that noble Benefactor to experimental
Philosophy, Mr. Robert Boyle, Dr. Wilkins, & other deserving Persons,
that he thought, he could easily contrive a Way, to convey any liquid
Thing immediately into the Mass of Blood, videl. by making Ligatures
on the Veins, & then opening them on the Side of the Ligature towards
the Heart, and by putting into them slender Syringes, or Quills, fasten'd
to Bladders (in the Manner of Clyster Pipes) containing the Matter to
be injected: performing that Operation upon pretty big and lean Dogs,
that the Vessels might be large enough, and easily accessible.

Philosophi-
cal Trans-
actions, No.
7. p. 128.
1665

This Proposition being made, Mr. Boyle soon gave Order for an Apparatus, to put it to Experiment; wherein at several Times, upon several Dogs, Opium, & the Infusion of Crocus Metallorum were injected into that Part of the hind Legs of those Animals, whence the larger Vessels, that carry the Blood, are most easy to be taken hold of; whereof the Success was, that the Opium being soon circulated into the Brain, did within a short Time stupify, tho' not kill the Dog; but a large Dose of the Crocus Metallorum, made another Dog vomit up Life and all: all which is more amply & circumstantially deliver'd by Mr. Boyle, in his excellent Book of the Usefulness of experimental Philosophy, Part 2. Postscript to Essay 2. Where 'tis also mention'd that the Fame of this Invention, and of the succeeding Trials being spread, and particularly coming to the Knowledge of a foreign Ambassador, that was curious, and then resided in London, it was by him tried with some Crocus Metallorum, upon a Malefactor, that was an inferiour Servant of his; with this Success, that the Fellow, as soon as ever the Injection began to be made, did, either really, or craftily, fall into a Swoon; whereby, being unwilling to prosecute so hazardous an Experiment, they desisted, without seeing any other Effect of it, save that it was told the Ambassador, that it wrought once downwards with him. Since which Time, it hath been frequently practised both in Oxford and London; as well before the Royal Society, as elsewhere. And particularly that learned Physician Dr. Timothy Clark, hath made it part of his Business, to pursue those Experiments with much Industry, great Accurateness, and considerable Observations thereon; which above two Years since were produc'd by him, and read before the Royal Society, who thereupon desir'd him, as one of their Members, to compleat what he had propos'd to himself upon that Subject, and then to publish the same; the Effect whereof 'tis hoped, will now shortly appear, and not prove unwelcome to the Curious.

Some whereof, though they may conceive, that Liquors thus injected into Veins without Preparation and Digestion, will make odd Commotions in the Blood, disturb Nature, and cause strange Symptoms in the Body; yet they have other Thoughts of Liquors, that are prepar'd of such Things as have pass'd the Digestion of the Stomach; for Example, of the Spirit of Urine, of Harts-horn, of Blood, &c. And they hope likewise, that besides the medical Uses, that may be made of this Invention, it may also serve for anatomical Purposes, by filling after this Way, the Vessels of an Animal as full as they can hold, & by exceedingly distending them, discover new Vessels, &c. But not now to enlarge upon the Uses, the Reader may securely take this Narrative, as the naked, real, Matter of Fact, whereby 'tis as clear, as Noonday, both from the Time, and irrefragable Testimony of very many considerable Persons in that University, who can jointly attest it; as well as from that particular unquestionable one of Mr. Boyle, and his worthy Company, who were the first eye-

62

witnesses of the Trials made, that to Oxford, and in it to Dr. Christopher Wren, this Invention is due; and consequently that all others, who discourse or write of it, do either derive it from him, or are fallen upon the same Devise several Years after him.

Mr. Boyle's Account of the above-mention'd Invention, and the Experiments thereon.

TO enable you (Pyrophilus) to gratify those inquisitive Persons· that have heard some, and yet but an imperfect Report of a much nois'd Experiment, that was some Years ago devis'd at Oxford, and since try'd in other Places, before very illustrious Spectators; I am content to take the Occasion afforded me, by what was in the foregoing Essay lately mention'd concerning the Application of Poisons, to inform you, That a pretty while after the Writing of that Essay, I happen'd to have some Discourse about Matters of the like Nature, with those excellent Mathematicians, Dr. J. Wilkins, & Mr. Christopher Wren; at which the Latter of those Virtuosi told us, that he thought, he could easily contrive a Way to convey any liquid Poison immediately into the Mass of Blood. Whereupon our Knowledge of his extraordinary Sagacity, making us very desirous to try what he propos'd, I provided a large Dog, on which he made his Experiments in the Presence & with the Assistance of some eminent Physicians, & other learned Men: his Way (which is much better learn'd by Sight than Relation) was briefly this: First, to make a small and opportune Incision over that Part of the hind Leg, where the larger Vessels that carry the Blood, are most easy to be taken hold of: then to make a Ligature upon those Vessels, and to apply a certain small Plate of Brass (of above half an Inch long, and about a quarter of an inch broad, whose Sides were bending inwards) almost of the Shape & Bigness of the Nail of a Man's Thumb, but somewhat longer. This Plate had four little Holes in the Sides, near the Corners, that by Threads pass'd through them, it might be well fasten'd to the Vessel, and in the same little Plate, there was also left an Aperture, or somewhat large Slit, parallel to the Sides of it, and almost as long as the Plate, that the Vein might be there exposed to the Lancet, and kept from starting aside. This Plate being well fastened on, he made a Slit along the Vein, from the Ligature towards the Heart, great enough to put in at it the slender Pipe of a Syringe; by which I had proposed to have injected a warm Solution of Opium in Sack, that the Effect of our Experiment might be the more quick & manifest. And accordingly our dexterous Experimenter having surmounted the Difficulties, which the tortured Dog's violent Strugglings interposed, conveyed a small Dose of the Solution or Tincture into the opened Vessel, whereby getting into the Mass of Blood, (some Quantity of which 'tis

Essays of nat. exper. philosophy, Part 2. *Postscript, Oxford,* 1663

difficult to avoid shedding in the Operation) it was quickly, by the circular Motion of that, carried to the Brain, and other Parts of the Body: So that we had scarce untied the Dog, (whose four Feet it had been requisite to fasten very strongly to the four Corners of the Table) before the Opium began to disclose its Narcotick Quality, and almost as soon as he was on his Feet, he began to nod with his Head, and faulter and reel in his Pace, & presently after appeared so stupified, that there were Wagers offered his Life could not be saved. But I, that was willing to reserve him for further Observation, caused him to be whipped up and down a neighbouring Garden, whereby being kept awake, and in Motion, after some Time he began to come to himself again; and being led home, and carefully tended, he not only recovered, but began to grow fat so manifestly, that 'twas admired: But I could not long observe how it fared with him: For this Experiment & some other Trials made upon him, having made him famous, he was soon after stolen away from me. Succeeding attempts informed us, that the Plate was not necessary, if the Fingers were skilfully employed to support the Vessel to be opened, & that a slender Quill fastened to a Bladder containing the Matter to be injected, was somewhat more convenient than a Syringe; as also that this notwithstanding, unless the Dog were pretty big and lean, that the Vessels might be large enough, and easily accessible, the Experiment would not well succeed.

The Inventor of it afterwards practised it in the Presence of that most learned Nobleman, the Marquis of Dorchester, & found that a moderate Dose of the Infusion of Crocus Metallorum did not much move the Dog to whom it was given; but once, that he injected a large Dose, (about two Ounces or more) it wrought so soon and so violently upon a fresh one, that within a few Hours after he vomited up Life and all, upon the Straw whereon they had laid him. I afterwards wished, that not only some vehemently working Drugs, but their appropriated Antidotes, (or else powerful liquid Cordials) and also some Altering Medicines might be in a plentiful Dose injected. And in Diureticks, a very ingenious Anatomist & Physician told me, he try'd it with very good Success. I likewise proposed, that if it could be done, without either too much Danger or Cruelty, Trial might be made on some human Bodies, especially those of Malefactors. And some Months after, a foreign Ambassador, a very curious Person, at that Time residing in London, did me the Honour to visit me, and informed me, that he had caused Trial to be made, with Infusion of Crocus Metallorum, upon an inferior Domestick of his that deserved to have been hanged; but that the Fellow, as soon as ever the Injection began to be made, did, (either really or craftily) fall into a Swoon: whereby, being unwilling to prosecute so hazardous an Experiment, they desisted, without seeing any other Effect of it, save that it was told the Ambassador, that it wrought once downward with him, which yet might be occasion'd, perhaps, by Fear or Anguish. But the Trials of a very dexterous Physician of my Acquaintance, in human Bodies, will, perhaps, when I shall have receiv'd a more circumstantial Account of them, be not unwelcome to you. And in Dogs, you may possibly from our own Observations, receive a further Account of an Experiment, of which, I now chiefly designed but to relate to you the Rise and first Attempts.

The French Journals in the Year 1667, affirmed with Confidence, as a Certainty, that the French gave the English the first Thought or Notion of this Experiment: And why? because (say they) we are Witnesses, that a Benedictine Friar, one Robert de Gabets, discoursed of it at Mons. de Montmor's, ten Years ago. Surely all ingenuous Men will acknowledge, that the certain Way of deciding such Controversies as these, is a publick Record, either written or printed, declaring the Time & Place of an Invention first proposed, the Contrivance of the Method to practise it, and the Instances of the Success in the Execution: All this appears in the Field for England. *Philosophical Transactions, Numb.* 28. 1667

Number 7, of the 'Transactions of the Royal Society,' (printed Anno 1665, in December) acquaints the World, how many Years since Dr. Christopher Wren proposed the Experiment of Infusion into Veins: And this was Hint enough for the Royal Society, some while after, to advance Infusion to Transfusion; for the Trial of which latter, they gave Order at their publick Meeting of May 17, 1665, as may be seen in their Journals, where it was registered by the Care of their Secretaries, obliged by Oath to Fidelity: The Trials proving then lame, for want of a fit Apparatus, & a well contrived Method of Operation, the learned Physician and expert Anatomist Dr. Lower, since found out such a Method, which is not only registered in the same Book, but also published in Print, Numb. 20, of the Transactions, before which Time it had been already practised by the said Doctor in Oxford, who was followed by several ingenious Men at London, who successfully practised it, by the publick Order of the Royal Society.

It seems strange, that so surprizing an Invention should have been conceived in France, as they will have it, ten Years ago, & lain there so long in the Womb, 'till the Way of midwiving it into the World was sent thither from London: To say nothing of the Disagreement, there seems to be about the French Parent of this Foetus: Mons. de Gurye in his Letter fathering it upon the Abbot Bourdelot, but the Author of the French Journals upon a Benedictine Friar. *Philosophical Transactions, Numb.* 35. 1668

Extract of part of a Letter written to Mr. Oldenburg, Secretary to the Royal Society, by the learned and experienced Dr. Timothy Clark, one of his Majesty's Physicians in Ordinary, concerning the Origin of the Injection into Veins, and the Transfusion of Blood.

CÆterum, cum tu ita velis, doctissime vir, & quod ita fieri opporteat credas, fideliter originem transfusionis sanguinis, ut ea apud nos saltem se habet, enarrabo. Misso testimonio illo, quod a viro fide digno, & Regalis Societatis consorte, penes te etiamnum reperitur, viz. rever. dominum Potter, theologum insignem, triginta abhinc annis, consideratâ circulatione Harveanâ, socio huic nostro, & aliis viris doctis, saepius sanguinis transfusionem proposuisse; ego equidem, quae mihi ipsi hac de re certo cognita sunt, solum referam. Circa finem Anni 1656, aut circiter, mathematicus ille insignissimus, D.D. Christop. Wren primus infusionem variorum liquorum in massam sanguineam viventium animalium excogitavit, & Oxonii peregit. Idem mihi tunc temporis, sanguinis naturam pro virili indaganti, quae ipse fecerat, etiam communicavit; ex quo tempore diligenter ad diversa hujusmodi experimenta facienda me accingebam : & inter alia, quae tunc temporis agenda decrevi, aquas, cerevisias cujusvis generis, lac, serum lactis, juscula, vina, sp. vini, & animalium diversorum sanguinem, injicienda mecum statui. Et praeter fistulas alias, ad varias operationes adaptatas, quasdam talem in modum, factas habui, ut uno extremo in arteriam unius animalis immisso, altero in venam alterius, sanguis ab uno animali in alterum facilius transfundi posset: & ut docto cuivis, quod debitum est, reddam, Dr. Henshaw, etiam è societate regia, vel ante hoc, vel circa idem tempus (uti & egomet) incassum tamen, eadem methodo, sanguinis transfusionem tentavit. Hinc fuit, quod cum in Regali Societate, inter alia experimenta (quod ex archivis illius satis liquet) sanguinis transfusio proponeretur, alii viri docti mecum opinabantur, ex operatione tali nil fortasse sperandum; atque ipsemet difficultates recitavi, quae mihi hanc operationem peragenti contigerant. Dehinc res denuo tentata, nobiscum non successit, donec doctissimus & exercitatissimus D. Dr. Lower, Oxonii, anno 1666. rem feliciter conficeret. Quo facto, tutemet sub ejusdem anni finem, totam rem cum operationis methodo, publicam fecisti. Anno sequenti, ex Galliâ etiam de hac operatione audivimus. Fateor, me totum gaudio perfusum fuisse, quum certus redderer, fiduciam Gallicam illud aggressam esse, quod timor vel ignavia fortasse nostra, vix tentare quidem ausa fuerat. Scis. doctissime vir, quanto cum applausu clariss. Denisio assurexi, qui non solum ingeniosissimè talem experimentorum defensionem suscepit, sed in hominibus etiam postea celebravit.

At tanti mihi non videtur, eruditum illum Gallum tam strenuè & animosè de primâ transfusionis sanguinis origine contendere; vel me etiam primam

ejus inventionem nobis ipsis vendicare. Tutemet, ni fallor, D. Olden-
burge, hunc Gallum in errorem duxisti. In philosophicis enim tuis transactionibus, mense Decembri, anno 1665. editis, ubi de origine infusionis
variorum liquorum in venas, rationem reddidisti; inquis sex ab illo tempore retrò annis ad minimum, D. D. Christophorum Wren, infusionem
illam primum omnium tentasse.

Nemo fortasse dubitabit, quin, si quis de hoc experimento promovendo
seriò cogitaret, & de variis cum sanguine miscendis attentè meditaretur,
mixtio sanguinis diversorum animalium facillimè tali meditationi sit oc-
cursura. Cum igitur infusio, secundùm calculum tuum, circà annum 1659
inventa fuerit, & propositio illa de sanguinis transfusione in aedibus D.
Montmori facta dicatur anno 1658, vel a clarissimo abbate Bourdelot,
vel a docto Benedictino, Roberto de Gabets (de primo enim propositore
necdum convenit) facilè quivis in illam duci potuit sententiam, quod
Galliae experimenti hujus mentio prima saltem debeatur. Sed illa opera-
tio, cujus in dictis illis transactionibus mentionem fecisti, infusio scil.
vini emetici in massam sanguineam, per venam brachii servi cujusdam,
in aedibus legati alicujus peregrini, Londini tunc temporis commorantis,
peracta, facta fuit anno 1657, in aedibus Gallici oratoris D. de Bourdeaux,
adstante D. Colladon, equite aurato, & hodiè reginae matri medico or-
dinario Quodque multa talia experimenta eodem anno à nobis repetita
fuerint, mecum multi viri docti testari possunt, quorum aliqua in aedibus
illustr. Marchionis Dorcestriae peracta etiam fuerunt.

Notatu etiam dignum est, quad tota illa methodus facilis D. Loweri,
transfusionis peragendae, mense Decembri anno 1666. a te edita fuit, &
non nisi mense Martii anni sequentis de tali operatione è Galliâ audivimus. Verisimilè ergò, ni fallor, videtur, palman hujus Inventionis (si
modo palmam mereatur) Anglis quam Gallis potuis deberi.

Caetera, libenter scirem, quibus rationibus ductus, Romanus ille doctissimus Manfredi judicarit, hanc inventionem Germaniâ primò conceptam
fuisse. Nobis enim adhuc nihil omnino occurrit, quod vel in minimam
ejusmodi suspicionem ducere potuerit. Tribus vel quatuor abhinc annis,
Major quidam, medicus Hambergensis, schedis quibusdam publice emis-
sis persuadere orbi literato nisus est, se ante biennium de tali re cogitasse.
Sed proculdubio malè hac de re edoctus fuit vir eruditus, & nimis festi-
nanter suas propalavit cogitationes. Dicit enim, se audivisse, talem operationem, viz. exhibitionem medicamenti chartice per infusionem in
venam coram principe quodam Palatino in Germaniâ peractam fuisse;
cum reverà hoc à me in aulâ nostrâ regiâ coram celsissimo principe Palatino, Ruperto, praestitum fuerit, unde posteà facilè Germanis potuit
communicari. Rem fideliter, temporum secutus ordinem, enarravi.—Et
hoc audacter assero, nos in Angliâ inventionem hanc a nullo accepisse
peregrino.

f 2

An Italian Philosopher, in a certain Tract, entitl'd 'Relatione dell' experientie fatte in Inghelterra, Francia, & Italia intorno la transfusione del sangue,' printed in Rome, undertook to prove, that the Transfusion was of greater Antiquity, as having been known to Libavius above fifty Years since. For which, that Roman Author alledg'd a Place out of the said Libavius, (in defensione syntagmatis arcanorum chymicorum, &c. anno 1615.) where the Transfusion is describ'd in these Words: Adsit juvenis robustus, sanus, sanguine spirituoso plenus; adstet exhaustus viribus, tenuis, macilentus, vix animam trahens. Magister artis habeat tabulos argenteos inter se congruentes, aperiat arteriam robusti, & tubulum inserat, muniatque; mox & aegroti arteriam findat, & tubulum faemineum infigat. Jam duos tubulos sibi mutuo applicet, & ex sano sanguis arterialis, calens, & spirituosus saliet in aegrotum, unaque vitae fontem afferet, omnemque languorem pellet. The Observator here rightly takes Notice, that Libavius did not propose this Operation, but only to mock at it, and that he contriv'd it with great Danger, both to the Recipient and Emittent, by proposing to open Arteries in both: But,

Dr King practis'd an easy and safe Way of transfusing Blood out of one Animal into another by the Veins only, without opening any Artery of either: the Success whereof in two Experiments he communicated to the Royal-Society. To enumerate briefly some of the first Trials perform'd in England, and in foreign Parts, in pursuance of, and after the Publication of Dr. Wren's noble Invention of Infusion, & in consequence Trans-

fusion; 'tis recorded, that in November, 1667, the Experiments of Transfusion of nine or ten Ounces of the arterial Blood of a young Sheep into a human Vein of the Arm, was successfully perform'd at Arundel-House, by the Doctors Lower and King, in the Presence of many considerable Persons; and the Relation communicated to the Royal Society.

Mons. Denys, Professor of the Mathematicks and natural Philosophy at Paris, related in a Letter to the Publisher of the Transactions, that they had transmitted the Blood of four Weathers into a Horse of twenty-six Years old, and that this Horse had thence receiv'd much Strength, and more than ordinary Stomach.

By the same Mons. Denys's Relation, in his printed Letter to Monsieur de Montmor; a young Man, after he had receiv'd the arterial Blood of a Lamb, was cured of an extraordinary Lethargy, consequent to a violent Fever, wherein he had been let Blood twenty Times. Among other successful Transfusions by the said Author, are those of Lambs Blood into Dogs, which after the Space of several Months from the Time of the Operation, did not only live, but were very well, and some of them grew fatter than they were before; and of Kids Blood into a little Spaniel Bitch of twelve Years of Age, which, a little while after the Operation grew vigorous and active, and even proud, in less than eight Days. To these he added a considerable Experiment, made upon a Person, who had been for three Weeks afflicted with the complicated Distempers of an hepatick Flux, a Lientery, and a bilious Diarrhaea, accompany'd with a very violent Fever, &c.

Some remarkable Experiments of injecting medicated Liquors into Veins, were communicated in a Letter from Dantzick, by Dr. Fabricius, Physician to that City.

Ibid. p. 564

FOrasmuch (said he) as we had a great Desire to experiment, what would be the Effects of the Chirurgery of injecting Liquors into human Veins, three fit Subjects presenting themselves in our Hospital, we thought good to make the Trial upon them. But seeing little Ground to hope for a manifest Operation from any altering Medecines, we esteem'd the Experiment would be more convenient, and conspicuous from Laxatives; which made us inject by a Syphon about two Drachms of such a kind of Physick into the Median Vein of the right Arm. The Patients were these, one was a lusty robust Soldier dangerously infected with the Venereal Disease, and suffering grievous Protuberatings of the Bones in his Arms· He, when the purgative Liquor was infus'd into him, complain'd of great Pains in his Elbows, and the little Valves of his Arm did swell so visibly, that it was necessary by a gentle Compression of ones Fingers to stroke up that Swelling towards the Patient's Shoulders. Some four Hours after, it began to work, not very troublesomely, and so it did the next Day; insomuch that the Man had five good Stools after it: Without any other Remedies those Protuberances were gone, nor are there any Footsteps left of the abovemention'd Disease. The two other Trials were made upon the other Sex. A married Woman of thirty-five, and a serving Maid of twenty Years of Age, had been both of them from their Birth, very grievously afflicted with epileptick Fits, so that there were little Hopes left to cure them. They both underwent this Operation, and there was injected into their Veins a laxative Rosin, dissolv'd in an anti-epileptical Spirit. The first of these had gentle Stools, some Hours after the Injection, & the next Day, the Fits recurring now and then, but much milder, are since altogether vanish'd. As for the other, viz. the Maid, she went the same Day to Stool four Times, and several Times the next: but by going into the Air, and taking Cold, and not observing any Diet, cast herself away.

Philos. Trans. Numb. 26
Philos. Trans. Numb. 42 *from the Italian Giornale de Literati*

Mons. Gayant at Paris shew'd the Effects of Transfusion of Blood, by putting that of a young Dog into the Veins of an old one, who, two Hours after, did leap and frisk; whereas he was almost blind with Age, & could hardly stir before.—A Spaniel thirteen Years old, was recover'd of Deafness, by transfusing into his Veins the Blood of a Lamb.

f 3

Dr. J. Denys above-mention'd, (in a Letter printed at Paris, and sent to the Publisher of the Transactions of the Royal Society by himself,) gave an Account with all the strange Circumstances of a Man cured of an inveterate and outragious Madness or Phrensy, by the Transfusion of the Blood of a Calf, five or six Ounces from the crural Artery, in lieu of about ten Ounces drawn from the Patient, out of a Vein of the right Arm.

After this, in the Year 1669, Dr. Denys was question'd before the Lieutenant Criminal, at Paris, for the Death of his Patient (a Man that had been stark mad for several Years) who had expired under his Hands, while he was transfusing Blood into him, according to the new Experiment. The Operation had been twice perform'd with good Success; the Patient having had thereupon a good Interval of two Months after the first, and all Hopes of a longer, after the second; had it not been for the Debauches of Wine and Brandy, that he fell to, soon after the Operation. He was a Britain by Birth, and the Original of his Madness, Love. That which Dr. Denys's Advocate, (who was the Son of Monsieur the premier President de Lamoignon) very much gloried in, was, that (besides that the Experiment had been practised with good, at least with no ill Success, in England, Germany, Italy, Holland, &c. and defended in Theses, in almost all the Universities of France) there were two Persons, a Man and Woman present in the Audience, that receiv'd a Benefit to Admiration from the Experiment, after they had been abandoned by all Physicians, and other Helps.

With the Accounts of Transfusion of Blood, one other memorable Instance, among many, may be further cited of the Success of some Experiments of infusing Medicines into human Veins: written from Dantzick, to the Honourable R. Boyle.

Mons. Smith, Physician in ordinary to this City, having Liberty granted him to try an Experiment upon some Persons desperately infected with the Pox, then in the publick Hospital here; adventur'd the opening a Vein, & infusing some Medicines into the Blood; which was try'd upon two Persons, whereof the one recover'd, and the other died. Yet being since further encourag'd by corresponding with some of the Royal Society in England, about a Month since, the said Physician, together with Mons. Scheffeler, another eminent Practitioner in this City, repeated the Experiment, by infusing altering Medicines into the Veins of the right Arms of three Persons; the one lame of the Gout; the other extremely Apoplectical; and the third, reduc'd to Extremity by that odd Distemper, the Plica Polonica. The Success of this, as Mons. Hevelius (who was the Person only admitted to be present at the Operation) informs me, was that the gouty Man found himself pretty well next Day, and shortly after went to work, it being Harvest-time, and has continu'd well ever since, leaving the Hospital yesterday, and professing himself cured. The Apoplectical hath not had one Paroxysm: & the several Sores which the Plica Polonica had occasion'd, are heal'd; and both these Persons have been able to work any Time these three Weeks. Dated August 18. 1668.

Was it not too ludicrous for the Subject, one might be apt to imagine, that the ancient Mythologists had some Notion of the Doctrine of Transfusion, and Infusion, and the wonderful sanative, and restorative Effects thereof; but not comprehending it could be possible to assign them to natural Causes; had recourse to the Powers of Enchantments, & magical Arts.—Thus Medea restor'd, (as 'tis said) Æson, when decrepid with Age, to his former Vigour of Life, by exhausting the old Blood, and infusing medicinal Juices, and new vital Blood into the empty'd Veins and Arteries.—The like Experiment she try'd on an old Ram, which became a sucking Lamb.—These Particulars, well adapted to Fable, are describ'd by the Roman Poet, with his usual Elegancy, & with this Conclusion—

        " stricto Medea recludit
" Ense senis jugulum; veteremque exire cruoreum
" Passa; replet succis: quos postquam combibit Æson
" Aut ore acceptos, aut vulnere; barba, comaeque
" Canitie positâ nigrum rapuère colorem:
" Pulsa fugit macies; abeunt pallorque, situsque;
" Adjectoque cavae supplentur sanguine venae;
" Membraque luxuriant. Æson miratur, & olim
" Ante quater denos hunc se reminiscitur annos.

          [*Ovid. Metam. L. VII. Fab. II.*]

        " When this Medea Spy'd,
" She cuts her Patient's Throat; Th'exhausted Blood
" Recruiting with her new enchanted Flood;
" While at his Mouth, and thro' his op'ning Wound,
" A double Inlet her Infusion found;
" His feeble Frame resumes a youthful Air,
" A glossy Brown his hoary Beard and Hair.
" The meagre Paleness from his Aspect fled,
" And in its Room sprang up a florid Red;
" Thro' all his Limbs a youthful Vigour flies,
" His empty'd Art'ries swell with fresh Supplies,   ⎫
" Gazing Spectators scarce believe their Eyes.   ⎬
   ⎭

Ovid. Met. translated by several Hands, Lond. 1717

f 4

" But Æson is the most surpriz'd, to find
" A happy Change in Body, and in Mind;
" In Sense and Constitution the same Man,
" As when his Fortieth active Year began.

Aries in agnum restitutus.
" Protinus innumeris effaetus laniger annis
" Attrahitur, flexo circum cava tempora cornu:
" Cujus ut haemonio marcentia guttura cultro
" Fodit, & exiguo maculavit sanguine ferrum;
" Membra simul pecudis, validosque Venesica succos
" Mergit in aere cavo minuuntur corporis artus.
" Cornuaque exuitur, nec non cum cornibus annos:
" Et tener auditur medio balatus aeno.
" Nec mora, balatum mirantibus exsilit agnus:
" Lascivitque fugâ; lactantiaque ubera quaerit.

" A Wreath'd-horn'd Ram is brought, so far o'er-grown
" With Years, his Age was to that Age unknown.
" Of Sense too dull the piercing Point to feel,
" And scarce sufficient Blood to stain the Steel.
" His Carcase She into a Cauldron threw,
" With Drugs whose vital Qualities She knew;
" His Limbs grow less, he casts his Horns and Years,
" And tender Bleatings strike their wondring Ears.
" Then instantly leaps forth a frisking Lamb,
" That seeks (too young to graze) a suckling Dam.

Dr. Wren's Operation of cutting out the Spleen of a Dog with Safety, and Method of Cure.

MR. Boyle in his Essays of experimental natural Philosophy, mentions the following Experiment of cutting out the Spleen of a Dog with Safety. The same Experiment was try'd by Dr Wren, who has describ'd the whole Operation, and given the Method of Cure, which being deficient in Mr. Boyle's Relation, is here subjoin'd thereunto.
Nor is it small Convenience to the Anatomist, that he may in the Bodies of Brutes make divers instructive Experiments, that he dares not venture on, in those of Men, as for Instance, that late noble, and by many not yet credited Experiment, of taking out the Spleen of a Dog without killing him: For, that this Experiment may be useful, we may elsewhere have Occasion to shew; and that it is possible to be safely made, (tho' many, I confess, have but unprosperously attempted it, and it hath been lately

72

pronounced impossible in Print) ourselves can witness. And because I have not yet met with any Author, that professes himself not to relate this Experiment (of the Exemption of a Dog's Spleen) upon the Credit of others, but as an Eye-witness; I am content to assure you, that that dexterous Dissector, Dr. Jolive, did the last Year, at my Request, take out the Spleen of a young Setting-dog I brought him; and that it might not be pretended, the Experiment was unfaithfully, or favourably made; I did Part of it myself, & held the Spleen (which was the largest in Proportion to his Body I ever saw) in my Hand, whilst he cut asunder the Vessels reaching to it, that I might be sure there was not the least Part of the Spleen left unextirpated; and yet this Puppy, in less than a Fortnight, grew not only well, but as sportive and as wanton as before, which I need not take Pains to make you believe, since you often saw him at your Mother's House, whence at length he was stol'n. And tho' I remember the famous Emperick Fiorovanti, in one of his Italian Books, mentions his having been prevail'd with by the Importunity of a Lady (whom he calls Marulla Graeca) much afflicted with splenetick Distempers, to rid her of her Spleen; and adds, That she outlived the Loss of it many Years· Yet he that considers the Situation of that Part, and the Considerableness of the Vessels belonging to it, in human Bodies will probably be apt to think, that tho' his Relation may be credited, his Venturousness ought not to be imitated.

The Operation and Method of Cure, by Dr. Wren.

PRovide a Dog, as big as a Spaniel, and having tied him in a fit Posture on the right Side, with a Cushion under him, that his Belly may turn a little up; first clip away the Hair, and mark with Ink the Place for Section, drawing a Line two Fingers breadth below the Short-ribs; cross the Abdomen at right Angles to the Musculus rectus, beginning short of it a Finger's breadth, & so carry it up the Length of three Finger's breadth towards the Back; then thrust in a sharp Knife, like a Sow-gelder's Knife, till you feel you have just pierced thro' the Muscles and Peritonaeum, having a Care of the Guts; thence rip up freely, carrying on the Point of the Knife to the End of the Line; then put in two Fingers, and while another presses down the Abdomen, draw out the Spleen just without the Wound, having a great Care of pulling it too far out, because of disordering the adhering Vessels within, the Stomach, the Caul, the Arteries, & Veins; then either tie the Veins and Arteries with untwin'd Thread, but strong, and in three or four Places, Caul and all, and so cut them off close to the Parenchyma of the Spleen, and anointing the Ends of the Vessels and Wound of the Caul with Balsam, or Oil of Hypericon, put them in their Places, or else sear off the Vessels, and anoint them with the Juice of Sengreen and Plantain beaten with Whites of Eggs; or else, cum Unguento Diacalcitheos dissolv'd with Vinegar and Oil of Roses, especially the Nerve; then sew up the Wound with the Suture call'd Gastroraphia, leaving at the lower End room enough for Matter to come out, first anointing the Wound with Balsam, then ℞ *Olei Mirtini & Rosarum,* ℥ *u. Ceræ alb.* ℥ *i. Farinæ hord.* ℥β. *Boli Armeni. & Terræ Sigillatæ, ana* ℥ *vi.* make a large Plaister of this to cover the Wound, and all the Muscles about; swath his Belly warm, and lay him upon his left Side in Straw; after six Hours let him Blood in the left hinder Leg, two or three Ounces, more or less, according to the Bigness of the Dog: The next Day if there

* This was a composition of his own Invention of excellent Use

seem to lye any clotted Blood in the Abdomen; out of a Glister-pipe (one holding the Dog in his Arm, or hanging over the Table, so that the Wound may be downward) inject half a Pint of Decoction of Barley with Honey of Roses & red Sugar, till you have wash'd out the clotted Blood, then tent the remaining Hole with the * yellow Salve, and wrap him up in the former Plaister as before till the Wound begins to suppurate.

He compos'd a Treatise of the Motion of the Muscles, explaining the whole Anatomy by Models form'd in Pasteboards. These were presented to that eminent Physician, and his excellent Friend, Sir Charles Scarborough: but lost at the Fire of London: there is extant only the first Draught of a Letter from Oxford to Sir Charles concerning the Bone of the Arm, wherein is a Hint of the Pasteboards.

Sprat's Hist. of the Royal Society, p. 317

" This is a short Account of the principal Discoveries which Dr. Wren
" presented or suggested to the Royal Society, I know very well that some
" of them he did only start and design, and that they have been since car-
" ried on to Perfection by the Industry of other Hands; I purpose not to
" rob them of their Share in the Honour; yet it is but reasonable, that the
" original Invention should be ascrib'd to the true Author, rather than
" the Finishers. Nor do I fear, that this will be thought too much which
" I have said concerning him; for, there is a peculiar Reverence due to so
" much Excellence, cover'd with so much Modesty; & it is not Flattery
" but Honesty, to give him his just Praise, who is so far from usurping
" the Fame of other Men, that he endeavours with all Care to conceal
" his own.

†*Mr. Addison*

It was well observ'd by a fine † Genius of our Country, "That when,
" without any Incentive of Vanity, a Person of great Abilities is zealous
" for the Good of Mankind; and as solicitous for the Concealment, as the
" Performance of illustrious Actions; we may be sure that he has some-
" thing more than ordinary in his Composition, & has a Heart fill'd with
" Goodness and Magnanimity.

Characters of Writers

" The very elegant Historian (Dr. Sprat) gives a faithful Account of the
" Beginning, Growth, and Settlement of that illustrious Company, the

74

*John
Pointer,
Lond.*
1718

" Royal-Society, together with some of its real Inventions and Experi-
" ments, by Dr. Wren and others; and concludes with a compleat, and
" noble Apology for so brave an Institution: the whole being enlighten'd
" with such Eloquence, as is above all Description.
" But if we enquire who it was that mov'd the first Springs of this famous
" Enterprize, we shall find both Historian (viz. Sprat) & Poet (Cowley)
" referring that Honour to the Lord Bacon, whose admirable Works,
" that especially, which is worthily entituled 'Of the Advancement of
" Learning,' establish'd the first Marriage Articles between the rational
" and experimental Philosophy, from which Alliance, has sprung all the
" fair Offspring of modern Discoveries.—If the Origin and Variety of
" Forms, has been so well traced, and pursu'd through all its intricate
" Mazes, by the excellent Mr. Boyle, and other Experimenters, as Na-
" turalists, and by Mr. Lock as a Metaphysician, we see who it was that
" gave them the Clue. And if Astronomy, grafted upon the Principles of
" Nature, and cultivated by the Mathematicks, has grown up into a Sci-
" ence, and become infallible; 'tis no less certain (with all due Respect to
" the Memory of the great Men of other Nations) that the Glory of Phil-
" osophy among the Moderns began with the Lord Bacon, continu'd im-
" proving principally by the above-mention'd Mr. Boyle; Drs. Seth
" Ward, Wilkins, Williams, Wren, Wallis, Mr. Rook; Hook; and Dr.
" Halley; and ends in Sir Isaac Newton.
The great Virtuoso John Evelyn, Esq.; in his excellent 'Discourse of
Medals,' collecting the Names of the most renowned, famous, and illus-
trions Persons, in all Professions of our own, and other Nations, worthy
the Honour of Medals,* terminates his Catalogue of Mathematicians,
with this Animadversion——
" To whom add those Viri ΠΟΑΤΜΑΘΕΣΤΑΤΟΙ, (highly meriting, and in-
" feriors to none we have celebrated) Sir Christopher Wren, Dr. Wallis,
" Newton, Flamstead, Hook, Halley, &c. Fellows of the Royal Society,
" whom none but the ΑΓΕΩΜΕΤΡΗΤΟΙ & Ignorant, such as have nothing
" to commend them, will envy the Honour of a Medal, even whilst they
" are living, and their Works speak for them.

75

PART I. SECT. III.

A CATALOGUE OF SOME OF THE PHILOSOPHICAL TRACTS, MANUSCRIPTS AND PRINTED, OF SIR CHR. WREN; SUCH AS, AT PRESENT, HAVE OCCURR'D TO THE COLLECTOR.

I.

16 OROLOGIORUM Sciotericorum in plano, geometricè solùm, sine calculo trigonometrico, delineandorum, modus facillimus: per quem meridiana substylaris & stylus ipse non investigantur modò, sed etiam in cujusvis generis plano, situ proprio inscribuntur, omniaque perspicuè demonstrantur. Ex Anglico idiomate Gulielmi Oughtred, Clavis mathematicae

II.

15 Sciotericon catholicum. The Art of Dialling, perform'd on all Planes, & in all Latitudes, with much Facility, by a peculiar Instrument. Serving also for many other Uses in the organical Part of Mathematicks.

III.

16 Trigonometriae sphericae institutio Neperiana ad praxin accommodata.

IV.

17 Epistolæ miscellaneae, de propositionibus in opticis, staticis & mechanicis.

V

Praelectiones Greshamenses in astronomiam Kepleri.

VI.

Praelectiones astronomicae. Oxoniae 1662.

76

VII.

Lecturae de problematibus sphericis.

VIII.

De natura & motibus cometarum.
Of the Comet in the Year 1664. N. B. Hypothesis and Theory of Comets; produc'd to the Royal Society. 1665.

IX.

Phases Saturni accuratè delineatae & illustratae ab Anno 1649. ad Annum 1656.

X.

Discourse of the Appearance of Saturn.

XI.

Tabulæ epactarum Lunae Saturninae conjunctionibus ejus cum ♄ infimis inveniendis inservientes.

XII.

Description of an Instrument for the observing Distances of fix'd Stars, & the Planets, and Appulses to the Moon; by two Telescopes join'd like a Sector, so as to give the true Angle of their Distances.

XIII.

A Method to make Telescopes with little Trouble and Expence, of great Length, to be used for any Altitude. A Corollary relating to Telescopes.

XIV.

Of the Longitude.

XV.

To observe the Variations of the magnetical Needle.

XVI.

De re nauticâ veterum.

XVII.

To find the Velocity of a Ship in sailing.

XVIII.

Of the Improvement of Gallies.

XIX.

Of an Instrument perpetually noting the Soundings in Shallows.

XX.

To recover Wrecks.

XXI.

A convenient Way of useing Artillery on Ship-board.

XXII.

To build in deep Water.

XXIII.

To build a Mole into the Sea, without Puzzolan Dust, or Cisterns.

XXIV.

Of the Improvement of River-navigation, by the joining of the Rivers.

XXV.

Diatribe algebraica, quâ annus periodi Julianae è datis cyclis indagari & erui docetur.—[Edita in 5tâ editione Helvici chronologiæ, post prolegomena.] Oxoniae 1651.

XXVI.

Ratiocinia anni Judaici.

XXVII.

De paschate.

XXVIII.

Lecturae anglicae & latinae, de luce & refractione.

XXIX.

Philosophical Transactions, Numb. 43

Theory concerning the general Laws of Motion; imparted to the Royal-Society, December 17, 1668. Tho' entertain'd by the Author divers Years before, and verify'd by many Experiments made by himself, & that other excellent Mathematician, Mr. Rook, before the said Society, as was attested by many worthy Members of that illustrious Body.

Lex naturae de collisione corporum.

N.B. All learned Men concerned in some historical Passages relating to this Treatise, and to those communicated to the Royal Society by Dr.

78

John Wallis, and Mr. Christian Hugens, on the same Subject; it was thought most proper to publish them in the Language of the Learned, viz.-

Cum novíssimis mensibus nonnullı è Societate Regia in publico ejusdem consessu enixius urgerent, ut gravissimum illud de Regulis Motus argumentum, non semel inter ipsos antehac agitatum, sed, pluribus aliis intercurrentibus rebus, nunquam, uti par erat, discussum expensumve, tandem aliquando examini rigido subjectum conficeretur; visum equidem fuit illustrissimo isto caetui decernere, ut quotquot è sociis suis indagandae Motus indoli prae caeteris incubuissent, rogarentur ut sua in rem illam meditata, & inventa depromere, simul & ea, quae ab illis viris precellentibus, Galilaeo puta, Cartesio, Honorato Fabri, Joachimo Jungio, Petro Borrelli, aliisque, de argumento isto fuerant excogitata, congerere & procurare vellent; eo scil. fine, ut consultis hoc pacto collatisque omnium sententiis, illa dehinc theoria, quae cum observationibus & experimentis, debitâ curâ & fide crebrò peractis, quam maximè congrueret, civitate philosophicâ suo jure donaretur.

Edito hoc celeusmate, incitati protinus e dictâ Societate fuerunt, imprimis Christianus Hugenius, Johannes Wallisius, Christophorus Wrennus, ut suas de Motu hypotheses & regulas, quibus condendis aliquandiu insudassent, maturare & expedire satagerent. Factum hinc, ut selectus ille virorum praestantissimorum trias, post paucarum septimanarum spatium, theorias suas, eleganter compendifactas, tantum non certatim transmitterent, Regiaeque Societatis super iis sententiam exquirerent. Primus omnium D. Wallisius, sua de Motibus aestimandis principia, literis die 15 Novemb. 1668, datis, ejusdemque mensis die 29, traditis & praelectis, communicavit. Mox eum excepit D. Christophorus Wren, qui naturae legem de collisione corporum, proximo mense Decembri, ejusque die 17. eidem Societati publicè exhiberi curavit; quae in mandatis mox dedit, (prae-habito tamen utriusque hujus authoris consensu) ut ad commodiorem horum scriptorum communicationem, discussionemque diffusiorem, res tota typis mandaretur.

Haec dum apud nos geruntur, ecce adfert nobis tabellarius die 4 Januarii insequentis (St. Ang.) D. Hugenii literas, ejusdem mensis die 5. (at St. nov.) exaratas, ejusque scripti, De motu corporum ex mutuo impulsu, priores regulas quatuor, unà cum demonstrationibus, continentes, habebam ego in promptu theoriae Wrennianae apographum, idque actutum eodem planè die, sic favente tabellione publico, D. Hugenio, hostimenti vice, remittebam, dilata interim literarum Hugenianarum, (quibus tale quid includi, ob molem, & antegressum authoris promissum suspicabar) resignatione, donec ferret occasio nobilissimum & sapientissimum Regiae Societatis praesidem, D. Vice comitem Brouncker, compellandi.

Per Henricum. Oldenburg, Soc. Reg. Secr.

Quo facto, amborum regulis in modò dictâ Societate collatis, mirus confestim in utroque consensus effulsit; id quod insignem in nobis libentiam pariebat, utrumque hoc scriptum praelo nostro committendi. Nihil hic nobis deerat a parte Hugenii, quam ejus consensus; absque quo fas nequaquam judicabamus, ipsius inventum, maximè cum illud haud integrum eo tempore nobis dedisset, in lucem emittere. Curae interim nobis erat, scriptum ipsius publicis Regiae Societatis monumentis inserendi simul & authori die II Januar. Solennes pro cordatâ illâ communicatione gratias reponendi; additâ dehinc die scil. 4 Februarii) sollicitâ commonefactione, ut suam hanc theoriam vel Parisiis, (quod proclive erat factu in Eruditorum, ut vocant, Diario) vel hic Londini in adversariis philosophicis, imprimendam curaret, vel saltem permitteret. Quibus expeditis literis, paulo post secundas accepimus ab Hugenio, scripti Wrenniani de hoc argumento rectè traditi mentionem facientes, nil tamen quicquam de suimet scripti editione, vel Parisiis vel Londini parandâ, commemorantes. Unde liquere omninò autumem, ipsum sibi defuisse Hugenium in illâ publicatione maturandâ; quin imo occasionem dedisse procrastinando, ut laudatus D. Wren, pro ingenii sui sagacitate geminam omnino theoriam eruens, in gloriae, huic speculationi debitae, partem jure veniret; cum extra omne sit dubium, neutrum horum theoriae illius quicquam, priusquam scripta eorum comparerent, rescivisse ab altero, sed utrumque, propriâ ingenii faecunditate, pulchellam hanc sobolem enixum fuisse.

Solvit equidem Hugenius, ante aliquot jam annos, Londini cum ageret, illos de Motu casus qui ipsi tunc proponebantur; luculento sanè argumento, eum jam tum exploratas habuisse regulas, quarum id evidentiâ praestaret. At non affirmabit ipse, cuiquam se Anglorum suae theoriae quicquam aperuisse; quin fateri tenetur, se ab eorum nonnullis ad communicationem ejus solicitatum, nec tamen unquam; nisi nuperrimè, ad id faciendum pertractum fuisse.

His itaque veritati & justitiae litatis, ipsas jam Hugenii regulas donamus &c.

Tabula refractionis radiorum in medio vitreo (suppositâ mâxima refractione vitri, 489.) secundum hypothesin exquisitissimam philosophi Angli calculata.

Letters, of Astronomy, from Sir Paul Neile, to Mr. Wren, in the Years 1655, 6, 7, *and* 9.

XXX.

To make an uncertain reciprocal Motion tend to the continual Progress of an uniform progressive Motion.

XXXI.

De cycloidibus, eorumque segmentis, nec non de sphaeroidibus cycloidalibus, & segmentorum cycloidalium solidis rotundis.

80

Literae ad D. Pascal. Parisiis. De doctrinâ cycloidum.

Literae à D. Pascal. De eodem argumento, datae Parisiis 1658.

Literae ad D. Carcavy, Parisiis 1658. Quibus continetur solutio problematis missi ex Galliâ ad doctorem Seth Ward. De cycloide, ejusque solidis, centrisque gravitatis.

A Letter to Mr. Wren from Mr. Hobbs, dated at Chatsworth, 1659,
concerning the Propositions in the Book of Mons. Dettonville, *alias* Pascal; about the Cycloid.

De problemate Kepleriano per cycloidem solvendo.

XXXII.

Solutio problematis missi ex Galliâ ad matheseœs professores, & alios in
Angliâ mathematicos: à *Jean de Monfert. (printed).

**A fictitious
Name**

XXXIII.

The Description of an Instrument (in the Musaeum of the Royal Society)
with the Figure, for drawing the Out-lines of any Object in Perspective.

*Philos.
Trans.
Numb.* 45

XXXIV.

Generatio corporis cylindroidis hyperbolici, elaborandis lentibus hyper-
bolicis accommodati.

Descriptio machinae unà cum icone brevi, cujus beneficio lentes elabor-
entur hyperbolici.

*Philos.
Trans.
Numb.* 48
*Philos.
Trans.
Numb.* 53

XXXV.

Of the true Shape of the Superficies of the terrestrial Globe.

XXXVI.

Of the rising of the Sap in Trees.

XXXVII.

Description of a Hot-house to produce the Plants of the Torrid Zone.

XXXVIII.

Of a Lamp to continue to any Length of Time.

XXXIX.

To heat any Quantity of Water without Fire under it, in Wood, or any
Sort of Vessel that may be damag'd by Fire.

XL.

Experiments of the Nature of Silk; Tenacity of Oyl; of the Parts of
Leather, &c.

XLI.

Of many useful Things in our Country, & to the Improvement of Trade, which have been neglected to be brought from foreign Parts.

XLII.

Of the Os Brachii, in a Letter to Sir Charles Scarborough.

XLIII.

Anatomia anguillae fluviatilis, longae plusquam 40 digitos, circuitu, (circà umbilicum) sex, cum figuris.

XLIV.

Of the Instruments of Respiration, &c.

A Catalogue, with Vouchers of several of the Works of Sir Christopher Wren: in the Method they are recited by Mr. Ward, (in his Account of the Lives of the Professors of Gresham-college.) exclusive of some Variations and Additions enumerated in the preceding Catalogue and Accounts.

o8,

1. HOrologiographia geometrica.

This was a Latin Version of an English Treatise. Written by Mr. Oughtred, while Mr. Wren was a Gentleman commoner at Wadham-college, in Oxford, and afterwards publish'd by Mr. Oughtred, at the End of his Clavis Mathematica, [Vid. Praef. G. O. ad Clav. Mathemat.]

2. Tractatulas ad periodum Julianam spectans, Chronologiae summè utilis.

This short Tract, which contains a Method to find any particular Year requir'd, upon giving the Cycles, is inserted in the Prolegomena of 'Helvicus's Theatrum historicum & chronologium,' Ed. Oxon. 1651. And continu'd in the Later Editions. The Author's Name is not mention'd; but that it was written by Mr. Wren, is manifest from a Note indorsed on the Title-page of the Book, in the Hand of his Father, the Dean, now in the Possession of Christopher Wren, Esq.; The Words are these: "Denique filio meo modestius renitenti incentivum adhibui, ut tractatulum illum algebraicum; Julianae periodo (e cyclis in historia datis) expiscandae accommodatissimum, sudante jam hoc praelo Oxoniensi, praefigi sineret." By the Time, in which this Tract was first publish'd it appears, that Mr. Wren could not be more than nineteen Years of Age, when he wrote it.

82

3. Oratio inauguralis habita Londoni, in Collegio Greshamensi, per Christophorum Wren, A. M. Astronomiae professorem electum, Anno 1657, Ætatis suae 25.

This Oration is now first publish'd in the Appendix, N. VIII. from a Copy communicated by Christopher Wren, Esq. to Dr. Mead, by whom I was favour'd with it.

4. De recta tangente cycloidem primariam.
ΕΤΘΥΣΜΟΣ curvae lineae cycloidis primariae secundum methodum antiquorum demonstratus.
De dimentione cycloidum contractarum & protractarum.
De problemate Kepleriano per cycloidem solvendo.

These four Tracts being communicated by him to Dr. Wallis, the beginning of July 1658, were afterward publish'd by the Doctor, as an Appendix to his tractatus de cycloide. [*vid.* J. W. 'opera mathemat.' vol. I. p. 533.]

5. Solutio problematis mathematici, Folio, one Sheet, printed.

This Problem, which came from France in the Year 1658, was thus introduc'd: "Spectatissimos viros matheseos professores, & alios praeclaros in Anglia mathematicos, ut hoc problema solvere dignentur *Jean de Montfert maxime desiderat." *A fictitious Name for Mons. Pascal
And it was, as follows: "Extremis ellipseos diametris, distantia centri ab aliquo puncto in axi transverso, ubi linea eundem secet sub angulo dato, in numeris datis: segmenta ejusdem lineae, (si opus est) productae, & intra transversum axem & ellipsin terminatae, in numeris invenire."
After the Solution of this Problem, Mr. Wren in the same Paper subjoins the following (propos'd formerly by Kepler) which he had himself solved geometrically. [*vid.* Wallis *ubi supra*, Page 540.] "Aream datam semicirculi dati, vel ellipseōs datae, ex quocunque puncto diametri cujuscunque, etiam si libet productae, in data ratione secare." And he adds: "Rogo igitur praestantissimos in Gallia mathematicos, ut problema Keplerianum solvere dignentur, numerice quidem, si fieri possit saltem geometrice."

6. A Method for the Construction of solar Eclipses.

This was discover'd by him in the Year 1660, and afterwards publish'd by Mr. Flamstead, in his 'Doctrine of the Sphere'; & has now for many Years been generally follow'd, as the most concise and plain. See Sir Jonas Moor's System of the Mathematicks, London 1681, Quarto.

7. Cerebri & Calvariae figurae eruditissimè [propriis manibus] delineatae.

These Figures were drawn at the Desire of Dr. Willis, for the Use of his
excellent Treatise, intitled Cerebri Anatome, publish'd in 1664; of which
the learned Author has given Account in his Preface. [Praeter suppetias, &c.]

8. An architectonical Account of the cathedral Church of Salisbury;
with Schemes for the Repairs.

The original Manuscript of this, in the Author's own Hand, and dated
1668, is yet in the Registry of the Dean and Chapter there. And it has
been since publish'd in a Book intitled, 'The History and Antiquities of
the cathedral Church of Salisbury, and the Abbey-church of Bath,'
London 1723, Octavo. Where it is called, "An excellent Piece wrote by
" an eminent Gentleman, who was invited thither by Dr. [Bishop] Ward,
" in 1668. [for his Opinion and Instructions for the Repairs,] where he
" then made the Survey."

Besides these, the following Papers, communicated by him to the Royal-
Society, are all of them, except the last, printed in their Transactions.

1. A Way to convey Liquors immediately into the Mass of Blood, No.
VII. p. 128. December 1665.
2. Lex naturae de collisione corporum, No. XLIII. p. 867. December
1668.

This is a Theory of what the Author had before proved by Experiments.

3. A Description of an Instrument for drawing the out Lines of any Object in Perspective, No. XLV. p. 898, March 1669.
4. Generatio corporis cyclindroidis hyperbolici, laborandis lentibus hy-
perbolicis accommodati, No. XLVIII. p. 961. June 1669.
5. A Description of an Engine design'd for grinding hyperbolical Glasses,
No. LIII. p. 1059, November 1669.
6. A Letter concerning the finding a straight Line equal to that of a Cycloid, in 1658, No. XCVIII. p. 6156, November 1673.
7. An Hypothesis and geometrical Problem about the Comets, in 1664,
and 1665.

This was publish'd by Mr. Hook in his 'Cometa' in 1670. page 40.

These Papers which follow, communicated by him to the Royal Society,
later than the History, and never publish'd are entered in their Registers,
and Letter-books.

1. A Description & Figure of a new Level for taking the Horizon every

Way in a Circle, Register III. p. 184. Produced before the Royal Society, December 12 and March 7, 1666.

This is describ'd by Mr. Hook in his Animadversions on Hevelius's machina coelestis, p. 65.

2. An Account of the uncommon Shape of Hail, that fell on the 26th of March 1667; about Four of the Clock in the Afternoon, Regist. III. p. 184. Communicated to the Royal Society, November 28, 1667.

3. A Letter to Mr. Oldenburgh about a Design of building a College for the Royal Society. Dated from Oxford, June 7, 1668.

4. A Cypher or Anagram, for concealing secret Inventions. Regist. IV. p. 49. Communicated to the Society, on the 4th of February, 1668.

This was transmitted to Mr. Huygens, upon his having sent one not explain'd.

5. A Description and Scheme of an Instrument for drawing up great Weights from deep Places; Register IV. p. 99. Read May 5, 1670.

To these may be added, the three following Manuscripts, yet remaining in other Hands.

1. Christophori Wren, Londini, in Collegio Greshamensi astronomiae professoris, de corpore Saturni, ejusque phasibus hypothesis.

This Lecture in the Author's own Hand, is now in Possession of William Jones, Esq.

2. An historical and architectonical Account of the collegiate Church of St. Peter, Westminster, and of the Repairs.

This was written by Sir Christopher, at the Desire of Dr. Atterbury, Bishop of Rochester, and principal Commissioner for the Repairs of that Church, about the Year 1714. The Heads of it, with a Letter to the Bishop, are enter'd in the Journal of the Antiquary Society; but the Discourse itself is in the Hands of Christopher Wren, Esq.

3. Extracts of some loose original Papers, & Minutes, written at sundry Times, relating to the Longitude.

By these Papers it appears, that Sir Christopher Wren had his Thoughts very early upon that Subject, and always kept it in his View afterwards. They are dispos'd in the Order of an Introduction, with a Discourse following it. The Introduction, which, excepting the last Paragraph, seems to have been written about the Year 1660, contains various Ways made use of by the Antients, & in later Times, for finding the Longitude. Some Parts of the Discourse, that follow it, were written in the Year 1612.—

Others so late as 1720; & the whole consists of Divers Methods proposed by Sir Christopher for that End, with Draughts of several Instruments proper for the Purpose, (engraved on Copper-plates) These Papers are also in the Hands of the same Gentleman, with the Discourse last mentioned.

This Catalogue in Mr. Professor Ward's Work, compared and adjusted with the Catalogues recounted before may be deemed the most perfect that at present occur.

Sir Christopher has been heard sometimes to reflect sharply on the Disingenuity of Mr. Oldenburg, who had neglected not only to enter divers Inventions and Experiments of his in the Registers of the Society, but conveyed the same into foreign Parts, France and Germany; where they were after published under other Names, as their own.

Hence Dr. Sprat in his History of the Royal Society, took Occasion, in the meer Consideration of Justice, to publish a separate Account of his Endeavours in promoting the Design of the Royal Society, because in turning over the Registers, he perceived, that many excellent Things, whose first Invention ought to be ascribed to him, were casually (rather designedly) omitted.

The Problem before recited Number XXXII, was sent from France by way of Challenge to the English Mathematicians, & a pecuniary Reward promised to the Person who should give a Solution: The Solution was given beyond Exception, and the Premium demanded, which yet at last, by some Chicanery, was dishonourably witheld.

His communicative Temper in lending out Papers, never recovered; his peculiar Modesty, and Disregard of publick Applause, and of those Methods by which Men of the World usually proclaim & support the Merits of their own Performances, prevented the Appearance in publick, under his own Name, of many useful Tracts, and occasioned his not carrying on divers Discoveries to Perfection.

N.B. Mr. Henry Oldenburgh, mentioned before, (P. 118) upon the Foundation of the Royal Society, was chosen Fellow & Secretary thereof. He hath collected & published Philosophical Transactions, commencing from March 6, 1664, and carried on to No. 136. Dated the 25th of June, 1677.

APPENDIX TO PART I. SECT. III.
OF ADDITIONAL RECORDS.

NUMB. I.

Dr. Flamstead's Reflections on Mons. Cassini's Remarks on his Letter to
Dr. Wallis, relating to the Earth's Motion, &c. referred to the Judgment of Sir Christopher Wren, in the Year 1702.

The Observatory, Nov. 19, 1702.

Honoured Sir,

I Send you included a long Letter whereby you will find, that Mons.
Cassini has performed nothing of what he proposed to shew concerning
the Effects of the Earth's Motion, or the Parallax of the Orb at the fixed
Stars. As to what he adds and of the Poles of the World and Ecliptick,
after you have perused the latter part of the Letter, it will appear to you,
he might have done better to have left it out, since the Parallaxes of the
fixed Stars are determined without moving these Poles at all; & making
them to move misrepresents the Parallaxes: so that on the whole, you
will conclude that he understood nothing of the Business.—This I mind
you of, because I have not mentioned it in the Letter, which I have wrote
after my usual Way with all the Plainness and Sincerity imaginable, and
so as not to give Mons. Cassini, or any other any Offence, or Cause to complain of uncivil Usage. It is something longer than I designed at first it
should be; being a new Subject, and uncommon, I thought it was better
to err on this Hand, than to make it obscure by my Brevity.

JOHN FLAMSTEAD.

SIR,

I Send you here some Reflections on Mons. Cassini's Remarks on my
Letter to Dr. Wallis, together with an Account of the Effects of the
Earth's Motion in changing the Longitudes, Latitudes, Right Ascensions and Declinations of the fixed Stars. 'Tis a new Subject, and never
that I know of handled before. For though Mr. Cassini proposes to himself to examine what will be the Result of the Hypothesis of the Earth's
Motion, with respect of the fixed Stars and the apparent Poles of the Earth
and the Ecliptick, in order to prove that the greatest Remove of the Pole-
star is from the Pole, is made about the Beginning of the foreign April,
and its nearest Approach of October; yet he has done it in such a Manner
as will make it appear to you, that though there be some Truth in the

" Il sera à
" propos
" d'examiner
" ce qui re-
" sulte de
" l'Hypo-
" these du
" mouvement
" de la terre,
" par rap-
" port aux
" etoiles fixes

" & aux po-
" les appar-
" ens de la
" terre et de
" l'ecliptique

Cassini's
2d. Fig.

Conclusion, yet it does not result from his Premises (as I asserted) or any deep Consideration of the Effects of the Earth's Motions, or geometrical Argumentation.

His first Figure represents mine well enough, and his Report of the Contents of my Letter is fair and candid, but the ground of his Error is laid in his second, where with me making IODR to represent the Earth's Orbit, he raises Perpendiculars from every Point of it 'till they intersect the Plane EQ, (supposed placed on the Surface of the Sphere parallel to the Plane of the Ecliptick) whereby they describe on it the Orbit EML which will therefore be an exact Representative of the Orbit DOIR, now this, all that allow the Motion of the Earth make an Ellipsis, therefore that must be an Ellipsis too, and the Point M in this will represent the Sun, or the Point S in the original Orbit DOIR; though in his 3d Fig. he makes and calls it a Circle wherein a moveable Pole of the Ecliptick is carried annually about a fixed & divides it into twelve Signs marked with their proper Characters: Again,

Drawing Lines parallel to the Earth's Axis to every Point of the Original Orbit DOIR, till they intersect the aforesaid Plane EQ, he projects another curve NPQ, which also shall be an Ellipsis (but more oblique than the former) and a distinct Representative of the Earth's Orbit the Sun's Place in it being at P, in the Line SP, drawn from the Sun S in the original Parallel to the Axis.

Yet in his 3d, Fig. he makes & calls it a Circle in which a moveable Pole of the World revolves annually about a fixed one, and this also he distinguishes with the twelve Signs, as he had done the other.

Near this last representative Orbit he lays of a Star at V, which he says shall be sometimes nearer, at other, farther off from the Pole of the World. He shews no Reason why this Star's Place may not be laid off with the same respect to the other distinct representative Orbit EML and to the original IODR: Let it be done for the first at V for the Original at Y, it appears now that as the Earth makes her annual Revolution, she sometimes comes nearest to it, and removes farther from it at others, by all the several Orbits; which imports nothing to his Purpose.

From these Preliminaries he proceeds and transfers the second representative Orbits of his 2d Fig. into his 3d, and making their Suns to be fix'd Poles of the Ecliptick at P, and of the World at A; he lays off the Pole Star A in the Surface of his Sphere, by its Longitude from the next Colure and Complement of its Latitude, and thereby finds its Place at S in his 3d Fig.

But it appears by what was remark'd before, that both his Circles describ'd about the two fix'd Poles are distinct Representatives of the Earth's Orbit (let him call 'em what he pleases) and their Centers represent the Sun's Places in them; he may and ought therefore to lay off the

88

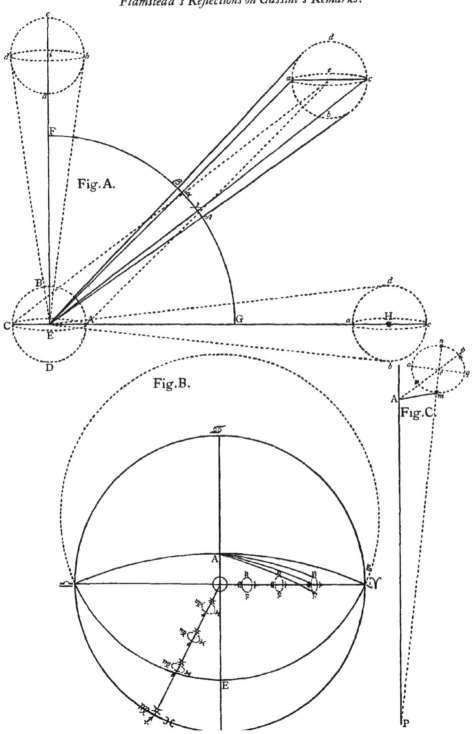

Fig. A.

Fig. B.

Fig. C.

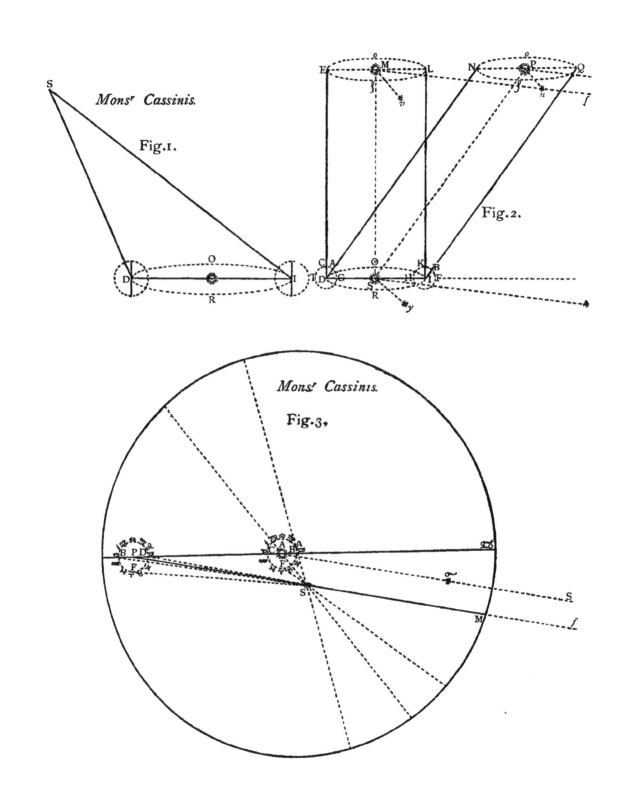

Monsr Cassinis.

Fig. 1.

Fig. 2.

Monsr Cassinis.

Fig. 3.

Star with the same Respect to the Pole A, that it has to the Pole P, and then its Place in the Surface of his Sphere will be at ♌.

And now as in his 2d Fig. we had three Orbits of the Earth, as many Suns and three Places of one fix'd Star; so in this third we have two Suns, two Fix'd Poles and two moveable of the World and Ecliptick: with two Places of the fix'd Star, which is a pretty Absurdity.

Let those who so fiercely assert Mr. Cassini's Conclusion, throw up which Pair of his Poles they please, it will be evident that his Conclusion vanishes, and that (as I affirm'd) it does not follow from these Premises.

I foresee an Evasion that Mr. Cassini may make, which I shall remember and answer in its proper Place. At present I shall only mind him, that those who understand how all the diurnal Appearances are made in the Hypothesis of the Earth's Motion, know also how to represent 'em by Lines describ'd in its Surface, or a fix'd Rete including it so close, that the Earth may only have Room to revolve within it; as I have shewn in my Doctrine of the Sphere (a Book printed above twenty Years ago, and which I am well assur'd, they are not ignorant of, at the French Observatory) and that by Lines design'd upon it, I shall endeavour to do what he has propos'd (how far he has perform'd judge you) that is to explicate the Effect of the Earth's Motion (or the Parallaxes of the annual Orb) in changing the Longitudes, Latitudes, right Ascensions, Distances from the Pole of the fix'd Stars.

Conceive the Eye plac'd at an infinite Distance in the Plane of the Earth's Orbit ABCD, it will be represented by the Line AC, its Diameter, and let the Sun's Place be at the Center at E: Again, *Fig. A.*

Conceive a Star plac'd in the North Latitude at e, Lines eA, eC drawn from the Star at e to the Extremities of the Diameter A and C, will form the Angle AEC, the greatest Parallax of the Orb at the Star; produce CA to H, then is the Angle eAH the greatest apparent latitude of the Star and the $\angle e$CH the least.

Through e the Place of the Star, draw the Line ac parallel to the Ecliptick EH, and about e let the Orbit of the Earth be describ'd equal and similar to the orginal Orbit, but contrary plac'd; and from the Extremities of its Diameter ac to E, draw the Lines AE, CE, 'tis evident to any tolerable Geometrician that the $\angle a$EC is equal to the $\angle$ CeA the greatest Parallax of the Orb.

And that instead of supposing the Star fix'd in e, and the Earth moving round in the Orbit ABCD; the Earth may be suppos'd fix'd at E, and the Star carry'd round in the representative Orbit $abcd$ whose Plane is parallel to the Plane of the Ecliptick.

Whereby the Parallaxes and the Star's apparent Place will be shewn the same in all respects, as if the original Orbit had been employ'd.

89

Let therefore E represent the Center of the Earth now fix'd, and FG a Quadrant of a Circle of Longitude on it, the Line Ea drawn from the Center of the Earth E to the nearest Point of the representative Orbit a, cuts the Periphery of the Earth in a, measuring the Arch of the Earth Ga= to the $\angle a$EH=eAH its greatest apparent Latitude: and in like Manner the Line Ec piercing the Periphery FG in r, makes rG = $\angle c$EH =eCH the least Latitude of the Star.

If further, Lines be drawn from the Center of the Earth E, touching the representative Orbit in d and b, these will cut the Earth's Periphery in p and ♂, and will give the greatest Diameter of the Curve; describ'd in the Superficies of the Earth, by Lines proceeding from its Center to the infinite Points of the representative Orbit.

The shortest was found in the preceding Paragraph to be ar which Curve (because all the Points in the Orbit $abcd$ are conceiv'd to be in a Plane parallel to the Ecliptick, and Lines drawn from E to every one of them describ'd a Cone), shall be an Ellipsis, whose Diameters are given.

1. Hence it follows that the longest or transverse Diameter of every Ellipsis or Curve, expressing the Parallax of the Orb, shall lie parallel to the Planes of the Ecliptick.

2. The conjugate or shortest at Right-angles to it, and the longer to the shorter, shall be as the Radius to the Co-sine of the Star's latitude.

3. The farther any Star is from the Earth or Sun, the lesser these Ellipses or parallactick Curves shall be: and farther,

4. If a star have no Latitude, then lying in the Plane of the Ecliptick, and the Earth moving always in the same Plane, its Latitude cannot be alter'd by the Parallax, but its Parallax of Longitude will cast it sometimes in Antecedence, sometimes in Consequence of its middle Place.

5. If a Star be conceiv'd also in the Pole of the Ecliptick at i, the Parallax of Longitude shall cast it always into the same Longitude with the Sun, and its Latitude shall be always the Complement of half the intire Parallax of the Orb; so that the Star with the Sun shall traverse all the Signs in the Space of one Year.

6. That from the Time of the first Quartile with the Sun, after its Emersion from his Rays, to the second Quartile (whilst the Earth moves from D by A to B, or the representative Point of the Star from d by a to b) the Star (suppos'd at H) appears to move always retrograde; from thence by the Conjunction to the first Quartile Star (whilst the Earth moves from B by C to D or the Star in its Representative from b by c to d) again continually direct; the Parallaxes of Longitude ceasing, and not changing its true or middle Place, at the Conjunction and Opposition to the Sun and being greatest in Antecedence at the first Quartile in Consequence at the second.

These are the Affections of the Parallactick Curves or Ellipses, and the Properties of the Parallaxes of the Orb at the Fix'd Stars, deduc'd from this Figure; we shall find more in the next Figure *B*.

Wherein let ♈♋♎♑ represent the Ecliptic, P its Pole, A the Pole of the Earth, ♎ E ♈ ♎ the Æquator; conceive a Star plac'd in the first Point of ♈, without Latitude, the Ellipsis that expresses its Parallax shall have no Latitude, and therefore will appear a straight Line, let it be represented by the short straight Line *lm* coinciding with the Ecliptick: At the Conjunction with the ☉ its primitive or middle Place is unalter'd; from thence after its Emersion from the Sun it moves in Consequence towards *m*, at which Point he arrives when he is in Quartile of it; and now 'tis evident by the Figure, that tho' its Latitude be not chang'd, yet by the Parallax of Longitude it has gotten North Declination from the Equator equal to $\frac{2}{3}$ of $\frac{1}{2}$ the intire Parallax of Longitude *lm*C; when afterwards the Sun comes into ♑, and the Point on which the Star appears to *l*; it has there as much South Declination as it had North at the 1st Quadrature in *m*, its Latitude remaining unchang'd.

But if the Star have 20, 40, or 60 Degrees North Latitude, the Parallaxes may be express'd by the three small Ellipses plac'd one above another, in the Line ♈P; and Lines drawn from the Pole of the Ecliptick P to the Place of the Sun design'd; and to be found in them, will shew which Way the Parallax carries the Star, in Consequence, or in Antecedence; and in what Proportion its Distance from the said Pole is augmented or diminish'd by it: But, for the Parallax of right Ascension and Distance from the Pole of the Globe; that narrow Ellipsis plac'd next the Ecliptick, represents the parallactick Curve of a Star that has 20 Degrees North Latitude. Let Arches of Hour-circles be struck from the Pole of the world A, to the nearest and remotest Points of this Ellipsis; they shew that the Star shall have its greatest Declination, or least Distance from the Pole, a little after its first Quartile with the Sun, he being in ♋; and its greatest Distance from the Pole, or least Declination, a little after the second Quadrature, he being in ♑.

The ingenious Reader will consider, that tho' I count the Sun's Longitude along these Curves, yet the Places design'd by them, shew only those Points in them, whereon the Star appears by Reason of the Parallax of the Orb; and the Distances of these Points from either of the said Poles in the Arch of a great Circle, represent the Distance as the Parallax makes it appear, augmented or diminish'd, with respect to either of them.

As the Latitude of the Star's Increase, the Parallaxes of Longitude, Latitude, right Ascension, and Declination, do all increase, as may be easily apprehended, by the sole Inspection & Consideration of this Figure; but with two many Varieties to be recounted, except by such as have a great deal of Leisure, & are desirous to let the World see their excellent Abilities, in retailing Things at length; I leave them to the sagacious Reader to collect from the Figure, and proceed to shew how the Appearances of the Pole-star shall be alter'd by the Parallax of the Orb, if sensible at it.

The present Longitude of the Pole-star is ♊, 24 Deg. $\frac{1}{3}$, it's Latitude 66 Deg. North. Let PA in Fig. C, represent an Arch of the solstitial Colure, equal to 23 Deg. $\frac{1}{2}$, the Distance of the Pole of the World and Ecliptick, Pe the Line of the Pole-star's Longitude, and its Distance from the Pole of the Ecliptick: About e let the parallactick Ellipsis *onqm* be describ'd in such sort, that its longer Diameter may lie parallel to the Ecliptick, and may be in Proportion to the shortest, as the Rad. is to the Line of its Latitude. 'Tis evident, by bare Inspection of the Fig. that its greatest Distance from the Pole of the Ecliptick shall then happen when the Star shall appear on *n:* And the Sun is in the same Longitude with it in the beginning of our June; it's least in December, when their Longitudes are opposite, or (to include both in our Expression) they shall both happen when the Sun, Earth, and Star, are all in the same Plane perpendicular to the Plane of the Ecliptick.

But the nearest Approach of the Pole-star to the Pole of the Globe, and its greatest Remove from it, will be distant from these Points about *q* and *o*, as appears by the Figure, perhaps not much different from the Times on which Mr. Cassini places them; but to determine exactly the Place of these Points on the Curve, the Resolution of this Problem will be required; "A Point being given, & an Ellipsis describ'd in the Superficies of the Sphere, to strike two Arches of great Circles through the said Point to the Ellipsis, so as one of them shall be the shortest, the other the longest that can be betwixt them." There is then an Oversight committed in my Letter to Dr. Wallis, where I place the greatest Remove of the Pole-star from the Pole in June, the nearest Approach in December, Mr. Halley acknowledges aloud, that Dr. Wallis, Dr. Gregory, and himself, saw it not: 'tis no very great Fault to have committed an Oversight, where they did not find it in four Years Time. We are oblig'd to Mr. Cassini for the Discovery of it; yet it appears, that he understood not the Effect of the Parallaxes of the Earth's Orb, in changing and varying the Distances of the fix'd Stars from the Pole of the Globe, since he endeavours to represent them by the Help of two Circles, placed about the Poles of the Ecliptick and Globe, when the Hypothesis neither requires nor admits of any such Thing, but only one Ellipsis, & that in numerous Cases a very narrow one *frustra fit*.

Mr. Cassini may say, that as I remove the Orbit of the Earth from about the Sun, and draw it about the Star to represent the Parallaxes, so he may in like Manner remove my Ellipses from about the Star, & draw a Circle or two about the two Poles to effect the same Thing; but he may re-

92

member that the parallactick Curves, are Ellipses, and not Circles; and that not Circles, but Ellipses, only serve to represent these Effects of Parallaxes in the Hypothesis of the Earth's Motion; and further, that it has been shew'd him, that his Circles are really Ellipses and Representatives of the Earth's Orbit, with Suns in them, & therefore no proper Exponents of the Parallaxes.

However, I am oblig'd to him for having given me an Occasion to clear up this Subject, that has not hitherto (as I know of) been handled by any Body; and now since it is evident, that the Parallaxes of such Stars as are nearest to us, and lie in the Neighbourhood to the equinoctial Colure, will (if sensible) be perceiv'd by the Change of the meridional Distances from the Pole, observ'd at six Months Distance, when they were in Quartile to the Sun, as appears by what I have remark'd: I shall return to my Stock of Night Observations, to seek out such as are most proper for discovering the Error of the Instrument; afterward those that are most convenient for shewing the Parallaxes of the Orb: And I shall copy the very first Notes of both, faithfully and exactly as they were transcrib'd from the Instrument, and compare them, to see what Parallax they allow, that the skilful Reader may both correct, examine, & compare them himself if he thinks he can do it more accurately, than I shall: Something is done towards this already; nothing is to be expected from the French, because their Instruments are commonly not above $\frac{1}{2}$ the Radius of mine; or if they be equal to mine, or bigger, as I think one of them is, they are not fix'd as they ought to be for this Purpose; which makes me wish I had a larger than my present, & a better Wall to fix it on than that is to which I have fitted the large & costly one I have made at my own great Charge: However, if the good Providence of Heaven, that has bless'd all my Labours hitherto, give me Health till after the Holidays, I hope I may by that Time give you a full Account of what it has afforded.

SIR,

Your faithful humble Servant,

JOHN FLAMSTEAD, M. R.

The Observatory, Nov. 19, 1702.

Honoured Sir,

I Send you included a long Letter, whereby you will find that Monsieur Cassini has performed nothing of what he proposed to shew concerning the Effects of the Earth's Motion on the Parallax of the Orb at the fixed Stars. As to what he adds, and of the Poles of the World and Ecliptick, after you have perused the latter Part of the Letter, it will appear to you, he might have done better to leave it out, since the Parallaxes of the fixed Stars are determined without moving these Poles at all, & making them to move misrepresents the Parallaxes; so that on the whole you will conclude that he understood nothing of the Business, and perhaps they as little, that affect him. This I mind you of, because I have not mentioned it in the Letter, which I have wrote after my usual Way, with all the Plainness and Sincerity imaginable, and so, as not to give Mons. Cassini, nor any other any Offence, or cause to complain of uncivil Usage. 'Tis something longer than I designed at first it should be; being a new Subject and uncommon, I thought it was better to err on this Hand, than to make it obscure by my Brevity.

But I am sorry, I must tell you this will not make me and Mr. Halley Friends: I have some Papers in my Hands that prove him guilty of disingenuous Practices, and know more of him than the Generality of the World does. He knows I cannot cover Dishonesty, or bear with any thing but what is just, honest and true; and that I know he regards nothing of these in his Practices: We must therefore keep at a Distance. I pray God make him sensible of his Faults; and as I told him at Brown's, whenever he becomes a sincere and honest Man, he is sure to have me his Friend.

I shall be at your End of the Town some Time next Week, when I will wait on you to clear up any Thing that may appear obscure in my long Letter, and pay you the sincere Respects of

SIR,

Your most humble Servant,

JOHN FLAMSTEAD, M. R.

I desire you to let your Son acquaint my Lord Pembroke that you have the included Letter from me; & present him with humble Respects and Services. I have acquainted Mr. Aston that I have sent you the included.

NUMB. II.

From the same Hand to Sir Christopher Wren.

An Account of the Heights of the Welch Hills, &c.

July 1, 1696.

Honoured Sir,

TO satisfy you that I was not mistaken in the Account of the Heights of the Welch Hills I gave you, I have examined some Letters I received from Mr. Caswell, in the Year 1682, who was employed by Mr. Adams in his Survey of Wales, wherein he gives me the Measures of them taken with good Instruments, made by my Directions.

The Wreckin in Shropshire, he says, by levelling by a long Pole he found 396 Yards above the Level of the Severn. But by a Base & Altitudes taken by a Quadrant with Telescope-sights, 30 Yards more; $396 + 30 + 40, = 466$ Yards.

The Severn in that Place to which he measured is 40 Yards higher than the Sea, and falls 3 Yards 3 Inches in five Miles.

Stiperstone Clee Hill, in Shropshire, he concludes 600 Yards high.

Penmenmaur in Caernarvonshire, 515 Yards.

Caddorydris in Merionethshire, 970.

Snowdown in Caernarvonshire (more than Caddorydris 270 Yards,) = 1240.

Snowdown distant from Caddorydris $27\frac{886}{1000}$ Miles. He gives me the Height of the ☿ on the Top of Snowdown $25\frac{6}{10}$ Inches, but notes not the Time: on Caddorydris (July 26, 1682.) $26\frac{45}{100}$ Inches.

Permit me to rectify a Mistake of yours concerning the Date of my Observations: All that I have made with the large mural Arch, (and which I use in rectifying the Places of the fixed Stars) are got since Michaelmas 1689, when that Instrument was scarce compleat; so that I have not yet spent seven Years in my exactest Observations. I began to rectify the Places of the fixed Stars for these Observations, but at Michelmas last, when I found I had a sufficient Stock for that Purpose, and since then I have rectify'd the eight Signs of the Ecliptick you saw, and some few more you saw not. Excuse the Trouble of this from

Your most humble Servant,

JOHN FLAMSTEAD.

NUMB. III.

Extract of a Letter from Mr. Sprat (afterwards Bishop of Rochester) to Mr. Wren, Professor of Astronomy at Gresham-College, Lond. in 1658, at which Time the College was garrison'd by the Rebels, and the Professors driven out.

Dear Sir,

THIS Day I went to visit Gresham-college, but found the Place in such a nasty Condition, so defil'd, and the Smells so infernal, that if you should now come to make Use of your Tube, it would be like Dives looking out of Hell into Heaven. Dr. Goddard of all your Collegues, keeps Possession, which he could never be able to do, had he not before prepar'd his Nose for Camp Perfumes, by his Voyage into Scotland, and had he not such excellent Restoratives in his Cellar. The Soldiers by their Violence which they put on the Muses' Seats, have made themselves odious to all the ingenious World; and if we pass by their having undone the Nation, this Crime we shall never be able to forgive them: And as for what concerns you, they have now prov'd, that their Pretensions to Religion were all feign'd, since by hindering your Lectures, they have committed so manifest a Mischief against Heaven. Yet your many Friends here hope you will hereafter recompense this unhappy Leasure which is afforded you, by making those admirable Discourses which you had intended for that Place more publick; and that you will imitate Cicero, who being hinder'd from pronouncing his Oration, 'pro Milone,' by the Guards of Pompey's Soldiers that incompass'd his Chair, set it forth afterwards more perfect than all the Rest.

To Mr. Christopher Wren, at All-Souls-College, in Oxford.

Dear Cousin,

Yesterday being the First of the Term, I resolv'd to make an Experiment, whether Dr. Horton entertain'd the new Auditory of Gresham with any Lecture, for I took it for granted, that if his Divinity could be spar'd your Mathematicks would not be expected. But at the Gate I was stop'd by a Man with a Gun, who told me there was no Admission upon that Account, the College being reform'd into a Garrison. Then changing my Pretension, I scarce got Permission to go in to Dr. Goddard, who gave me Assurance enough, that none of your Collegues intend to appear this Term, unless the Soldiers be remov'd of which there is no Probability. Upon these Premises, it is the Conclusion of all your Friends, that you may save that Journey hither, unless some other Occasions call you: and for these, I expect you will make me your Agent, if they be such as I am capable of dispatching. But it will not perhaps be amiss to take from hence the Occasion of a short and civil Letter to the Committee, signifying, that you hope you have not deceiv'd their Expectation, in choosing you, and that you are ready to attend your Duty, but for this publick Interruption and Exclusion from your Chamber, or what else you will, that looks towards this. I know no more of domestick News, than what every Body talks of: Yesterday I was in Westminster Hall, and saw only Keudigate and Windham in the two Courts, and Wild and Parker in the Exchequer, in the Chancery none at all, for Bradshaw keeps the Seal, as if it were to be carried before him in the other World, whither he is going. Glyn and Fountain pleaded at the Bar. They talk much of the

96

Mediation of the two Crowns, and proceed so far as to name Marshal de Clerambault, for the Embassador, who is to come hither from France.

My Service to all Friends,

Dear Cousin,

Your most humble Servant,

Oct. 25, 1658. *M. W.

*Matthew Wren, eldest Son of Matthew, Bishop of Ely.

From the abovementioned Mr. Sprat, to Mr. Wren, on his Translation of Horace's Epistle to Lollius.

My Dear Friend,

I Receiv'd two of your Letters together, for both which I very heartily thank you; but you must give me Leave to dissent from your Sense in one of them, wherein you maintain, that Horace cannot be well translated; for, by that elegant Epistle ad Lollium, which you sent me, you have confuted yourself: You have admirably well hit his Genius; your Verse is numerous; your Philosophy very instructive for Life; your Liberty in translating, enough to make it seem to be an English Original, and yet not so much, but that the Mind of the Author is still religiously observ'd: so that if you have not adorn'd the Fat-droll (as you most pleasantly call him) with Feathers, yet you have with Jewels, which is a more stately, though not so flanting a Bravery. Most other Attempts on him (nay even those of Ben Jonson himself) appear to me to have been hitherto very unfortunate, and his Translators have seem'd not so much to have remember'd that he was Friend to Augustus, as that he was *libertino Patre natus*: so rudely and so clownishly have they handled him.

You perfectly well agree with my Opinion, in approving this Poet above others; for, ever since I have had the good Fortune to read him otherwise than as a Schoolboy, I have always respected him as one of the most accomplish'd Men of that incomparable Age. He was almost the first Writer that brought Poetry from the Fables of their ridiculous Religion, and from flattering Womens Beauties, to speak of human Affairs, and to shew Mankind to themselves. The Decency of his Order and Invention is admirable; all Things so justly, and measuredly said, that even the hypercritical Matt. Clifford himself cannot find one Word in him whereon to use his Sponge: so natural he is, that every Fancy seems to flow into his Pen, without any Contention of Brain, and yet he was the slowest and severest of his Time; the Wit which he shews, is just enough for the subjects which he undertakes; and no more. This I esteem one of

h 1

the surest and noblest of Perfections, that belongs to an excellent Pen; and I like very well what Jack Berkenhead has somewhere said: "That a great Wit's great Work is to refuse." Moderation of Fancy is a Thing most commendable, and most difficult; it being hard for Men of hot and violent Minds (such as most commonly great Writers have) to stop themselves in full Speed, and to understand when they have done enough.

He meets, I confess, with some Tuccas, that blame him for his many downright and proverbial Sentences, and for the Roughness of his Style. But, as for the first, it must be said, that if his plain Morals are not Wit in this Age, yet they were then, and that too so great, that we have nothing else left us of all the eldest and most applauded Grecians, but some few such Sayings, of which we meet many hundreds in Horace. And if we consider his Stile too, we shall find it was very smooth, compar'd to those who writ before him; for, the best Judge of Poetry in the World gives this Judgment of the best of the ancienter Romans, Lucilius,

Hor. Sat. iv. Lib. 1.

that he was 'durus componere Versus.'* Nor can his Way of writing be call'd crabbed, or harsh, but rather a masculine Plainness, and ductile Course of Verse. If there be any Unevenness, or Ruggedness in it, it is such as that of his own Rome was, to which it was not an Injury but Advantage, that it was built on Hills. Nor are all Things presently to be prais'd that are smooth, for then it might be Quarles might come in Competition with Cowley; and if to be oyl'd were to be harmonious, I know not why a Coach-wheel, or a Jack, does not make good Musick.

They who blame him for the Equality and Familiarity of his Stile, are not worth confuting; let such be still ignorant, who admire nothing but what is lofty and swelling; such who prefer

" The fair Abbess of the Skies,
" With all her Nunnery of Eyes;

or, (to make another Instance of the same Author, not yet puplish'd)

* An eminent Oculist of that Time

" Go, call me *Stepkins for the Sun,
" And hang green Sarcenet 'fore the Moon,
" For, since my Celia's Eyes appear'd,
" Those illustrious Lights are blear'd.

Before

" Fountains and Trees our wearied Pride do please,
" Even in the midst of gilded Palaces;
" And in our Towns, that Prospect gives Delight,
" Which opens round the Country to our Sight.

And that much, my dear Friend, for your Poet.

98

To Mr. Wren, from the same Hand.—Recital of a mutual Discourse on the Subject of the Wit of Conversation. 1663.

I Owe you, my dear Friend, an ill Turn, your late Plot against me was most barbarous, your Design was as bloody as Venner's; you endeavour'd to raise a new Rebellion in my Heart, just after a long civil War; for this I have vow'd a severe Revenge, and have laid a thousand Policies to catch you; I have looked over all my Treasures of Malice, and have at last found a good old Engine, which never fail'd me in Time of Need, and that is the writing a long Letter: With this I have made many fatal Experiments, & have on all Occasions satisfy'd my Wrath on those that have displeas'd me; so that for fear of it, some have wholly forsaken my Acquaintance, and rejected my Passion; some have fled the Kingdom; and some (for what I know) have gone into another World. It is with this murd'rous Instrument that I now come to assault you; and I trust its Operation will confirm the Opinion of you Philosophers, that any Thing tho' never so innocent may be a Poison, if taken in too great a Quantity. It shall, I promise you, be as long as the Paper will give me Leave, and to the Length of it I will also add, that it shall be written on a Subject, on which I have heard you yourself speak many admirable Things; that so you may undergo the Torment to read your own Thoughts disfigur'd by my Expressions; which, I hope, will be as great a Grief to you, as it was to that King (whose Name I have forgot) when the Scythians sent home his own Ambassadors to him with their Ears, and Noses, and lips cut off. Now then, my dearest Friend, you may recollect we went lately from Axeyard to walk in St. James's-park, and tho' we met not the incomparable Person, whose Company we sought, yet he was not enough present to our Thoughts, to bring us to discourse of that in which he so much excels, the Wit of Conversation. Some Part of what you then said, you shall now hear over again; for tho' I have a most treacherous Memory in other Matters, yet my Love to Kit Wren makes it always faithful in preserving whatever he commits to it. The Wit therefore of Discourse is as different among the several Parts of Mankind, as the Temper ot their Air, and Constitution of their Bodies; and so it is to be divided into general, and particular. The general is that which consists of Terms, and Similitudes, and Humours, which are receiv'd by many Nations. This either prevails by Conquest, and so the Roman Language and Wit have obtain'd over all the Countries where they sow'd Civility by their Victories: Or else, by the Situation, Authority, and commanding Genius of one People above another. Thus the Grecians became Teachers of the Arts of Talking to the Ancients; and the French of late to the Moderns; whose Tongue and Customs have gone farther in Europe, than their present King, how terrible soever he appears, is likely to carry their

h 2

Armies. Of this general Wit there are manifest Differences to be observ'd.
That of the Chinese consists in the Skill of writing several Characters.
That of the Egyptians in giving Things themselves, instead of Words,
for Similitudes; in painting a Snake with its Tail in its Mouth, to signify
the Year; a Lyon for Courage; the Sun, Moon, and Stars, for a thousand
Conceipts. A strange Kind of laborious expressing their Minds, which
if the Orators of our Time should use in their Luxuriancy of Metaphors,
they would stand in Need of the Ark, to carry about with them any one
of their Orations. The Eastern Wit in all Ages has been principally made
up of lofty and swelling Comparisons, as we may see at this Day in the
Titles of the Sophy, and Grand Seignor, which no doubt are some of
their noblest Fancies; and yet to our Understanding, they require the
Assistance of Mahomet's Dove to make Sense of them. That of the
Moors was the same as the Spanish at this Time. The Italian, French,
English, Dutch (if they have any) is something alike, according to their
common Original the Latin. Of the Muscovitish, or Tartarian, I can
give but little Account: But I assure you, even the Irish had a Wit of
their own, tho' you will hardly believe it, till some of our Friends went
thither; nay, to say more to their Advantage, they had this peculiar to
themselves, that almost all their whole Nation was at the same Time
both Poets and Saints. The particular Wit is that which arises from the
frequent Meetings of private Assemblies: And this too is capable of infinite Divisions; for, there is hardly the least Company in the World
which rendezvouses together, but has its common Sayings, Figures,
Characters, and Observations, which are great Raillery in their proper
Compass, but tasteless to Strangers. This is evident in several Shires of
England. When I was in the North, there was a Buffoon that was a
dreadful Droll among the Yorkshire Gentlemen, and yet scarce spoke a
Grain of Salt to our Southern Tastes. This likewise appears in several
Professions of Men. The Lawyers will laugh at those Jests in the Temple,
which it may be will not move us at Charing-cross. And it is likely that
Tom Killigrew himself would not seem good Company to a Table of
Benchers. The Wit beyond Fleet-bridge has another Colour from that
on this Side. The very Watermen on the Bank-side have their Quipps,
and their Repartees, which are not intelligible but upon the Thames.
But to say no more; this is to be seen in every private Family: I had
almost gone so far as to say, that there is scarce a Husband and Wife in
the World, but have a particular Way of Wit among themselves; but
this I will not affirm, because this evil Age believes, that few married
Persons are wont to delight so much in one another's Company, as to be
merry & witty alone. Now then having discovered this mighty Proteus,
which puts on so many various Shapes in several Places, and Occasions,
let us try to define it. The Wit of Discourse is (to speak magnificently)

the greatest Art about the smallest Things: For to confess a Secret, as Sir W. Davenant's Way differs very little from Frank Bowman's, and yet the one is the gayest and the other the most insipid; so the true pleasant Talk, and the vainest Tattle, are not very much distinguished: The Subjects of both of them are a thousand little Trifles, and the Difference lies only in the Management. Nor does this Meanness of Matter prejudice the Art, for then it would follow, that your* divine Works in the King's Closet are the worse, because they are the Descriptions of a Louse, a Flea, and a Nit. This Wit therefore is made up of many inexpressible Excellences. It must have a general Evenness of Humour; it must perfectly observe all the Rules of Decency, to know when enough is said; to forbear biting Things not to be touched; to abstain from abusing honest & vertuous Matters.

Forms of little Animals, & minute Bodies, drawn by the Help of Microscopical Glasses

It must apply itself to the Condition, and Inclination of the Company; it must rather follow than lead; it must not always strain to speak extraordinary Things; for that is a constant walking on the Ropes, in which though a Man does often well, yet he may have one Fall, that may chance to break his Neck: It must allow every one their Turn of speaking; for it is natural to all, better to love their Company who give them Occasions of speaking well, than those that do it themselves. It must mingle Stories with Argument, pleasant Things with solemn; it must vary the Subject often, & not pump itself dry at once. This, if you will believe Mr. Cowley, is a wise Quality: for in a Copy of Verses which you have not yet seen, he says

> "So the Imperial Eagle does not stay
> "'Till the whole Carcase he devour
>   "That's fallen into his Power,
> "As if his generous Hunger understood,
> "That it can never want Plenty of Food;
>   "He only sucks the tasteful Blood,
> "And to fresh Game flies chearfully away,
> "To Kites and meaner Birds he leaves the mangled Prey.

This generous Eagle-wit therefore uses the best and easiest Words, is not the first that takes up new ones, nor the last that lays down old ones. But above all, its chiefest Dominion is in forming new Significations, and Images of Things & Persons. And this may be so suddenly practised, that I have known in one Afternoon, new Stamps, and Proverbs, & Fashions of Speech raised, which were never thought of before, & yet gave Occasion to most delightful Imaginations. You see now, my dear Friend, of what Extent and Difficulty this Art is. The Truth is, it is seldom to be found among Men of large and full and high Thoughts; because such Minds overlook the little Passages, and fly presently to general Axioms,

which it may be are more useful, yet they do not affect our Thoughts
with such an Immediate and familiar Delight. But to speak Truth, the
Perfection of this glorious Faculty, without which, Life were no Life,
belongs not so much to Men, as to the softer Sex: for they have usually
their heads less disturbed with busy Thoughts, their Minds are quicker
& readier for new Impressions, they talk more of circumstantial Things,
they sit longer together, and (which you used to say is of great Concernment in our northern and phlegmatick Climate) they keep their Feet
warmer and drier, and go less into the moist and open Air. But that
Women are the best Speakers, I could give you two undeniable Instances,
in your Laura (as I think you call her) and her who was once my Clelia;
the one speaks with a great Freedom and Spirit, and Abundance of excellent Words; the other talks less, but with as much Sweetness& Nature;
from the one nothing can be taken away; to the other nothing ought to
be added. But I dare not go farther in this Description on Remembrance
of an old Story: That while a Painter was drawing a most beautiful Lady,
he fell desperately in Love with her, & it had cost him his Life, had not
Alexander bestowed her on him! The first Part of this Tale, I am sure
would be my Fortune, if I should longer employ my Thoughts on such
a lovely Object; and I am as certain, that I should perish long enough,
before I should find an Alexander to pity me. To go on then in my first
Purpose. Wit consists in a right ordering of Things & Words for delight.
But—Stay— Now I look about me, What Need have I to go any farther?
you are without Question already sufficiently tired, and so my End is
obtained; and then it will be useless to speak more on this Subject, seeing
the Age wherein we live runs already so mad after the Affairs of Wit.
All the World are at present Poets: the poetical Bees are all at Work:
Comedies, Tragedies, Verses, Satyrs, Burleques, Songs buzz everywhere
about our Ears; and (to ease my Hand a little by changing my Pace)

    " Wits we have now as many (if not more)
    " As we had Sects, or Preachers, heretofore:
    " And Heaven in Mercy grant this crying Sin
    " Don't the same Judgments once more usher in.
    " We have our Northern Wits, Wits of all the East,
    " Wits of the South, and Witlings of the West;
    " South and by West, South-East, East and by North,
    " From ev'ry Point like Winds they Bluster forth.
    " We have our Wits that write only to sway
    " At York, or Hull, or ten Miles thence each Way.
    " Each Corporation, Sea-Port, Borough Town,
    " Has those that will this glorious Title own.

" Like Egypt's Frogs they swarm, and like them too
" Into the Chambers of our Kings they go.

What is to be done with this furious Generation of Wits and Writers?
To advise them to leave off is in vain.

" ——— Too strong the Infection is
" To be destroy'd by such quick Remedies:
" No no, it is a sweet and flatt'ring Kind
" Of Poison, and deceives the clearest Mind:
" Cowley himself (Cowley whom I adore)
" Often resolv'd, nay, and I think he swore,
" That he no more those barren Lands would plow,
" Where flow'ry Weeds instead of Corn do grow.
" Perchance (as Jesuit's Powder does) each Vow
" Kept the Fit off from him three Weeks, or so,
" But yet at last his Vows were all in vain,
" This Writing Ague still returns again.

Well, then, if they are incurable let them write on. But while others are
exalting such dangerous Trophies of their Wit I will be content to give
but one Instance of my own; but it is such that no Critick can lay hold
on; and it is that I infinitely love one of Sir Harry Savil's Professors: You
may easily guess which I mean, or whether it be to Dr. W. or yourself,
that I am

A most affectionate Servant,

THO. SPRAT.

From the same Hand, from Oxford, to Dr. Wren in London, 1663.

My dear Sir,

I Must confess I have some little Peek against you——therefore am not
much displeased, that I have this Occasion of telling you some ill News.
The Vice-Chancellor did yesterday send for me, to inquire where the Astronomy Professor was, and the Reason of his Absence, so long after the
Beginning of the Term——I used all the Arguments I could for your Defence. I told him, that Charles the Second was King of England, Scotland, France and Ireland; that he was by the late Act of Parliament de-
clar'd absolute Monarch in these his Dominions; and that it was this
mighty Prince who had confin'd you to London. I endeavour'd to per-
swade him that the drawing of Lines in Sir Harry Savill's School was not

‡Dr. Rich. Bayly, President of St. John's and Dean of Sarum

altogether of so great a Concernment for the Benefit of Christendom, as the rebuilding of * St. Paul's, or the fortifying (a) of Tangier: (for I understood those were the great Works, in which that extraordinary Genius of yours was judg'd necessary to be employ'd) All this I urged, but after some Discourse, he told me, that he was not to consider you now as ‡ Dr. Bayly, (for so he ow'd you all Kindness) but as Vice-Chancellor, & under that Capacity he most terribly told me, that he took it very ill, you had not all this while given him any Account what hinder'd you from the Discharge of your Office. This he bid me tell you, & I do it not very unwillingly, because I see that our Friendships are so closely ty'd together, that the same Thing which was so great a Prejudice to me, (my losing your Company all this while here) does also something redound to your Disadvantage. And so, my dear Sir, now my Spite and Spleen is satisfied, I must needs return to my old Temper again, and faithfully assure you, that I am with the most violent Zeal and Passion,

Your most affectionate and devoted Servant,

THO. SPRAT.

NUMB. IV.

IN the Year 1665, Mr. Wren took a Journey to Paris, where, at that Time all Arts flourish'd in a higher Degree than had ever been known before in France; and where there was a general Congress of the most celebrated Masters in every Profession, encourag'd by Royal Munificence, and the Influence of the great Cardinal Mazarine.

How he spent his Time, in that Place, will in Part appear from a short Account he gave by Letter to a particular Friend; wherein he returns Thanks for his Recommendation of him to the Earl of St. Albans, who in the Journey, and ever since, had us'd him with all Kindness and Indul-

(a) *A Commission to survey and direct the Works of the Mole, Harbour & Fortifications of the Citadel and Town of Tangier in Africa, was at this Time proposed for him, (being then esteemed one of the best Geometricians in Europe) with an ample Salary, and Promise of other royal Favours, particularly a Dispensation for not attending the Business of his Professorship, during his Continuance in his Majesty's Service abroad; and a Reversionary Grant of the Office of Surveyor-General of the royal Works, on the Decease of Sir John Denham: all which was signified to him by Letter from Mr. Matthew Wren, Secretary to the Lord Chancellor Hyde. This Employment he had no Inclination to accept, (being not then consistent with his Health,) but humbly prayed his Majesty to allow of his Excuse, and to command his Duty in England.*

gence imaginable, and made good his Character of him, as one of the best Men in the World. He then proceeds to the following Particulars; I have, says he, busied myself in surveying the most esteem'd Fabricks of Paris, & the Country round; the Louvre for a while was my daily Object, where no less than a thousand Hands are constantly employ'd in the Works; some in laying mighty Foundations, some in raising the Stories, Columns, Entablements, &c., with vast Stones, by great and useful Engines; others in Carving, Inlaying of Marbles, Plaistering, Painting, Gilding, &c. Which altogether make a School of Architecture, the best probably, at this Day in Europe. The College of The four Nations is usually admir'd, but the Artist hath purposely set it ill-favouredly, that he might shew his Wit in struggling with an inconvenient Situation.—An Academy of Painters, Sculptors, Architects, and the chief Artificers of the Louvre, meet every first and last Saturday of the Month. Mons. Colbert, Superintendant, comes to the Works of the Louvre, every Wednesday, and, if Business hinders not, Thursday. The Workmen are paid every Sunday duly. Mons. Abbè Charles introduc'd me to the Acquaintance of Bernini, who shew'd me his Designs of the Louvre, and of the King's Statue.—Abbè Bruno keeps the curious Rarities of the Duke of Orleans's Library, well fill'd with excellent Intaglio's, Medals, Books of Plants, and Fowls in Miniature. Abbè Burdelo keeps an Academy at his House for Philosophy every Monday Afternoon.—But I must not think to describe Paris, and the numerous Observables there, in the Compass of a short Letter.—The King's Houses I could not miss; Fontainbleau has a stately Wildness and Vastness suitable to the Desert it stands in. The antique Mass of the Castle of St. Germains, & the Hanging-gardens are delightfully surprising, (I mean to any Man of Judgment) for the Pleasures below vanish away in the Breath that is spent in ascending. The Palace, or if you please, the Cabinet of Versailles call'd me twice to view it; the Mixtures of Brick, Stone, blue Tile and Gold make it look like a rich Livery: Not an Inch within but is crouded with little Curiosities of Ornaments: the Women, as they make here the Language and Fashions, and meddle with Politicks and Philosophy, so they sway also in Architecture; Works of Filgrand, and little Knacks are in great Vogue; but Building certainly ought to have the Attribute of eternal, and therefore the only Thing uncapable of new Fashions. The masculine Furniture of Palais Mazarine pleas'd me much better, where is a great and noble Collection of antique Statues and Bustos, (many of Porphyry) good Basso-relievos; excellent Pictures of the great Masters, fine Arras, true Mosaicks, besides Pierres de Raport in Compartiments and Pavements; Vases on Porcelain painted by Raphael, and infinite other Rarities; the best of which now furnish the glorious Appartment of the Queen Mother at the Louvre, which I saw many Times.—After the incomparable Villas of Vaux and Maisons,

I shall but name Ruel, Courances, Chilly, Essoane, St. Maur, St. Mande, Issy, Meudon, Rincy, Chantilly, Verneul, Lioncour, all which,& I might add many others, I have survey'd; and that I might not lose the Impressions of them, I shall bring you almost all France in Paper, which I found by some or other ready design'd to my Hand, in which I have spent both Labour and some Money. Bernini's Design of the Louvre I would have given my Skin for, but the old reserv'd Italian gave me but a few Minutes view; it was five little Designs in Paper, for which he hath receiv'd as many thousand Pistoles; I had only Time to copy it in my Fancy and Memory; I shall be able by Discourse, and a Crayon, to give you a tolerable Account of it. I have purchas'd a great deal of *Taille-douce*, that I might give our Country-men Examples of Ornaments and Grotesks, in which the Italians themselves confess the French to excel. I hope I shall give you a very good Account of all the best Artists of France; my Business now is to pry into Trades and Arts, I put myself into all Shapes to humour them; 'tis a Comedy to me, and tho' sometimes expenceful, I am loth yet to leave it. Of the most noted Artisans within my Knowledge or Acquaintance I send you only this general Detail, and shall inlarge on their respective Characters and Works at another Time.

ARCHITECTS.

Sig. Cavalier Bernini, Mons. Mansart, Mons. Vaux, Mons. Gobert, Mons. Le Pautre.

Messieurs Anguiere and Sarazin; Sculptors and Statuaries.

Mons. Perrot; famous for Basso-relievos.

Van Ostal, Mr. Arnoldin; Plaisterers, perform the admirable Works at the Louvre.

Mons. Orphelin, Mons. de Tour; Gravers of Medals and Coins.

PAINTERS IN HISTORY.

Mess. Le Brun, Bourdon, Poussin, Ruvine, Champeine, Vilcein, Loyre, Coypel, Plcard.

Miniard, in History and Portraits.

Mons. Beaubrun; in Portraits for Women.

Mess. Baptist, Robert, for Flowers.

Mr. Matthews, an English Painter, at the Rue-Gobelins; works for the Arras-weavers; where Mons. Bruno is the Designer, and an excellent Artist.—There I saw Goldsmiths working in Plate admirably well.

Abbè Burdelo works in Enamel.

Mons. de la Quintinye, has most excellent Skill in Agriculture, Planting, and Gardening.

106

My Lord Berkley returns to England at Christmass, when I propose to take the Opportunity of his Company, and by that Time, to perfect what I have on the Anvil; Observations on the present State of Architecture, Arts, and Manufactures in France.

N.B. "Painting & Sculpture, (said the judicious Sieur de Cambray) are "the politest and noblest of antient Arts, true, ingenuous, and claiming "the Resemblance of Life, the Emulation of all Beauties, the fairest Re- "cords of all Appearances whether celestial or sublunary, whether an- "gelical, divine or humane. And what Art can be more helpful, or more "pleasing to a philosophical Traveller, an Architect, & every ingenious "Mechanician? All which must be lame without it.

PART II.
OF THE WORKS OF SIR CHRISTOPHER WREN IN ARCHITECTURE.

PART II.
OF THE WORKS OF SIR CHRIS-TOPHER WREN IN ARCHITEC-TURE.

INTRODUCTION.

AFTER the most dreadful Conflagration of London, in the fatal Year 1666. Dr. Christopher Wren was appointed Surveyor-general and principal Architect for rebuilding the whole City; the Cathedral Church of St. Paul; all the parochial Churches (in Number Fifty-one, enacted by Parliament, in lieu of those that were burnt and demolished) with other publick Structures; and for the Disposition of the Streets: A Charge so great and extensive, incumbent on a single Person, disposed him to take to his Assistance Mr. Robert Hook, Professor of Geometry in Gresham College, to whom he assigned chiefly the Business of measuring, adjusting, and setting out the Ground of the private Street-houses to the several Proprietors; reserving all the publick Works to his own peculiar Care and Direction.

On the 6th of March, 1667-8. He receiv'd his Majesty's Warrant under the Privy-seal (in Confirmation of a Deputation from Sir John Denham, Knight of the Bath) to execute the Office of Surveyor-general of the Royal-works: Upon whose Decease in the same Month, his Majesty was pleas'd to grant him Letters Patents, under the Great-seal to succeed in that Employment (a). Dr. Wren had the Honour of Knighthood confer'd on him, in the Year 1674.

(a) *By the Way; this Sir John Denham, the only Son of Sir John Denham Knight, sometime one of the Barons of the Exchequer; was a celebrated Poet, and an eminent Royalist. King Charles I. granted to him the Reversion of the Office of Surveyor-general of the Works; after the Decease of the great Architect Inigo Jones; which Office he entered upon at the Restoration of King Charles II. Anno 1660. (for the said Inigo Jones deceas'd 21 July, Ann. 1651, aged about 79 years). At the Coronation of King Charles II. he was made a Knight of the Bath. He died at his Office in Scotland-yard near Whitehall, at the Time above-mentioned, and was buried in Westminster-abbey, near the Graves of Jeffery Chaucer, and Abra. Cowley.*

At Ox 2. p

In 1684, Sir Christopher Wren was constituted by Patents under the Great-seal, the principal Officer, by the Stile of Comptroller of the Works in the Castle of Windsor; and of all Mannors, Lodges, &c., in the Forrest thereof; in the Room of Hugh May, Esq.; deceas'd.

In 1698, he was appointed Surveyor-general, and a Commissioner of the Works and Repairs of the ancient Abbey-church of St. Peter, in Westminster; (upon the passing of an Act of Parliament, charging a Branch of the Duty on Coals, for that Purpose) and furthermore, was occasionally nominated a Commissioner in divers other publick Commissions.

A View (however short and imperfect) of the Surveyor's Proceedings, in Relation to the Buildings of London; the royal & other publick Works pursuant to the several above-mention'd Appointments, may be taken from the following Sections, put together out of some scatter'd Papers, and publick Accounts, such as the Collector hath hitherto met with.

PART II. SECT. I.

OF LONDON IN ANCIENT TIMES, AND THE BOUNDARY OF THE ROMAN COLONY, DISCERN'D BY THE SURVEYOR, AFTER THE GREAT FIRE.

TO have a right Idea of London of old, it will be necessary to consider the State of the Britains, at the Time the Romans made their first Descent on the Island; and surely we cannot reasonably think them so barbarous, at least in that Age (and the Accounts before that, are too fabulous) as is commonly believ'd. Their Manner of Fighting was in Chariots, like the ancient Heroes of Greece, in the Trojan War, & occasionally on Foot, with such good Order and Discipline, as much embarrass'd the Roman Legions, and put a Stop to the Progress of the invincible Cæsar; who could do nothing great, nor conquer any part, but, says Tacitus, only shew'd the Country to the Romans; and, according to Lucan, was oblig'd shamefully to retreat.

Territa quæsitis ostendit terga Britannis.

The Britains went to Sea in Vessels cover'd with Hides, for they wanted Pitch: They traded chiefly with the Gauls, and certainly the principal Emporium, or Town of Trade to which the Gallic Ships resorted, must be London; tho' situated far up the Country, yet most commodiously accessible by a noble River, among the thickest Inhabitants; taking its Name (according to some Derivations from the old British Term) of Ship-hill; or otherwise, a Harbour of Ships.

Here the Romans fix'd a civil, or trading Colony, in the Reign of Claudius, which greatly increas'd under Nero, by the Concourse of Merchants, and Convenience of Commerce, and was inhabited by Christians and Heathens together.

The Extent of the Roman Colony, or Præfecture, particularly Northward, the Surveyor had Occasion to discover by this Accident. The parochial Church of St. Mary-le-Bow, in Cheapside, requir'd to be rebuilt after the great Fire: the Building had been mean and low, with one Corner taken out for a Tower, but upon restoring that, the new Church could be render'd square. Upon opening the Ground, a Foundation was discerned firm enough for the new intended Fabrick, which (on further Inspection, after digging down sufficiently, and removing what Earth or Rubbish lay in the Way) appear'd to be the Walls, with the Windows also, and the Pavement of a Temple, or Church, of Roman Workmanship, intirely bury'd under the Level of the present Street. Hereupon, he determin'd to erect his new Church over the old; & in order to the necessary Regularity and Square of the new Design, restor'd the Corner; but then another Place was to be found for the Steeple: The Church stood about 40 Feet backwards from the high Street, and by purchasing the Ground of one private House not yet rebuilt, he was enabled to bring the Steeple forward so as to range with the Street-houses of Cheapside. Here, to his Surprise, he sunk about 18 feet deep through made-ground, and then imagin'd he was come to the natural Soil, and hard Gravel, but upon full Examination, it appear'd to be a Roman Causeway of rough Stone, close and well rammed, with Roman Brick and Rubbish at the Bottom, for a Foundation, and all firmly cemented. This Causeway was four Feet thick [the Thickness of the via Appia, according as Mons. Montfaucon measur'd, it was about three Parisian Feet, or three Feet two Inches & a half English]. Underneath this Causeway lay the natural Clay, over which that Part of the City stands, & which descends at least forty Feet lower. He concluded then to lay the Foundation of the Tower upon the very Roman Causeway, as most proper to bear what he had design'd, a weighty and lofty Structure.

He was of opinion for divers Reasons, that this High-way ran along the North Boundary of the Colony. The Breadth then North and South, was from the Causeway now Cheapside, to the River Thames; the Extent East and West, from Tower-hill to Ludgate, and the principal middle Street, or Prætorian Way, was Watling-street.

The Colony was wall'd next the Thames, and had a Gate there called Dow-gate, but anciently Dour-gate, which signified the Water-gate.

On the North Side, beyond the Causeway, was a great Fen, or Morass, in those Times; which the Surveyor discover'd more particularly when he had Occasion to build a new East-front to the parochial Church of St. Lawrence near Guildhall; for the Foundation of which, after sinking seven Feet, he was obliged to pile twelve Feet deeper; and if there was no Causeway over the Bog, there could be no Reason for a Gate that Way.

At length, about the Year 1414, all this moorish Ground was drain'd by the Industry and Charge of Francerius, a Lord-mayor, and still retains the Name of Moor-fields, and the Gate, Moor-gate. London-stone, as is generally suppos'd, was a Pillar, in the Manner of the Milliarium Aureum, at Rome, from whence the Account of their Miles began; but the Surveyor was of Opinion, by Reason of the large Foundation, it was rather some more considerable Monument in the Forum; for in the adjoining Ground on the South Side (upon digging for Cellars, after the great Fire) were discovered some tessellated Pavements, and other extensive Remains of Roman Workmanship and Buildings.*

On the West-side was situated the Prætorian Camp, which was also wall'd in to Ludgate, in the Vallum of which, was dug up near the Gate, after the Fire, a Stone, with an Inscription, and the Figure of a Roman Soldier, which the Surveyor presented to the Archbishop of Canterbury, who sent it to Oxford, & it is reposited among the Arundellian Marbles. This is a sepulchral Monument dedicated to the Memory of Vivius Marcianus, a Soldier of the second Legion, stil'd Augusta, by his Wife Januaria Matrina. The Inscription is in this Manner.

Camden's Britannia, 2d Edit. by Bp. Gibson, vol. 1. p. 375

D. M.
VIVIO MARC·
-ANO ML. LEG. II.
AVG. IANVARIA
MARINA CoNIVNX
PIENTISSIMA POSV
-IT ME MORAM.

N.B. The Extract of this Inscription published in the Marmora Oxoniensia, Numb. 147, is erroneous.

The Soldiers used to be buried in Vallo, as the Citizens, *extrà Portas in Pomaerio;* there 'tis most probable the Extent of the Camp reached to Ludgate, to the declining of the Hill, that Way. The Surveyor gave but little Credit to the common Story, that a Temple had been here to Diana (which some have believed, upon the Report of the digging up, formerly, and of later Years, Horns of Stags, Ox-heads, Tusks of Boars, &c.) meeting with no such Indications in all his Searches; but that the North-side of this Ground had been very anciently a great Burying-place, was mani-

See Part 2, Sect. 7

Probably this might in some aegree, have imitated the Milliarium Aureum at Constantinople, which was not in the Form of a Pillar as at Rome, but an eminent Building; for under its Roof (according to Cedrenus and Suidas) stood the Statues of Constantine and Helena; Trajan; an equestrian Statue of Hadrian; a Statue of Fortune; and many other Figures and Decorations.

fest; for upon the digging the Foundations of the present Fabrick of St.
Paul's, he found under the Graves of the latter Ages, in a Row below
them, the Burial Places of the Saxon Times: the Saxons, as it appeared,
were accustomed to line their Graves with Chalk-stones, though some
more eminent were entombed in Coffins of whole Stones. Below these
were British Graves, where were found Ivory and wooden Pins, of a hard
Wood seemingly Box, in Abundance, of about 6 Inches long; it seems
the Bodies were only wrapped up, & pinned in woollen Shrouds, which
being consumed, the Pins remained entire. In the same Row & deeper,
were Roman Urns intermixed: This was eighteen Feet deep or more,
and belonged to the Colony when Romans and Britains lived and died
together.

The most remarkable Roman Urns, Lamps, Lacrymatories, and Fragments of Sacrificing-vessels, &c., were found deep in the Ground, towards the North-east Corner of St. Paul's Church, near Cheapside;
these were generally well wrought, and embossed with various Figures
and Devices, of the Colour of the modern red Portugal Ware, some
brighter like Coral, and of a Hardness equal to China Ware, and as well
glaz'd. Among Divers Pieces which happened to have been preserved,
are, a Fragment of a Vessel, in Shape of a Bason, whereon Charon is represented with his Oar in his Hand receiving a naked Ghost; a Patera
Sacrificalis with an Inscription PATER.CLO. a remarkable small Urn
of a fine hard Earth, and leaden Colour, containing about half a Pint,
many Pieces of Urns with the Names of the Potters embossed on the
Bottoms, such as, for Instance, ALBUCI. *M. VICTORINUS.
PATER. †F. MOSSI. M.‡OF. NIGRI. AↃ. MAPILII. M., &c., a
sepulchral earthen Lamp, figured with two Branches of Palms, supposed
Christian; and two Lacrymatories of Glass.

Among the many Antiquities, the Surveyor had the Fortune to discover
in other Parts of the Town, after the Fire, the most curious was a large
Roman Urn, or Ossuary of Glass, with a Handle, containing a Gallon
and half, but with a very short Neck, and wide Mouth, of whiter Metal,
encompassed Girthwise, with five parallel Circles. This was found in
Spital-fields, which he presented to the Royal Society, and is preserved
in their Museum.

PART II. SECT. II.

PROPOSALS FOR REBUILDING THE CITY OF LONDON, AFTER THE GREAT FIRE.

THE Manner of building in the City of London, practised in all former Ages, was commonly with Timber, a Material easily procured, and at little Expence, when the Country was over-burthened with Woods. This often subjected the Town to great & destructive Fires, some-times to the Ruin of the whole, as happened, for Instance, in the Year 1083, & Reign of Wil-liam the Conqueror, the Street-houses being then of Timber covered with Thatch. Not-withstanding these Incidents, this Mode continued until the two fatal Years 1665 and 6; but then the successive Calamities of Plague & Fire, gave all People Occasion seriously to reflect on the Causes of the Increase of both to that excessive Height; viz. Closeness of Buildings, and com-bustible Materials, and hence the Wishes for the necessary Amendment of both, by widening the Streets, and building with Stone and Brick, be-came universal.

Some intelligent Persons went farther, and thought it highly requisite, the City in the Restoration should rise with that Beauty, by the Straight-ness and Regularity of Buildings, & Convenience for Commerce, by the well disposing of Streets and publick Places, and the Opening of Wharfs, &c. which the excellent Situation, Wealth, and Grandeur of the Metro-polis of England did justly deserve; in respect also of the Rank she bore with all other trading Cities of the World, of which tho' she was before one of the richest in Estate & Dowry, yet unquestionably the least beau-tiful. *Informe, ingens, cui lumen ademptum.*

In order therefore to a proper Reformation, Dr. Wren (pursuant to the royal Commands) immediately after the Fire, took an exact Survey of the whole Area and Confines of the Burning, having traced over, with great Trouble and Hazard, the great Plain of Ashes and Ruins; and designed a Plan or Model of a new City, in which the Deformity and Inconveni-ences of the old Town were remedied, by the inlarging the Streets and Lanes, and carrying them as near parallel to one another as might be; avoiding, if compatible with greater Conveniences, all acute Angles; by seating all the parochial Churches conspicuous and insular; by forming the most publick Places into large Piazzas, the Centers of eight Ways; by uniting the Halls of the twelve chief Companies, into one regular Square annexed to Guild-hall; by making a commodious Key on the whole Bank of the River, from Blackfriars to the Tower.

Moreover, in contriving the general Plan, the following Particulars were chiefly consider'd and propos'd.

The Streets to be of three Magnitudes; the three principal leading straight through the City, and one or two Cross-streets to be at least 90 Feet wide; others 60 Feet; & Lanes about 30 Feet, excluding all narrow dark Alleys without Thorough-fares, and Courts.

The Exchange to stand free in the Middle of a Piazza, and be, as it were, the Nave or Center of the Town, from whence the 60 Feet Streets as so many Rays, should proceed to all principal Parts of the City: the Building to be contriv'd after the Form of the Roman Forum, with double Porticos.

Many Streets also to radiate upon the Bridge. The Streets of the first and second Magnitude to be carried on as straight as possible, and to center into four or five Piazzas.

The Key or open Wharf on the Bank of the Thames, to be spacious & convenient, without any Interruptions; with some large Docks for Barges deep loaden.

The Canal to be cut up Bridewell, 120 Feet wide, with Sasses at Holborn Bridge, and at the Mouth to cleanse it of all Filth; & Stores for Coal on each Side.

The Churches to be design'd according to the best Forms for Capacity and Hearing, adorn'd with useful Porticos, and lofty ornamental Towers and Steeples, in the greater Parishes. All Church-yards, Gardens, & unnecessary Vacuities; and all Trades that use great Fires, or yield noisome Smells, to be placed out of the Town.

The Model or Plan form'd on these Principles, delineated by Dr. Wren, was laid before the King and the honourable House of Commons; and is thus explain'd.

From that Part of Fleet-street which remain'd unburnt, about St. Dunstan's Church, a straight Street of 90 Feet wide, crosses the Valley, passing by the South Side of Ludgate Prison, and thence in a direct Line ends gracefully in a Piazza at Tower-hill; but before it descends into the Valley where now the great Sewer (Fleet-ditch) runs, about the once Middle of Fleet-street, it opens into a round Piazza, the Center of eight Ways, where at one Station are these Views. — First, straight forward quite through the City· Second, obliquely towards the Right Hand, to the Beginning of the Key, that runs from Bridewell Dock to the Tower. Third, obliquely on the left to Smithfield. Fourth, straight on the Right, to the Thames. Fifth, straight on the left, to Hatton-street, and Clerkenwell.

118

Sixth, straight backwards, towards Temple-barr. Seventh, obliquely on the right, to the Walks of the Temple. Eighth, obliquely on the left, to Cursitor's Alley.

Passing forward we cross the Valley, once sullied with an offensive Sewer, now to be beautified with a useful Canal, passable by as many Bridges as Streets that cross it.—Leaving Ludgate Prison on the left Side of the Street, (instead of which Gate, was design'd a triumphal Arch to the Founder of the new City, King Charles the Second.) This great Street presently divides into another as large, which carries the Eye and Passage to the South-front of the Exchange, (which we leave as yet for a second Journey) and before these two Streets spreading at acute Angles, can be clear of one another, they form a triangular Piazza, the Basis of which is fill'd by the cathedral Church of St. Paul.

But leaving St. Paul's on the left, we proceed as our first Way led us to-towards the Tower, the Way being all along adorn'd with parochial Churches.

We return again to Ludgate, and leaving St. Paul's on the right Hand, pass the other great Branch to the Royal-exchange, seated in the Place where it was before, but free from Buildings, in the Middle of a Piazza included between two great Streets; the one from Ludgate leading to the South-front, & another from Holborn, over the Canal to Newgate, and thence straight to the North-front of the Exchange.

The Practicability of this whole Scheme, without Loss to any Man, or Infringement of any Property, was at that Time demonstrated, & all material Objections fully weigh'd, and answer'd: the only, &, as it happened, insurmountable Difficulty remaining, was the obstinate Averseness of great Part of the Citizens to alter their old Properties, and to recede from building their houses again on their old Ground & Foundations; as also, the Distrust in many, & Unwillingness to give up their Properties, tho' for a Time only, into the Hands of publick Trustees, or Commissioners, till they might be dispens'd to them again, with more Advantage to themselves, than otherwise was possible to be effected; for, such a Method was propos'd, that by an equal Distribution of Ground into Buildings, leaving out Church-yards, Gardens, &c. (which were to be removed out of the Town) there would have been sufficient Room both for the Augmentation of the Streets; Disposition of the Churches, Halls, & all publick Buildings; and to have given every Proprietor full Satisfaction; and although few Proprietors should happen to have been seated again, directly upon the very same Ground they had possess'd before the Fire, yet no Man would have been thrust any considerable Distance from it, but been placed at least as conveniently, and sometime more so, to their own Trades than before.

By these Means, the Opportunity, in a great Degree, was lost, of making the new City the most magnificent, as well as commodious for Health and Trade of any upon Earth; and the Surveyor being thus confin'd and cramp'd in his Designs, it requir'd no small Labour and Skill, to model the City in the Manner it has since appear'd.

In the Acts of Parliament, 19 and 22 Car. II. for the rebuilding the City of London; among other Rules and Directions consistent with the Surveyor's Opinion & Advice, it is enacted: "That there shall be left a Key, " or open Wharf, from London-bridge to the Temple, forty Foot broad; " and in order thereunto, all Buildings, Sheds, &c. within forty Feet " Northward of the Thames, shall within eight Months ensuing be taken " down, and remov'd; and the Buildings to front the said Key, shall be of " the second or third Rate of Buildings, observing Uniformity as in other " Streets, &c.

A Clause so well calculated for the Ornament, & Advantage of the City, requir'd to have been punctually observ'd and executed by the Citizens, according to the full Extent and Virtue of the Law.

Critical Review of the Buildings of London, p. 2 Lond. 1734

The Observations of a late Critick, (allowing for some Mistakes in his Description of Sir Christopher Wren's Scheme for rebuilding the City) are judicious and right.

" Towards the End of King James I.'s Reign, and in the Beginning of his " Son's, Taste in Architecture made a bold Step from Italy to England at " once, and scarce staid a Moment to visit France by the Way. From the " most profound Ignorance in Architecture, the most consummate Night " of Knowledge, Inigo Jones started up, a Prodigy of Art, and vied even " with his Master Palladio himself. From so glorious an Out-set, there " was not any Excellency that we might not have hoped to obtain; Bri- " tain had a reasonable Prospect to rival Italy, and foil every Nation in " Europe beside. But in the midst of these sanguine Expectations, the fatal " Civil-war commenc'd, and all the Arts and Sciences were immediately " laid aside, as no Way concern'd in the Quarrel. What follow'd was all " Darkness and Obscurity, and 'tis even a Wonder they left us a Monu- " ment of the Beauty, 'twas so agreeable to their Natures to destroy.

" Wren was the next Genius that arose, to awake the Spirit of Science, " and kindle in his Country a Love for that Science which had been so " long neglected: during his Time a most melancholy Opportunity of- " fer'd for Art to exert itself, in the most extraordinary Manner; but the " Calamities of the present Circumstance were so great and numerous, " that the Pleas of Elegancy and Beauty could not be heard; and Neces- " sity and Conveniency took Place of Harmony and Magnificence.

" What I mean is this; The Fire of London, furnish'd the most perfect " Occasion that can ever happen in any City, to rebuild it with Pomp " and Regularity: this, Wren foresaw, &, as we are told, offer'd a Scheme " for that Purpose, which would have made it the Wonder of the World.

" He propos'd to have laid out one large Street from Aldgate to Temple-
" bar, in the Middle of which was to have been a large Square, capable
" of containing the new Church of St. Paul's, with a proper Distance for
" the View all round it; whereby that huge Building would not have
" been cooped up, as it is at present, in such a Manner, as no where to be
" seen to Advantage at all; but would have had a long and ample Vista
" at each End, to have reconcil'd it to a proper Point of View, and gave
" it one great Benefit, which, in all probability, it must now want for ever.
" He further propos'd to rebuild all the Parish Churches in such a Man-
" ner as to be seen at the end of every Vista of Houses, and dispersed in
" such Distances from each other, as to appear neither too thick, nor thin
" in Prospect; but give a proper heightening to the whole Bulk of the
" City, as it fill'd the Landscape. Lastly, he propos'd to build all the Houses
" uniform, and supported on a Piazza, like that of Covent-Garden: And,
" by the Water-side, from the Bridge to the Temple, he had plan'd a long
" & broad Wharf, or Key, where he design'd to have rang'd all the Halls
" that belong to the several Companies of the City, with proper Ware-
" houses for Merchants, between, to vary the Edifices, & make it at once
" one of the most beautiful, and most useful Ranges of Structure in the
" World.——But the Hurry of Rebuilding, and the Disputes about Pro-
" perty, prevented this glorious Scheme from taking Place."

There is scarce any Instance in History and Antiquity, of a Conflagration comparable in its Celerity and Extent, to the fatal Fire of the City of
London. What seems to come nearest, and to be almost a parallel Case,
was the Burning of Lyons in Gaul, thus describ'd by Seneca.

"Lugdunensis colonia exusta est. Hoc tam inopinatum malum, & penè
"inauditum, non miror si sine metu fuit, cum esset sine exemplo. Multas
"enim civitates incendium vexavit, nullam abstulit. Nam etiam ubi
"hostili manu in tecta ignis immissus est, multis locis deficit; & quamvis
"subinde excitetur, rarò tamen sic cuncta depascitur, ut nihil ferro re-
"linquat. Terrarum quoque vix unquam tam gravis & perniciosus fuit
"motus, ut tota oppida everteret. Nunquam denique tam infestum ulli
"exarsit incendium, ut nihil alteri superesset incendio. Tot pulcherrima
"opera, quae singula illustrare singulas urbes possent, una nox stravit,
"& in tanta pace, quantum de bello quidem timeri potest, accidit. Quis
"hoc credat? Ubique armis quiescentibus, cum toto orbe terrarum dif-
"fusa securitas sit, Lugdunum quod ostendebatur in Galliâ quaeritur.
"Omnibus fortuna quos publicè afflixit, quod passuri erant, timere
"permisit. Nulla res magna, non aliquod habuit ruinae suae spacium. In
"hac* una nox interfuit inter urbem maximam & nullam. [Epist.
"XCII."]

*N.B. Lon-
dinum, nobil-
issimam ur-
bem cui nulla
gens habuit
parem, flam-
ma triduo in
cineres re-
degit

PART II. SECTION III.

OF THE ANCIENT CATHEDRAL CHURCHES OF ST. PAUL; FROM THE FIRST AGE OF CHRISTIANITY, TO THE LAST GREAT FIRE OF LONDON, IN MDCLXVI.

AND OF THE SURVEYOR'S DESIGN FOR REPAIRING THE OLD RUINOUS STRUCTURE, MADE (BY ORDER OF HIS MAJESTY, AND THE COMMISSIONERS) UPON AN ACCURATE SURVEY, ABOUT FOUR MONTHS BEFORE THE CONFLAGRATION.

Stillingfleet see Bp. of Worcester's Origines Britanicae

‡*Rapin's Hist. of Eng. Lib. I.*

THE christian Faith, without doubt, was very early received in Britain; and without having recourse to the monkish Tale of Joseph of Arimathea, & other legendary Fictions; there is authentick Testimony of a Christian Church planted here by the Apostles themselves, and, in particular, very probably by St. Paul.

‡It is very certain this Apostle, from his first Imprisonment at Rome, to his Return at Jerusalam, had spent eight Years in preaching in divers Places, but more especially in the Western Countries. We know he design'd for Spain, and it is not improbable, but his Earnestness to convert the Britains might have carried him to this Island.

This Opinion may be strengthened by the Evidence of Vanutius Fortunatus, who says the same Thing, speaking of the Travels of St. Paul, in his Poem on the Life of St. Martin.

> Transit & oceanum, vel quà facit insula portum,
> Quasque Britannus habet terras, quasque ultima Thule.

Every Christian Church derived from the Apostles, had a Succession of Bishops from them too, and the Condition of the British Church was so early establish'd, that some maintain there were Bishops of the Britains at the Council of Nice, assembled in 325: and 'tis certain, that twenty-two Years after, Restitutus Bishop of London was one of the three British Bishops present at the Council of Arles.

Some British Prelates were likewise at the Council of Ariminum, assembled in 359, and these were of such Dignity, that they refused the

122

Emperor's † Allowance, thinking it beneath them not to bear their own
Expences.

The first Cathedral of this episcopal See of London (built in the Area,
where had been the Roman Praetorian Camp; the Situation of all the
succeeding Fabricks to this Time) was demolished under the great and
general Persecution by Dioclesian; But although in Pursuance of the
Strictness of his Edicts, the Christian Churches in all the Provinces of
the Roman Government were ordered to be pull'd down, yet possibly
the Praefects might not take the Pains, when they had made them unfit
for Use, to tear up the Foundations also. The Time of the Persecution
was short, for under Constantine, the Church flourish'd again; the
Churches in Rome, and other Parts of the Empire were soon rebuilt, and
most likely ours among the first, after the Pattern of the Roman Basilica
of St. Peter, and St. Paul, in the Vatican; and, as the Surveyor conceiv'd,
upon the old Foundations left by the Persecutors; for, the Christians
were zealous, and in haste to be settled again.

The Church thus re-edified under Constantine, was afterwards destroy'd
by the Pagan Saxons; and restor'd again, upon the old Foundations, when
they embrac'd Christianity, in the seventh Century, by Mellitus, Bishop
of London, under Ethelbert King of Kent, the first Saxon King of the
Christian Faith.

This Church, together with the whole City was destroy'd by a casual
Fire in the Year 1083. Mauritius then Bishop of London, obtain'd of the
King, the old Stone of a spacious Castle in the Neighbourhood, call'd
the Palatine Tower, demolished by the same Fire; (this Fort stood at the
Entrance of the Fleet-river, as if to defend the little Haven, then capable
of Ships) & began the Building, upon the old Foundations, a fourth Time
of that Pile; which after Additions, at several Times, to the East and
West, continu'd till the last general Conflagration of the City, in 1666.

The Fabrick thus began by Mauritius, had originally, as the Surveyor
believ'd, a semicircular Presbyterium or Chancel, after the usual Mode
of the Primitive Churches, and came near the Form of a Cross, short to
the East; as he concluded for this Reason; a Quire in after Times was
added to give a greater Length Eastward than at first; this Building was
apparently of a more modern Gothick-stile, not with Round (as in the
old Church) but sharp-headed Arches; to make Way for which, the
semicircular Presbyterium had been taken down. Upon demolishing the
Ruins, after the last Fire, and searching the Foundations of this Quire,
the Surveyor discover'd nine Wells in a Row; which, no doubt, had
anciently belong'd to a Street of Houses, that lay aslope from the High-
street (then Watling-street) to the Roman Causeway (now Cheapside)
and this Street, which was taken away to make room for the new Quire,
came so near the old Presbyterium, that the Church could not extend

123

farther that Way at first. He discover'd also, there had been a considerable Addition, and a new Front to the West, but in what Age is not
ascertain'd.

The Reason the Surveyor was of Opinion, that though several Times
the Fabrick had been ruin'd, yet that the Foundations might remain, as
originally they were laid, was upon his observing, that they consisted of
nothing but Kentish-rubble-stone, artfully work'd, and consolidated
with exceeding hard Mortar, in the Roman Manner, much excelling
what he found in the Superstructure; the Outside of which was built
chiefly with the Free-stone of the old Palatine Tower, and Free-stone
suppos'd from the Quarries of Yorkshire, & in every Part was apparently
less skilfully perform'd, and with worse Mortar.

*Dugdale's
St. Paul's,
p. 6*

Tho' there be now no History or Record notifying directly the first
Building of the first new Quire, yet 'tis probable it might have been exe-
cuted by Richard who was Bishop of London in the first Year of the
Reign of King Richard the First, & had been Treasurer to King Henry

*Godwin de
Praesul,
p. 237*

the Second; who is said to have expended a vast Sum of Money on the
Buildings of his Church, &c.

*Dugdale's
St. Paul's,
p. 12*

But the said Quire being, afterwards, not thought beautiful enough, and
a Resolution taken for an Improvement, they began with the Steeple,
which was finish'd in the Year 1221 (5 Hen. III.) & then going on with
the Quire, perfected it in 1240 (24 Hen. III.) in the Form it continued
to the last great Fire, 1666.

Under the Quire was a noble Vault, wherein were three Ranks of large
and massy Pillars, which being made a Parish-church, was dedicated to
St. Faith.

Upon the happy Restoration of King Charles II. it was determin'd to
proceed in the Repairs of the old cathedral Church, which had been interrupted by the great Rebellion; and Dr. Wren was order'd to prepare
proper Designs for that Purpose· his Predecessor Mr. Inigo Jones had
(pursuant to a Royal-commission in 1631, 7 Car. I.) put the Quire, of a
more modern Gothick Stile, as before specified, than the rest of the
Fabrick, into very good Repair; he had proceeded to case great Part of
the Outside with Portland-stone; had rebuilt the North & South-fronts;
and also the West-front, with the Addition of a very graceful Portico of
the Corinthian Order, built of large Portland-stone. The great Tower
remained to be new cased Inside and Outside; and the whole Inside from
the Quire to the West-door to be new cased, and reformed in some
Measure.

The Vaulting wanted much to be amended, in order to which it was all
well center'd, & upheld with Standards of some hundreds of tall Masts.
In this State was the Fabrick when the great Rebellion began; "but in
"1643, all the Materials, &c., assign'd for the Repairs were Seized, the

"Scaffolds pull'd down; and the Body of the Church converted to a *Dugdale's*
"Horse-quarter for Soldiers; the beautiful Pillars of Inigo Jones's Por- *St. Paul's*
"tico were shamefully hew'd and defaced for support of the Timber- *p. 146 &c.*
"work of Shops, for Seamstresses, and other Trades; for which sordid
"Uses, that stately Colonade was wholly taken up, and defil'd. Upon
"taking away the inner Scaffolds, which supported the arched Vaults,
"in order to their late intended Repair, the whole Roof of the South-
"cross tumbled down; and the rest in several Places of the Church, did
"often fall, so that the Structure continued a woful Spectacle of Ruin,
"till the happy Restoration.
"In 1662, the Dean and Chapter had taken Care to fit up for divine Ser-
"vice, the East-part of the Church, beyond the old Quire, enlarging the
"length of one Arch, into the Quire, until the Repairs of the remaining
"Part of the old Fabrick should be perfected.
"For the expediting of which general Repair, a royal Commission pass'd *Continuation*
"in 1663. After this, the Time was spent, in taking down Houses and *of Dugdale's*
"Nusances that had been rais'd by the late Usurpers, at the West-end, *St. Paul's*
"and Sides of the Church; in clearing the Rubbish; searching the *p. 149*
"Decays; repairing the Portico; in Provision of Stone, Timber, and all
"necessary Preparations; until the Beginning of the Year 1666. By which
"Time Dr. Wren had finish'd and adjusted his Designs for the whole
"Reparation, and laid the same before the King, & the Commissioners."
The first Business Dr. Wren had enter'd upon, previous to the forming
Designs for the general Repairs, was to take an exact Plan, Orthography,
and Section, upon an accurate Survey of the whole Structure, even to
Inches; in the Prosecution of which, he was astonish'd to find how negli-
gent the first Builders had been; they seem'd Normans, and to have used
the Norman Foot; but they valu'd not Exactness: some Inter-columns
were one Inch and a half too large, others as much, or more, too little.
Nor were they true in their Levels. It consisted in great Part of old
Materials, which the Founder, Mauritius Bishop of London, had pro-
cur'd of King William the First, out of the Ruins of the Palatine Tower;
these were small Yorkshire Free-stone, Kentish-ashler, and Kentish-rag
from Maidstone. They made great Pillars without any graceful Manner;
and thick Walls without Judgment. They had not as yet fallen into the
Gothick pointed-arch, as was follow'd in the Quire of a later Date, but
kept to the circular Arch; so much they retain'd of the Roman Manner,
but nothing else: Cornices they could not have, for want of larger Stones;
in short, it was a vast, but heavy Building. Adjoining to the South-cross
was a Chapter-house of a more elegant Gothick Manner, with a Cloyster
of two Stories high.
The lofty Spire which anciently rose from the great middle Stone-tower,
the Surveyor observed, was not originally intended of Stone, for there

were no diagonal Arches to reduce it into an Octagon, 'twas therefore finish'd of Timber cover'd with Lead: this was twice fir'd by Lightning, and the last Time, in 1561, totally consum'd.

Antiquaries differ in their Accounts of its Altitude, By Stow's Measures, the Stone-tower, and Spire, were equally 260 Feet each in height, the whole 520 Feet. Mr. Camden's Dimensions rise to 534 Feet. Dugdale (seemingly by good Authority, who took his Relation from a Brass-table heretofore hung on a Pillar on the north Part of the Quire) makes the Heighth of the Tower 260 Feet, and of the Spire 274 Feet, and yet the whole, viz. both of Tower and Spire did not exceed 520 Feet, as is testified by the Table (whereof there is a MS Copy also in the publick Library in Cambridge) which is 14 Feet short of the Height of the two Dimensions of the Tower and Spire added together; "This (says the "Right Rev. and Learned Editor of Camden's 'Britannia') must indeed "have been true, had the Spire risen from the Summit of the Battlements: "whereas, I suppose, it rose (as the Spires of most Steeples do) much be- "low them; the Battlements here rising 14 Feet above the Base of the "Spire, must occasion the Difference."

All the stone Tower was standing when the Surveyor measur'd it before the Fire, and, agreeable with the other Accounts, was in Height 260 Feet; the Basis of the Spire he found was 40 Feet, therefore according to the usual Proportion of Spires in Gothick Fabricks, which was 4 Diameters, or 5 at most, it could rise no higher than 200 Feet, and make the whole Altitude not to exceed 460 Feet to the Ball of Copper gilt & Cross: upon which after the first Fire by Lightning was added a Weathercock representing an Eagle, of Copper gilt likewise.

The Proportions of these copper Ornaments are thus recorded; the Ball was in Circumference 9 Feet one Inch. The Height of the Cross from the Ball, 15 Feet 6 Inches, and its Traverse 5 Feet 10 Inches. The Eagle from the Bill to the Tail, 4 Feet, the Breadth over the Wings, 3 Feet and a half.

In order to a further View of this ancient cathedral Church, some Particulars relating to the Architecture, the original Defects, and at length ruinous Parts thereof; the Design for the Repairs, and for erecting a new Cupola in the Place of the great Tower; will most properly & distinctly appear from an Extract of the Proposals of Dr. Wren, to the Right Honourable the Commissioners for the Reparation, upon an accurate Survey taken in 1666; which, together with the several respective Drawings, were laid before the King and Commissioners, some Months before the great Fire of London.

"Amongst the many Propositions, that may be made to your Lordships, "concerning the Repair of St. Paul's, some may possibly aim at too great "a Magnificence, which neither the Disposition, nor Extent of this Age

"will probably bring to a Period. Others again may fall so low as to think
"of piecing up the old Fabrick, here with Stone, there with Brick, and
"cover all Faults with a Coat of Plaister, leaving it still to Posterity, as
"a further Object of Charity.
"I suppose your Lordships may think proper to take a middle Way, and
"to neglect nothing that may conduce to a decent uniform Beauty, or
"durable Firmness in the Fabrick, or Suitableness to the Expence
"already laid out on the Outside: especially since it is a Pile both for
"Ornament & Use. For, all the Occasions either of a Quire, Consistory,
"Chapter-house, Library, Court of Arches, Preaching-auditory, might
"have been supplied in less Room, with less Expence, & yet more Beauty;
"but then it had wanted of the Grandeur, which exceeds all little Curio-
"sity; this being the Effect of Wit only, the other a Monument of
"Power, and mighty Zeal in our Ancestors to publick Works in those
"Times, when the City had neither a fifth Part of the People, nor a
"tenth Part of the Wealth it now boasts off.
"I shall presume therefore to enumerate as well the Defects of Comeli-
"ness as Firmness, that no one may be reconcil'd with the other in the
"Restitution. And yet I should not propose any Thing of meer Beauty
"to be added, but where there is a Necessity of rebuilding, and where it
"will be near the same Thing to perform it well as ill.
"First, it is evident by the Ruin of the Roof, that the Work was both ill
"design'd, and ill built from the Beginning: ill design'd, because the
"Architect gave not Butment enough to counterpoise, and resist the
"Weight of the Roof from spreading the Walls; for, the Eye alone will
"discover to any Man, that those Pillars as vast as they are, even eleven
"Foot diameter, are bent outwards at least six Inches from their first
"Position; which being done on both Sides, it necessarily follows, that
"the whole Roof must first open in large and wide Cracks along by the
"Walls and Windows, & lastly drop down between the yielding Pillars.
"This bending of the Pillars was facilitated by their ill Building; for,
"they are only cased without, and that with small Stones, not one greater
"than a Man's Burden; but within is nothing but a Core of small Rub-
"bish-stone, and much Mortar, which easily crushes and yields to the
"Weight: and this outward Coat of Free-stone is so much torn with Age,
"and the Neglect of the Roof, that there are few Stones to be found that
"are not moulder'd, and flaw'd away with the Salt-peter that is in them,
"an incurable Disease, which perpetually throws off whatever Coat of
"Plaister is laid on it, and therefore not to be palliated.
"From hence I infer, that as the Outside of the Church was new flagg'd
"with Stone of larger Size than before, so ought the Inside also: And in
"doing this, it will be as easy to perform it, after a good Roman manner,
"as to follow the Gothick Rudeness of the old Design; & that, without

" placing the Face of the new Work in any Part many Inches farther out
" or in, than the Superficies of the old Work; or adding to the Expence
" that would arise were it perform'd the worse Way.

" This also may be safely affirm'd, not only by an Architect, taking his
" Measures from the Precepts and Examples of the Antients, but by a
" Geometrician (this Part being liable to Demonstration) that the Roof
" is, and ever was, too heavy for its Butment, and therefore any Part of
" the old Roof new pieced, will still but occasion further Ruin, and the
" second Ruin will much sooner follow than the first, since 'tis easier to
" force a Thing already declining. It must therefore be either a timber
" Roof plaister'd (which, in such Buildings where a little Soke of Weather
" is not presently discover'd or remedied, will soon decay) or else a
" thinner and lighter Shell of Stone, very geometrically proportion'd to
" the Strength of the Butment. The Roof may be Brick, if it be plaister'd
" with Stucco, which is a harder Plaister, that will not fall off with the
" Drip of a few Winters, and which to this Day remains firm in many
" ancient Roman Buildings.

" The middle Part is most defective both in Beauty and Firmness, with-
" out and within; for, the Tower leans manifestly by the settling of one
" of the ancient Pillars that supported it. Four new Arches were, there-
" fore, of later Years, incorporated with the old ones, which hath
" straighten'd and hinder'd both the room, and the clear thorough View
" of the Nave, in that Part, where it had been more graceful to have been
" rather wider than the rest.

" The excessive Length of Building is no otherwise commendable, but
" because it yields a pleasing Perspective by the continu'd optical Dimi-
" nution of the Columns; & if this be cut off by Columns ranging within
" their Fellows, the Grace that would be acquir'd by the Length is to-
" tally lost.

" Besides this Deformity of the Tower itself within, there are others near
" it; as, the next Intercolumnation in the Navis or Body of the Church,
" is much less than all the rest. Also the North & South-wings have Ailes
" only on the West-side, the others being originally shut up for the Con-
" sistory. Lastly, the Intercolumnations or Spaces between the Pillars of
" the Quire next adjoining to the Tower are very unequal. Again, on the
" Outside of the Tower, the Buttresses that have been erected one upon
" the Back of another to secure three Corners on the inclining Sides, (for
" the fourth wants a Buttress) are so irregular, that upon the whole Mat-
" ter, it must be concluded, that the Tower from Top to Bottom, and the
" next adjacent Parts, are such a Heap of Deformities, that no judicious
" Architect will think it corrigible, by any Expence that can be laid out
" upon new dressing it, but that it will still remain unworthy the rest of

128

" the Work, infirm and tottering; and for these Reasons, as I conjecture,
" was formerly resolv'd to be taken down.

" I cannot propose a better Remedy, than by cutting off the inner Cor-
" ners of the Cross, to reduce this middle Part into a spacious Dome or
" Rotundo, with a Cupola, or hemispherical Roof, and upon the Cupola,
" (for the outward Ornament) a Lantern with a Spiring Top, to rise pro-
" portionably, tho' not to that unnecessary Height of the former Spire of
" Timber and Lead burnt by Lightning.

" By this Means the Deformities of the unequal Intercolumnations will
" be taken away, the Church, which is much too narrow for the Heighth,
" render'd spacious in the Middle, which may be a very proper Place for
" a vast Auditory: the outward Appearance of the Church will seem to
" swell in the middle by Degrees, from a large Basis, rising into a Ro-
" tundo bearing a Cupola, & then ending in a Lantern: and this with in-
" comparable more Grace in the remoter Aspect, than it is possible for
" the lean Shaft of a Steeple to afford. Nor if it be rightly order'd, will the
" Expence be much more than that of investing the Tower and Corners
" yet unfinish'd, with new Stone, and adding the old Steeple anew; the
" Lead of which will be sufficient for a Cupola; and the same Quantity
" of Ashler makes the Corners outward, that would make them inward
" as they now are: And the Materials of the old Corners of the Ailes will
" be filling Stone for the new Work; for I should not persuade the Tower
" to be pull'd down at first, but the new Work to be built round it, partly
" because the Expectations of Persons are to be kept up; for, many Un-
" believers would bewail the Loss of old Paul's Steeple, and despond if
" they did not see a hopeful Successor rise in its stead; & chiefly because
" it would save a great Quantity of scaffolding Poles; the Scaffolds which
" are needful being fix'd from the old to the new Work; and when the
" Tholus or inward Vault is to be laid, the Tower taken down to that
" Height will rest the Centers of the Vault with great Convenience, and
" facilitate the planting of Engines for raising the Stones; and after all is
" finish'd and settl'd, the Tower that is left may be taken clear away from
" within. All which can only from the Designs be perfectly understood.

" And for the Encouragement and Satisfaction of Benefactors that com-
" prehend not readily Designs and Draughts on Paper, as well as for the
" inferior Artificers clearer Intelligence of their Business, it will be requi-
" site that a large & exact Model be made; which will also have this Use,
" that if the Work should happen to be interrupted, or retarded, Pos-
" terity may proceed where the Work was left off, pursuing still the same
" Design.

" And as the Portico built by Inigo Jones, being an intire and excellent
" Piece, gave great Reputation to the Work in the first Repairs, and oc-

" casion'd fair Contributions; so to begin now with the Dome may prob-
" ably prove the best Advice, being an absolute Piece of itself, and what
" will most likely be finished in our Time; will make by far the most
" splendid Appearance; may be of present Use for the Auditory, will
" make up all the outward Repairs perfect; and become an Ornament to
" his Majesty's most excellent Reign, to the Church of England, & to this
" great City, which it is pity, in the Opinion of our Neighbours, should
" longer continue the most unadorn'd of her Bigness in the World.
" In the mean Time, till a good Quantity of Stone be provided, Things
" of less Expence, but no less Consequence, ought to be regarded; such as
" fixing again all Cramps that the Roof hath been spoil'd of; covering all
" Timber from Weather; taking down the falling Roofs; searching the
" Vaults beneath, & securing them. And before the Foundations be digg'd
" for the Dome, the Arches on which the Tower stands must be secur'd
" after a peculiar Manner represented in the Designs.

" P. S. I shall crave leave to subjoin, that if there be Use of Stucco, I have
" great Hopes, from some Experience already had, that there are English
" Materials to be brought by Sea at an easy Rate, that will afford as good
" Plaister as is any where to be found in the World; and that with the
" Mixture of cheaper Ingredients than Marble-meal, which was the old,
" and is now the modern Way of Italy.
" The Proposer also, (considering that high Buildings grow more and
" more expensive as they rise, by reason of the Time and Labour spent in
" raising the Materials,) takes this Occasion to acquaint your Lordships,
" that having had the Opportunity of seeing several Structures of greater
" Expence than this, while they were in raising, conducted by the best
" Artists, Italian and French; & having had daily Conference with them,
" and observing their Engines and Methods, he promoted this geomet-
" rical Part of Architecture yet farther, & thinks the raising of Materials
" may yet be more facilitated, so as to save in lofty Fabricks, a very con-
" siderable part of the Time, and Labourers Hire.

N. B. The original Designs under the Hand of the Surveyor, consisting
of Plans, Elevations, and Sections, propos'd for this Renovation of old
viz. 1728 Paul's, are *still extant.
Notwithstanding the very ruinous Condition of the old Tower (as specified above) and that the Surveyor had prepar'd so proper and beautiful a
Design for the Restitution, yet great Opposition was made by some to
the taking it down, with strong Application to his Majesty, that, (however difficult and expenceful the Work might prove) the Tower by all
Means should continue, and be repair'd, without deviating from the old

Gothick-stile: but the great Fire intervening, decided the Matter for that Time. This remarkable Circumstance recollected by that very ingenious and worthy Gentleman John Evelyn, Esq.; is recorded in his Dedication to the Surveyor, of his Account of Architecture, &c.

"I have nam'd, says he, St. Paul's, and truly, not without Admiration, as *Lond.* 1728.
"oft as I recall to Mind (as frequently I do) the sad and deplorable Con- *Account of*
"dition it was in; when (after it had been made a Stable of Horses, and a *Architects,*
"Den of Thieves) You, (with other Gentlemen and myself) were by King *and Archi-*
"Charles, named Commissioners to survey the Dilapidations, & to make *tecture. De-*
"Report to his Majesty, in order to a speedy Reparation; you will not, *dication to*
"I am sure, forget the Struggle we had with some, who were for patch- *Sir Chris-*
"ing it up any how, (so the Steeple might stand) instead of new building, *toph. Wren,*
"which it altogether needed: when (to put an End to the Contest) five *Knt.*
"Days after that dreadful Conflagration happen'd; out of whose Ashes
"this Phoenix (new St. Paul's) is to rise, and was by Providence design'd
"for you.

The great and dreadful Fire of London which began the 2nd of Septem- *Dugdale's*
ber, Anno 1666, consum'd the greatest Part of the City; the parochial *History of*
Churches were destroy'd, & the ancient Cathedral of St. Paul miserably *St. Paul's*
shatter'd, and demolish'd; the Roof fell down, and with a mighty Force *2d Edit,*
through those Vaults, call'd the Undercroft, &c. The first Thing design'd *p.* 153
after this deplorable Fire, was to fit some Part of the Church, thus ruin'd,
for a Quire; wherein the Dean and Prebends might have divine Service,
until the Repair of the whole, or a new Structure could be accomplish'd:
To which End, upon a View thereof, it was resolv'd, that Part of the
Body of it, towards the West-end, might, with the least Charge, be made
useful for that Purpose. Whereupon Workmen were set upon it, & Scaffolds rais'd for Search of the Walls, and cutting the Remainder of the un-
melted Lead from the high Roof, and other Parts of the Church.

In which Employment, as also in digging up the melted Lead, clearing
the Rubbish, taking down the Remainder of the vaulted Roof and Walls,
with the greatest Part of the Tower-steeple, digging up the Floors, sort-
ing the Stone, and carrying it to several Places, repairing the Convoca-
tion-house, & building new offices for the Work; no less than two Years,
(viz. the rest of the Year 1666, the whole Year 1667, and Part of the Year
1668) were spent. Towards the latter End of which two Years, they fell
to casing some of those great and massy Pillars, which stood betwixt the
middle Aile, and the side Ailes; beginning with those below the little
North-door, towards the West: But before the third Pillar was perfectly
cased, so weak & unsound had the excessive Heat of the Fire left it, with
the remaining Pillars and Walls, which were all miserably scaled with
the Flame, and shatter'd; that upon farther Search into them, they were

found to be altogether uncapable of any substantial Repair· It was therefore fully concluded, that, in order to a new Fabrick, the Foundations of the old Cathedral, thus made ruinous, should be totally clear'd; and Preparation of Materials, and all Things needful made ready, conducing to a new Fabrick. Which Work continu'd until the last of April 1674.

The State of the old Fabrick after the Fire; the unsuccessful Attempts to repair the Ruins, with the Defects of Inigo Jones's Work, are farther explain'd in the following Transcript of a Letter from the Rev. Dr. William Sancroft, then Dean of St. Paul's; afterwards (viz. 1677.) Arch-bishop of Canterbury.

To my worthy Friend Dr. Christopher Wren, Professor of Astronomy in Oxford, April 25, 1668.

SIR,

As he said of old, *Prudentia est quaedam divinatio*, so Science (at the Height you are Master of it) is prophetic too. What you whisper'd in my Ear at your last coming hither, is now come to pass. Our Work at the West-end of St. Paul's is fallen about our Ears. Your quick Eye discern'd the Walls and Pillars gone off from their Perpendiculars, and I believe other Defects too, which are now expos'd to every common Observer.

About a Week since, we being at Work about the third Pillar from the West-end on the South-side, which we had new cased with Stone, where it was most defective, almost up to the Chapitre, a great Weight falling from the high Wall, so disabled the Vaulting of the Side-aile by it, that it threaten'd a sudden Ruin, so visibly, that the Workmen presently remov'd; and the next Night the whole Pillar fell, & carry'd Scaffolds and all to the very Ground.

The second Pillar (which you know is bigger than the rest) stands now alone, with an enormous Weight on the Top of it; which we cannot hope should stand long, and yet we dare not venture to take it down.

This Breach has discover'd to all that look on it, two great Defects in Inigo Jones's Work; one, that his new Case of Stone in the upper Walls (massy as it is) was not set upon the upright of the Pillars, but upon the Core of the Groins of the vaulting: the other, that there were no Keystones at all to tie it to the old Work; and all this being very heavy with the Roman Ornaments on the Top of it, and being already so far gone outward, cannot possibly stand long. In fine, it is the Opinion of all Men, that we can proceed no farther at the West-end. What we are to do next is the present Deliberation, in which you are so absolutely and indispensably necessary to us, that we can do nothing, resolve on nothing without you.

'Tis therefore, that in my Lord of Canterbury's Name, and by his Order, (already, as I suppose, intimated to you by the Dean of Christ-church) we most earnestly desire your Presence and Assistance with all possible Speed.

You will think fit, I know, to bring with you those excellent Draughts and Designs you formerly favour'd us with; and in the mean Time, till we enjoy you here, consider what to advise, that may be for the Satisfaction of his Majesty, and the whole Nation; an Obligation so great and so publick, that it must be acknowledg'd by better Hands than those of—

Your very affectionate Friend, and Servant,

W. SANCROFT.

From the same Hand.—To Dr. Wren, at Oxford, London, July 2, 1668.

SIR,

Yesterday my Lords of Canterbury, London, and Oxford, met on purpose to hear your Letter read once more, and to consider what is now to be done in order to the Repairs of St. Paul's. They unanimously resolv'd, that it is fit immediately to attempt something; and that without you they can do nothing.

I am therefore commanded to give you an Invitation hither, in his Grace's Name, and the rest of the Commissioners with all Speed; that we may prepare something to be propos'd to his Majesty (the Design of such a Quire at least, as may be a congruous Part of a greater and more magnificent Work to follow) and then for the procuring Contributions to defray this, we are so sanguine, as not to doubt of it, if we could but once resolve what we would do, and what that would cost. So that the only Part of your Letter we demurr to, is the Method you propound of declaring first, what Money we would bestow; and then designing something just of that Expence; for quite otherwise, the Way their Lordships resolve upon, is to frame a Design handsome and noble, and suitable to all the Ends of it, and to the Reputation of the City, and the Nation, and to take it for granted, that Money will be had to accomplish it; or however, to let it lie by, till we have before us a Prospect of so much as may reasonably encourage us to begin.

Thus far I thought good to prepare you for what will be said to you, when you come, that you may not be surprised with it; and if my Summons prevail not, my Lord the Bishop of Oxford, hath undertaken to give it you warmer, *ore tenus*, the next Week, when he intends to be with you, if at least you be not come towards us before he arrives; which would be a very agreeable Surprise to us all, and especially to—

Your very affectionate humble Servant,

W. SANCROFT

Le Neve's Lives of Archbishops, vol. 1, *p.* 199 This excellent Man was nominated Dean of St. Paul's in 1664, where he set himself with unwearied Diligence to repair that Cathedral, till the Fire in 1666, employed his Thoughts on the more noble Undertaking of rebuilding it; towards which he gave £1400, besides what he contributed by his Industry and Endeavours.

PART II. SECT. IV.
OF THE NEW CATHEDRAL CHURCH OF ST. PAUL'S.

REPARATION for the new Structure being thus made, and several Designs presented to the King for the Form and Fashion thereof; which was intended to equal, if not exceed the Splendor and Magnificence of the old Cathedral, when it was in its best Estate; his Majesty well approving one of them, commanded a Model to be made thereof in so large & exact a Manner, that it might remain as a perpetual and unchangeable Rule and Direction for the Conduct of the whole Work. And for the more speedy Procedure in this vast and mighty Building, issued out his Letters Patents under the Great Seal of England, bearing Date the 12th day of November in the 25th Year of his Reign Anno scil. 1673, unto several Lords spiritual and temporal, and other Persons of eminent Rank and Quality, and Christopher Wren Doctor of Laws, Surveyor General of the Royal Works; authorizing them, or so many of them, as are therein appointed and enabled to act, to proceed in that great Undertaking, & to endeavour the perfecting thereof, by such Ways and Means, and according to such Rules & Orders as are therein mentioned. A Transcript of the Preamble of which Commission is here inserted.

Whereas—Since the issuing out of our Commission (viz. Anno 1663, 15 Car. II.) the late dreadful Fire in London hath destroyed & consumed the cathedral Church of St. Paul to such a Degree, that no Part of the ancient Walls or Structures can with any Safety be relied upon, or left standing; insomuch, that it is now become absolutely necessary totally to demolish and raze to the Ground all the Relicks of the former Building, and in the same Place, but upon new Foundations, to erect a new Church; (which that it may be done to the Glory of God, & for the promoting of his divine Worship and Service therein to be celebrated; and to the End the same may equal, if not exceed the Splendor and Magnificence of the former cathedral Church, when it was in its best Estate, and so become much more than formerly, the principle Ornament of our royal City, to the Honour of our Goverment, and of this our Realm, we have caused several Designs to that Purpose to be prepared by Dr. Christopher Wren, Surveyor General of all our Works and Buildings, which we have seen, and one of which we do more especially approve, & have commanded a Model thereof to be made after so large & exact a Manner, that it may remain as a perpetual unchangeable Rule and Direction for the Conduct of the whole Work) And whereas our former Commission, in which the upholding and repairing the ancient cathedral Church, is only designed and mentioned, doth not sufficiently authorize & impower our said Commissioners therein named, to begin and compleat a new Fabrick upon new Foundations.

Know ye, &c.

The Royal Warrant under the Sign-manual & Privy-seal for beginning the Works of the new Cathedral of St. Paul, transcribed from the Original annexed to the Surveyor's Drawings.

CHARLES R.

WHeras We have been informed that a Portion of the Imposition laid on Coals, which by Act of Parliament is appointed and set apart for the rebuilding of the cathedral Church of St. Paul, in our capital City of London, doth at present amount to a considerable Sum, which, tho' not proportionable to the greatness of the Work, is notwithstanding sufficient to begin the same; & with all the Materials, and other Assistances, which may probably be expected, will put a new Quire in great Forwardness: and whereas among divers Designs which have been presented to Us, We have particularly pitched upon one, as well because We found it very artificial, proper, and useful; as because it was so ordered that it might be built and finish'd by Parts: We do therefore by these Presents signify Our Royal Approbation of the said Design, hereunto annexed; and do will and require you forthwith to proceed according to the said Design, beginning with the East-end or Quire, and accomplishing the same with the present Stock of Money, & such Supplies as may probably accrue, according to the Tenor of the Commission to you directed; and for so doing this shall be your Warrant. Given at Our Court at Whitehall, the 14th Day of May, 1675, in the 27th Year of our Reign.

By His Majesty's Command,

HENRY COVENTRY.

To Our Commissioners for rebuilding the
Cathedral of St. Paul, London.

In the Management of the former Repairs of the old Fabrick, under the Conduct of Inigo Jones, Surveyor of the royal Works, no other Fund was advanced towards defraying the Expence, but the voluntary Contributions of pious and charitable People, which came in so slowly, in proportion to the greatness of the Work, that notwithstanding the royal Munificence, the considerable Sums of Money brought, from Time to Time, into the Chamber of London, from private Benefactions; the Zeal of Archbishop Laud, for the Honour of God, and the Church of England, in promoting by his own Example, and exciting others to liberal Donations for the Restitution of so signal a Monument of the Piety of our Ancestors, being the principal Ornament of the Realm, that celebrated Architect was not able to execute a third Part of what was necessary.

Before such Time, therefore, as a Tax on Sea-coal had been granted by Parliament, for the Building the Church (which duty commenced not till the first of May, 1670) it seemed in vain in any new Designs, to propose an Edifice too large and costly to be brought to a good and timely Period.

Upon this Consideration the Surveyor was at first directed to contrive a Fabrick of moderate Bulk, but of good Proportion; a convenient Quire, with a Vestibule, and Porticoes, and a Dome conspicuous above the Houses. A long Body with Ailes was thought impertinent, our Religion not using Processions. It was to be vaulted underneath for Burials, that the Pavement above might be preserved. A Model in Wood was made of this Church, which tho' not so large, would have been beautiful, and very fit for our Way of Worship; being also a convenient Auditory (for the Sermons anciently accustomed to be without Doors from a Stone Pulpit in the Church-yard, were now to be brought into the Church) and by the Help of the Vestibule, it was capable of any grand Ceremony. It had Porticoes on the Outside, which might prevent Disturbance within. This was applauded by Persons of good Understanding, as containing all that was necessary for the Church of a Metropolis; of a beautiful Figure, and of an Expence that reasonably might have been compass'd; but being contriv'd in the Roman Stile, was not so well understood & relish'd by others, who thought it deviated too much from the old Gothick Form of cathedral Churches, which they had been used to see and admire in this Country. Others observed it was not stately enough, and contended, that for the Honour of the Nation, and City of London, it ought not to be exceeded in Magnificence, by any Church in Europe.

After this, in order to find what might satisfy the World, the Surveyor drew several Sketches meerly for Discourse-sake, and observing the Generality were for Grandeur, he endeavour'd to gratify the Taste of the Connoiseurs and Criticks, with something coloss and beautiful, with a Design antique & well studied, conformable to the best Stile of the Greek and Roman Architecture. Some Persons of Distinction, skill'd in An-

137

tiquity and Architecture, express'd themselves much pleased with the Design, and wished to see it in a Model; The Surveyor comply'd with their Desires as well as his own and made a very curious large Model in Wood, accurately wrought, and carv'd with all its proper Ornaments, consisting of one Order, the Corinthian only (as St. Peter's in Rome.) This Model was for many Years kept in the Office of the Works at St. Paul's, in a Shed built for that Purpose; thence, after the finishing the new Fabrick, it was deposited (together with the other Models, and par-

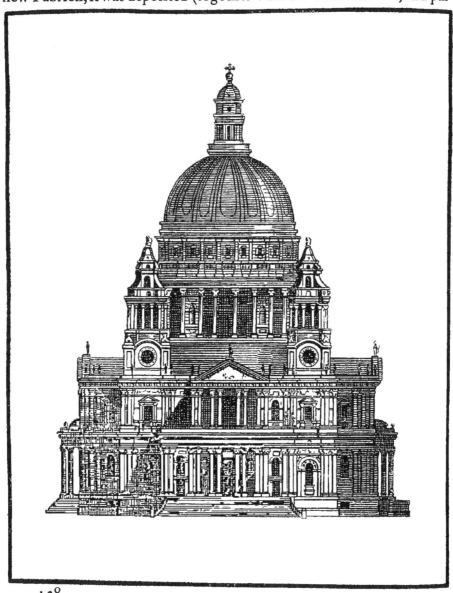

ticularly one for the high Altar, to consist of rich Marble-columns writhed, &c., in some Manner like that of St. Peter's at Rome) over the Morning-prayer-chapel, on the North-side; where, it is to be hoped, such publick Care will be taken, that it may be preserv'd, &, if damag'd, repair'd, as an eminent and costly Performance, & a Monument, among the many others of the Skill of the greatest Geometrician and Architect of his Time. [The original Designs drawn in a large Scale for the King's Use, are extant.] (a).

Thus much is specified, upon Recollection, that the Surveyor in private Conversation, always seem'd to set a higher Value on this Design, than any he had made before or since; as what was labour'd with more Study and Success; and (had he not been over-rul'd by those, whom it was his Duty to obey), what he would have put in Execution with more Chearfulness, and Satisfaction to himself than the latter.

But as yet nothing could be fully resolv'd upon; the Chapter, and some others of the Clergy thought the Model not enough of a Cathedral-fashion; to instance particularly, in that, the Quire was design'd Circular, &c., in the mean Time, the Money granted by Parliament upon the Coal-duty began to come in; something was to be done in order to make a Beginning without more Delay. The Surveyor then turn'd his Thoughts to a Cathedral-form (as they call'd it) but so rectified, as to reconcile, as near as possible, the Gothick to a better Manner of Architecture; with a Cupola, and above that, instead of a Lantern, a lofty Spire, and large Porticoes.

King Charles approved those Designs, & that there might be no further Interruption, the *Warrant, as before recited, was issued under the Privy-seal, for beginning the Works.

From that Time, the Surveyor resolved to make no more Models, or publickly expose his Drawings, which (as he had found by Experience) did but lose Time, & subjected his Business many Times, to incompetent Judges.

By these Means, at last, the Scheme of the present mighty Structure (different in some Manner from the former, & preferable in his Majesty's own Judgment, upon After-thoughts) was no sooner concluded on, and order'd by his Majesty, but begun and prosecuted by his Surveyor, with Vigour, in the Year 1675. And the King was pleas'd to allow him the Liberty in the Prosecution of his Work, to make some Variations, rather ornamental, than essential, as from Time to Time he should see proper; and to leave the Whole to his own Management.

* 1

(a) *The Model of Bramante's first Design of St. Peter's Church is preserved with great Care in the Vatican Palace.*

PART II. SECT. V.

OF THE TAKING DOWN THE VAST RUINS OF THE OLD CATHEDRAL, AND OF THE FOUNDATIONS OF THE OLD AND NEW STRUCTURE.

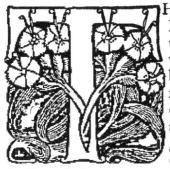

THE pulling down the Walls, being about 80 Feet high, and 5 Feet thick, was a great and troublesome Work; the Men stood above, and work'd them down with Pickaxes, whilst Labourers below moved away the Materials that fell, and dispersed them into Heaps: the want of Room made this Way slow, and dangerous, and some Men lost their Lives; the Heaps grew steep and large; and yet this was to be done before the Masons could begin to lay the Foundations.

The City having Streets to pave anew, bought, from the Rubbish, most of the Stone, call'd Kentish-rag, which gave some Room to dig, and to lay Foundations; which yet was not easy to perform with any Exactness, but by this Method.

The Surveyor placed Scaffolds high enough to extend his Lines over the Heaps that lay in the Way; and then by Perpendiculars set out the Places below, from the Lines drawn with Care upon the level Plan of the Scaffold.

Thus he proceeded, gaining every Day more Room, till he came to the middle Tower that bore the Steeple; the Remains of the Tower being near 200 Feet high, the Labourers were afraid to work above, thereupon he concluded to facilitate this Work by the Use of Gunpowder.

He dug a Hole of about 4 Feet wide, down by the Side of the North-west Pillar of the Tower, the 4 Pillars of which were each about 14 Feet diameter; when he had dug to the Foundation, he then, with Crows & Tools made on purpose, wrought a Hole 2 Feet square, level into the Center of the Pillar; there he placed a little Deal-box, containing eighteen Pounds of Powder, & no more: a Cane was fix'd to the Box with a Quick-match, (as Gunners call it) within the Cane, which reach'd from the Box to the Ground above, and along the Ground was laid a Train of Powder, with a Match: after the Mine was carefully clos'd up again with Stone and Mortar to the Top of the Ground, he then observ'd the Effect of the Blow.

This little Quantity of Powder not only lifted up the whole Angle of the Tower, with two great Arches that rested upon it, but also two adjoining Arches of the Ailes, and all above them; and this it seem'd to do somewhat leisurely, cracking the Walls to the Top, lifting visibly the whole Weight about nine Inches, which suddenly jumping down, made a great Heap of Ruin in the Place without scattering, it was half a Minute before the Heap already fallen open'd in two or three Places, and emitted some Smoke. By this Description may be observ'd the incredible Force of Powder: 18 Pounds only of which lifted up above 3000 Tun, & saved the Work of 1000 Labourers.

The Fall of so great a Weight from an Height of 200 Feet, gave a Concussion to the Ground, that the Inhabitants round about took for an Earthquake.

Encourag'd by this Success, he thought to proceed this Way, but being oblig'd to go out of Town in the King's Service, he left the Management of another Mine begun, to the Care of his next Officer, who too wise in his own Conceit, put in a greater Quantity of Powder, and neither went low enough, nor sufficiently fortified the Mouth of the Mine; and tho' it had the Effect, yet one Stone was shot out to the opposite Side of the Church-yard, through an open Window, into a Room of a private House, where some Women were sitting at Work, without any Harm done; this Accident frighted the Neighbours to that Degree, that he was importun'd to use no more Powder, and was so directed also by his Superiors; tho' with due Caution it might have been executed without Hazard, and sav'd much Time and Money.

He then turn'd his Thoughts to another Method; to gain Time, prevent much Expence, and the endangering of Men's Lives; and that was, to make an Experiment of that ancient Engine in War, the Battering-ram. He took a strong Mast of about 40 Feet long, arming the bigger End with a great Spike of Iron, fortified with Bars along the Mast, & Ferrels; this Mast in two Places was hung up to one Ring with strong Tackle, and so suspended level to a Triangle-prop, such as they weigh great Guns with: thirty Men, fifteen on a Side, vibrated this Machine to and again, and beat in one Place against the Wall the whole Day; they believ'd it was to little Purpose, not discerning any immediate Effect; he bid them not despair, but proceed another Day: on the second Day the Wall was perceiv'd to tremble at the Top, and in a few Hours it fell. The Reason to be given for it may be this; 'tis not by any present Violence the Ram is able to overturn a Wall of such Bulk & Compacture, but incessantly vibrating by equidistant Pulses, it makes a small intestine Motion through all the insensible Parts of the Wall, and by Degrees loosens all the Bond of the Mortar, and moves every Stone from its Bed, and tho' not the hundredth Part of an Inch at every Blow, yet this Motion once begun hath its Effects more and more, till at length it is quite loose & falls. He made good Use of this Machine in beating down all the lofty Ruins; & pleas'd himself that he had recover'd this notable Engine, of so great Service to the Ancients in besieging of Towns; tho' great Guns have now put them out of Use, as more expeditious, and requiring fewer Men to manage.

It has been before observ'd, (SECT. I.) that the Graves of several Ages and Fashions in strata, or Layers of Earth one above another, particularly at the North-side of Paul's, manifestly shew'd a great Antiquity from the British and Roman Times, by the Means whereof the Ground had been raised; but upon searching for the natural Ground below these Graves, the Surveyor observed that the Foundation of the old Church stood upon a layer of very close and hard Pot-earth, and concluded that the same Ground which had born so weighty a Building, might reasonably be trusted again. However, he had the Curiosity to search further, and accordingly dug Wells in several Places, and discern'd this hard Pot-earth to be on the North-side of the Church-yard about six Feet thick, & more, but thinner and thinner towards the South, till it was upon the declining of the Hill scarce four Feet: still he searched lower, and found nothing but dry Sand, mix'd sometimes unequally, but loose, so that it would run through the Fingers. He went on till he came to Water and Sand mixed with Periwincles and other Sea-shells; these were about the Level of Low-water Mark. He continued boreing till he came to hard Beach, and still under that, till he came to the natural hard Clay, which lies under the City, and Country, and Thames also far and wide.

By these Shells it was evident the Sea had been where now the Hill is, on which Paul's stands.

The Surveyor was of Opinion, the whole Country between Camberwell-hill, and the Hills of Essex might have been a great Frith or Sinus of the Sea, & much wider near the Mouth of the Thames, which made a large Plain of Sand at Low-water, through which the River found its Way; but at Low-water, as oft as it happen'd in Summer-weather, when the Sun dried the Surface of the Sand, & a strong Wind happen'd at the same Time, before the Flood came on, the Sands would drive with the Wind, and raise Heaps, and in Time large and lofty Sand-hills; for so are the Sand-hills rais'd npon the opposite Coasts of Flanders and Holland. The Sands upon such a Conjuncture of Sun-shine and Wind, drive in visible Clouds: this might be the Effect of many Ages, before History, and yet without having Recourse to the Flood.

142

This mighty broad Sand (now good Meadow) was restrained by large Banks still remaining, and reducing the River into its Channel; a great Work, of which no History gives Account: the Britains were too rude to attempt it; the Saxons too much busied with continual Wars; he concluded therefore it was a Roman Work; one little Breach in his Time cost £17000 to restore.

The Sand-hill at Paul's in the Time of the Roman Colony, was about 12 Feet lower than now it is; & the finer Sand easier driving with the Wind lay uppermost, and the hard Coat of Pot-earth might be thus made; for Pot-earth dissolv'd in Water, and view'd by a Microscope is but impalpable fine Sand, which with the Fire will vitrify; and, of this Earth upon the Place, were those Urns, sacrificing Vessels, and other Pottery-ware, made, which (as noted before) were found here in great Abundance, more especially towards the North-east of the Ground.

In the Progress of the Works of the Foundations, the Surveyor met with one unexpected Difficulty; he began to lay the Foundations from the West-end, & had proceeded successfully through the Dome to the East-end, where the Brick-earth Bottom was yet very good; but as he went on to the North-east Corner, which was the last, and where nothing was expected to interrupt, he fell, in prosecuting the Design, upon a Pit, where all the Pot-earth has been robb'd by the Potters of old Time: Here were discovered Quantities of Urns, broken Vessels, and Pottery-ware of divers Sorts and Shapes; how far this Pit extended northward, there was no Occasion to examine; no Ox-sculls, Horns of Stags, and Tusks of Boars were found, to corroborate the Accounts of Stow, Camden, and others; nor any Foundations more Eastward. If there was formerly any Temple to Diana, he supposed it might have been within the Walls of the Colony, and more to the South. It was no little Perplexity to fall into this Pit at last: He wanted but six or seven Feet to compleat the Design, and this fell in the very Angle North-east; he knew very well, that under the Layer of Pot-earth, there was no other good Ground to be found till he came to the Low-water Mark of the Thames, at least forty Feet lower: his Artificers propos'd to him to pile, which he refus'd; for, tho' Piles may last for ever, when always in Water (otherwise London-Bridge would fall) yet if they are driven through dry Sand, tho' sometimes moist, they will rot: His Endeavours were to build for Eternity. He therefore sunk a Pit of about eighteen Feet square, wharfing up the Sand with Timber, till he came forty Feet lower into Water and Sea-shells, where there was a firm Sea-beach which confirmed what was before asserted, that the Sea had been in Ages past, where now Paul's is; he bored through this Beach till he came to the original Clay; being then satisfied, he began from the Beach a square Peer of solid good Masonry, ten Feet square, till he came within fifteen Feet of the present Ground, then he turned a short Arch under Ground to the former Foundation, which was broken off by the untoward Accident of the Pit. Thus this North-east Coin of the Quire stands very firm, &, no doubt, will stand. This Narrative may be of Use to others not to trust Piles, unless always, and in all Parts wet; for almost all Sorts of Timber under Water will prove everlasting, but wet and dry will soon perish. The same cannot be said of Iron, for that will decay under Water: but this has been observ'd, in taking out Cramps from Stone-work at least four hundred Years old, which were so bedded in Mortar, that all Air was perfectly excluded, the Iron appear'd as fresh as from the Forge. Therefore in cramping of Stones, no Iron should lye within nine Inches of Air, if possible; for the Air is the Menstruum that consumes all Materials whatever. When there is a Necessity to use Iron for Want of Stones large enough, Care is to be taken to exclude sufficiently the Air from it. To mention another Caution of Use to Artificers; some Cornices of large Projections, tho' the upper Joints are as close fitted as good Workmen can make them, yet in the melting of Snow, the Water will dribble through, and stain the Cornice. The Surveyor thus avoided this Inconvenience; he caused the Masons so to work the Stone next the Joint, as to leave half a Quarter of an Inch rising on each Side, that the Water might soon fall off, then soak to the Joint; and this he observ'd in the Paveing of the upper Portico of the principal Front of St. Paul's; besides, that the Joints are run with Lead: and the same is done, where-ever he was obliged to cover with Stone only.

The Reasons for changing the Site of the Church, and taking up all the old Foundations, were chiefly these; first, the Act of Parliament for re-building the City had enacted, that all the high Streets (of which that which leads round the South-side of St. Paul's was one) should be forty Feet broad, but the old Foundations streightened the Street towards the East-end to under 30 Feet.

Secondly, the Church-yard on the North-side was wide, and afforded Room that Way to give the new Fabrick a more free and graceful Aspect.

Thirdly, To have built on the old Foundations must have confined the Surveyor too much to the old Plan and Form; the ruinous Walls in no Part were to be trusted again, nor would old and new Work firmly unite, or stand together without Cracks.

It being found expedient therefore to change the Foundations, he took the Advantage of more Room northward, and laid the middle Line of the new Work more declining to the North-east than it was before, which was not due East and West; neither did the old Front of the Cathedral lie directly from Ludgate, as it does not at present, which was not practicable, without purchasing and taking down a great Number of Houses; and the Aid of Parliament. This, tho' much wished for, he was not able to effect; the Commissioners for rebuilding the City, had, in the first Place, marked and staked out all the Streets, and the Parliament confirmed their report, before any Thing had been fully determined about the Design for the new Fabrick. The Proprietors of the Ground with much Eagerness and Haste, had begun to build accordingly; an incredible Progress had been made in a very short Time; many large & fair Houses erected; and every Foot of Ground in that trading and populous Part of the Town was highly estimated.

PART II. SECT. VI.

ANSWERS TO OBJECTIONS; & SOME ACCOUNT OF THE NEW FABRICK.

IN order to satisfy such Persons who are charmed with the Grandeur of the Vatican Church of St. Peter at Rome; with the stately Colonades, and spacious Area in the Front; and think no Structure of this Sort is to be esteemed truly noble and majestic, that does not arise, or nearly approach to that Magnificence; it is to be considered, that at St. Paul's the Surveyor wanted Room, and had but small Hopes of procuring more than he found, for the Reasons above-mentioned; and when all the adjacent Ground & new-built Streets were in private Possessions, under various Titles, which on account of their good Situation for Trade in the greatest and richest City in all Europe, were valued at a very high Rate; so that proper & necessary Ground as well for the Grandeur as graceful Approach to all Parts of the Fabrick could only be had by a special Act of Parliament, to oblige the numerous Proprietors to part with their Estates upon equitable Terms; and for applying a Part of the Fund on Coals or otherwise to that particular Purpose; which alas! was never obtained. And for this Reason, no more Space was left, especially before the West-front, and to the North-west, tho' great Sums of Money were expended, even with the Assistance of Parliament to purchase Houses, and to gain what present Room there is.*

Some have enquired why the Surveyor chose to make two Orders, rather than one single Order, with an attick Story, as at St. Peter's in Rome. It is most certain his Intention and Desires from the Beginning were to have followed that Example, had all Things succeeded to his Wish. This appears by all his first Designs, and in particular by the great Model before mentioned.

---

* *The magnificent Portico before the Church of St. Peter is not to be equalled, but yet the whole Front of that Structure terminating in a strait Line at the Top, cannot be said to afford so agreeable an Aspect, nor that rational Variety as is discerned by the Elevation of the Pediment in the Middle, and beautiful, Campanile Towers at each End of the Front of St. Paul's.*

146

Bramante knew the Quarries of Tivoli* would yield Blocks large enough for his Columns at St. Peter's, of nine Feet Diameter, but then he was at a Loss to find Stones for his Cornices; & this was the Reason that obliged him to diminish the Proportions of the proper Members of his Cornice At St. Paul's the Surveyor was cautious not to exceed Columns of four Feet, which had been tried by Inigo Jones in his Portico; the Quarries of the Isle of Portland would just afford for that Proportion, but not readily, for the Artificers were forced sometimes to stay some Months for one necessary Stone to be raised for their Purpose, and the farther the Quarry-men pierced into the Rock, the Quarry produced less Stones than near the Sea. All the most eminent Masons of England were of Opinion, that Stones of the largest Scantlings were there to be found, or no where. An Enquiry was made after all the good Stone that England afforded. Next to Portland, Rock-abbey Stone, & some others in Yorkshire seemed the best and most durable; but large Stone for the Paul's Works was not easily to be had even there.

For these Reasons the Surveyor concluded upon Portland-stone, & was also to use two Orders, and by that Means to keep the just Proportions of his Cornices; otherwise he must have fallen short of the Heighth of the Fabrick, which now exerts itself over all the Country, as well as City, as it did of old, when that Structure, tho' rude, was lofty & majestick.

At the Vatican Church, Bramante was ambitious to exceed the ancient Greek and Roman Temples, which generally were built from the noble Quarries of Marble of the Isles of the Archipelago, and Egypt, where Stones were to be had of the largest Size Architects could have Occasion to use, and altho' by Necessity he failed in the due Proportions of the proper Members of his Cornice, because the Tivoli stone would not hold out for the Purpose; yet (as far as we can find) he succeeded in the †Diameter of his Columns, for the greatest of the antique Pillars that remain (supposed to have been of the Frontispiece of Nero's golden House, thence brought by Vespasian to the Temple of Peace, and now before the Temple of Santa Maria Major) is less in ‡Diameter than those of St. Peter's. The Glory however of the Roman Pillar must be acknowledged in this wonderful Particular, that consists but of one solid‖ Stone of Parian Marble, of the Corinthian Order.

A Query has been made, why all the Pilasters of the Outside were doubled? They are of the same Use as Buttresses, and to give Space for large Windows between, which in our darker Weather is necessary: as also for the good Regularity of the Arcades within, and the Roof, they will appear proper to those who consider well the whole Design together. Again, why were the Columns of the West Portico doubled? This, no doubt, is not according to the usual Mode of the Ancients in their ordinary Temples, which, for the Generality, were small; but was followed

*No fine Stone, but yellowish & porous

†Viz. nine Feet. Q.

‡Viz. 6 Feet, 2 Inches one Quarter English. Palm 8 Pal 3 Overbeke, 2 tom. p. 43 ‖Above 60 Feet English in Heighth

§ See the
Plan in the
Architec-
ture of Sebas-
tian Serlio

in their Coloss, or greater Works; for Instance, in the Portico of the §Temple of Peace, the most magnificent in old Rome, the Columns were very properly & necessarily doubled to make wider Openings, after the Manner of the middle Openings in the Porticies of the Greek Temples, to five Doors at unequal Distances, viz., three near together, which lead into the great Middle Nave, or Body of the Temple, and one to each Side-aile, at greater Distances. (a) Bramante used double Columns without Scruple, as did Michael Angelo within and without the Cupola of St. Peter's, in the Vatican: the like is done in the Portico of the Church of Santa Maria Major in Rome; and also in other public and private Edifices by the most celebrated Architects; to instance among others, in the

*Palazzi
di Roma
da Pietro
Ferrerio

*Facade of the Palace of SSrs. Caffarelli alla Valle, built by Raphael Urbin in the Year 1515; which contains 26 duplicated Columns in Front. The French Architects have practised the same to a good Effect, especially in the beautiful Facade of the Louvre. It is to be observed in the Portico of St. Paul's, two Columns are brought nearer together, to make greater Inter-columns alternately, to give a proper Space for three Doors. The Ancients, particularly the Greeks, in their Temples, generally made the middle Inter-column wider than the rest; and as they shifted the Columns of the Portico for the better Approach to one Door; so at St. Paul's, for the same Reason, where there are three Doors (the two Side-doors are for daily Use, and the middle for Solemnities) the Columns are widened, to make a more open and commodious Access to each; and this falls out gracefully, by placing the Pillars alternately, Eustyle, and Pyenostyle. Hermogenes, who first contrived the Pseudo-dipteron, by taking away a whole Range of Columns to enlarge the Portico, went farther than his Masters durst before him, yet is commended by Vitruvius for this very Thing, because useful. The Romans, after the Greek Examples, not only widened the middle Openings in the Colonades before their Temples, but followed the like Manner in Arcades also: thus in the Colosseum, or Amphitheatre of Vespasian in Rome, of the eighty Arches, four which lead principally to the Arena, were made wider than all the rest. They generally took such Liberties, well knowing that the Orders were to be adapted to their proper Use, and not the Design too servilely to the Orders; of which a hundred Examples may be given. Those who duly examine by Measure the best Remains of the Greek or Roman Structures, whether Temples, Pillars, Arches or Theatres, will soon discern, that even among these is no certain general

(a) *The Cupola of the Temple of Bacchus, near the Gate of St. Agnes at Rome, anciently the Porta Viminalis, was supported on the Inside by twenty-four coupled Columns of the Composite Order, or Oriental Granite [Palladio. Desgodetz. Seb. Serlio.]*

Agreement; for it is manifest the ancient Architects took great Liberties in their Capitals and Members of Cornices, to shew their own Inventions, even where their Design did not oblige them, but where it did oblige them to a rational Variation, still keeping a good Symmetry, they are surely to be commended, and in like Cases to be followed. We now most esteem the Learning of the Augustan Age, yet, no question there were then many different Styles in Oratory, and perhaps some as good as Cicero's. This is not said as any Inducement to Masons, or every Novice that can draw Lines, to fall into crude Gothick Inventions, far from the good Examples of the Ancients, no more than to encourage a barbarous Style in Latin, & yet surely we cannot but with Erasmus, laugh at him who durst not use one Word that he could not find in Tully.

To proceed in examining what has been further objected, particularly why the Architrave within is cut off by the Arch. In this the Surveyor always insisted that he had the Ancients on his Side; in the Templum Pacis, and in all the great Halls of the Baths, and in all the great Structures of three Ailes, this was done, & for this Reason: in those wide Intercolumns the Architrave is not supposed to lye from one great Column to another, but from the Column to the other Wall of the Aile, so the End of it will only appear upon the Pillar of the Inside of the great Navis. Vitruvius tells us, that Architecture took its Beginning from wooden Porticoes; suppose therefore a Portico of three Ailes in Wood, or at least with the Roof of Timber, the Architraves must join the Pillars of the Ailes, and not be in Range with the inside Pillars, but cross to that Line; so nothing will appear upon the Pillars of the Navis but the Ends of the Architraves. If it be said that in the Templum Pacis the Cornice is cut off as well as the Architrave, the Answer is plain, there is not the same Reason to cut off the Cornice of the Arches at St. Paul's, which rise not so high; for a Cornice may be carried within, even without Pillars (provided the Proportion be kept of its due Height) much more with Pillars.

The Surveyor followed the Templum Pacis as near as our Measures would admit, having but three Arcades in each of the Bodies East and West, as there; but where there are no Arcades, and next the Dome, he has continued the whole Entablature.

One Thing he seems to have varied from the Ancients, in that he has incorporated lesser Pilasters with the greater, and that of the same Corinthian Order: 'tis true the Imposts of old upon which the Arches rested, had a particular Capital of the Dorick Manner, and not of the same Capital with the Pillar, as is to be seen in the triumphal Arches, and Theatres that remain; but above all Things, they were careful, that this Capital of the Impost should not have more Sally or Projection than to lie upon the great Pillar or Pilaster: and this was easily done in the Outside of Buildings, where there was Room enough to advance the Pilaster till it could receive the Impost Mouldings to lie against the Side of the Pilaster; but in the Inside of St. Paul's it would have streightened the great Nave, & made the Breaks of the Cornice above too heavy. Whether Bramante was aware of this in St. Peter's, it may be questioned, till after he had laid the Bases of the great Pilasters; for he has chopped off the Cornice Mouldings of the Imposts to give Way for the Pilaster to break through them; which is ungraceful, & without Authority, or good Reason. Whatever Veneration we may have for this great Man, yet surely in this it must be owned, he hath confessed an Oversight. If any Man thinks it improper to incorporate great and small Pillars together; as is done in the Ailes at St. Paul's, let him consider the Basilica of the Colonia Julia, at Fanum; which is the only Piece Vitruvius owns himself to be the Author of; he will easily perceive, that there must be small Pillars incorporated into the great, to bear the Galleries; and he will find, that the whole Frize is taken up by Vitruvius to give Light.

Bramante makes no Scruple of incorporating Pilasters in his whole Outside of St. Peter's: the Surveyor at St. Paul's chose to make the little Pilasters of the same Order with the great, in the Ailes, because the opposite Wall is beautified with the same smaller Order; so the Aile of the whole Length of the Church is of itself a long and graceful Portico, without being interrupted by the Legs of the Dome.

The Surveyor in giving the Entablature to this Order, has taken the Liberty to leave out Members, as the Ancients did the Inside of Porticoes; the Architrave is essential in all Works, but they often used in the Inside to leave out the Frize and Cornice also, except some of the lower Members which they added to the Architrave, that it might not appear too meagre. By this Liberty, (in which he was authorised by the best Ancient Porticoes) he could couch most of the Members of the Entablature of the little Order within the Sally of the great Pilaster, without chopping off short the Members of an Impost. If it be said still by any, the little Pillars should not have been of the same Order, let them examine the Templum Pacis, they will find a little Colonade continued through every Arch, and that of the Corinthian Order, as appears by some small Corinthian Capitals still adhering to the great Pile.

This Temple, being an Example of a three ailed Fabrick, is certainly the best and most authentic Pattern of a cathedral Church, which must have three Ailes, according to Custom, and be vaulted: tho' it may not be always necessary to vault with Diagonal-cross Vaults, as the Templum Pacis, and Halls of the Roman Baths are: the Romans used hemispherical Vaultings also in some Places: the Surveyor chose those as being demonstrably much lighter than the other; so the whole Vault of St. Paul's consists of 24 Cupolas cut off semicircular with Segments to join to the

great Arches one Way, and which are cut cross the other Way with eliptical Cylinders to let in the upper Lights of the Nave: but in the Ailes
the lesser Cupolas are both Ways cut in semicircular Sections; and altogether make a graceful geometrical Form, distinguished by circular
Wreaths, which is the horizontal Section of the Cupola, for the Hemisphere may be cut all Manner of Ways into circular Sections; and the
Arches and Wreaths being of Stone carved, the Spandrels between are
of sound Brick invested with Stucco of Cockleshell Lime, which becomes
as hard as Portland Stone; and which having large Planes between the
Stone Ribs, are capable of further Ornaments of Painting, if required. Be-
esides these 24 Cupolas, there is a half Cupola at the East, and the Great
Cupola of 112 Feet Diameter, in the Middle of the Crossing of the great
Ailes. In this the Surveyor has imitated the Pantheon, or Rotundo in
Rome, excepting only that the upper Order is there but umbratile, not
extant as at St. Paul's, out of the Wall, but only distinguished by different
coloured Marbles The Pantheon is no higher within than its Diameter;
St. Peter's is two Diameters; this shews too high, the other too low; the
Surveyor at St. Paul's took a mean Propottion, which shews its Concave
very Way; and is very lightsome by the Windows of the upper Order,
which strike down the Light through the great Colonade that encircles
the Dome without, & serves for the Butment of the Dome, which is Brick
of two Bricks thick, but as it rises every five Feet high, has a Course of
excellent Brick of 18 Inches long, banding through the whole Thickness. (a) The Concave was turned upon a Centre; which was judged necessary to keep the Work even and true, tho' a Cupola might be built
without a Centre; but this is observable, that the Centre was laid without any Standards from below to support it; and as it was both Centering
and Scaffolding, it remained for the Use of the Painter. Every Story of
this Scaffolding being circular, and the Ends of all the Ledgers meeting
as so many Rings, and truly wrought, it supported itself. This Machine
was an Original of the Kind, & will be a useful Project for the like Work
to an Architect hereafter; for since he must have Scaffolds for the Inside
Ornaments, the same thus contrived will also serve for the Builders, and
bear all the Weight till the Cupola be turned, & that without any Standards. It was necessary to give a greater Height than the Cupola would
gracefully allow within, tho' it is considerably above the Roof of the
Church; yet the old Church having had before a very lofty Spire of

(a) *The Bricks in the Ruins of the Roman Wall, and multangular Tower at*
York, are about seventeen Inches of English Measure long, and about eleven
inches broad, and two Inches and a half thick, measured by the ingenious Mr.
Lister, and communicated to the Royal Society, 1683.
Phil. Tranf. No. 149.)

Timber and Lead, the world expected, that the new Work should not in this Respect fall short of the old (tho' that was but a Spit, and this a Mountain) He was therefore obliged to comply with the Humour of the Age, (tho' not with ancient Example, as neither did Bramante) and to raise another structure over the first Cupola; & this was a Cone of Brick, so built as to support a Stone Lantern of an elegant Figure, and ending in Ornaments of Copper gilt.

As the whole Church above the Vaults is covered with a substantial oaken Roof, and Lead, (for no other Covering is so durable in our Climate) so he covered and hid out of Sight the Brick Cone with another Cupola of Timber and Lead; and between this and the Cone are easy Stairs that ascend to the Lantern.

He took no Care to make little luthern Windows in the leaden Cupola, as are done out of St. Peter's, because he had otherwise provided for Light enough to the Stairs from the Lantern above, and round the Pedestal of the same, which are not seen below; so that he only ribb'd the outward Cupola, which he thought less Gothick, than to stick it full of such little Lights in three Stories, one above the other, (as is executed in the Cupola of St. Peter's at Rome) which could not without Difficulty be mended, and if neglected would soon damage the Timbers.

The Inside of the whole Cupola is painted, and richly decorated, by an eminent English Artist, Sir James Thornhill, containing, in eight Compartments, the Histories of St. Paul. In the Crown of the Vault, as in the Pantheon, is a circular Opening, by which not only the Lantern transmits Light, but the Inside Ornaments of the painted and gilded Cone, display a new and agreeable Scene (a)

(a) *The Judgment of the Surveyor was originally, instead of painting in the Manner it is now perform'd, to have beautified the Inside of the Cupola, with the more durable Ornament of the Mosaic-work, as is nobly executed in the Cupola of St. Peter's in Rome, which strikes the Eye of the Beholder with a most magnificent and splendid Appearance; & which, without the least Decay of Colours, is as lasting as Marble, or the Building itself. For this Purpose he had projected to have procured from Italy four of the most eminent Artists in that Profession; but as this Art was a great Novelty in England, and not generally apprehended, did not receive the Encouragement it deserved; it was imagined also the Expence would prove too great, and the Time very long in Execution; but tho' these and all Objections were fully answered, yet this excellent Design was no further pursued.*

The Painting and Gilding of the Architecture of the East-end of the Church over the Communion Table was intended only to serve the present Occasion, till such Time as Materials could have been procured for a magnificent Design of an Altar, consisting of four Pillars wreathed, of the richest Greek Marbles, sup-

Altho' the Dome wants no Butment, yet, for greater Caution, it is hooped with Iron in this Manner; a Chanel is cut in the Bandage of Portland-stone, in which is laid a double Chain of Iron strongly linked together at every ten Feet, and the whole chanel filled up with Lead.

Among all the Composures of the Ancients, we find no Cupolas raised above the necessary Loading of the Hemisphere, as is seen particularly in the Pantheon. In after Ages the Dome of Florence, and of the great Church of Venice, was raised higher. The Saracens mightily affected it, in Imitation of the first most eminent Pattern, given by Justinian, in his Temple of Sancta Sophia, at Constantinople. Bramante would not fall short of those Examples; nor could the Surveyor do otherwise than gratify the general Taste of the Age, which had been so used to Steeples, that these round Designs were hardly digested, unless raised to a remark-able Height.

Thus St. Paul's is lofty enough to be discerned at Sea Eastward, and at Windsor Westward; but our Air being frequently hazy, prevents those distant Views, except when the Sun shines out, after a Shower of Rain has washed down the Clouds of Sea-coal Smoke that hang over the City from so many thousand Fires kindled every Morning, besides Glass-houses, Brew-houses, & Founderies, every one of which emits a blacker Smoke than twenty Houses.

In the beginning of the new Works of St. Paul's, an Incident was taken notice of by some People as a memorable Omen, when the Surveyor in Person had set out upon the Place, the Dimensions of the great Dome, and fixed upon the Centre; a common Labourer was ordered to bring a flat Stone from the Heaps of Rubbish (such as should first come to Hand) to be laid for a Mark and Directions to the Masons; the Stone which was immediately brought & laid down for that Purpose, happened to be a piece of a Grave-stone, with nothing remaining of the Inscription but this single Word in large Capitals, RESURGAM.

The first Stone of this Basilica was laid in the Year 1675, and the Works carried on with such Care and Industry, that by the Year 1685 the Walls of the Quire and Side-ailes were finished, with the circular North and South Porticoes; and the great Pillars of the Dome brought to the same Height; and it pleased God in his Mercy to bless the Surveyor with

porting a Canopy hemispherical, with proper Decorations of Architecture and Sculpture: for which the respective Drawings, and a Model were prepared.
Information, & particular Descriptions of certain Blocks of Marble were once sent to the Right Reverend Dr. Compton, Bishop of London, from a Levantine Merchant in Holland, and communicated to the Surveyor, but unluckily the Colours and Scantlings did not answer his Purpose; so it rested in Expectance of a fitter Opportunity, else probably this curious and stately Design had been finished at the same Time with the main Fabrick.

Health and Length of Days, and to enable him to compleat the whole Structure in the Year 1710 to the Glory of his most holy Name, & Promotion of his divine Worship, the principal Ornament of the Imperial Seat of this Realm. * 'Majestas convenit ista Deo.'

I   The highest or last Stone on the Top of the Lantern was laid by the Hands of the Surveyor's Son, Christopher Wren, deputed by his Father, in the Presence of that excellent Artificer Mr. Strong, his Son, and other Free & Accepted Masons, chiefly employed in the Execution of the Work. Thus was this mighty Fabrick, the second Church for Grandeur in Europe, in the space of 35 Years, begun and finished by one Architect, and under one Bishop of London, Dr. Henry Compton: the Charge supported chiefly by a small and easy Imposition on Sea-coal brought to the Port of London: whereas the Church of St. Peter in Rome (the only Edifice that can come in Competition with it) continued in the Building the Space of 145 Years, carried on by no less than 12 Architects successively; assisted by the Police and Interests of the Roman-See; the ready Acquisition of Marble, and attended by the best Artists of the World in Sculpture, Statuary, Painting, and Mosaic-work, during the Reigns of 19 Popes, as may be discerned in the following View.

Names of the ARCHITECTS.	POPES.
1. Bramante	under Julius II.
2. Julianus a Sancto Gallo	
3. Frater Jucundus Veronensis Dominicanus	} Leo X.
4. Raphael Urbino	
5. Balthazarus Perusius	Hadrianus VI.
6. Michael Angelo Bonarota	Clemens VII.
7. Pyrrhus Lygorius	Paulus III.
8. Jacobus Barocius	Julius III.
9. Jacobus a Porta	Paulus IV.
10. Dominicus Fontana	Pius IV.
	Pius V.
	Gregorius XIII.
	Sixtus V.
	Urbanus VII.
	Gregorius XIV.
11. Carolus Modernus	Innocentius IX.
	Clemens VIII.
	Paulus V.
	Alexander VII.
12. Eques Berninus	Urbanus VIII.
	Innocentius X.

154

INSCRIPTION OVER THE MIDDLE GREAT GATE O
ST. PETER'S.

Basilicam
Principus Apostolorum
In hanc Molis Amplitudinem.
Multiplici Romanorum Pontificum
Ædificatione Perductam
Innocentius X. Pont. Max., &c.

* * * * * * * * *
* * * * Terminavit.

THE DIFFERENCE BETWEEN THE DIMENSIONS OF S'
PETER'S CHURCH AT ROME, AND ST. PAUL'S I
LONDON.

N.B. The Proportion of the Roman Palm to the English Foot is as 7
is to 1000. 1000=732. 914=669,048, and so of the rest, ut infra.

	St. Peter's	2.	3.	St. Paul's.	Excess (St. Pete above St. Paul
	Roman Palms.	English Feet.	Fraction of a Foot.	English Feet.	Differ ence o Feet.
Long within	914	669	048	500	169
Broad at the En-trance	310	226	920	100	126
Front without	540	395	280	180	215
Broad at the Cross	604	442	128	223	219
Cupola Clear	190¾	139	629	108	031
Cupola & Lantern high	591	432	612	330	102
Church high	200	146	404	110	036
Height of Pillars in the Front	125	091	500	040	051

155

"The grand Cathedral of St. Paul's (says an ingenious Writer) is un-
"doubtedly one of the most magnificent modern Buildings in Europe;
"all the Parts of which it is composed are superlatively beautiful and
"noble; the North & South Fronts in particular are very perfect Pieces
"of Architecture, neither ought the East to go without due Applause.
"The two Spires at the West-end are in a finished Taste; & the Portico
"with the Ascent, and the Dome that rises in the Centre of the whole,
"afford a very august & surprizing Prospect."-*N.B.* The Critical Objections of this Author, subsequent to this his general Character of St. Paul's
delivered with Candour and Modesty, are chiefly answered in the above
Section VI. Part II.

"The Parts (says a judicious Traveller) of the Front of that most admir-
"able Fabrick of St. Peter's in Rome are certainly very beautiful, grand,
"and noble, the Pillars being nine Feet in Diameter; but the whole is
"terminated by a straight Line at Top, which (without any Prejudice
"in favour of my own Country) I cannot think has so good an Effect as
"the agreeable Variety, which is given by the Turrets at each End, and
"the Pediment rising in the Middle of the Front of St. Paul's."

A List of Drawings, relating to the Architecture of the cathedral
Church of St. Paul.

A Plan of the old Gothick Cathedral, with the Chapter-house, &c., in a
large Scale, on Vellum, used by the Surveyor for adjusting the proposed
Repairs, before the great Fire, Anno 1666.

P. 98 A Plan of Part of the old Cathedral reformed; together with the Plan,
Orthography, and Section of a Dome, Lantern and Spire, contrived to
have been erected in the Place of the old, ruinous, middle Tower, as
presented to King Charles II. and Commissioners for the Repairs of that
Fabrick, before the great Fire.

P 116 Plan, Elevation, and Section of a Design after the great Fire; but before
a Fund was granted by the Parliament for the Building.

P 117 Plan, Elevation, Section, and diagonal View, according to a Design after
the Coal-duty was appropriated by Parliament for the Fabrick; of which
a large and curious Model was made in Wood, approved by the Royal
Commission under the Great Seal, Anno 1673.

P. 118 The same Designs in a large Scale, drawn for his Majesty's Perusal.

Plan, Elevation, & Section of another Design, in a Style more conform-
*Original able to the old Cathedral Form, with his Majesty's *Approbation, and
Warrant to begin the Works, under the Sign-manual, and Privy-seal,
annexed to the Drawings, Anno 1675.

Plans general and particular of the new Fabrick, as it is executed.

Orthography of the whole Church from West to East, with the Section;

in which the Dome and Western Towers are represented, as once intended.

Orthography and View of the whole Fabrick to the West, the Dome, and upper Parts of the Towers, according to a prior Intention, not executed.

Orthography and Sections of the whole, and distinct Parts of the Structure, as it is executed, viz.

The Peristyles of the Dome, outward and inward, with the Section.

Section of the whole Cupola, Cone, & Stone Lantern, with the Copper-work, Ball and Cross.

Section of the Cross-aile.

Elevation and Section of the West-towers.

Designs of the great Portico, the two circular Porticoes, and their Architraves, &c.

Designs in Orthography, and Perspective of the Inside of the Church, Quire and Chapels.

Designs of the Doors, Windows, Niches, the exterior & interior Finishings and Ornaments.

Designs for Marble Altar-Pieces.

Designs of the Morning-prayer-chapel, and Consistory.

Design of the Organs, and their Ornaments.

Design of the Centering of the great Cupola, &c.

PART II. SECT. VII.

NOTHER eminent Work, in a different Style of Architecture, was the Reparation of the ancient Abbey-church of St. Peter, in Westminster, prosecuted by the Surveyor, to the Time of his Death, the Space of 25 Years, with all the Application, that the Branch of the Coal-duty given by Parliament for that Purpose, would admit. A particular Account of which will be best understood from his own Words, in the following Memorial to the Bishop of Rochester, in the Year 1713.

" When I had the Honour to attend your Lordship to congratulate your Episcopal Dignity, and pay that Respect which particularly concerned myself as employed in the chief Direction of the Works and Repairs of the Collegiate-church of St. Peter in Westminster; you was pleased to give me this seasonable Admonition, that I should consider my advanced Age; and as I had already made fair Steps in the Reparation of that ancient and ruinous Structure, you thought it very requisite for the publick Service, I should leave a Memorial of what I had done; and what my Thoughts were for carrying on the Works for the future.

In order to describe what I have already done, I should first give a State of the Fabrick as I found it; which being the Work of 500 Years, or more, through several Ages and Kings Reigns, it will come in my Way to consider the Modes of Building in those Times, and what Light Records may afford us; such as at present I am able to collect, give me leave to discourse a little upon.

That a Temple of Apollo was here in Thorny-island (the Place anciently so called, where the Church now stands) and ruined by an Earthquake in the Reign of the Emperor Antoninus Pius, I cannot readily agree. The Romans did not use, even in their Colonies, to build so lightly; the Ruins of ancienter Times shew their Works to this Day; the least Fragment of Cornice, or Capital, would demonstrate their Handy-work. Earthquakes break not Stones to Pieces, nor would the Picts be at that Pains: but I imagine the Monks finding the Londoners pretending to a Temple of Diana, where now St. Paul's stands; (Horns of Stags, Tusks of Boars, &c., having been dug up there in former Times, and it is said also, in later Years) would not be behind Hand in Antiquity: but I must assert, that having changed all the Foundations of Old Paul's, and upon that Occasion rummaged all the Ground thereabouts, and being very desirous to find some Footsteps of such a Temple, I could not discover any, and therefore can give no more Credit to Diana than to Apollo.

158

To pass over the fabulous Account, that King Lucius first founded a little Church here, A.D. 170, out of the Ruins of the Temple of Apollo, destroyed by an Earthquake a little before: but it is recorded with better Authority, that Sebert, King of the East-Saxons, built a Monastery and Church here in 605, which being destroyed by the Danes, was about 360 Years after repaired by the pious King Edgar. This, it is probable, was a strong good Building, after the Mode of that Age, not much altered from the Roman. We have some Examples of this ancient Saxon Manner, which was with Peers or round Pillars, much stronger than Tuscan, round headed Arches, and Windows; such was Winchester Cathedral of old; and such at this Day the Royal Chapel in the White-tower of London; the Chapel of St. Crosses; the Chapel of Christ-church in Oxford, formerly an old Monastery, & divers others I need not name, built before the Conquest; & such was the old Part of St. Paul's built in King Rufus's Time.

King Edward the Confessor repaired, if not wholly rebuilt this Abbey-church of King Edgar; of which a Description was published by Mr. Camden in 1606, from an ancient Manuscript in these Words: " Princi-
"palis area domûs, altissimis erecta fornicibus quadrato opere, parique
"commissura circumvolvitur; ambitus autem ipsius aedis duplici lapi-
"dum arcu ex utroque latere hinc inde fortiter solidata operis compage
"clauditur. Porrò crux templi quae medium canentium domino chorum
"ambiret, & sui gemina hinc inde sustentatione mediae turris celsum
"apicem fulciret, humili primùm & robusto fornice simpliciter surgit;
"deinde cochleis multipliciter ex arte ascendentibus plurimis intumes-
"cit; deinceps vero simplici muro usque ad tectum ligneum plumbo dil-
"igenter vestitum pervenit."

The Sense of which I translate into Language proper to Builders, as I can understand it.

"The principal Aile or Nave of the Church being raised high, & vaulted
"with square and uniform Ribs, is turned circular to the East. This on
"all Sides is strongly fortified with double Vaulting of the Ailes in two
"Stories, with their Pillars and Arches. The Cross-building fitted to con-
"tain the Quire in the Middle, and the better to support the lofty Tower,
"rose with a plainer and lower Vaulting; which Tower then spreading
"with artificial Winding-stairs, was continued with plain Walls to its
"Timber Roof, which was well covered with Lead."

These ancient Buildings were without Buttresses, only with thicker Walls: the Windows were very narrow, and latticed, for King Alfred is praised for After-invention of Lanterns to keep in the Lamps in Churches. In the Time of King Henry the Third, the Mode began, to build Chapels behind the Altar to the Blessed Virgin: what this Chapel here was, is not now to be discovered, I suppose the Foundations of it, are under the Steps of King Henry the Seventh's Chapel, and this Work probably semicircular (as afterwards four more were added without the Ailes) was also intended for his own Sepulture; some of his own Relations lying now, just below those Steps, and may be supposed to have been within his Chapel. of this he laid the first Stone, Anno 1220, and took down the greatest Part of St. Edward's Church to rebuild it according to the Mode, which came into Fashion after the Holy War.

This we now call the Gothick Manner of Architecture (so the Italians called what was not after the Roman Style) tho' the Goths were rather Destroyers than Builders; I think it should with more Reason be called the Saracen Style; for those People wanted neither Arts nor Learning; and after we in the West had lost both, we borrowed again from them, out of their Arabick Books, what they with great Diligence had translated from the Greeks.

They were Zealots in their Religion, and where-ever they conquered, (which was with amazing Rapidity) erected Mosques and Caravansara's in Haste; which obliged them to fall into another Way of Building; for they built their Mosques round, disliking the Christian Form of a Cross, the old Quarries whence the Ancients took their large Blocks of Marble for whole Columns and Architraves, were neglected, and they thought both impertinent. Their Carriage was by Camels, therefore their Buildings were fitted for small Stones, and Columns of their own Fancy, consisting of many Pieces; and their Arches were pointed without Keystones, which they thought too heavy.

The Reasons were the same in our Northern Climates, abounding in Free-stone, but wanting Marble.

The Crusado gave us an Idea of this Form; after which King Henry built his Church, but not by a Model well digested at first; for, I think, the Chapels without the Ailes were an After-thought, the Buttresses between the Chapels remaining being useless, if they had been raised together with them; & the King having opened the East-end for St. Mary's Chapel, he thought to make more Chapels for Sepulture; which was very acceptable to the Monks, after Licence obtained from Rome to bury in Churches, a Custom not used before.

The King's Intention was certainly to make up only the Cross to the Westward, for thus far it is of a different Manner from the rest more Westward built after his Time, as the Pillars and Spandrils of the Arches shew.

I am apt to think the King did not live to compleat his Intention, nor to reach four Inter-columns West of the Tower; the Walls of this Part might probably be carried up in his Time, but the Vaulting now covering the Quire, tho' it be more adorned and gilded, is without due Care in the Masonry, and is the worst performed of all done before. This Stone Vault was finished 23 Years after his Decease, in the Reign of King Edward the First, so that the old Verse is not punctually right,

"Tertius Henricus est templi conditor hujus."

But alas! it was now like to have been all spoiled; the Abbots would have a Cloyster, but scrupled, I suppose, at moving some venerable Corpses laid between the Outside Buttresses; then comes a bold, but ignorant Architect, who undertakes to build the Cloyster, so that the Buttresses should be without the Cloyster spanning over it, as may be seen in the Section.

This was a dangerous Attempt. It is by due Consideration of the Statick Principles, and the right Poising of the Weights of the Butments to the Arches, that good Architecture depends; and the Butments ought to have equal Gravity on both Sides. Altho' this was done to flatter the Humour of the Monks, yet the Architect should have considered that new Works carried very high, and that upon a newer Foundation, would shrink: from hence the Walls above the Windows are forced out ten Inches, and the Ribs broken. I could not discern this Failure to be so bad, till the Scaffold over the Quire was raised to give a close View of it; and then I was amazed to find it had not quite fallen. This is now amended with all Care, and I dare promise it shall be much stronger, and securer than ever the first Builders left it.

After what had been done by King Henry the Third and his Successor, it is said, the Work was carried further by the Abbots and Monks toward the West, and I perceive also the contiguous Cloyster after the Manner it was begun by King Henry the Third with Butments spanning over the Cloyster, which they were necessitated to proceed upon, according as it had been begun, tho', by Error, not to be amended till it was carried beyond the Cloyster; but then they proceeded with regular Butments answerable to the North-side, till they came to the West-front. This West-vault was proceeded on with much better Care and Skill, and was a Work of many Years, during the Reigns of the three succeeding Edwards, and King Richard the Second. I suppose there was a great Intermission or Slackness of Work, till the Lancastrian Line came in; for then, in the very first Bay of this Work, I find in the Vaulting, and the Keystones, the Rose of Lancaster.

In the tumultuous and bloody Wars between the two Houses of York & Lancaster, little was done to the Abbey, but by the Zeal of the Abbots, who drove the Work on as well as they were able, tho' slowly, to the West-end, which was never compleatly finished.

When King Henry the Eighth dissolved the Monastery, the Cloyster was finished, and other Things for the Convenience of the Abbey.

The Consistory (no contemptible Fabrick) was, I think, done in the

Time of King Edward the First, and, in order to join it to the Church, the East-side of the Cloyster was taken out of the West-side of the cross Part of the Church (by ill Advice) for it might have otherwise been done by a more decent Contrivance, but it may be the King was to be obeyed, who founded this octagonal Fabrick: the Abbot lent it to the King for the Use of the House of Commons, upon Condition the Crown should repair it, which, tho' it be now used for Records, hath lately been done. The Saracen Mode of Building seen in the East, soon spread over Europe, and particularly in France; the Fashions of which Nation we affected to imitate in all Ages, even when we were at Enmity with it.

Nothing was thought magnificent that was not high beyond Measure, with the Flutter of Archbuttresses, so we call the sloping Arches that poise the higher Vaultings of the Nave. The Romans always concealed their Butments, whereas the Normans thought them ornamental. These I have observ'd are the first Things that occasion the Ruin of Cathedrals, being so much exposed to the Air and Weather; the Coping, which cannot defend them, first failing, & if they give way, the Vault must spread. Pinnacles are of no Use, and as little Ornament. The Pride of a very high Roof raised above reasonable Pitch is not for Duration, for the Lead is apt to slip; but we are tied to this indiscreet Form, & must be contented with original Faults in the first Design. But that which is most to be lamented, is the unhappy Choice of the Materials, the Stone is decayed four Inches deep, and falls off perpetually in great Scales. I find, after the Conquest, all our Artists were fetched from Normandy; they loved to work in their own Caen-stone, which is more beautiful than durable. This was found expensive to bring hither, so they thought Rygate-stone in Surrey, the nearest like their own, being a Stone that would saw and work like Wood, but not durable, as is manifest; and they used this for the Ashlar of the whole Fabrick, which is now disfigur'd in the highest Degree: this Stone takes in Water, which, being frozen, scales off, whereas good Stone gathers a Crust, and defends itself, as many of our English Free-stones do. And though we have also the best Oak Timber in the World, yet these senseless Artificers in Westminster-hall, & other Places, would work their Chesnuts from Normandy; that Timber is not natural to England, it works finely, but sooner decays than Oak. The Roof in the Abbey is Oak, but mixed with Chesnut, and wrought after a bad Norman Manner, that does not secure it from stretching, & damaging the Walls, and the Water of the Gutters is ill carried off. All this is said, the better, in the next Place, to represent to your Lordship what has been done, and is wanting still to be carried on, as Time and Money is allowed to make a substantial and durable Repair.

First, in Repair of the Stone-work, what is done shews itself: beginning from the East-window, we have cut out all the ragged Ashlar, & invested it with a better Stone, out of Oxfordshire, down the River, from the Quarries about Burford. We have amended and secured the Butresses in the Cloyster-garden, as to the greatest Part; and we proceed to finish that Side; the Chapels on the South-side are done, and most of the Arch-buttresses all along as we proceeded. We have not done much on the North-side, for these Reasons: the Houses on the North-side are so close, that there is not Room left for the raising of Scaffolds and Ladders, nor for Passage for bringing Materials: besides, the Tenants taking every Inch to the very Walls of the Church to be in their Leases, this Ground already too narrow, is divided as the Backsides to Houses, with Wash-houses, Chimnies, Privies, Cellars, the Vaults of which, if indiscreetly dug against the Foot of a Buttress, may inevitably ruin the Vaults of the Chapels (and indeed I perceive such Mischief is already done, by the Opening of the Vaults of the octagonal Chapel on that Side) and unless effectual Means be taken to prevent all Nusances of this Sort, the Works cannot proceed, and if finished, may soon be destroyed. I need say no more, nor will I presume to dictate, not doubting but proper Means will be taken to preserve this noble Structure from such Nusances, as directly tend to the Demolition of it.

And now, in further Pursuance of your Lordship's Directions, I shall distinctly set down, what yet remains to finish the necessary Repairs for Ages to come. And then, in the second Place (since the first Intentions of the Founders were never brought to a Conclusion) I shall present my Thoughts and Designs, in order to a proper compleating of what is left imperfect, hopeing we may obtain for this, the Continuance of the Par-liamentary Assistance.

I have yet said nothing of King Henry the Seventh's Chapel, a nice embroidered Work, and performed with tender Caen-stone, & tho' lately built, in Comparison, is so eaten up by our Weather, that it begs for some Compassion, which, I hope, the sovereign Power will take, as it is the regal Sepulture.

I begin, as I said, to set down what is necessary for compleating the Re-pairs, tho' Part thereof at present I can only guess at, because I cannot as yet come at the North-side to make a full Discovery of the Defects there, but I hope to find it rather better than the South-side; for it is the Vicis-situdes of Heat and Cold, Drought and Moisture, that rot all Materials more than the Extremities that are constant, of any of these Accidents. this is manifest in Timber, which, if always under Ground & wet, never decays, otherwise Venice and Amsterdam would fall: it is the same in Lead-work, for the North-side of a steep Roof is usually much less de-cayed than the South; and the same is commonly seen in Stone Work; besides, the Buttresses here are more substantial than those of the South-side, which I complained before were indiscreetly altered for the sake of the Cloyster; and I find some Emendations have been made about eighty Years since, but not well. Upon the whole Matter I may say, that of the necessary Repairs of the outward Stone Work, one third Part is already compleated. The most dangerous Part of the Vaulting over the Quire now in Hand will be finished in a few Months, but the Roof over it cannot be opened till Summer. The Repairs of the Stone Work, with all the Chapels, Arch-buttresses, Windows, and Mouldings of the North-side are yet to be done, excepting Part of the North-cross Aile: a great Part of the Expence will be in the North Front, and the great Rose Window there, which being very ruinous, was patched up for the present to prevent further Ruin, some Years since, before I was concerned, but must now be new done: I have prepared a proper Design for it. The Timber of the Roof of the Nave, and the Cross, is amended and secured with the Lead; and also the Chapels. but the whole Roof, & Ailes from the Tower Westward, with Lead & Pipes to be new-cast, remains yet, with all the Timber Work, to be mended, as hath been done Eastward of the Tower already. The Chapels on the North-side must have their Roofs amended, when we can see how to come at them, after the Removal of one little House.

And now having given a summary Account of what will perfect the meer Repairs, let me add what I wish might be done to render those Parts with a proper Aspect, which were left abruptly imperfect by the last Builders, when the Monastery was dissolved by King Henry the Eighth. The West-front is very requisite to be finished, because the two Towers are not of equal Height, and too low for the Bells, which hang so much lower than the Roof, that they are not heard so far as they should be: the great West-window is also too feeble, & the Gabel-end of the Roof over it, is but Weather-boards painted.

The original Intention was plainly to have had a Steeple, the Beginnings of which appear on the Corners of the Cross, but left off before it rose so high as the Ridge of the Roof, & the Vault of the Quire under it, is only Lath and Plaister, now rotten, and must be taken care of.

Lest it should be doubted, whether the four Pillars below, be able to bear a Steeple, because they seem a little swayed inward, I have considered how they may be unquestionably secured, so as to support the greatest Weight that need be laid upon them; & this after a Manner that will add to their Shape and Beauty.

It is manifest to the Eye, that the four innermost Pillars of the Cross are bended inward considerably, and seem to tend to Ruin, and the Arches of the second Order above are cracked also: how this has happened, and how it is to be secured, I shall demonstrate.

I conceive the Architect knew very well, that the four Pillars above the Intersection of the Cross-nave would not prove a sufficient Butment to

164

stand against the Pressure of so many Arches, unless they were very much bigger than the other Piers; but that could not be without cumbering up the principal Part of the Church: but tho' these angular Pillars could not be made bigger, yet they could be made heavier to stand against the Pressure of the several Rows of Arches, which might prove an Equivalent, as may appear thus:

Let A B C be an Arch resting at C, against an immoveable Wall K M, but at A upon a Pillar A D, so small as to be unable to be a sufficient Butment to the Pressure of the Arch A B: what is then to be done? I cannot add F G to it to make it a Butment, but I build up E so high, as by Addition of Weight, to establish it so firm, as if I had annexed F G to it to make it a Butment: it need not be enquired how much E must be, since it cannot exceed, provided A D be sufficient to bear the Weight imposed on it: and this is the Reason why in all Gothick Fabricks of this Form, the Architects were wont to build Towers or Steeples in the Middle, not only for Ornament, but to confirm the middle Pillars against the Thrust

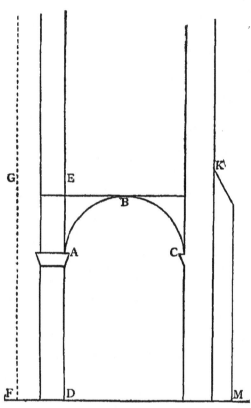

of the several Rows of Arches, which force against them every Way. The Architect understood this well enough, but knowing that it might require Time to give such a Butment as the Tower to his Arches, which was to be last done; and lest there should be a Failing in the mean Time, he wisely considered, that if he tied these Arches every Way with Iron, which were next to the Middle of the Cross: this might serve the Turn, till he built the Tower to make all secure, which is not done to this Day. These Irons which were hooked on from Pillar to Pillar have been stolen away; and this is the Reason of the four Pillars being bent inward, and the Walls above cracked; but nothing can be amended, till first the Pillars are restored, which I have considered how to perform, and repre-

m 3

165

sented in a Model. This must be first done, otherwise the Addition of Weight upon that which is already crooked and infirm, will make it more so: but the Pillars being once well secured from further Distortion, it will be necessary to confirm all by adding more Weight upon them, that is, by building a Tower according to the original Intention of the Architect, and which was begun, as appears by the Work, but left off before it rose to the Ridge of the Roof. In my Opinion the Tower should be continued to at least as much in Height above the Roof, as it is in Breadth; and if a Spire be added to it, it will give a proper Grace to the whole Fabrick, and the West-end of the City, which seems to want it.

I have made a Design, which will not be very expensive but light, and still in the Gothick Form, and of a Style with the rest of the Structure, which I would strictly adhere to, throughout the whole Intention: to deviate from the old Form, would be to run into a disagreeable Mixture, which no Person of a good Taste could relish.

I have varied a little from the usual Form, in giving twelve Sides to the Spire instead of eight, for Reasons to be discerned upon the Model.

The Angles of Pyramids in the Gothic Architecture, were usually inriched with the Flower the Botanists call Calceolus, which is a proper Form to help Workmen to ascend on the Outside to amend any Defects, without raising large Scaffolds upon every slight Occasion; I have done the same, being of so good Use, as well as agreeable Ornament.

The next Thing to be considered is, to finish what was left undone at the West-front.

It is evident, as is observed before, the two West-towers were left imperfect, and have continued so since the Dissolution of the Monastery, one much higher than the other, though still too low for Bells, which are stifled by the Height of the Roof above them; they ought certainly to be carried to an equal Height, one Story above the Ridge of the Roof, still continuing the Gothick Manner, in the Stone-work, and Tracery.

Something must be done to strengthen the West-window, which is crazy; the Pediment is only boarded, but ought undoubtedly to be of Stone. I have given such a Design, as I conceive may be suitable for this Part: the Jerusalem-Chamber is built against it, and the Access from Tothill-street not very graceful.

The principal Entrance is from King-street, and I believe always will continue so, but at present, there is little Encouragement to begin to make this North-front magnificent in the Manner I have designed, whilst it is so much incumbered with private Tenements, which obscure and smoke the Fabrick, not without danger of fireing it.

The great North-window had been formerly in danger of Ruin, but was upheld, and stopt up, for the present, with Plaister. It will be most necessary to rebuild this with Portland-stone, to answer the South-rose-win-

166

dow, which was well rebuilt about forty years since; the Stair-cases at the Corners must now be new ashlar'd, & Pyramids set upon them conformable to the old-Style, to make the Whole of a Piece. I have therefore made a*Design in order to restore it to its proper shape first intended, but which was indiscreetly tamper'd with some years since, by patching on a little Dorick Passage before the great Window, & cropping off the Pyramids, and covering the Stair-cases with very improper Roofs of Timber and Lead, which can never agree with any other part of the Design.

For all these new Additions I have prepared perfect Draughts & Models, such as I conceive may agree with the original Scheme of the old Architect, without any modern Mixtures to shew my own Inventions; in like manner as I have among the Parochial Churches of London given some few Examples (where I was oblig'd to deviate from a better Style) which appear not ungraceful, but ornamental, to the East part of the City; and it is to be hoped, by the publick Care, to the West part also, in good Time, will be as well adorned; and surely by nothing more properly than a lofty Spire, and Western-towers to Westminster-Abbey.

*This front, commonly called Solomon's Porch, the Surveyor lived to finish in the Year 1722

N.B. By the foregoing Epistle, at the Beginning, and also in Part II. Sect. I It appears that Sir Christopher Wren gave no Credit to the Stories; how, of old, a Temple of Diana stood on the Situation of the present Church of St. Paul, in London; & another of Apollo, in Thorney-Island, the Site of Westminster Abbey; what induced him to reject these Accounts as fabulous, was, that in digging the Foundations of St. Paul's Cathedral, he could make no Discoveries in favour of such Conceits; no doubt, the many Antiquities said to have been found there, in proof of those Relations, were never brought to his View; however, the following Extracts from good Authority, shew the Conjecture, particularly in Reference to the Temple of Diana, was not groundless.

" Erasmus observed, while he was in England, a popular Custom at
" London, that on such a Day, viz. St. Paul's Conversion, the People in
" a sort of wild Procession, bring into the Church of St. Paul, the Head
" of a kind of Deer frequent in that Island, fixed upon the Top of a long
" Spear or Pole, with the whole Company blowing Hunters-horns in a
" sort of hideous Manner, and so in this rude Pomp they go up to the
" High-Altar, and offer it there; you would think them all the mad Vo-
" taries of Diana." This, probably at first Pagan Custom, continued to, and could hardly be swept away at the Reformation. Though the Church was now dedicated to the Memory of the great Apostle St. Paul; yet they seemed willing not to forget the Goddess Diana, to whom (we are told) in this very Place, was anciently a Temple erected; and that in the Time of Melitus, the first Bishop of London, Ethelbert, King of Kent, built a Church to the Honour of St. Paul, where before stood a Temple of

Erasmi Ecclesiastae

Dr. Knight's Life of Erasmus, p. 298

m 4

Ib. 299 Diana, as an antient Manuscript in the Cotton Library tells us. 'Immolat Dianae Londonia, thurificat Apollini suburbana Thorneia' (Thorney is now Westminster).

Ib. 301 An earthen Lamp was found in digging the Foundation of St. Paul's, representing the Figure of a Building, which the late Mr. Kemp, into whose Hands this Lamp came, supposed to be the Temple of Diana; and he was the more confirmed in this Opinion, from another Lamp of the same Sort, which was found in the same Place, & at the same Time with the former, together with several Boars Tusks.*

*Monument Kemp. Par. 1. p. 179, 180 Mr. Camden thinks it not improbable, that there was antiently a Temple of Diana, where St. Paul's Church now stands, from the great Number of Ox-heads that were found there in digging up the Church-yard, in the Reign of K. Edw. I. and were looked upon as Gentile Sacrifices, and in this Opinion he is followed by his learned Editor; as also by Mr. Samms, Mr. Howel, and others; particularly the ingenious Dr. Wood-

Ib. 302 ward acquaints us, that he has in his Collection, Tusks of Boars, Horns of Oxen, and of Stags, as also the Representations of Deer, and even of Diana herself, upon the sacrificing Vessels digged up near St. Paul's Church; and likewise a small Image of that Goddess, found not far off. Now it appears from ancient Writers, that not only Stags, but Oxen and Swine also were sacrificed to Diana.

There is extant an earthen Lamp, which was procured of the above-mentioned Mr. Kemp, and is supposed to have been dug up among the other Lamps and Antiquities at St. Paul's; on it is embosssed the Figure of Diana in a Hunting-posture, in the same Manner as she is represented on the ancient Greek Coins of Ephesus, and conformable to an antique Statue of Marble in the Gallery of the King of France at Versailles. This Lamp, as the other before-mentioned, is of very mean Work; on the Reverse, in the Center are some Letters, probably the Potter's Name, as usual, but so ill executed as to be hardly legible.

PART II. SECT. VIII.

THE large, and magnificent Cathedral-church of Salisbury, (in like manner as Westminster-Abbey) discovering manifest Decays, and threatening Ruin, arising partly from the Want of true Judgment in the first Architect, partly from Injuries of Time and Weather, the lofty Spire especially having been much shaken and crackt by some Tempest & Storm of Lightning, required the Skill and Direction of the Surveyor for a speedy Amendment; in order to which, the Faults of the Steeple of Necessity claimed the first consideration, because it could not be ruined alone, without drawing with it the Roof and Vaults of the Church. This therefore he took special Care to strengthen, and effectually secure, by bracing with Bandages of Iron wrought by Anchor-smiths, accustomed in great Work for Ships, and these so judiciously placed, and artfully performed, that it continues demonstrably stronger than at the first Erection.

He had taken an accurate Survey in the Year 1669, of the whole Structure of this ancient Cathedral, at the Request of his excellent Friend Dr. Seth Ward, Bishop of that See; in his Report to whom, & the Dean and Chapter, after enumerating the fundamental Errors, Defects, & present Decays, he gave his Advice & full Instructions, for the necessary amending, restoring, and keeping it from farther Declension, together with the Diseases suggesting the Cures. As this Church is justly esteemed one of the best Patterns of Gothick-building, a short Architectonical Account, thereof, taken from the first Part of the Surveyor's Report, may bespeak the Attention of the Curious, as a further Taste of that Style of Architecture.

" The Figure of the Church is a Cross, upon the Intersection of which,
" stands a Tower and Spire of Stone, as high from the Foundation, as the
" whole Length of the Navis, or Body of the Church; and it is founded
" only upon the four Pillars and Arches of the Intersection. Between the
" Steeple and the East-end is another crossing of the Navis, which on the
" West-side only wants its Ailes; all other Sides of the main Body & the
" Crosses are supported on Pillars with Ailes annexed, and buttressed
" without the Ailes, from whence arise Bows or flying Buttresses to the
" Walls of the Navis which are concealed within the Timber Roof of the
" Ailes. The Roof is almost as sharp as an Æquilateral Triangle, made of
" small Timber after the ancient Manner without principal Rafters; but
" the Wall-plats are double, and tied together with Couples above forty
" Feet long. The whole Church is vaulted with Chalk between Arches

169

" and Cross-springers only, after the ancienter Manner, without Orbs
" and Tracery, excepting under the Tower, where the Springers divide,
" and represent a wider Sort of Tracery; and this appears to me to have
" been a later Work, and to be done by some other Hand than that of the
" first Architect, whose Judgment I must justly commend for many
" Things, beyond what I find in divers Gothick Fabricks of later Date,
" which, tho' more elaborated with nice and small Works, yet want the
" natural Beauty which arises from the Proportion of the first Dimen-
" sions. For here the Breadth to the Height of the Navis, and both to the
" Shape of the Ailes bear a good Proportion. The Pillars and the Inter-
" columnations, (or Spaces between Pillar and Pillar) are well suited to
" the Height of the Arches, the Mouldings are decently mixed with
" large Planes without an Affectation of filling every Corner with Orna-
" ments, which, unless they are admirably good, glut the Eye, as much
" as in Musick, too much Division the Ears. The Windows are not made
" too great, nor yet the Light obstructed with many Mullions and Tran-
" somes of Tracery-work; which was the ill Fashion of the next follow-
" ing Age: our Artist knew better, that nothing could add Beauty to
" Light, he trusted to a stately and rich Plainness, that his Marble Shafts
" gave to his Work. I cannot call them Pillars, because they are so small
" and slender, and generally bear nothing, but are only added for Orna-
" ment to the Outside of the great Pillars, and decently fastened with
" Brass.
" Notwithstanding this Commendation of the Architect, there are some
" original Errors, which I must lay to his Charge, the Discovery of
" which will give us light to the Cause of the present Decays.
" First, I must accuse him, that building in a low and marshy Soil, he did
" not take sufficient Care of the Foundation, especially under the Pillars.
" That Foundation which will bear a Wall, will not bear a Pillar, for
" Pillars thrust themselves into the Earth, & force open the solid Ground,
" if the Foundation under them be not broad; and if it be not hard Stone,
" it will be ground and crushed as Things are bruised in a Mortar, if the
" Weight be great.
" A second Fault, was the not raising the Floor of the Church above the
" Fear of Inundations; many sufficient Foundations have failed after the
" Earth hath been too much drenched with unusual Floods; besides, it
" is unhandsome to descend into a Place.
" The third Fault, is in the Poise of the Building: generally the Substruc-
" tions are too slender for the Weights above.
" The Pillars appear small enough, and yet they shew much greater than
" they are; for the Shafts of Marble that encompass them, seem to fill out
" the Pillars to a proportionable Bulk; but indeed they bear little or no
" Weight, and some of those that are pressed, break and split; if those

170

" Ornaments should be taken off, the Pillar would then appear too little
" for its Burthen; but this no where so enormous as under the Steeple,
" which being four hundred Feet in Height, is borne by four Pillars, not
" much larger than the Pillars of the Ailes: and therefore out of Fear
" to over-burden them in the Inside of the Tower, for forty Feet high
" above, the Navis is made with a slender hollow Work of Pillars and
" Arches; nor hath it any Buttresses, and the Spire itself is but seven
" Inches thick, tho' the Height be above one hundred and fifty Feet.
" This Work of Pillars and Arches within the Tower, makes me believe
" that the Architect laid his first Floor of Timber forty Feet higher than
" the Vault beneath, (which, as I said, was since added) and without
" doubt intended a Belfry above (as appears by Places left in the Walls
" for Timber, and fastening of the Frames for the Bells) and so would
" have concluded with the Tower only, without a Spire. And if this
" Addition of a Spire was a second Thought, the Artist is more excusable
" for having omitted Buttresses to the Tower; & his Ingenuity commend-
" able for supplying this Defect, by bracing the Walls together with
" many large Bands of Iron within and without, keyed together with
" much Industry, and Exactness: and besides these that appear, I have
" Reason to believe, that there are divers other Braces concealed within
" the Thickness of the Walls; and these are so essential to the Standing
" of the Work, that if they were dissolved, the Spire would spread open
" the Walls of the Tower, nor could it stand one Minute. But this Way
" of tying Walls together with Iron, instead of making them of that
" Substance and Form, that they shall naturally poise themselves upon
" their Butment, is against the Rules of good Architecture; not only be-
" cause it is corruptible by Rust, but because it is fallacious, having un-
" equal Veins in the Metal, some Pieces in the same Bar being three
" Times stronger than other; and yet all sound to Appearance. I shall
" not impute to our Artist those Errors which were generally the Mis-
" takes of Builders in that Age; yet it will not be amiss to insist a little
" upon those which seem to concern us, and to occasion some of the In-
" firmities in our Buildings.
" Almost all the Cathedrals of the Gothick Form are weak & defective
" in the Poise of the Vault of the Ailes; as for the Vault of the Navis, both
" Sides are equally supported, and propped up from the Spreading by the
" Bows or flying Buttresses, which rise from the outward Walls of the
" Ailes; but for the Vaults of the Ailes, they are indeed supported on the
" Outside by the Buttresses, but inwardly they have no other Stay but
" the Pillars themselves, which (as they are usually proportioned) if they
" stood alone without the Weight above, could not resist the Spreading
" of the Ailes one Minute. True indeed, the great Load above the Walls
" and Vaults of the Navis, should seem to confirm the Pillars in their

" perpendicular Station, that there should be no need of the Butment
" inward; but Experience hath shewn the contrary, and there is scarce
" any Gothick Cathedral, that I have seen, at home or abroad, wherein
" I have not observed the Pillars to yield and bend inwards from the
" Weight of the Vault of the Aile; but this Defect is most conspicuous
" upon the angular Pillars of the Cross, for there, not only the Vault
" wants Butment, but also the angular Arches that rest upon that Pillar,
" and therefore both conspire to thrust it inward towards the Center of
" the Cross: and this is very apparent in the Fabrick we treat of: for this
" Reason, this Form of Churches has been rejected by modern Archi-
" tects abroad, who use the better and Roman Art of Architecture."

These Surveys, & other occasional Inspections of the most noted cathedral Churches & Chapels in England, and foreign Parts; a Discernment
of no contemptible Art, Ingenuity, and geometrical Skill in the Design
and Execution of some few, and an Affectation of Height and Grandeur,
tho' without Regularity and good Proportion, in most of them, induced
the Surveyor to make some Enquiry into the Rise and Progress of this
Gothick Mode, and to consider how the old Greek and Roman Style of
building, with the several regular Proportions of Columns, Entablatures, &c. came within a few Centuries to be so much altered, and almost
universally disused.

He was of Opinion (as has been mentioned in another Place) that what
we now vulgarly call the Gothick ought properly and truly to be named
the Saracenick Architecture refined by the Christians; which first of all
began in the East after the Fall of the Greek Empire by the prodigious
Success of those People that adhered to Mahomet's Doctrine, who out
of Zeal to their Religion, built Mosques, Caravansaras, & Sepulchres,
wherever they came.

These they contrived of a round Form, because they would not imitate
the christian Figure of a Cross; nor the old Greek Manner, which they
thought to be idolatrous, and for that Reason all Sculpture became offensive to them.

They then fell into a new Mode of their own Invention, tho' it might
have been expected with better Sense, considering the Arabians wanted
not Geometricians in that Age, nor the Moors, who translated most of
the most useful old Greek Books. As they propagated their Religion with
great Diligence, so they built Mosques in all their conquered Cities in
Haste. The Quarries of great Marble, by which the vanquished Nations
of Syria, Egypt, and all the East had been supplied; for Columns, Architraves, and great Stones, were now deserted; the Saracens therefore were
necessitated to accommodate their Architecture to such Materials,
whether Marble or Free-stone, as every Country readily afforded. They
thought Columns, and heavy Cornices impertinent, & might be omitted;

172

snd affecting the round Form for Mosques, they elevated Cupolas in ome Instances, with Grace enough. The Holy War gave the Christians, who had been there, an Idea of the Saracen Works, which were afterwards by them imitated in the West; and they refined upon it every Day, as they proceeded in building Churches. The Italians (among which were yet some Greek Refugees) and with them French, Germans, and Flemings, joined into a Fraternity of Architects, procuring papal Bulls for their Encouragement, & particular Privileges; they stiled themselves Freemasons, and ranged from one Nation to another, as they found Churches to be built (for very many in those Ages were every where in Building, through Piety or Emulation.) Their Government was regular, and where they fixed near the Building in Hand, they made a Camp of Huts. A Surveyor govern'd in chief; every tenth Man was called a Warden, and overlooked each nine: the Gentlemen of the Neighbourhood, either out of Charity or Commutation of Pennance, gave the Materials and Carriages. Those who have seen the exact Accounts in Records of the Charge of the Fabricks of some of our Cathedrals near four hundred Years old, cannot but have a great Esteem for their Economy, & admire how soon they erected such lofty Structures. Indeed great Height they thought the greatest Magnificence; few Stones were used, but what a Man might carry up a Ladder on his Back from Scaffold to Scaffold, tho' they had Pullies, and spoked Wheels, upon Occasion, but having rejected Cornices, they had no need of great Engines; Stone upon Stone was easily piled up to great Heights; therefore the Pride of their Works was in Pinnacles & Steeples. In this they essentially differed from the Roman Way, who laid all their Mouldings horizontally, which made the best Perspective: the Gothick Way on the contrary carried all their Mouldings perpendicular, so that the Ground-work being settled, they had nothing else to do but to spire all up as they could. Thus they made their Pillars of a Bundle of little Torus's, which they divided into more, when they came to the Roof; and these Torus's split into many small ones, and traversing one another, gave Occasion to the Tracery-work, (as they called it) of which this Society were the Inventors. They used the Sharp-headed-arch, which would rise with little centering, required lighter Key-stones and less Butment, & yet would bear another Row of doubled Arches rising from the Key-stone; by the diversifying of which, they erected eminent Structures, such as the Steeples of Vienna, Strasburg, and many others. They affected Steeples, though the Saracens themselves most used Cupolas. The Church of St. Mark at Venice, is built after the Saracen Manner. Glass began to be used in Windows, & a great part of the Outside-ornament of Churches consisted in the Tracery Works of disposing the Mullions of the Windows, for the better fixing in of the Glass. Thus the Work required fewer Materials, & the Workmanship was for the most part performed by Flat-moulds, in which the Wardens could easily instruct hundreds of Artificers. It must be confessed, this was an ingenious Compendium of Work, suited to these northern Climates; and I must also own, that Works of the same Height and Magnificence in the Roman Way, would be very much more expensive, than in the other Gothick manner managed with Judgment. But, as all Modes, when once the old rational Ways are despised, turn at last into unbounded Fancies; this Tracery induced too much mincing of the Stone into open Battlements and spindling Pinnacles, and little Carvings without Proportion of Distance; so the essential Rules of good Perspective and Duration were forgot. But about two hundred Years ago, when ingenious Men began to reform the Roman Language to the Purity, which they assigned and fixed to the Time of Augustus & that Century. the Architects, also, ashamed of the modern Barbarity of Building, began to examine carefully the Ruins of Old Rome, and Italy; to search into the Orders and Proportions, and to establish them by inviolable Rules; so to their Labours and Industry, we owe in a great Degree the Restoration of Architecture.

Account of Architecture, p. 9 The ingenious Mr. Evelyn, makes a general and judicious Comparison, in his Account of Architecture, of the ancient and modern Styles, with Reference to some of the particular Works of Inigo Jones, and the Surveyor; which in few Words, gives a right Idea of the majestick Symmetry of the one, and the absurd System of the other.

" The ancient Greek & Roman Architecture answer all the Perfections
" required in a faultless and accomplished Building; such as for so many
" Ages were so renowned and reputed by the universal Suffrages of the
" civilised World, and would doubtless have still subsisted, & made good
" their Claim, and what is recorded of them; had not the Goths, Van-
" dals, and other barbarous Nations, subverted and demolished them, to-
" gether with that glorious Empire, where those stately and pompous
" Monuments stood; introducing in their stead, a certain fantastical and
" licencious Manner of Building, which we have since called Modern or
" Gothick. Congestions of heavy, dark, melancholy, and monkish Piles,
" without any just Proportion, Use or Beauty, compared with the truly
" ancient, so as when we meet with the greatest Industry, and expensive
" Carving, full of Fret and lamentable Imagery; sparing neither of Pains
" nor Cost; a judicious Spectator is rather distracted or quite confounded,
" than touched with that Admiration, which results from the true & just
" symmetry, regular Proportion, Union, and Disposition; and from the
" great and noble Manner in which the august and glorious Fabricks of
" the Ancients are executed.

It was after the Irruption & Swarms of those truculent People from the North; the Moors and Arabs from the South and East, over-running the

174

civilised World; that where-ever they fixed themselves, they soon began to debauch this noble and useful Art; when instead of those beautiful Orders, so majestical & proper for their Stations, becoming Variety, and other ornamental Accessories; they set up those slender and misshapen Pillars, or rather Bundles of Staves and other incongruous Props, to support incumbent Weights, & ponderous arched Roofs, without Entablature; and though not without great Industry (as M. D'Aviler well observes) nor altogether naked of gaudy Sculpture, trite & busy Carvings; 'tis such as gluts the Eye, rather than gratifies and pleases it with any reasonable Satisfaction: For Proof of this (without travelling far abroad) I dare report myself to any Man of Judgment, and that has the least Taste of Order and Magnificence; if after he has looked a while upon King Henry the VIIth's Chapel at Westminster, gazed on its sharp Angles, Jetties, narrow Lights, lame Statues, Lace, and other Cut-work, and Crincle-crancle; and shall then turn his Eyes on the Banquetting-hall built at Whitehall by Inigo Jones, after the ancient Manner; or on what his Majesty's Surveyor, Sir Christopher Wren, has advanced at St. Paul's, and consider what a glorious Object the Cupola, Porticoes, Colonades, and other Parts present to the Beholder, or compare the Schools and Library at Oxford with the Theatre there; or what he has built at Trinity-College, in Cambridge, & since all these, at Greenwich and other Places; by which Time our Home-traveller will begin to have a just Idea of the ancient and modern Architecture: I say, let him well consider, and compare them judicially, without Partiality and Prejudice; and then pronounce which of the two Manners strikes the Understanding as well as the Eye, with the more Majesty and solemn Greatness; tho' in so much a plainer and simple Dress, conform to the respective Orders and Entablature; and accordingly determine to whom the Preference is due: Not as we said, that there is not something of solid, and odly artificial too, after a Sort: but then the universal and unreasonable Thickness of the Walls, clumsy Buttresses, Towers, sharp-pointed Arches, Doors, & other Apertures, without Proportion: nonsensical Insertions of various Marbles impertinently placed; Turrets and Pinnacles thick set with Monkies and Chimeras, and Abundance of busy Work & other Incongruities dissipate and break the Angles of the Sight, and so confound it, that one cannot consider it with any Steadiness, where to begin or end; taking off from that noble Air and Grandeur, bold and graceful Manner, which the Ancients had so well, and judiciously established: but, in this Sort have they and their Followers ever since filled not Europe alone, but Asia and Africa besides, with Mountains of Stone, vast and gigantick Buildings indeed, but not worthy the Name of Architecture, &c.

PART II. SECT. IX.

A CATALOGUE, SHORT DESCRIPTION, AND GENERAL DIMENSIONS OF FIFTY-ONE PAROCHIAL CHURCHES OF THE CITY OF LONDON, ERECTED ACCORDING TO THE DESIGNS, AND UNDER THE CARE & CONDUCT, OF SIR CHRISTOPHER WREN, IN LIEU OF THOSE WHICH WERE BURNT AND DEMOLISH'D BY THE GREAT FIRE IN THE YEAR 1666. TOGETHER WITH OTHER CHURCHES BUILT, AND REPAIR'D; AND PUBLICK BUILDINGS.

New View of London, 1708

ALLHALLOWS Bread-street Church, in the Ward of Bread-street within the Walls of London, was rebuilt, & finish'd in 1684, and the Steeple, in 1697. It is a pleasant Church of the Tuscan Order; the Length 72, Breadth 35, and Altitude 30 Feet. The Steeple, (as the Church) is of Stone, built square, of the Dorick Order, & well adorn'd; the Key-stones over the Windows being Carved Heads, and between each a large Festoon; its Height is about 86 Feet.

II. Allhallows the Great, situated on the South-side of Thames-street, in the Ward of Dowgate, within the Walls of London, was re-erected, and finished in 1683, of the Tuscan Order, supported & adorn'd with Pillars and Membrettos of that Order, and strong built of Stone. Its Length is about 87 Feet, Breadth 60, Height 33, with a square Stone Tower, 86 Feet high.

III. Allhallows Lombard-street Church, situated on the North-side of that Street, in the Ward of Langbourn, was rebuilt and finish'd in 1694. In the Church is only one Pillar, which, as also the Pilasters, are of the Tuscan Order; the Length is 84 Feet, Breadth 52, Height about 30; the Altitude of the Tower is about 85, built square.

176

IV. St. Alban Wood-street Church, situated on the East-side of Great-Wood-street, in the Ward of Cripple-Gate, was rebuilt & finished in 1685; the Building both of the Outside and Inside is Gothick, as the same was before the Fire, in Length about 66, Breadth 59, Height 33 Feet; the Tower is of Stone, built square, with Gothick Pinnacles; its Altitude is $85\frac{1}{2}$ Feet, or to the Top of the Pinnacles 92.

V. The Church of St. Anne & Agnes, situated on the North-side of St. Anne's-lane, within Aldersgate, was re-erected and finish'd in 1680, and beautify'd in 1703, very pleasant, and ornamental, tho' small; 53 Feet square, and about 35 Feet high; & the Tower to the Top of the Turret, about 84. The Roof is supported by four handsome Corinthian Pillars, which are posited in a Geometrical Square, from each other; its Ornament consists of four Arches of Fret-work, with Flowers, Fruit, Leaves, Cherubims, &c. At the four Angles, the Roof is lower, & consists of four Quadrangles, within each of which, is a Circle form'd by a Circumference of very rich Fret-work.

VI. St. Andrew's Wardrobe Church, situated on the East-side of Puddle-dock-hill, in the Ward of Castle-Baynard, was re-edify'd and finish'd in 1692, built of Brick, but finished or rendered over in imitation of Stone; the Facias and Corners are Stone, and very good rustick Quoins. The Roof is supported by twelve Tuscan Pillars, and well ornamented with Fret-work:

ST ALBAN

ALLHALLOWS·BREAD ST

n 1

The Length of this Church is about 75, Breadth 59, Altitude 38 Feet; and that of the square Tower about 86.

VII. St. Andrew's Holbourn Church, situated on the South-side of Holbourn-hill, in the Ward of Farendon, without the Walls of London, but within the Liberty, was rebuilt and finished in 1687, beautiful, and spacious; the Columns that support the Roof; adorn'd with Fret-work, are of the Corinthian Order; the Walls of Stone; the Length is 105, Breadth 63, and Height 43 Feet; the Altitude of the Tower, or square Steeple, is 110 Feet; it has four large Windows frontting E. W. N. & S. adorn'd with Pilasters, Architrave, Friese, Cornice, Pediments, and of the Dorick Order; finish'd in 1704.

ST AUGUSTIN'S

VIII. St. Anthony's, *alias* St. Antholin's Church, situated at the Westend of Watlin-street, in Cordwainer-street Ward, was re-erected and finish'd in 1682, built of Stone, the Outside of the Tuscan Order, but the Roof within (which is an eliptical Cupola adorn'd with Fret-work of Festoons, with four Port-hole Windows) is supported by eight Pillars of the Composite Order; the Length is about 66, Breadth 54, & Height within 44 Feet. It has a neat Spire Steeple, in Altitude about 154 Feet.

IX. St. Augustin's neat little Church, situated on the North-side of Watlin-street, near St. Paul's Cathedral, was finish'd in 1683, and the Steeple in 1695; the Church and Steeple are of Stone, the latter being a Tower with Acroteria, a Cupola, a Lantern adorn'd with Vases, and a Spire whose lower Part is of a parabolical Form. The Roof is camerated, divided into Pannels, adorn'd with Fret-work, & supported with Pillars of the Ionick Order; the Length of the Church is about 51, Breadth 45, and Height 30 Feet; and that of the Steeple 145 Feet.

X. St. Benedict (vulgarly St. Bennet) Gras-church situated on the Eastside of Gras-church-street, in the Ward of Bridge-within, *i.e.* within the Walls of London, was re-edify'd and finished in 1685; its Length within is about 60, Breadth 30, Height 32; and of the Steeple 149 Feet.

178

XI. St. Bennet's Paul's Wharf Church, situated on the North-side of Thames-street, in the Ward of Castle-Baynard, was rebuilt in 1683, of Brick and Stone, ornamented on the Outside with Festoons carv'd in Stone round the Fabrick; the quadrangular Roof within is supported by four Pillars and Pilasters of the Corinthian Order, with their Architrave, Friese, and Cantaliever Cornice; the Length within is 54, Breadth 50, Height 36 Feet; the Steeple (which is of Brick and Stone, as the Church) consists of a Tower, Dome and Turret, the Altitude about 118 Feet.

St BENNET'S ✠

XII. St. Benedict's (vulgò St. Bennet) Fink-church, situated on the North side of Thread-needle-street, in the Ward of Broad-street, was built in 1673, of Stone, and is a fine Piece of Architecture; the Body of the Church within is a compleat elipsis, (a very commodius Form for the Auditory) and the Roof is an eliptical Cupola, (at the Center of which is a Turret glaz'd round) environ'd with a Cantaliever Cornice, & supported by six Columns of the Composite Order; between each of which is a spacious Arch, and six large light Windows, with strong Munions and Transums: The Length (or greater Diameter) of the Church is 63, the Breadth, (or lesser Diameter) 48, the Altitude 49 Feet. The Steeple consists of a square Tower, over which is a large Cupola, and above that a Spire, which are together above 110 Feet; and the Tower is adorn'd with Fresco-work of Festoons &c.

XIII. St. Bartholomew's Exchange (or the Little) Church, situated on the East-side of Bartholomew-lane, and near the Royal Exchange, in the Ward of Broad-street, was rebuilt in 1679; 'tis a strong Building, the Roof flat, adorn'd with Fret-work, and supported with Columns of the Tuscan Order, and large Arches. Here are three fine Door-cases, on the N.S. and W. Sides of the Church, whose Pilasters, Entablature, & Pediments are of the Corinthian Order, adorn'd with Cherubims, Shields, Festoons, &c. that towards the South being more particularly spacious and fine: The Length is 78, Breadth 60, Height 41; and that of the square Tower, about 90 Feet.

ST BRIDE'S

XIV. St. Bridget, *alias* St. Bride's Church, situated on the South-side of Fleet-street, in the Ward of Farendon, without the Walls of London, but within the Liberty of the City, was rebuilt with great Beauty & Strength, in 1680, and further adorn'd in 1699; the Roof is elevated on Pillars, and Arches, with Entablaments of the Tuscan Order; the Length is 111, Breadth 57, Height 41 Feet; The Altitude of the Steeple is 234 Feet; it consists of a Tower, and lofty Spire of Stone, adorn'd with Pilasters, and Entablature of the Corinthian Order, arched Pediments, Urns, &c. & spiry Arcades, of a most elegant Effect.

XV. Christ-church, situated on the North-side of Newgate-street, was rebuilt in 1687; the Fabrick is of Stone, spacious & beautiful, with Buttresses on the Out-side, and adorn'd with Acroteria, Pine-apples, Pediments, &c. the Spire was finish'd in 1704, which is likewise of Stone, adorn'd with Vases, &c. the Roof of the Nave of the Church is camerated, and those of the two Side-ailes are flat; the first supported by ten Pillars of the Composite Order, the others by as many Pilasters of the same Order; the Length is 114 Feet, Breadth 81, Height 38; the Altitude of the Steeple (which consists of a Tower and Spire) is about 153 Feet.

XVI. St. Christopher's Church, situated on the North-side of Threadneedle-street, in the Ward of Broadstreet, was not totally destroy'd by the great Fire, (the Walls partly escaping the Flames) & had probably far'd bet-

ST BRIDE'S

180

ter, had it not been fill'd with Paper.
It was soon after the Fire repair'd, in
1671; afterwards beautify'd in 1696;
all the Old Part left by the Fire is
Gothick, but the Pillars within are
Tuscan; the Length is 60, Breadth
52, Height 40 Feet; Altitude of the
Tower about 80 Feet

XVII. St. Clements Danes Church,
situated on the North-side of the
Strand, a little Westward of Temple-
Bar, in the Liberty of Westminster,
" being greatly decay'd, was taken
" down in the Year 1680, and rebuilt
" and finish'd in 1682, &c. Sir Chris-
" topher Wren his Majesty's Survey-
" or, freely and generously bestowing
" his great Care and Skill towards the
" contriving and building of it, &c."
The Fabrick is of Stone, strong and

CHRIST-CHURCH ☒

*Inscribed on
a Stone of
white Mar-
ble on the
North-side
of the chancel
*by Mr.
Gibbs*

beautiful, of the Corinthian Order, with a Tower, and the late Addition
thereon of an ornamental *Steeple. The East-ends both of the Church
and Chancel are eliptical. The Roof is camerated, supported with Corinthian Columns, & enrich'd with Fret-work. On the South, fronting the
Strand, is a circular Portico of six Ionick Pillars. The Length is 96 Feet,
Breadth 63, Height 48; Altitude of the Tower about 116 Feet.

XVIII. St. Clements East-cheap Church, situated on the East-side of St.
Clements-lane, near great East-cheap, in the Ward of Candlewick-
street, was rebuilt of Brick and Stone, in 1686, of the Composite Order,
having a Tower, flat Roof, and Pilasters round the Inside of the Church.
The Ceiling is adorn'd with a spacious Circle, whose Periphery is curious
Fret-work. The Length is 64, Breadth 40, Height 34; and that of the
Tower 88 Feet.

XIX. St. Dionis Back Church, situated on the West-side of Lime-street,
in the Ward of Langbourn, was rebuilt in 1674; & the Steeple, in 1684.
The Building is chiefly of Stone; the Tower, and the Pillars within are
strong; but part of the Walls are of Brick finish'd-over, the said Pillars
and the Pilasters that strengthen the Walls within, & support the Roof,
are of the Ionick Order; as is also the End fronting Lime-street. The
Length is 66 Feet, Breadth 59, Height 34; and that of the Tower and
Turret 90 Feet.

ST DUNSTAN'S

XX. St. Dunstan's in the East, is situated in the Middle-way between Tower-street, North, and Thames-street, South; in Tower-street Ward. The Church was only repair'd, and new beautify'd, but the Steeple was erected as it now appears, in 1698. The Windows and Steeple are of a modern Gothick Stile, but the Pillars and Arches within are Tuscan. The Altitude of the Steeple, consisting of a Stone-tower & Spire, at each Corner of which Tower are four neat smaller Spires, & the fifth or principal erected on four Gothick Arches is 75 Feet.

XXI. St. Edmund the King, situated on the North-side of Lombard-street, in Langbourn Ward, is well built of Stone, and of the Tuscan Order: The Roof is flat, and there are no Pillars within to support it. The Length is 69 Feet, Breadth 39, Height 33; and that of the Tower about 90 Feet, the Church was rebuilt in 1690.

XXII. St. George Botolph-lane Church, situated on the West-side of Botolph-lane, in the Ward of Belinsgate, was rebuilt of Stone, in 1674. The Roof over the two Side-ailes is flat, but that over the Nave is camerated, and supported by Columns of the Composite Order. The Outside of the East-end is adorn'd with a Stone Cornice and Pediment, and enrich'd with a Cherub and Festoons; the Roof with fretted Arches; and an Entablament above the Columns. The Length is 54 Feet, Breadth 36, Height 36; and of the Steeple about 84 Feet.

XXIII. St. James's Garlick-hill Church, situated on the East-side of that Hill, near Thames-street, in the Ward of Vintry, was rebuilt, in 1683, of Stone, with handsome outer Door-cases of the Corinthian Order. The Roof within is flat, and supported with 12 Columns, besides Pilasters, of the Ionick Order. The Length is 75, Breadth 45, Height 40 Feet; and of the Steeple (which is a Tower, with Rail and Banister above the Cornice) about 90 Feet.

XXIV. St. James's, Westminster, Church, situated on the North-side of Jermyn-street, fronting towards St. James's-square, within the Liberty of

182

the City of Westminster, was erected at the Charge and Credit of Henry Jermyn, Earl of St. Albans, and of the Inhabitants, Owners & Occupiers of the Houses & Lands in this Precinct; and with the Authority of an Act of Parliament passed 3tio Jacobi 2di. constituting this Church parochial. The Walls are of Brick, with Rustick Quoins, Facias, Doors, and Windows of Stone. The Roof is arched, supported by Pillars of the Corinthian Order; & the Door-cases of the Ionick Order. The Beauty of this Church consists chiefly, 1st. in its Roof within, divided into Pannels of Crocket and Fret-work, and the twelve Columns that support it; and in the Cornice. 2dly, In the Galleries. 3dly, In the Door-cases, especially that fronting Jermyn-street. 4thly, In the Windows, especially two at the East-end;

St MAGNUS

the Upper Order a Venetian Window, adorned with two Columns and two Pilasters, of the Composite Order; the lower of the Corinthian: The Length is 84, Breadth 63, Height 42; & that of the Steeple, which consists of a Tower and Clock-spire, 149 Feet.

XXV. St. Lawrence Jewry Church, situated on the North-side of Cateaton-street, and West-side of Guildhall-yard, in the Ward of Cheap, was rebuilt in 1677 of Stone, and in the Corinthian Order. The Roof is flat, adorned with Fret-work; and the Columns, Pilasters, and Entablement, of the same Order. The Length is 81, Breadth 68, Height 40 Feet; and that of the Steeple, (which is a Tower-lanthorn, and small Spire) about 130 Feet.

XXVI. St. Magnus Church, situated on the East-side, and North-end of London Bridge, in Bridge-ward, was rebuilt in 1676, and the Steeple in 1705, of Stone. The Roof over the Nave or middle Aile is camerated, and enriched with Arches of Fret-work; also an Architrave, Frieze, and Cornice, round the Walls. Over the two other Ailes flat, supported by Columns of the Ionick Order, &c. The Steeple consists of a Tower, a Lanthorn, a Cupola, and spiry Turret. The Length is 90, Breadth 59, Height 41 Feet.

n 4

S.ᵗ MARGARET'S PATTENS

XXVII. St. Margaret Lothbury Church, situated on the North-side of Lothbury, in the Ward of Coleman-street, was re-edified and finish'd in 1690, of Stone; with a Steeple, consisting of a spacious Tower, on which is a small Dome, and on that a Spire: The Roof is flat, supported with Columns on the South, & Pilasters on the North-side, of the Corinthian Order. The Length is 66, Breadth 54, Height 36 Feet; and that of the Steeple 140 Feet.

XXVIII. St. Margaret's Pattens Church, situated on the North-side of Little Tower-street, in the Ward of Belinsgate, was rebuilt in 1687. The Walls at the West-end are of Stone, but fronting Southward of Brick covered with a Finishing, and Quoins of Stone. The Tower is also of Stone, with Acroteria & Spire, of the Dorick Order. The outer Door-case at the West-end is Tuscan, and the Pillars & Pilasters within are Corinthian. The Roof is flat, having a Quadrangle of Fret-work, and the Arches adorned with the like. The Length is 66, Breadth 52, Height 32; & that of the Steeple, which consists of a spacious Tower and Spire, is 198 Feet 2 Inches.

XXIX. St. Martin's Ludgate Church, situated on the North-side of Ludgate-street, in the Ward of Farrendon, was rebuilt and finished, with the Steeple, in 1684. The Walls, and four Columns near the four Angles of the Church that support the camerated Roof, are of Stone, of the Composite Order: The Steeple consists of a handsome Tower, Cupola, and Spire, of the Tuscan Order: Above which Cupola is a Balcony. The Length is 57, Breadth 66, Height 59 Feet; and of the Steeple to the Top of the Spire 168 Feet.

XXX. St. Mary Abchurch, situated on the West-side of Abchurch-lane, in the Ward of Candlewick-street, was rebuilt in 1686, of Brick, with Stone-Quoins, Windows, and Door-cases: The Tower also is of the like Materials, which has a Cupola and Spire. The Length is 63, Breadth 60, Height 51 Feet; and of the Steeple about 140 Feet.

184

XXXI. St. Mary-at-hill Church, situated on the West-side of the Street, called St. Mary-hill, in the Ward of Belinsgate, was rebuilt in 1672. The Front towards the Hill is Stone; the rest of the Walls Stone, covered with a Finishing; the Tower is also of Stone; the Inside of the Roof over the middle Aile is a little Arching, in the Middle whereof is a handsome Cupola: The Roofs of the side Ailes are flat, and lowest at the four Angles, supported with four Columns: At each End of the Church are two Pilasters, of no Order at all; but a Species, partly composed of the Dorick & Corinthian. The Roof of the Cupola is adorned with Cherubims, Arches, and Leaves, & the rest of the Church-ceiling with quadrangular Figures, all of Fret-work; under which is a

St MARTIN'S & St PAUL'S

Cantaliever Cornice. The Length is 96, Breadth 60, Altitude to the Ceiling of the Roof 26, and to the Center of the Cupola 38 Feet; and that of the Steeple, consisting of a Tower and Turret, about 96 Feet.

XXXII. St. Mary Aldermary Church, situated on the East-side of Bow-lane, in the Ward of Cordwainers-street, was rebuilt by a private Benefaction, before the Publick Fund was settled by Parliament on Coals, for rebuilding the Churches demolished by the Fire. The lower Part of the Tower was repaired by the Surveyor, and the upper Part new-built in 1711. The Altitude to the Vertex of the Pinnacles 135 Feet.

XXXIII. St. Mary Magdalen, Old Fish-street Church, situated on the North-side of Little Knight-rider-street, in the Ward of Castle-Baynard, was rebuilt in the Year 1685, mostly of Stone; with Rail and Banister round the Outside. There are three Ailes, and a handsome Stone-Tower. The Length is 60, Breadth 48, Height 30 Feet.

XXXIV. St. Mary Somerset Church, situated on the North-side of Thames-street, in the Ward of Queenhyth, was rebuilt in 1695, of Stone, with the Tower. Here are two Ailes, with a flat Roof, adorned with a Cornice; and between the Windows with Fret-work of Cherubims, &c. The Length is 83, Breadth 36, Height 30 Feet; and of the Tower, to the Top of the highest Pinnacles, 120 Feet.

185

ST MARY-LE-BOW ✠

XXXV. St. Mary-le-bow, situated on the South-side of Cheapside, in the Ward of Cordwainer - street. This Church was rebuilt and finished in 1673, upon the Walls of a very ancient Church, about the early Time of the Roman Colony, which by the Rising of the Gound in succeeding Ages, were entirely buried under the Level of the present Street of Cheapside. It is built of Brick and Stone; the Walls covered with a Finishing; the Roof is arched, & supported with ten Corinthian Columns; there are three Ailes, besides the cross Aile at the West-end. The Model is after that of the Templum Pacis.

But the principal Ornament of this Church is the Steeple, erected near the North-west Angle, & made contiguous by a Lobby between the Church and Steeple, which is founded upon an old Roman Causeway, lying about 18 Feet below the Level of the Street. It is accounted by judicious Artists an admirable Piece of Architecture, not to be parallel'd by the Steeple of any parochial Church in Europe. It was designed by the incomparable Sir Christopher Wren, begun in 1671, and finished in 1680. It is built of Portland-stone, consisting of a Tower and Spire: The Tower is square; in the North-side thereof is a Door and beautiful Doorcase, the Peers and Arch are of the Tuscan Order, and is adorned with two Columns and Entablement of the Dorick Order; the Metops enriched with Cherubims; above the Cornice is an elliptical Aperture, on the Keypiece a Cherub, whence (by way of Compartment) extend two Festoons of large Fruit, sustain'd lower by two Cupids in a sitting Posture, their Feet resting on the Cornice; and the whole farther adorned with Rustick-work, and another Door-case of the same Form, on the West-side; above which, on the said North-side, is another Aperture and Balcony; and a little higher a Modillion Cornice; above that are four Windows, (on each Side one) each adorned with four Pilasters, with Entablement, of the Ionick Order: Over the Cornice a Ballustrade, and at each Angle four Cartouches, erected tapering; &, on the Meeting of the upper Ends, a spacious Vase, which terminates the Tower.

The Spire begins with a circular Mure; and on that, a little higher than the tops of the said Vases, is a Range of Columns with Entablature, and
186

Acroteria, of the Corinthian Order. This Balcony is adorned with Bows or Arches, all which you pass under in walking round this Part of the Spire, which (a little higher) is adorned with Pedestals, their Columns and Entablature of the Composite Order; so that here are all the five Orders, regularly executed. On the Cornice of this last Order stand Cartouches, whereon is erected an Obelisk of a considerable Altitude, and at the Vertex thereof a spacious Ball; and above that (as a Weather-cock) is the Figure of a Dragon of Brass gilt, about ten Feet long; in the expanded Wings is figur'd a Cross, (the Supporter of the Ensigns-armorial of the City of London.) The Dimensions of the Church within, are, Length 65½ Feet, Breadth 63, Altitude 38; and that of the famous Steeple 225 Feet.

To give the Sentiments of an Author we have took Occasion sometimes to quote:—"The Steeple of Bow-church, says he, is another Master- *Critical Review of Buildings, London, 1734, Page 13*
" piece [of Sir Christopher Wren's] in a peculiar Kind of Building, which
" has no fixed Rule to direct it, nor is it to be reduced to any settled Laws
" of Beauty; without doubt, if we considered it only as a Part of some
" other Building, it can be esteemed no other than a delightful Absurdity;
" But if either considered in itself, or as a Decoration of a whole City in
" Prospect, not only to be justified, but admir'd. That which we have
" now mentioned is beyond Question as perfect as human Imagination
" can contrive or execute, & till we see it outdone, we shall hardly think
" it to be equalled."

XXXVI. St. Mary Woolnoth Church, situated on the South-side of Lombard-street, was repaired in 1677. The Sides, the Roof, and Part of the Ends, having been damnified by the great Fire: The Steeple was old, and wanted rebuilding, which, together with the whole Church, is now very substantially performed by the ingenious and skilled Architect Mr. Nicholas Hawksmoor; who formerly was, and continued for many Years, a Domestick-clerk to the Surveyor, and was afterwards employed under him in the royal, and other publick Works.

XXXVII. St. Mary Aldermanbury Church, situated near the middle of Aldermanbury, in the Ward of Cripplegate, was rebuilt in 1677, of Stone, with the Steeple, consisting of a Tower and Turret. The Roof within is camerated, & supported with twelve Columns of the Composite Order: At the East-end is a large Cornice and Pediment; also two large Cartouches, and Pine-Apples of Stone carved; the Inside of the Roof is adorned with Arches of Fret-work, & the said Columns with an Entablature; the Cornice Cantaliever. The Length 72, Breadth 45, Height 38 Feet; and of the Steeple, about 90 Feet.

XXXVIII. St. Matthew Friday-street Church, situated on the West-

St MICHAEL ROYAL ✠

side of Friday-street, near Cheapside, in the Ward of Farrendon, was rebuilt in 1685. The Walls and Tower are of Brick, the Windows and Door-cases Stone; as is all the Front towards Friday-street. The Length is 60, Breadth 33, Height 31; and of the Tower, 74 Feet.

XXXIX. St. Michael Basingshall (*alias* Bassishaw) Church, situated on the West-side of Basinghall-street, in the Ward of Bassishaw, was rebuilt and finish'd in 1679. The Walls are brick; the Tower of Stone; three Ailes, the Apertures of each Side similar to those of their Opposites in Number and Model; Pillars of the Corinthian Order: The Roof is camerated, & divided into Quadrangular Pannels of Crocket-work; also a Cantaliever Cornice, Friese, &c. enrich'd with Foliage, &c. the Length 70, Breadth 50, Height 42 Feet; and of the Tower, 75 Feet.

XL. St. Michael Royal Church, on the East-side of College-hill, in the Ward of Vintry, was rebuilt in 1694. The Walls are of Stone, and at the East-end some Brick; a flat square Roof, adorned with Fret & Crocket-work. The Length is 86, Breadth 48, Height 40; and of the Tower, about 90 Feet.

XLI. St. Michael Queenhyth Church, on the South-west Angle of Little Trinity-lane, in Thames-street, in the Ward of Queenhyth, was rebuilt in 1677. The Walls are of Stone; there are three Ailes; the Roof is square and flat, with the Ornament of a Quadrangle bounded with Fret-work. The Length 71, Breadth 40, Height 39; and that of the Steeple, consisting of a Tower and Spire, 135 Feet.

XLII. St. Michael Wood-street Church, on the West-side of Great Wood-street, in the Ward of Cripplegate, was rebuilt in 1675, of Stone; the Roof flat, and adorned with Fret and Crocket-work, the Walls with Arches & Imposts; the Front towards Wood-street, with Stone Pilasters, Entablature, and pitched Pediment of the Ionick Order. The Length within is 63, Breadth 42, Height 31 Feet; of the Tower, 90 Feet.

188

XLIII. St. Michael Crooked-lane
Church, on the East-side of St. Michael's-lane, in the Ward of Candlewick-street, was rebuilt in 1688, of
Stone. The Length is 78, Breadth 46,
Height 32 Feet; and of the Tower
to the Top of the Pinnacles, about
100 Feet.

XLIV. St. Michael Cornhill Church,
on the South-side of Cornhill, in the
Ward of Cornhill, being demolished
by the great Fire (except the Tower),
was rebuilt in 1672, mostly of Stone,
and with three Ailes; the Roof camerated, having Groins and Imposts
covered with Lead, & supported with
Tuscan Columns. The Length is 87,
Breadth 60, Height 35 Feet; and, of
the Tower to the Top of the small
ones at the Angles, 130 Feet.

Sᵀ MICHAEL: CORNHILL

XLV. St. Mildred Bread-street
Church, on the East-side of Bread-
street, & in the Ward of Bread-street,
was rebuilt in 1683. The Front towards Bread-street is well-built of
Free-stone; the rest of the Walls, and
Tower, of Brick; the four Sides within the Structure are uniform, each
having one Window under a spacious
graceful Arch; & the Roof is a Dome,
whose Base's Circumference touches
the four Arches aforesaid. Here are
two Ailes, and the Steeple is placed at
the South-east Angle of the Church.
The Arches and Walls within are a-
dorned with great Variety of Fret-
work, &c. The Length is 62, Breadth
36, Height 40 Feet, & to the Top of
the Dome 52 Feet; and of the Steeple
to the Top of the Spire 140.

Sᵀ MILDRED·BREAD Sᵀ

189

St PETER'S ✠

St PETER'S ✠

XLVI. St. Mildred Poultry Church, on the North-side of the Poultry, near Stocks-market, in the Ward of Cheap, was rebuilt in 1676, of Stone, and has three small Ailes, with a flat quadrangular Roof, adorned with Fret-work, &c. The Outside next the Poultry has a Cornice, Pediment, and Acroters, with Enrichments of Foliage, &c. all cut in Stone. The Length is 56, Breadth 42, Height 36 Feet; & of the Stone Tower 75.

XLVII. St. Nicholas Coleabbey Church, on the South-side of Fish-street, in the Ward of Queenhyth, was rebuilt in 1677. The Walls are well built of Stone; the Steeple is a Tower, and a Frustum of a Pyramid covered with Lead, and a Balcony at the upper End; there are three Ailes; the Roof is flat, adorned with Pannels of Crocket-work; & the Walls with Corinthian Pilasters. The Length is 63, Breadth 43, Height 36 Feet; and of the Steeple 135.

XLVIII. St. Olaves Jewry Church, on the West-side of the Old Jewry, in the Ward of Coleman-street, was rebuilt in 1673. The Walls are partly Brick, with Stone Facias, Windows, Door-cases; the Outside of the East-end is adorned with Pilasters, Cornice, and a spacious pitched Pediment; the upper Part of the Walls, at the meeting with the Roof round the Church, is enriched with Cherubims, Festoons, and Cartouches: There are two Ailes, and a very large Chancel. The Steeple is of Stone, consisting of a handsome Tower, with Pinnacles. The Length is 78, Breadth 34, Height

36 Feet; and of the Tower, to the Top of its Pinnacles, about 88 Feet.

XLIX. St. Peter's Church in Cornhill, was rebuilt in 1681, of Stone, except Part of the South-side, and the Tower, which is Brick; the rest of the Steeple, viz. the Dome and Spire, are covered with Lead, the Roof within is camerated, and supported with square Pillars, adorned with Pilaster of the Corinthian Order; and there are three Ailes. The Length is 80, Breadth 47, Height 40; and of the Steeple, about 140 Feet.

L. St. Sepulchre's Church, on the North-side of Snow-hill, in the Ward of Farendon without, being almost demolished by the great Fire, (except part of the Wall and Steeple) was re-

St STEPHEN'S

built in 1670. The Walls are of Stone strengthened with Buttresses; the Tower is also of Stone, with four small Spires, one at each Angle, which, as also the Windows, are modern Gothick; the Roof over the Nave is camerated, but is flat; and lower about 8 Feet over the Side-ailes, supported with twelve strong Stone Columns of the Tuscan Order. The Length is (besides the Passage or Ambulatory at the West-end) 126 Feet, Breadth (excluding the Chapel on the North side) 58, Height of the Roof over the Middle-aile 35; and of the Tower and Spires, about 140 Feet.

LI. St. Stephen's Coleman-street, was rebuilt in 1676, chiefly of Stone, with two Ailes. The Roof is flat, without Pillars to support it. On the Outside, the Front of the East-end is adorned with a Cornice & circular Pediment between two Pine-apples, &c. The Length is 75, Breadth 35, Height 44; and of the Tower, besides the Turret, 65 Feet.

LII. St. Stephen's Wallbrook Church, near Stocks-market, was rebuilt in 1676. The Walls and Tower are of Stone; the Roof within, over the Middle-aile is arched, in the Center of which is a spacious Cupola, & a Lantern in the middle of that: Over the rest of the Church the Roof is flat, supported by Corinthian Columns and Pilasters. Here are three Ailes, and a Cross-aile. The Length is 75, Breadth 56, Altitude of the

ST STEPHEN'S

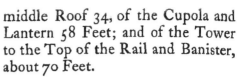

middle Roof 34, of the Cupola and Lantern 58 Feet; and of the Tower to the Top of the Rail and Banister, about 70 Feet.

" Walbrook Church, so little known
" among us, is famous all over Europe,
" & is justly reputed the Masterpiece
" of the celebrated Sir Christopher
" Wren. Perhaps Italy itself can pro-
" duce no modern Building that can
" vie with this, in Taste or Propor-
" tion: There is not a Beauty which
" the Plan would admit of, that is not
" to be found here in its greatest Per-
" fection; and Foreigners very justly
" call our Judgment in question for
" understanding its Graces no better,
" and allowing it no higher Degree
" of Fame." [*Critical Review of Pub-*
" *lick Buildings in London, P. 12, 1734.*]

LIII. St. Swithin's Church, on the North-side of Cannon-street, near London-stone, in the Ward of Walbrook, was rebuilt in 1679, of Stone, with the Tower, the Roof supported with Demi-columns of the Composite Order. Here are three Ailes; and the whole is commodious & pleasant, though small. The Length is 61 Feet from North to South, from East to West 42, Height 40; & of the Tower and Spire 150 Feet.

LIV. St. Vedast, *alias* Foster Church, on the East-side of Foster-lane, in the Ward of Farendon, was rebuilt in 1697, of Stone, with three Ailes; the Roof flat, supported on the South-side with Tuscan Columns, and adorned with an eliptical Figure within a Parallelogram, environed with curious

ST VEDAST

Fret-work, &c. The Length is 69 Feet, Breadth 51, Altitude 36; and of the Tower, about 90 Feet.

In the ninth Year of the Reign of Queen Anne, 1708, an Act of Parliament passed to erect Fifty new additional Parish Churches in the Cities of London and Westminster: The Surveyor, being appointed one of the Commissioners for carrying on the Works, attended that Service with all the Application his other Offices would permit; & preparatory thereunto, took occasion to impart his Thoughts to this Effect, in a Letter to a Friend in that Commission.

SINCE Providence, in great Mercy, has protracted my Age, to the finishing the cathedral Church of St. Paul, and the parochial Churches of London, in lieu of those demolished by the Fire; (all which were executed during the Fatigues of my Employment in the Service of the Crown, from that Time to the present happy Reign;) and being now constituted one of the Commissioners for Building, pursuant to the late Act, Fifty more Churches in London and Westminster; I shall presume to communicate briefly my Sentiments, after long Experience; and without further Ceremony exhibit to better Judgment, what at present occurs to me, in a transient View of this whole Affair; not doubting but that the Debates of the worthy Commissioners may hereafter give me occasion to change, or add to these Speculations.

1. First, I conceive the Churches should be built, not where vacant Ground may be cheapest purchased in the Extremities of the Suburbs, but among the thicker Inhabitants, for Convenience of the better sort, although the Site of them should cost more; the better Inhabitants contributing most to the future Repairs, and the Ministers and Officers of the Church, and Charges of the Parish.

2. I could wish that all Burials in Churches might be disallowed, which is not only unwholesom, but the Pavements can never be kept even, nor Pews upright: And if the Church-yard be close about the Church, this also is inconvenient, because the Ground being continually raised by the Graves, occasions, in Time, a Descent by Steps into the Church, which renders it damp, and the Walls green, as appears evidently in all old Churches.

3. It will be enquired, where then shall be the Burials? I answer, in Cemeteries seated in the Outskirts of the Town; and since it is become the Fashion of the Age to solemnize Funerals by a Train of Coaches, (even where the Deceased are of moderate Condition) though the Cemeteries should be half a Mile, or more, distant from the Church, the Charge need be little or no more than usual; the Service may be first performed in the Church; But for the Poor, & such as must be interred at the Parish

Charge, a publick Hearse of two Wheels and one Horse may be kept at small Expence, the usual Bearers to lead the Horse, and take out the Corpse at the Grave. A Piece of Ground of two Acres in the Fields will be purchased for much less than two Roods among the Buildings: This being inclosed with a strong Brick Wall, and having a Walk round, and two cross Walks, decently planted with Yew-trees, the four Quarters may serve four Parishes, where the Dead need not be disturbed at the pleasure of the Sexton, or piled four or five upon one another, or Bones thrown out to gain Room. In these Places beautiful Monuments may be erected; but yet the Dimensions should be regulated by an Architect, and not left to the Fancy of every Mason; for thus the Rich, with large Marble Tombs, would shoulder out the Poor; when a Pyramid, a good Bust, or Statue on a proper Pedestal, will take up little Room in the Quarters, & be properer than Figures lying on Marble Beds: The Walls will contain Escutchions and Memorials for the Dead, & the Area good Air and Walks for the Living. It may be considered further, that if the Cemeteries be thus thrown into the Fields, they will bound the excessive Growth of the City with a graceful Border, which is now encircled with Scavengers Dung-stalls.

4. As to the Situation of the Churches, I should propose they be brought as forward as possible into the larger and more open Streets, not in obscure Lanes, nor where Coaches will be much obstructed in the Passage. Nor are we, I think, too nicely to observe East or West, in the Position, unless it falls out properly: Such Fronts as shall happen to lie most open in View should be adorn'd with Porticos, both for Beauty and Convenience; which, together with handsome Spires, or Lanterns, rising in good Proportion above the neighbouring Houses (of which I have given several Examples in the City of different Forms) may be of sufficient Ornament to the Town, without a great Expence for enriching the outward Walls of the Churches, in which Plainness and Duration ought principally, if not wholly, to be studied. When a Parish is divided, I suppose it may be thought sufficient, if the Mother-church has a Tower large enough for a good Ring of Bells, & the other Churches smaller Towers for two or three Bells; because great Towers, & lofty Steeples, are sometimes more than half the Charge of the Church.

5. I shall mention something of the Materials for publick Fabricks. It is true, the mighty Demand for the hasty Works of thousands of Houses at once, after the Fire of London and the Frauds of those who built by the great, have so debased the Value of Materials, that good Bricks are not to be now had, without greater Prices than formerly, and indeed, if rightly made, will deserve them; but Brick-makers spoil the Earth in the mixing & hasty burning, till the Bricks will hardly bear Weight; though the Earth about London, rightly managed, will yield as good Brick as

194

were the Roman Bricks, (which I have often found in the old Ruins of the City) & will endure, in our Air, beyond any Stone our Island affords: which, unless the Quarries lie near the Sea, are too dear for general Use; The best is Portland, or Roch-abbey Stone; but these are not without their Faults. The next Material is the Lime; Chalk-lime is the constant Practice, which, well mixed with good Sand, is not amiss, though much worse than hard Stone-lime. The Vaulting of St. Paul's is a rendering as hard as Stone; it is composed of Cockle-shell-lime well beaten with Sand; the more Labour in the beating, the better and stronger the Mortar. I shall say nothing of Marble, (though England, Scotland, and Ireland, afford good, and of beautiful Colours) but this will prove too costly for our Purpose, unless for Altar-pieces. In Windows and Doors Portland-Stone may be used, with good Bricks, and Stone Quoyns. As to Roofs, good Oak is certainly the best; because it will bear some Negligence: The Church-wardens Care may be defective in speedy mending Drips; they usually white-wash the Church, and set up their Names, but neglect to preserve the Roof over their Heads: It must be allowed, that the Roof being more out of Sight, is still more unminded. Next to Oak is good yellow Deal, which is a Timber of Length, and Light, and makes excellent Work at first, but if neglected will speedily perish, especially if Gutters (which is a general Fault in Builders) be made to run upon the principal Rafters, the Ruin may be sudden. Our Sea-service for Oak, and the Wars in the North-sea, make Timber at present of excessive Price. I suppose 'ere long we must have recourse to the West-Indies, where most excellent Timber may be had for cutting and fetching. Our Tiles are ill-made, and our Slate not good; Lead is certainly the best and lightest Covering, and being of our own Growth and Manufacture, and lasting, if properly laid, for many hundred Years, is, without question, the most preferable; though I will not deny but an excellent Tile may be made to be very durable; our Artisans are not yet instructed in it, & it is not soon done to inform them.

6. The Capacity & Dimensions of the new Churches may be determined by a Calculation. It is, as I take it, pretty certain, that the Number of Inhabitants, for whom these Churches are provided, are five times as many as those in the City, who were burned out, & probably more than 400,000 grown·Persons that should come to Church, for whom these fifty Churches are to be provided, (besides some Chapels already built, though too small to be made parochial.) Now, if the Churches could hold each 2000, it would yet be very short of the necessary Supply. The Churches therefore must be large; but still, in our reformed Religion, it should seem vain to make a Parish-church larger, than that all who are present can both hear & see. The Romanists, indeed, may build larger Churches, it is enough if they hear the Murmur of the Mass, and see the Elevation

of the Host, but ours are to be fitted for Auditories. I can hardly think it practicable to make a single Room so capacious, with Pews & Galleries, as to hold above 2000 Persons, and all to hear the Service, and both to hear distinctly, and see the Preacher. I endeavoured to effect this, in building the Parish Church of St. James's, Westminster, which, I presume is the most capacious, with these Qualifications, that hath yet been built; and yet at a solemn Time, when the Church was much crowded, I could not discern from a Gallery that 2000 were present. In this Church I mention, though very broad, and the middle Nave arched up, yet are there no Walls of a second Order, nor Lanterns, nor Buttresses, but the whole Roof rests upon the Pillars, as do also the Galleries; I think it may be found beautiful and convenient, & as such, the cheapest of any Form I could invent.

7. Concerning the placing of the Pulpit, I shall observe . . . A moderate Voice may be heard 50 Feet distant before the Preacher, 30 Feet on each Side, and 20 behind the Pulpit, and not this, unless the Pronunciation be distinct and equal, without losing the Voice at the last Word of the Sentence, which is commonly emphatical, and if obscur'd spoils the whole Sense. A French Man is heard further than an English Preacher, because he raises his Voice, and not sinks his last Words: I mention this as an insufferable Fault in the Pronunciation of some of our otherwise excellent Preachers; which School-masters might correct in the young, as a vicious Pronunciation, and not as the Roman Orators spoke: For the principal Verb is in Latin usually the last Word; and if that be lost, what becomes of the Sentence?

8. By what I have said, it may be thought reasonable, that the new Church should be at least 60 Feet broad, and 90 Feet long, besides a Chancel at one End, and the Bellfrey and Portico at the other. These Proportions may be varied; but to build more room, than that every Person may conveniently hear and see, is to create Noise and Confusion. A Church should not be so fill'd with Pews, but that the Poor may have room enough to stand and sit in the Alleys, for to them equally is the Gospel preach'd. It were to be wish'd there were to be no Pews, but Benches; but there is no stemming the Tide of Profit, & the Advantage of Pew-keepers; especially too since by Pews, in the Chapels of Ease, the Minister is chiefly supported. It is evident these fifty Churches are not enough for the present Inhabitants, & the Town will continually grow; but it is to be hoped, that hereafter more may be added, as the Wisdom of the Government shall think fit; and therefore the Parishes should be so divided, as to leave room for Sub-divisions, or at least for Chapels of Ease.

I cannot pass over mentioning the Difficulties that may be found, in obtaining the Ground proper for the Sites of the Churches among the

Buildings, and the Cæmeteries in the Borders without the Town; and therefore I shall recite the Method that was taken for purchasing in Ground at the North-side of St. Paul's Cathedral, where in some Places the Houses were but eleven Feet distant from the Fabrick, exposing it to the continual Danger of Fires. The Houses were seventeen, and contiguous, all in Leasehold of the Bishop, or Dean alone, or the Dean and Chapter, or the Petty-canons, with divers Undertenants. First we treated with the superior Landlords, who being perpetual Bodies were to be recompens'd in Kind, with Rents of the like Value for them and their Successors; but the Tenants in Possession for a valuable Consideration; which to find what it amounted to, we learn'd by diligent Inquiry, what the Inheritance of Houses in that Quarter were usually held at: This we found was fifteen Years Purchase at the most, and proportionably to this the Value of each Lease was easily determin'd in a Scheme, referring to a Map. These Rates, which we resolv'd not to stir from, were offered to each; and, to cut off much Debate, which may be imagin'd every one would abound in, they were assur'd that we went by one uniform Method, which could not be receded from. We found two or three reasonable Men, who agreed to these Terms: Immediately we paid them, and took down their Houses. Others who stood out at first, finding themselves in Dust and Rubbish, & that ready Money was better, as the Case stood, than to continue paying Rent, Repairs, and Parish Duties, easily came in. The whole Ground at last was clear'd, and all concern'd were satisfied, and their Writings given up. The greatest Debate was about their Charges for fitting-up their new Houses to their particular Trades: For this we allow'd one Year's Purchase, & gave leave to remove all their Wainscote, reserving the Materials of the Fabrick only. This was happily finish'd without a Judicatory or Jury; altho' in our present Case, we may find it perhaps sometimes necessary to have recourse to Parliament.

In the Year 1671, the Surveyor began the Building of the great fluted Column of Portland Stone, and of the Dorick Order, (commonly call'd the Monument of London, in Memory of the burning, and rebuilding of the City) and finish'd it in 1677. The Artificers were oblig'd to wait sometimes for Stones of proper Scantlings; which occasion'd the Work to be longer in Execution than otherwise it would have been. It much exceeds in *Height the Pillars at Rome, of the Emperors Trajan, and Antoninus, the stately Remains of Roman Grandeur; or that of Theodosius at Constantinople. In forming this Coloss Column, the Surveyor took the Liberty to exceed the received Proportion of the Order, one Module, or Semi-diameter. In the Place of the Brass-Urn on the Top, (which is not artfully perform'd and was set up contrary to his Opinion) was originally intended a Coloss Statue in Brass gilt, of King Charles the Second, as Founder of the new City; in the Manner of the Roman Pillars,

*The greatest of the R. m. Columns, viz. that of Antoninus, was 172½ Feet in Height, and

12 *Feet,*
three Inches,
in Diameter,
English
Measure

which terminated with the Statues of their Caesars; or else, a Figure erect of a Woman crown'd with Turrets, holding a Sword, and Cap of Maintenance, with other Ensigns of the City's Grandeur, and Re-erection. The Altitude, from the Pavement, is 202 Feet; the Diameter of the Shaft (or Body) of the Column is 15 Feet; the Ground bounded by the Plinth or lowest Part of the Pedestal is 28 Feet square; and the Pedestal in Height is 40 Feet. Within, is a large Stair-case of black Marble, containing 345 Steps, 10½ Inches broad, and six Inches Risers. Over the Capital is an Iron Balcony encompassing a Cippus, or Meta, 32 Feet high, supporting a blazing Urn of Brass gilt. Prior to this, the Surveyor (as it appears by an original Drawing) had made a Design of a Pillar of somewhat less Proportion, viz: 14 Feet in Diameter, and after a peculiar Device; for, as the Romans express'd by Relievo, on the Pedestals, and round the Shafts of their Columns, the History of such Actions and Incidents as were intended to be therby commemorated; so this Monument of the Conflagration, and Resurrection of the City of London, was represented by a Pillar in Flames; the Flames blazing from the Loopholes of the Shaft, (which were to give Light to the Stairs within) were figur'd in Brass-work gilt; and on the Top was a Phaenix rising from her Ashes, of Brass gilt likewise.

Mr. Evelyn
of Medals,
Page 162.
London.
1697

" Our late Discoveries of new Worlds, and Conflicts at Sea; the sanglant " Battles that have been fought at Land; the Fortitude and Sufferings of " an excellent Prince; the Restoration of his Successor; the Conflagra- " tion, and Re-edifying of the greatest City of the World in less than " twenty Years (which had been near two thousand Years in building, " nor then half so vast, &c.) call aloud for their Medals apart: We yet see " in Medal none of the Column erected in Memory of that dreadful Fire,

*Trajan's
Col. 147
Roman Feet,
Antonine's
175, *Lon-*
don, 202,
English Feet

" the biggest and *highest all Europe has to shew; and infinite Pity 'tis, " that it had not been set up where the Incendium and Burning ceas'd, " like a Jupiter stator, rather than where it fatally began; not only in re- " gard to the Eminency of the Ground, but for the Reason of the Thing, " since it was intended as a grateful Monument and Recognition to Al- " mighty God for its Extinction, and should therefore have been plac'd " where the devouring Flames ceas'd and were overcome, more agree- " ably to the stately Trophy, than where they first took Fire, and broke " out; and where a plain lugubrous Marble with some apposite Inscrip- " tion had perhaps more properly become the Occasion. But this was " over-ruled, and I beg Pardon for this Presumption; tho' I question not " but I have the Architect himself on my side, whose rare and extraor-

*The Thea-
tre of Oxon,
St. Paul's
Chelsea

" dinary Talent, and what he has *perform'd of great and magnificent, " this Column, and what he is still about, and advancing under his Di- " rection, will speak and perpetuate his Memory, as long as one Stone " remains upon another in this Nation."

"The Monument, says a modern Critick, is undoubtedly the noblest
"modern Column in the World; nay in some respects, it may justly vie
"with those celebrated ones of Antiquity, which are consecrated to the
"Names of Trajan, and Antonine. Nothing can be more bold and sur-
"prizing, nothing more beautiful and harmonious: The Bas-relief at the
"Base, allowing for some few Defects, is finely imagin'd, and executed as
"well; and nothing material can be cavilled with, but the Inscriptions
"round about it. Nothing, indeed, can be more ridiculous than its Situ-
"ation, unless the Reason which is assigned for so doing. I am of Opin-
"ion, if it had been raised where Cheapside Conduit stood, it would have
"been as effectual a Remonstrance of the Misfortune it is designed to
"record, & would at once have added an inexpressible Beauty to the Vista,
"and received as much as it gave."   [*Critical Review of London*, p. 9.]

Coll. Hamp-
ton Court,
Churches of
London, the
Library at
Trinity Coll.
Camb. &c.

AN ACCURATE ACCOUNT OF THE QUANTITY BY MEA-
SUREMENTS, OF THE GREAT COLUMN OF LONDON.

THE Solidity of the whole Fabrick, from the Bottom of
the lowest Plinth, to the black Marble under the Urn, the
Cylinder of the Stair-case only deducted, and the Stone   } 37396 Feet.
for the Carving not allowed for, is   -   -   -   -

The black Marble that covers the Capital   -   -   -   -   287
The black Marble that covers the Lanthorn   -   -   -   64

From this Solidity deduct,
For 8 great Niches   -   -   -   281
For 3 Doors and Passages   -   -   289
For 3 Sides reveyled   -   -   486
For rough Block --   -   -   1499
For Rubble-work   -   -   7185

In all 9740
The Remainder is 27656

To this add, upon the account of the
  Carvings in the Front, the 4 great   } 540
Dragons, and Festoons   -   -

28196 Feet of solid
Portland
Stone.

343 black Marble Steps.
The whole Shaft fluted after it was built, being
     4784 superficial Feet.
Marble Harch-pace 56 Feet.
Marble Paving, and other small Articles, not in this Measurement.

INSCRIPTION FOR THE GREAT PILLAR, OR MONUMENT, OF LONDON, ACCORDING TO THE FIRST CONCEPTION OF SIR C. W.

QUI celsam spectas Molem, idem quoque infaustum & fatalem toti quondam Civitati vides Locum. Hic quippè, Anno Christi MDCLXVI. 2 Sept. alterâ post mediam Noctem Horâ, ex Casâ humili, prima se extulit Flamma, quae, Austro flante, adeò brevi invaluit, ut non tantum tota ferè intra Muros Urbs, sed et Aedificia quaecunque Arcem, et Templariorium Hospitium; quaecunque denique Ripas Fluminis, et remotissima Civitatis interjacent Maenia, ferali absumpta fuerint Incendio. Tridui spatio, C. Templa, Plateae CCCC. et plura quam XIV. Domorum Millia Flammis absorpta fuêre. Innumeri Cives omnibus suis fortunis exuti, et sub dio agitare coacti, infinitae, et toto Orbe congestae opes in Cinerem et Favillam redactae: ita ut de Urbe omnium quotquot Sol aspicit amplissimâ, et faelicissimâ, praeter Nomen et Famam, et immensos Ruinarum Aggeres, vix quicquam superesset.

Carolus Secundus, Dei Gratiâ, Rex Magnae Britanniae, Franciae, et Hiberniae, Anno Regni XVIII. et plerique Angliae Proceres, consumptâ Incendio Urbe penè universâ, eâdemque triennio Spatio in ampliorem Modum instauratâ, et non ut antè ligneis aut luteis, sed partim lateritiis, partim marmoreis Aedificiis, et Operibus ita ornatâ, ut è suis Ruinis pulcrior multò prodiisse videatur; auctis praetereà ad immensam Magnitudinem Urbis Pomaeriis; ad aeternam utriusque Facti Memoriam, hic ubi tantae Cladis prima emicuit Flamma

Monumentum Posuère.

Discat Praesens et Futura Aetas, nequà similis ingruat Clades, tempestivis Numen placare votis: Beneficium verò Regis, et Procerum, quorum Liberalitate, praeter Ornatum, major etiam Urbi accessit Securitas, grata mente recognoscat.

> O quantum tibi debet AVGVSTA,
> Tot nascentia Templa, tot renata,
> Tot Spectacula?   *Mart.*

As Augustus said of Rome, lateritiam inveni, marmoream reliqui, so the Rebuilder of London might as properly say, luteum et ligneum inveni, lateritium et lapideum reliqui.

Saepe majori fortunae locum fecit Injuria: multa ceciderunt, ut altius surgerent, et in majus. Timagenes felicitati Urbis inimicus aiebat, Romae sibi Incendia ob hoc unum dolori esse, quod sciret meliora resurrectura, quam arsissent.

[*Senecae, Epist.* 92.]

Mensurae Columnarum, apud Antiquos, maximarum.

Tota Columna Imp. Antonini Romae, Alta est Palmos Romanos CCXXX. *Reliquiæ* Diametros Scapi continet Palmos XVI. et IV Pollices. *Antiquae* Tota Columna Imp. Trajani, Romae, ab ejus Imo Usque ad Statuae Sancti *Urbis Romæ* Petri verticem, alta est Palmos Romanos CXCIII. cum Dimidio; Dia- *per Mic.* metros ejus prope Basin complectitur Palmos XVI. cum Sesqui-pollice; *Overbeke* ita ut hic Diametros totidem in se continet Pollices, quot Moles tota Palmos alta esse cognoscitur.

N.B. Palmus Romanus architectonicus continet IX. Pollices Anglicanos. Columna, dicta Historica, Constantinopoli, sive Imp. Theodosii, sive Arcadii, alta est CXLVII. Pedes. Secundum computum Petri Gylii.

The Custom-house for the Port of London, situated on the South-side of Thames-street; was erected in 1668, adorned with an upper and lower Order of Architecture: In the latter are Stone Columns, and Entablement of the Tuscan Order; in the former are Pilasters, Entablature, and five Pediments of the Ionick Order. The West-end is elevated on Columns, forming a Piazza. The Length of this Building is 189 Feet, Breadth in the middle Part 27 Feet, at the West-end, &c. 60 Feet.

The Frontispiece of the Middle-temple, towards Fleet-street, was erected in the Year 1684, of Stone and Brick. The Basis is a Rustick Arcade of Stone, supporting four Pilasters, Entablature, and triangular Pediment of the Ionick Order, and the rest of rubbed Brick.

PART II. SECT. X.

A CATALOGUE AND SHORT DESCRIPTION OF THE SURVEYOR'S BUILDINGS, IN THE SERVICE OF THE CROWN.

ENERAL Plan of the Situation, with the Plan and Orthography of the royal Palace at the City of Winchester (the Venta Belgarum of the Romans, a military Station, the Seat of the West Saxon Kings.) ⟨⟩ This Palace was begun by the Commands of King Charles the Second, (March 23, 1683) & prosecuted with that Expedition, that the greatest Part was covered in, and finished, as to the Shell, before the King's Decease, February 1684-5. It extends to the West 326 Feet, to the South 216 Feet. "There was par-
Camden's Britannia, 2d. Edit. p. 141
" ticularly intended a large Cupola, 30 Feet above the Roof, which would " have been seen a great Way to the Sea; & also a regular Street of hand- " some Houses, leading in a direct Line down the Hill, from the Front of " the Palace to the West-gate of the Cathedral; for which, & for the Parks, " the Ground was procured;" and Preparations made for proper Plantations, a necessary Ornament for that open Situation. The Surveyor had projected also to have brought from the Downs a River through the Park, which would have formed a Cascade of 30 Feet Fall. The whole Disposition of this Palace was such, as made it esteemed by the best Judges an excellent Model of a Royal-hunting seat. In this Place, (where probably had been the Roman Prætorium) "stood an ancient Castle, which "had been often besieged, but never so straitly, as when Maud the Em- "press maintained it against King Stephen. In digging for the new " Foundations, were discovered divers Roman and Saxon Antiquities, as " Coins of Constantine the Great, and others; a Brick Pavement of the
Penes Collectorem
" tessellated Work; a round* Brass Seal, with a Head engraved, and this " Inscription in Saxon Characters,

SIGILLUM SECRETI. ✠ &c.

From 'A Journey Through England.'

Vol. II. p. 21, Lond. 1722
KING Charles the second taking a Liking to the Situation of Winchester, by reason of the Deliciousness of the Country for all manner of Coun-

try Sports, set Sir Christopher Wren, that great Architect, (who had the Honour of making the Plan of St. Paul's Church in London, laying the first Stone, and living to see it finished) to make a Plan for a Royal Palace where the old Castle stood; and King Charles was so fond of it, and forwarded it with so much Diligence, that the whole Case of the Palace was roofed, and near finished, when that Prince died. It will be the finest Palace in England, when finished, and inferior to few abroad. It fronts the City to the East, by a noble Area between two Wings. The Marble Pillars sent by the Duke of Tuscany, for supporting the Portico of the great Stair-case, lie half buried in the Ground. The Stair-case carries up to the great Guard-hall, from whence you enter into sixteen spacious Rooms on each Wing, nine of which make a Suite to the End of each Wing. There are also two Entries under the Middle of each Wing, to the South and North, above which are to be two Cupola's; & the Front to the West extends 326 Feet, in the Middle of which is another Gate, with a Cupola to be also over it. Under the great Apartment, on each Side from the Ground, is a Chapel on the left for the King, and another on the right for the Queen; and behind the Chapels are two Courts, finely piazza'd, to give Light to the inward Rooms. There was to be a Terrass round it, as at Windsor, and the Ground laid out for a Garden, very spacious, with a Park marked out, of eight Miles Circumference, and that Park to open into a Forest of twenty Miles Circumference, without either Hedge or Ditch. The King designed also a Street from the Area to the East, in a direct Line, by an easy Descent, to the great Door of the Cathedral.

Queen Anne came once to see Winchester, where she staid seventeen Days, and designed to have finished it, as a Jointure-house to her Consort Prince George of Denmark; but an expensive War, and the Prince's Death before her, prevented it. Whether his Majesty, or the Prince, when they please to make a Circuit through their Dominions, may not think it worth while to finish so noble a Structure, Time will discover.

Bishop Morley, who had been an Exile with King Charles, and made Bishop of this See after the Restoration, seeing his Majesty designing to make Winchester a royal Residence, thought himself obliged to keep pace with the King; and therefore pulled down a great Part of the old episcopal Palace, and, under the Direction of the same Architect, Sir Christopher Wren, began a new one; but he dying about the Time with the King, his Palace stood still with the King's. However he had compleated one Wing in his Life-time, & left Money for finishing the rest; but Bishop Mew, his Successor, seeing no Probability of a Court at Winchester, never minded it. Sir Jonathan Trelawny succeeding Bishop Mew, in Queen Anne's Time, called for the Money left by Bishop Morley, and finished it. It is a very handsome Palace *à la moderne*.

II. Plans, Elevations, & Sections, of the two royal Apartments at Hampton-court, being a Part only of the Surveyor's Design for a new Palace there.

This Edifice was begun by the Commands of King William and Queen Mary, in the Year 1690 (to make room for which, the principal Part of the old Fabrick fronting the House-park was taken down) and finished in 1694, just before the much lamented Death of that incomparable Princess.

> Quâ nihil majus meliusve Regnis
> Fata donavère, bonique Divi,
> Nec dabunt, quamvis redeant in Aurum
> Tempora priscum.

The Queen, upon observing the pleasant Situation of the Palace, proposed a proper Improvement with Building and Gardening, & pleased herself from time to time, in examining and surveying the Drawings, Contrivances, and whole Progress of the Works, and to give thereon her own Judgment, which was exquisite; for there were few Arts, or Sciences, in which her Majesty had not only an elegant Taste, but a Knowledge much superior to any of her Sex, in that, or (it may be) any former Age. This is not said as a Panegyrick, but a plain & well-known Truth, which the Surveyor had frequent Experience of, when, (by that Favour and Esteem the Queen was graciously pleased publickly to shew him, upon a Discernment & Trial of his Worth) he had many Opportunities of a free Conversation with her Majesty, not only on the Subject of Architecture, but other Branches of Mathematicks, and useful Learning.

Certified to the Collector by the Right Honourable Thomas Earl of Pembroke

King William was pleased so far to approve of the Surveyor's Service in the Designs, & Execution of this Fabrick, as occasionally to deliver his Opinion, (and once particularly in the Hearing of some noble Persons of the first Quality in England) That these two Apartments, for good Proportion, State, and Convenience, jointly, were not parallelled by any Palace in Europe; &, at the same time, to excuse his Surveyor, for not raising the Cloysters, under the Apartments, higher; which were executed in that Manner, according to his express Orders. The Façade, or King's Apartment, fronting the Privy-garden, & Thames, extends 328 Feet; the Façade, or Queen's Apartment fronting the House-park, extends 330 Feet; the Access to the principal Stair-case leading to the King's-side, is

Camden's Britannia, 2d Edit. P. 368

through a beautiful Portico of about 90 Feet long, consisting of a Colonade of 16 duplicated Pillars, of the Ionick Order. " Both House & Parks " being environ'd on three Sides with the River Thames, & consequently " enjoying as pleasant a Situation as the Prudence of its first Founder Car- " dinal Wolsey could select for it, was indeed a Piece of Work of great " Beauty & Magnificence for the Age it was built in. But the Additions " made to it by King William and Queen Mary do so far excel what it

" was before, that they evidently shew what vast Advancements, Archi-
" tecture has receiv'd since that Time."

Sic Partem Ille Domûs, quam vix Faelicior AEtas Finiat, exegit. . . .

If the World had not been depriv'd so soon of the inestimable Life of
Queen Mary, and had the Surveyor been impower'd to have finish'd his
whole Design, Leland's Description of Hampton Court would have been
a truer Resemblance of its latter than primitive State.

> Est locus insolito rerum splendore superbus,
> Alluiturque vagâ Tamisini fluminis undâ,
> Nomine ab antiquo jam tempore dictus Avona,
> Hic rex Wilhelmus tales hic condidit aedes
> Magnificas, quales toto sol aureus orbe
> Non vidit.

III. Design of the Mausoléum which was erected in Westminster-abbey,
at the Funeral-obsequies of Queen Mary the Second, March 5, 169$\frac{4}{5}$.

IV. Plans, Elevations, and Views of Chelsea-college. This noble Hospital was founded, and near finish'd, by King Charles the Second; prosecuted by King James the Second; and compleated, and furnish'd with all
sorts of Necessaries, and Conveniences for the comfortable Maintenance
of maim'd and superannuated Soldiers, by King William & Queen Mary.
The Industry, and Conduct of the Surveyor, and Sir Stephen Fox, jointly
in the Erection and Settlement hereof, are worthy Remembrance : Sir
Stephen Fox, a Lord of the Treasury, took care for the due Payment of
the Works; whilst the Surveyor vigorously prosecuted his Part in the
Buildings; and lastly prescrib'd the Statutes, and whole Oeconomy of
the House, which for Cleanliness, Health, & Convenience, is deservedly
esteem'd one of the best regulated in Europe; well suiting, in every particular, the pious Design, and Munificence of its royal Founders.

V. Designs of the royal Hospital at Greenwich, for disabled and superannuated Seamen, begun in 1699. The Surveyor was among the first who
address'd their Majesties King William and Queen Mary, to convert the
Site and Buildings of their royal Palace to this most charitable Use; which
was also industriously promoted by the Lord Sommers, Mr. Evelyn, Mr.
Bridgman Secretary of the Admiralty, and Mr. Lownds Secretary of the
Treasury. This extensive Charity was not only calculated for the Relief
and Support of the veteran Seamen, and such as had been wounded or
disabled in the Service, but also for the Relief & Maintenance of such
Widows, and the Education of such Orphans, whose Husbands, and Pa-

rents had been slain in the Defence of the Nation at Sea. A Project so seasonably adjusted for the Encouragement and Improvement of that other most important Branch of the national Defence, the naval Arms of Great-Britain. After the Grant had pass'd the great Seal, and an ample Commission appointed, with Powers to conduct and regulate all Affairs, relating to the building of the Hospital; and the Surveyor nominated a Director, and chief Architect of this great Undertaking, he chearfully engag'd in the Work, gratis, and contriv'd the new Fabrick extensive, durable, and magnificent, conformable to the graceful Pavilion, which had been erected there by King Charles the Second, and originally intended for his own Palace; contributing his Time, Labour, & Skill, and prosecuting the Works for several Years, with all the Expedition the Circumstances of Affairs would allow; without any Salary, Emolument, or Reward (which good Example, 'tis to be hoped, has been since follow'd;) preferring in this, as in every other Passage of his Life, the publick Service to any private Advantage of his own, by the Acquest of Wealth, of which he had always a great Contempt.

Extracts from the Account of the Buildings of Greenwich Hospital, publish'd by the Deputy-surveyor Mr. Hawksmoor, Anno 1728 for the Perusal of the Parliament.

HER Majesty Queen Mary, the Foundress of the marine Hospital, enjoin'd Sir Christopher Wren to build the Fabrick with great Magnificence and Order; and being ever sollicitous for the Prosecution of the Design, had several times honour'd Greenwich with her personal Views of the Building erected by King Charles II. as Part of his Palace, & likewise of that built by Mr. Inigo Jones, call'd the Queen's House, &c. On which Views She was unwilling to demolish either, as was propos'd by some. This occasion'd the keeping of an Approach from the Thames quite up to the Queen's House, of 115 Feet broad, out of the Grant that was made to the Hospital, that her Majesty might have an Access to that House by Water as well as by Land; and she retain'd a Desire to add the four Pavilions to that Palace, according to Inigo Jones's Design, that She might make that little Palace compleat, as a royal Villa for her own Retirement, or from whence Embassadors, or publick Ministers, might make their Entry into London.
Her Majesty's absolute Determination to preserve the Wing built by her Uncle King Charles II. to keep the Queen's House, and the Approach to it, on the Considerations abovesaid, naturally drew on the Disposition of the Buildings, as they are now placed and situated.
The principal Front of this great Building lies open to the Thames; from whence we enter into the Middle of the royal Court, near 300 Foot

square, lying open to the North, and cover'd on the West with the Court of King Charles II. and on the East with that of Queen Anne, equal to it; and on the South, the great Hall and Chapel.

The Court of Queen Anne contains the great Range or Wing next the royal Court, as aforesaid, and holds 140 Men. To the East of this Court of Queen Anne, is another Range of Building, which contains 66 Persons, &c.

The great Pavilion next the Thames contains four very commodious Apartments for Officers.

The great Pavilion, at the South-end of Queen Anne's Court, contains Lodgings for Officers, and some proper Rooms for the entertaining of the Widows and Children.

The Court of King Charles II. contains the great Wing on the West of the royal Court above mention'd, built by that Prince as Part of his own intended Palace. It is a noble Pile, having in the middle a tetrastyle Portico, with Arcades; the Walls are rusticated, all in Portland Stone; the Windows artfully decorated and proportion'd; the Order is Corinthian; the Body of the Building is crown'd with an Entablement of that Order; and the two Extreams in two great Pavilions (all in the same Style) rising with an Attick Order above the other Part, & make two eminent Towers. This Wing, together with the Bass-wing to the West of the Court of King Charles II. contain 206 Persons, &c.

The great Pavilion to the Thames, closing the North-side of this Court, contains four Apartments for Officers, and other Conveniences.

The great Pavilion on the South-end of this Court, contains several Lodgings for Officers, and the great Kitchen, and Rooms belonging to it. The Wing to the West, which was built for Offices for immediate Service, contains Chambers for Servants and other Uses of the Family. This is call'd the Bass-wing of King Charles II.

Keeping the central Lines of the whole Projection that runs through the royal Court and the Esplanade in the Park, the next Buildings we come at lie on the South-side of the royal Court, and are 1st.,

The Colonade, having a Portico on the right and left Hands of Doric Pillars 20 Feet high, is crown'd with an Entablement and Balustrade of Portland Stone, each of which Porticos is in Length 430 Feet, and both together sustain'd by 300 Pillars and Pilasters.

These Porticos are intended for Communication from the Hall & Chapel to the Wards and Dormitories; and to protect the Men from the Inclemency of Weather, and give them Air, at any time, without incommoding them; very useful where a Number of People are to inhabit in one College.

On the West-side of this Colonade is built the Court of King William, containing the great Hall, Vestibule and Cupola: The Tambour of the

Cupola is a Peristylium of Pillars duplicated, of the Composite Order, and broke upon the Quoins with Groups of Pillars; the Attick is a Circle without Breaks, cover'd with a Tholus and small Lantern.

Under is a less Hall, and Room for the Guard, & common Rendez-vous of the House. On the West-side of this Court is a large Dormitory, and sundry Lodgments, This Wing will contain 200 Persons.

On the South-side of King William's Court is another large Dormitory with several Rooms. This Wing will contain 320 Persons.

On the East of the Colonade is the Court of Queen Mary, which contains the royal Chapel, with the Vestibule and Cupola; and a large Dormitory to the South, like that of King William, holding 320 Persons; and a Dormitory, on the East-side of this Court, to hold 100 Persons. Besides the Grandeur, Regularity, and Beauty of this publick Building, the capacious Accommodations, the Wards and Chambers, can entertain 1352 Men, excluding Officers and Servants, & Rooms of publick Use. There was once this only Exception: some Gentlemen thought the Bass-wing of Offices was too mean for the rest of the Building, and desir'd a Proposal might be made to alter that, to the Style and Dignity of King Charles's Front; which was done, & shew'd to the Persons then in Power: And this occasion'd the doubling the great North Pavilion, and making it so large as now it is, with the Flag-tower upon the Center, which compleated the Strength and Beauty of the North Front of this royal Hospital towards the Thames.

VI. Design of the Altar-piece of the old Chapel of Whitehall, destroy'd, with the Palace, by the Fire in 1697.

VII. Design of the Marble Altar-piece, with the original Ornaments, and Statues, erected in King James the Second's Chapel at Whitehall, which was sav'd from the Fire, and given by Queen Anne to the collegiate Church of St. Peter in Westminster.

Preface to the following Account (in Section XI.) of the Design for the Tomb of King Charles the First.

Echard's
Hist. of
England,
Vol. II.
p. 649

Vol. III.
p. 200

" IT has been made a Question, and a Wonder by many, why a particu-
" lar Monument was not erected at Windsor for King Charles the First,
" after the Restoration of his Son; especially when the Parliament was
" well inclined to have given a good Sum for that grateful Purpose. This
" has caused several Conjectures and Reflections; and Intimations have
" been given, as if the royal Body had never been deposited there, or else
" had been afterwards removed by the Regicides; & the Lord Clarendon
" himself speaks softly and suspiciously of this Matter, as if he believed

"the Body could not be found. But to remove all Imaginations, we shall
"here insert a Memorandum, or Certificate, sent by Mr. John Sewell,
"Register at Windsor. Anno 1696, September 21. The same Vault in
"which King Charles the First was buried, was opened to lay in a still-
"born Child of the then Princess of Denmark, now our gracious Queen.
"On the King's Coffin the Velvet Pall was strong and sound, and there
"was about the Coffin a leaden Band, with this Inscription cut through
"it, King Charles, 1648. Queen Jane's Coffin was whole and entire; but
"that of King Henry the Eighth was sunk in upon the Breast Part, and
"the Lead and Wood consumed with the Heat of the Gums he was em-
"balmed with; and when I laid my Hand on it, it was run together, and
"hard, and had no noisome Smell. As a further Memorandum relating
"to the King's Interment, he says, That when the Body of King Charles
"the First lay in the Dean's Hall, the Duke of Richmond had the Coffin
"opened, and was satisfied that it was the King's Body. This several
"People have declared they knew to be true, who were alive, and then
"present, as Mr. Randue of Windsor, and others; so that he thinks the
"Lord Clarendon was misled in that Matter, and that King Charles the
"Second never sent to enquire after the Body, since it was well known
"to the Inhabitants of the Castle and Town, that it was in that Vault."
To this may be added, that Mr. Fishborne, Gent. of Windsor, a Relation
of Sir Christopher Wren's, was among those who were present at the Interment of the King, went into the Vault, and brought away a Fragment
of King Henry's Pall; he observed the Vault was so narrow, that it was
some Difficulty to get in the King's Coffin by the side of the others.

> At non Vinsorae manes jacuère cavernâ,
> Nec cinis exiguus tantam compescuit umbram;
> Prosiluit busto, dissectaque membra relinquens,
> Degeneremque rogum, sequitur convexa tonantis.
> . . . . . . Illic postquam se lumine vero
> Implevit, stellasque vagas miratur et astra
> Fixa polis, vidit quantâ sub nocte jaceret
> Nostra dies, risitque sui ludibria trunci.

Lucan

PART II. SECT. XI.

A CATALOGUE, AND SHORT ACCOUNT OF DESIGNS, IN PURSUANCE OF THE ROYAL COMMANDS, FOR BUILDINGS, WHICH HAVE NOT YET BEEN PUT IN EXECUTION.

GENERAL Plan, Orthography, & Section, with the Statues and Ornaments, designed for the Tomb of King Charles the First. 🖝 King Charles the Second was pleased to order the Surveyor to design a Mausolèum, or Tomb, for his Father, the Royal Martyr, after that the House of Commons had voted, upon the Motion of the Lord O-Brien, on the (a) 30th of January, 1677-8, (the House having sat on Part of that Day) "The Sum of

Echard's History of England, Vol. III. p. 441

"Seventy Thousand Pounds, for a solemn Funeral of his late Majesty "King Charles the First, and to erect a Monument for the said Prince

London, printed for Henry Brome; at the Gun in St. Paul's Church- yard, 1678, Page 4

(a) N.B. *The Historian mistakes the Day; the Vote passed on the 29th, as is seen in Dr. Sprat's Sermon before the House of Commons, at St. Margaret's, Westminster, Jan. 30, 1677-8.*
The beautiful Paragraph runs thus;
" *I confess I might, and, give me leave to say it, I intended to have complained,*
" *that the present Age had not made that Use of him [King Charles] which it*
" *ought; his Enemies for their Repentance and Amendment, nor even his Friends*
" *for his Praise and Honour. But, blessed be God, I am happily prevented in*
" *one Part of the Complaint; I have nothing now to wish, but that his Enemies*
" *would as well perform their Duty to him, as, it must be acknowledged, you*
" *[the House of Commons] his Friends have done yours, by that much desired,*
" *long expected, Yesterday's Vote; in which you have given a Resurrection to his*
" *Memory, by designing magnificent Rites to his sacred Ashes. So that now, for*
" *the future, an Englishman abroad will be able to mention the Name of King*
" *Charles the First, without blushing; and his heroick Worth will be delivered*
" *down to Posterity, as it always deserved to be, not only freed from Calumny,*
" *or Obscurity, but, in all Things, most illustrious; in all Things to be com-*

" of glorious Memory; the said Sum to be raised by a Two Months Tax,
" to begin at the Expiration of the present (*b*) Tax for building Ships."
The Form of this Structure (as appears by the Surveyor's original Drawings, which were laid before the King) is a Rotundo, with a beautiful
Dome and Lantern; a circular Colonade without, of the Corinthian Order, resembling the Temple of Vesta. The Enrichments on the Outside
and within, are designed costly & magnificent: to instance only in a few
Articles taken from the first Estimate, and, particularly, of the Inside,
viz.: " Eight Bases of black Marble for the great Pillars under the Dome,
" at £30 each. Eight Shafts of rich Marble in whole Stones, 28 Feet long,
" 3½ Feet Diameter, to be brought from the Levant, valued at £400 each.
" Eight Capitals of Brass-work gilt, for the above-named Pillars, at £250
" each. 3520 Feet of Incrustation with various Marbles in the lower Or-
" der of Pilasters within the Niches. Entablatures of white Marble. In
" the Spandrils over the Niches, Marbles inlaid. 1606 Feet superficial of
" Mosaic-work, in the Heads of Niches. 4620 Feet superficial, of the
" best Painting in Fresco, in the Cupola. Ten Figures of great Life, cast
" in Brass and gilt, at £400 each. Seven Genii, or Cherubims, of Brass
" gilt, with the Ornaments appertaining, at £150 each. A Coloss Statue
" of Fame, of gilt Brass, on the Summit of the Lantern. Twenty Statues
" of great Life, the Acroteria of the Order, on the Outside. Twenty Fes-
" toons of Marble between the Capitals on the Outside, &c. The whole
" Charge estimated at £43,663."
The Monument, thus designed, was approved by the King, and determined to be erected at Windsor Castle, at the East-end of St. George's
Chapel, in the Place where now stands " a little Gothick Building raised
" by Cardinal Wolsey, called the Tomb-house, in the Middle whereof
" he designed to erect a goodly Monument for King Henry the Eighth,
" and had well nigh finished it before he died. But this was demolished
" in April 1646, by Command of the long Parliament; and the Statues
" and Figures provided to adorn it, being all Copper gilt, & exceedingly
" enriched,* were taken thence.
" This Place King Charles the First, of ever blessed and glorious Me-

*Ashmole of
the Garter,
p. 136*

**By an
eminent
Italian
Statuary*

" mended; in most Things to be imitated; in some Things scarce imitable, & only
" to be admired."
*After divine Service, the House sat, (as appears by the Order of Thanks) viz.
Mercurii 30 Die Jan. 1677-8, Ordered, That the Thanks of this House be returned to Dr. Sprat, for his Sermon this Day preached before the House at St.
Margaret's, Westminster, and that he be desired to preach the same, &c.*
*(b) Apr. 16, 1677, Car. II. 29. An Act for raising the Sum of Five hundred
eighty-four thousand Pounds, &c. for the speedy building thirty Ships of War.*
[*Echard, Hist. England, Vol. III. p. 421.*]

" mory, intended to enlarge and make fit & capable, not only for the In-
" terment of his own royal Body, but also for the Bodies of his Successors
" Kings of England, had not bad Times drawn on, & such as, with much
" ado, afforded him but an obscure Grave, near the first Haut-pace in the
" Quire of the Chapel, his Head lying over-against the eleventh Stall on
" the Sovereign's Side, and in the same Vault where the Bodies of King
" Henry the Eighth, and his *Queen Jane, yet remain." [Echard's His-
" tory of England, Vol. II. p. 649. Athenæ Oxon. p. 528.]

The Tomb-house, which had been long neglected, & in a ruinous State,
was therefore proposed to be taken down, & the Ground thereof judged
to be a most proper Situation for the new Mausolèum. After some Time,
the King returned the Drawings and Estimates to the Surveyor, with
Orders to keep them till called for again: But, in conclusion, the whole
Design of the Funeral and Tomb, through Incidents of the Times, or
Motives unknown to the Publick, were laid aside.

Upon his Majesty's Decease, King James II. ordered the old Fabrick to
be put into immediate Repair, and the Cieling to be painted by Signior
Vario, as it now remains, with Intention, 'tis said, to convert the Room
to a Chapter-house, for the Use of the Order of the Garter.

In the Surveyor's original Designs (still extant) of the Mausolèum, are
three grand Niches, (besides that which the Portal at the Entrance breaks
into) rising from the Pavement to the Entablature of the great Columns
within-side: Whether by these was intended, that the three royal Coffins, upon finishing the Tomb, were to have been translated thither, and
proper monumental Statues and Ornaments placed in the respective
Niches, or whether the two Niches were to have been left in reserve for
other regal Monuments, is uncertain. In the Middle-niche fronting the
Entrance, was designed the King's Monument, after this Manner. Four
Statues, Emblems of heroick Virtues, standing on a square Basis, or
Plinth, & pressing underneath, Prostrate Figures of Rebellion, Heresy,
Hypocrisy, Envy, &c. support a large Shield, on which is a Statue erect
of the royal Martyr, in modern Armour; over his Head is a Group of
Cherubims, bearing a Crown, Branches of Palm, and other Devices.
There are two Draughts of this statuary Design,* one adapted for Brass-
work, the other for Marble, as should have been most approved.

Interea in chartâ tumulum signemus inanem,
Ut nota sit busti, si quis placare peremptum
Fortè volet, plenos et reddere mortis honores.
Proderit hoc olim, quod non mansura sepulcri
Ardua marmoreo surrexit pondere moles.
Pulveris exigui sparget non longe vetustas
Congeriem, bustumque cadet, mortisque peribunt

Argumenta tuæ. Veniet fælicior ætas
Quâ sit nulla fides saxum monstrantibus istud
Et Vinsora fuat populis fortasse, nepotum
Tam mendax Caroli tumulo, quam Creta tonantis.
                                        ˈ[*Lucan.*

In the Year 1674, at which Time the Surveyor was rebuilding some
Parts of the Tower of London, it happened, that the Bones of King Edward the Fourth's Children (those two innocent Princes, King Edward
the Fifth, and his Brother, Richard Duke of York, the one of thirteen,
the other of eleven Years of Age, most Barbarously murdered there, in
their Bed, by their unnatural Uncle, the Ursurper Richard the Third)
were, after 191 Years, found, about 10 Feet deep in the Ground, in a
wooden Chest, as the Workmen were taking away the Stairs, which led
from the royal Lodgings into the Chapel of the White-tower. The Circumstances of this Discovery being fully represented to the King by the
Surveyor, Sir Thomas Chicheley, then Master of the Ordnance, & other
Persons of Worth and Credit, Eye-witnesses in the whole Scrutiny, the
following Warrant from the Lord Chamberlain of his Majesty's House-
hold was directed to the Surveyor; in pursuance whereof, he designed an
elegant Urn of white Marble, on a Pedestal, with an Inscription ; all
which being approved by his Majesty, was erected in the East-wall of
the North-aile of King Henry the Seventh's Chapel.

" These are to signify his Majesty's Pleasure, That you provide a white   *Ex Auto-*
" Marble Coffin for the supposed Bodies of the two Princes lately found   *graph*
" in the Tower of London; & that you cause the same to be interred in
" Henry the Seventh's Chapel; in such convenient Place as the Dean of
" Westminster shall appoint: & this shall be your Warrant. Given under
" my Hand, this 18th Day of February, 1674-5.
                                        ARLINGTON.

To Sir Christopher Wren, Knt, Surveyor
    General of his Majesty's Works.

                              H. S. S.
                             Reliquiæ.
          Edwardi Vti. Regis Angliæ, et Richardi Ducis Eborac.
             Hos Fratres germanos in Arce Londinensi conclusos,
                    Injectisque culcitris suffocatos,
                   Abditè et inhonestè tumulari jussit
                   Patruus Richardus perfidus Regni
                              Prædo

P 3   213

Ossa desideratorum diù et multùm quæsita
Post Annos CXCI.
Scalarum in ruderibus (scalæ nuper istæ ad sacellum
Turris albæ ducebant)
Altè defossa Indiciis certissimis sunt reperta,
xvii. Die Julii, Anno Domini MDCLXXIIII.

Carolus Secundus, Rex clementissimus, acerbam
Sortem miseratus,
Inter avita Monumenta Principibus infelicissimis
Justa persolvit.
Anno Domini 1678, Annoque Regni sui, 30.

II. A Catalogue of Designs for rebuilding the royal Palace of Whitehall.
Sketch of a Plan for Whitehall.
Façade of the Palace of Whitehall, designed for King Charles II.
Part of the said Front in a large Scale.
1. General Plan of the Site, Palace, Gardens, &c. of Whitehall, designed pursuant to Order, and offered to his Majesty King William, after the Fire of the old Palace, in the Year 1697.
2. General Plan of the Palace, a Gallery of Communication with the Parliament-house, consisting of a long Portico of Dorick Columns on the Bank of the Thames, extending from Whitehall to Westminster. Together with the Plan and Orthography of the new Parliament-house, as intended.
3. Plan of the Palace, Gardens, Canals, and Decorations.
4. Orthography of the Palace fronting the Thames.
5. Orthography fronting the Park, or Gardens.
6. Orthography fronting Charing-cross, and Westminster.
7. Sciography of the whole Structure.
8. Façade of the Gallery of Communication next the River; and of the new Parliament-house.

1. Plan of another Design of a Palace for Whitehall, offered to his Majesty King William, in the Year 1697.
2. Orthography fronting the River Thames.
3. Front to the Park.
4. Front to Westminster.

III. Divers Designs of new Buildings, Alterations, and Improvements, in the Castle of Windsor, in 1698, and since; with several Dispositions for Gardens there.
2. Plan for rebuilding the royal Mews at Charing-cross, to contain 388

Horses, and 42 Coaches, with all Accommodations. Designed by Order, for the Service of King Charles the Second.

3. Plan of Barracks proposed in Hyde-park, for a Body of Guards of 1000 Horse, with Houses for Officers, Commissary, Farriers, Sadlers, Courts of Guard, Haybarns, Granaries, &c. by Order.

4. Plan of Barracks in Hyde-park, for 2000 private Men, and Officers, and Infirmary for 160 Men, a Chapel, & all Accommodations. By Order, in 1713; the Estimate of the whole computed at £48,118.

Sir Christopher Wren was one of the Commissioners, who, at the Motion of Sir Jonas Moore, Surveyor General of the Ordnance, had been appointed by his Majesty to find a proper Place for erecting a royal Observatory; and he proposed Greenwich, which was approved of: And August 10, 1675, the Foundation of the Building was laid; and when finished, under the Conduct of Sir Jonas, with the Advice and Assistance of Sir Christopher, was furnished with the best Instruments for making astronomical Observations, and the celebrated Mr. John Flamstead constituted his Majesty's first Professor there. (a)

(a) *Praef. ad Hist. Cœlest. Johann. Flamsteadii, p. II. Edit.* 1712. *J. Ward's Addition to the Lives of Gresham Professors, p.* 337.

PART II. SECT. XII.

A CATALOGUE, AND ACCOUNT OF DESIGNS OF BUILDINGS IN THE UNIVERSITIES OF OXFORD, AND CAMBRIDGE.

PLAN & ELEVATIONS OF THE THEATRE OF OXFORD, AND SCHEME OF THE ROOF.

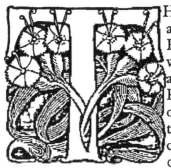HIS Theatre, a Work of admirable Contrivance and Magnificence, was the first publick Performance of the Surveyor, in Architecture; which however had been executed in a greater and better Style, with a View to the ancient Roman Grandeur discernable in the Theatre of Marcellus at Rome; but that he was obliged to put a Stop to the Bolder Strokes of his Pencil, & confine the Expence within the Limits of a private Purse. What (among other beautiful and distinguished Parts of this Structure) has been esteemed very observable, is the geometrical Flat-roof, which Dr. P—t has particularly *described, in his 'Natural History of Oxfordshire,' as follows:

*Natural History of Oxon. Chap. ix.

" It was an excellent Device, whoever first contrived it, of making Flat-
" Floors or Roofs of short Pieces of Timber continued to a great Breadth,
" without either Arch or Pillar to support them, but sustained only by
" the Side-walls, and their own Texture; for by this means many times
" the Defect of long Timber, or Mistakes of Workmen are supply'd, and
" rectified without any Prejudice to the Building. Of this Sort of Work
" we have an Example in the Schools, in the Floor of the uppermost
" Room of the Tower. There is also a Diagram of such Work in the *Ar-

*Lib. 1. de Geom. Cap. 1.

" chitecture of Sebastian Serlio. But Dr. Wallis was the first that demon-
" strated the Reason of this Work, and has given divers Forms of it, be-
" side the fore-mentioned, in his Book De Motu, whence are taken the

See Tab. xiii. Dr. Plot

" *Diagrams, Tab. Fig. 1, 2, 3, 4, 5. Upon the two first whereof depend
" the three last; and all others of the Kind whatever, whether made up
" of Quadrats, or oblong Parallelograms, of which there are some other
" Forms in the fore-cited Book de Motu, beside that markt Fig. 3, con-
" sisting of great and small Quadrats; or Triangles alone, as Fig. 4, or
" mixed with Hexagons, as Fig. 5."

A Model of a geometrick Flat-floor, contrived by the fore-mentioned

216

The Roof of the Theatre at Oxford.

Fig. 1.

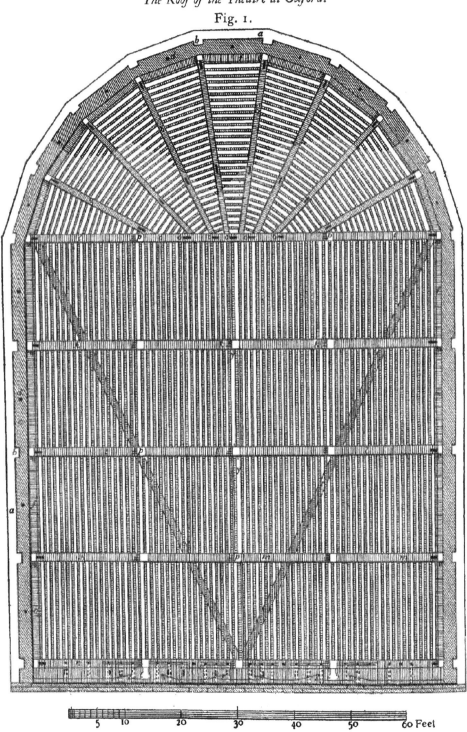

5   10   20   30   40   50   60 Feet

Fig. 3.

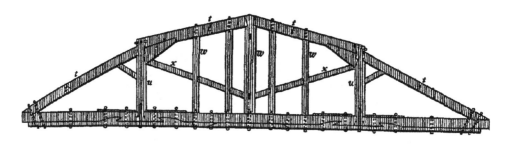

Fig. 4

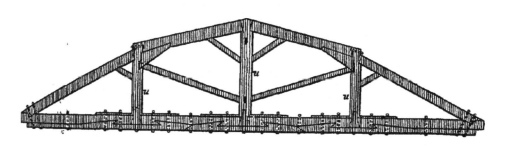

Fig. 5.

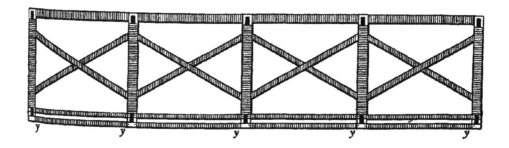

5   10   20   30   40   50   60 Feet

Dr. Wallis, & given to the Museum of the royal Society, is in the Design *Dr. Grew's*
obvious to the Eye. The Outsides represent the Walls of the Building, on *Musaeum of*
which the Flat-floor or Roof is to be laid. The Beams next adjoining to *the R S.*
the Sides, have one End lodged on those Walls; the other End sustained *Pag* 362
by another Beam, lying cross; both Ends of which, are, in like manner,
sustained by other cross Beams; and those again by others; till they reach
the other Walls. So that no one of them can fall, unless the Walls fail, or
the Beams break; all mutually sustaining each other, without any Pillar
or Prop to support them, besides the outer Walls.

" But of all the Flat-floors having no Pillars to support them, and whose *Dr. Plot*,
" Main-beams are made of divers Pieces of Timber, the most admirable *ditto*
" is that of the Theatre of Oxford, from Side-wall to Side-wall, 80 Foot
" over one Way, and 70 the other; whose Lockages being so quite dif-
" ferent from any before-mentioned, and in many other Particulars per-
" haps not to be parallel'd in the World, I have taken care to represent
" an exact Draught of it."

See Plate, Fig. I. &c. annexed.

" Wherein *a a a* and *b b b* shew the Walls of the Theatre that support this
" Frame of Timber, and the Places of the Pilasters of the Rail and Bal-
" lister round it: *c c c* and *d d d* the Leads & Pipes let down into the Wall
" for Conveyance of Water; *e e e* and *f f f* the Wall-plate or Lintal, and
" Places of its Joints; *g g g* the Girders of the Semi-circle, each supported
" by a King-piece or Crown-post cut off at *h h h* and screwed into the
" Binding-beam *i i i;* which is somewhat different from the rest of the
" Binding-beams *k k k, l l l, m m m, n n n,* having several Prick-posts let
" into it at *o o o o o,* beside the King-posts that support this and the rest at
" *p p p p p,* &c. The Letters *q q q q* shew the Purlines between the Binding-
" beams, not set right against one another, because of Room to turn the
" Screws whereby they are fastened, and *r r r r* two Dragon (perhaps
" rather Trigon) Beams or Braces lying under the Joists *s s s s s,* &c. The
" true Lengths and Distances whereof, and of all other Pieces of Timber
" and Places whatever, are all shewn by the Scale, Fig. 2. And so are the
" Lengths & Distances of the several Pieces of Timber set over this Flat-
" floor, such as the principal Rafters *t t t t,* the Crown-posts or King-
" pieces *u u u u u,* the Prick-posts *w w w,* Braces or Puncheons *x x x,* by
" all which together, the Binding-beams, Girders, Joists, &c. are all held
" up as it were by an Arch above, as in Fig. 3, which is all the Band of
" Timber that stands next the Semi-circle, having Prick-posts, and dif-
" ferent Lockages, from the rest of the four Bands, as is sufficiently repre-
" sented by one Half of one of them, Fig. 4. Which is all I think need be
" said concerning this fine Piece of Timber-work, only that there are
" Cross-braces between the middle Crown-posts as they stand in a Line
" from the Front to the Semicircle, as is represented, Fig. 5, marked

" with the Letters *y y y y y y*, both here, and as they stand, Fig. 1. And
" that it was contrived by our English Vitruvius, the Right Worship-
" ful and Learned Sir Christopher Wren, and erected at the sole Charge
" of his Grace Gilbert Sheldon, Archbishop of Canterbury, and Chan-
" cellor of the University; who, besides the Expence of the Structure,
" gave £2000 to purchase Lands for the perpetualRepair of it, which is
" like to stand a most magnificent and lasting Monument of his Grace's
" Munificence, and Favour of good Learning to all Posterity (*a*)."
" The Painting of the Cieling of the Theatre is worth Examination; for
" in Imitation of the Theatres of the ancient Greeks and Romans, which
" were too large to be covered with Lead or Tile, this, by the Painting of
" the Flat-roof within, is represented open : And, as they stretched a
" Cordage from Pilaster to Pilaster, upon which they strained a Covering
" of Cloth, to protect the People from the Injuries of the Weather, so
" here is a Cord-molding gilded, that reaches cross and cross the House
" both in Length and Breadth, which supporteth a great Drapery, sup-
" posed to have covered the Roof, but now furled up by the Genii round
" about the House toward the Walls, which discovereth the open Air,
" and maketh way for the Descent of the Arts and Sciences, that are con-
" gregated in a Circle of Clouds, &c.
" The great bivalve Wooden-windows in the upper Gallery of the The-
" atre are so ingeniously contrived, that notwithstanding their great
" Weight, yet can never sink so as to be brought out of a Square, as 'tis
" usual in such Windows; for the Iron-bars crossing them from Side to
" Side, not being set at Right-angles, but diagonally like Struts or Braces,
" as in Fig. 6, must necessarily bend or break, before the Window can
" sink. Nor are the Round-windows below, unworthy Consideration,

(*a*) *Dr. Gilbert Sheldon, educated in the University of Oxford, became Warden
of All-Souls, and having been Chaplain to King Charles the First, and run
through many Difficulties, was, after the Restoration, made first, Bishop of London, and lastly Archbishop of Canterbury; which See he held with great Honour
and Reputation for above 14 Years, when he died at Seventy-nine Years of Age,
Anno 1677. Besides his Learning and Piety, he is particulary distinguished by
his munificent Benefactions, in which no Man more readily signalized himself;
and especially he immortaliz'd his Name, in that glorious Work the Theatre of
Oxford, which cost him more than Sixteen Thousand Pounds; besides the Gift of
Two Thousand Pounds, to buy Lands worth £100 per Ann. to keep it in Repair. We are assured from his Relations, That from the Time of his being Bishop
of London, to that of his Death, it appeared in his Book of Accounts, that upon
publick, pious, and charitable Uses, he had bestowed about Threescore and Six
Thousand Pounds.*

218

" being contrived to admit Air in foul Weather, yet not one Drop of
" Rain; for being opened and set obliquely, as in Fig. 7, it receives the
" Rain within at *a*, & casts it out again at *b;* much less will it admit Rain
" any-ways when shut, it closing within its Frame at the Top, & without
" it at the Bottom."

On the 9th of July, 1669, the new Theatre was opened with great Solemnity, and followed with a most splendid Act, such as had not been
equalled in the Memory of Man. The munificent Founder honoured the
Architect, on this first Essay of his Skill, with the Present of a golden
Cup; & by his Statutes, appointed him jointly with the Vice-chancellor
perpetual Curator of the Fabrick.

" We William Townsend of Oxford, Mason, & Jeremiah Franklin, and
" Thomas Speakman of the same, Carpenters, do hereby certify, that by
" the Command of the Reverend Robert Shippen, Doctor in Divinity,
" Vice-chancellor of the University of Oxford, we did, on the Day of the
" Date hereof, survey, and strictly examine the whole Fabrick of the
" Theatre in the said University, and do find, that all the same is in per-
" fect Repair, and good Order; all the Walls thereof no where appearing
" to be in the least defective; and the Roof which has been formerly
" swayed or sunk in the Middle about eleven Inches, occasioned by the
" shrinking of some of the Timber and great Weight of Books formerly
" laid upon it, appearing to us to be in as good a Condition as it was above
" twenty Years since, when the like Examination was made: And we do
" further certify, That the whole Fabrick of the said Theatre is, in our
" Opinion, like to remain and continue in such good Repair and Condi-
" tion, for one hundred or two hundred Years yet to come. In Testimony
" whereof we have hereunto put our Hands the eighth Day of March,
" Anno Dom. 1720.

WILLIAM TOWNESEND.

JEREMIAH FRANKLIN.

THOMAS SPEAKMAN.

N.B. This Certificate, from Builders of the best Repute in Oxford, was
occasioned by a groundless Rumour, at that time, that the Fabrick was
in want of Repairs.

After the Description of this geometrical Flat-roof, it may be expedient
to examine the Diagrams of such Work, by the old Architect Sebastian-

Serlio: and much later, by Dr. Wallis; in order to discern in one View, how much this of the Oxford Theatre has excell'd the other two; though it is not known that either of those Schemes was ever put in Practice, except that of Dr. Wallis in a small Model.

Sebastiani Serlii Architectura, Lib. i. de Geometria.

Complura praeter opinionem Architecto saepius accidere solent: verbi gratiâ, ut hujusce rei exemplum aliquod offeramus: contignatio ei forte fortuna pedum XV. spatio ac intervallo producenda extruendaque committetur: verùm, compluribus tignis ipsi propositis, nullum eorum ad tantam utique longitidinem pertinget, quinimo singula bipedali quantitate, a praedicta deficient longitudine; quibus tamen, nulla alia prorsus suppetente materia, pro contignatione conficienda necessariò erit utendum: Quid obsecro miser ille Architectus sibi consilii capiet? Rationem hîc descriptam persequetur, et opus suum quam solidissimun reddet, altero nimirum tignorum capite parieti infixo, reliquoque absque ulla fultura suspenso remanente, quemadmodum ex subjectâ perspici potest Figurâ.

Sebastiani Serlii Diagramma Contignationis planae
Geometricae.

Dr. Grew's Description of the Musaeum of the Royal Society, Pag. 361

A model of a geometrical Flat-floor, contrived by Dr. J. Wallis, was given to the Royal Society by Bishop Wilkins; the following Account of which, by the Author, is an Abstract of that he hath published in his Book De Motu, Cap. vi. Prop. 10, Fig. 243.

I did first, saith the Doctor, contrive and delineate it, in the Year 1644, at Queen's-college in Cambridge. When afterwards I was made Professor of Geometry at Oxford, about the Year 1650, I caused it to be framed of small Pieces of Timber, prepared by a Joiner, and put together by myself.

This I shewed soon after to divers in Oxford, & particularly to Dr. Wilkins, then Warden of Wadham College. After the King's Restauration, I caused another to be made; and in the Year 1660, presented it to his Majesty, who was well pleased with it, and caused it to be reposited in his closet.

On the Model first-mentioned, I read two publick Lectures at Oxford; the one in the Year 1652, as to the Construction of it; the other, in the Year 1653, as to the Computation of what Weight every Joint of it sustains; whereby it might be the better judged how far it may be safely practised. The greatest Weight charged on any one Joint, doth not amount to ten times the Weight of one Beam; and the greatest Weight borne by one Beam, not to seventeen times its own Weight· And even this, not laid all on the same Part, but distributed to several Parts of it.

A third Lecture, much to the same purpose, I read May 1669, in the same Place, before the Grand Duke of Tuscany.

The Contrivance is obvious to the Eye. The Outsides represent the Walls of the Building, on which this Flat-floor or Roof is to be laid. The Beams next adjoining to the Sides, have one End lodged on those Walls; the other End sustained by another Beam, lying cross; both Ends of which, are in like manner sustained by other Cross-beams; and, those again by others; till they reach the other Walls. So that no one of them can fall, unless the Walls fail, or the Beams break: All mutually sustaining each other, without any Pillar or Prop to support them, besides the outer Walls.

The Models I caused to be made, and that of the Royal Society in Imitation thereof, are in Breadth about four times as much as the Length of the longest Beam; but may be continued, at Pleasure, to farther Breadth, as shall be thought fit; with this Caution, that the farther the Work is continued, the greater Weight will be charged on every Joint; especially near the Middle. And tho' in this Model, no one Beam is charged with so much as seventeen times its own Weight; yet if the Work be continued to a greater Breadth, the proportional Weight will be thereby increased. And therefore must be limited, according to the Strength of the Timber, able to bear more or fewer times its own Weight.

I do not know, that yet it hath been reduced to Practice, in more than four Pieces in this Form. Such is one of the Floors in the Tower of the publick Schools at Oxford: The Breadth whereof, to the Length of the Beams, is as three to two. But may doubtless be continued much further; especially in such a Roof, as is not to bear much more than its own Weight.

Thus, for Instance, a Bowling-green of near an Acre of Ground, may be covered with a Frame of long slender Pieces, without any other Prop than on the Sides, for Vines, or other like Plants to run upon, so as to shade the whole.

Note here, That whereas the Ends of the several Pieces are to lie upon those that cross them, about the Middle thereof, it will be necessary at every Joint to abate both Pieces half-way, or near it; that one may be thus let into the other, & the whole reduced to a Flat. But whether such Piece, so abated, doth end even with that on which it lies, or doth lie over somewhat beyond it, is indifferent. And though that may seem more elegant, this, perhaps, may be fitter for Use.

Each Piece, I say, must be so abated half-way, or near it; For, whereas those Beams, especially of a considerable Length, will, with the Weight, bow a little; if this Abatement be somewhat less then half-way, (whereby without such bowing, the whole would somewhat rise in the Middle) it will by such bowing be reduced to a Flat.

Note also, That a Frame thus contrived, needs neither Nail nor Pin; the several Pieces fastening, as well supporting one another. Yet, if it be to bear a great Weight more than its own, it will be convenient to fasten each Joint with Pins; and, if Need be, to strengthen it with Iron-plates, or line it with other Pieces of Timber, to be fastened with Iron-bolts, to make amends for what is weakened by the Abatements at the Joints; which will make the whole Frame exceeding strong.

Guil. Wal-
ker
 " Theatrum Oxoniense, in toto hoc nostro Britannico, an non e terrarum
" orbe? nec habet ullum sibi par, nec ullum secundum; Theatrum quod
" exoptet Apollo templum, Musae Parnassum, Plato academiam, Aris-
" toteles Lyceum, Cicero Tusculanum, Gratiae omnes, Veneresque
" domum.

Carmen Pindaricum in Theatrum Sheldonianum, et ejus Architectum.

I.

Authore
Corb. Owen,
ex Æde
Christi.
Musae Ang.
Vol. I.

QUousque linguas oculis, litamus
  Victimas tacentes?
Quousque defixi stupemus
  Saxei saxa, plumbeique plumbum,
Tanquam Nos vacuis parata conchis
Simulacra coelo dedolasset artifex?
Vocales ecce lapides et trabes sonorae
  Ingratam humanis taciturnitatem
Cognatis exprobrant, Dryas quos Obstetrix
Eduxit rupto frustrà de robore, frustrà
Deucalioneo mollibant numina jactu.

  Eja quae doctis musica pulsibus
Tot malleorum suave concinentium
  Agrestes cicurat sonos!
Cedant Orphei tandem miracula plectri,
  Atque Amphionae fides;
Ille feras olim sylvasque sequaces
  Excivit et montes vagos:
Hic Architecto maenia carmine
  Stupendia Thebis addidit:
At ecce jam blando fragore
Ipsos murorum symphonia
Vates attonitos trahit:

At ecce ruderibus prosae jacentem
Me me poetam extruit:
Cui tantos liceat sonos
Confusae saltem pro more imitarier Echûs.

II.

At nullum eloquium nulla sonantium
Decora verborum strues,
Vastarum trabium non enerrabile textum
Æquabit, solidamve exprimet harmoniam.
En ut sublimi pensilis aëre
Tenditur campus juga ponderosi
Sustinens plumbi, gravidumque faeto
Culmine montem:
O quam justa fides nectit amantes
Arbores, quondam solitas procari
Blando murmure, nutibusque blandis:
Connubio junctas stabili vis nulla revellet,
Divortium sera non facient saecula.
En audax quanto machina nisu
Muros deserit hinc et hinc relictos,
Metumque subjectis jocosum
Salvis incutit usque et usque tutis!
Non illa planisspherii minacis
Secura lapsum magis expavescit,
Firma quam coeli camera arcuati
Æterni fornicis ruinam.
Tam stabilem jubet esse vastitatem
Ingenium potentis architecti,
Quo nil soliduisve latiusve,
Quod molem aetheream vi sustinet Atlanteâ,
Carcere quod veterum teneri
Orbiculorum nesciens
Augusti extendit latèpomeria coeli.

III.

Divina WRENNVS heu! diu Mathemata
Vel docto nimium pulvere sordida
Evexit assurgens in altum,
Interque stellas luce donavit novâ
Stellis vel ipsis invidenda.
Illic sydereo spectator in Amphitheatro
Vidit ferarum splendida praelia,

Iratisque coruscantes
Faucibus atque oculis rogos.
Illic serenarum pictis noctium scenis
Vidit planetas praescios coeli mimos
Humana ludentes fata,
Nunc ore risus comico futuros
Festivosque sales, atque hilares jocos,
Æthereis celebrare choris,
Nunc face lugubri radiisque pullis,
Et scelera, & caedes nepotum
Fingere materiem cothurnis.
Tandem rependit gratus hospes aetheris
Spectaculorum syderibus vices,
Mirantur astra posse mortales manus
Ditare terras aemula coeli domo.
Quin et rivalem lustrat amabilem,
Suamque coelum deperiens imaginem,
Ut penitùs speculo fruatur
Jam plures oculos, & lumina plura requirit.

IV.

Quamvis hianti subtrahat popello
Modesta frontem fabrica, sicut decet
Sacro parente procreatem virginem
Non turbâ genitam promiscuâ;
Profanis subducat licet
Oculis plebis malè feriatae
Intemerandum vultûs eximii decus;
Quale nec Etruscâ miratus victor in urbe
Negavit olim Carolus
Cuivis mortali fore fas profestâ
Luce videre;
Non illa coeli tamen intuentis
Criticum lumen fugit; ultro solem
Lynceum vocat, astraque curiosa
Centum receptat fenestris,
Ingentis populi videt capaces
Pegmatum moles attonitus sol,
Mundi Supervisor supremus,
Interque varios undique miratur foros
Tam bellam ordinis benignitatem,
Dum nulla lucem pars queratur amissam,

Tristemque pulla lugeat eclipsin.
Hic sole melius quilibet vel ipso
Et cunctos vidisse potest, cunctisque videri.

V.

Celandum nihil est, nihil tegendum;
    Nullus hic error latebras requirit;
Perfecta surgit undiquaque moles,
Et merito duplicis gerit ornamenta coronae:
Quanta debitur quotuplexque WRENNO
Laurea victori, servatori civica,
    Capitique decentior Architecto
      Turrita Cybeles corona?
Devictam nimium diu
Oppressamque suis miserabilem ruinis
    Tectonicen benignus
    Artium civem reddidit urbi
Olim quae rudibus dedit vagisque
        Artibus urbem.
Longa nequicquam rabies Gothorum,
    Quae citò Romanum perdidit imperium,
    Bello terebat usque pervicaci
    Artem vastoribus inimicam.
Auxiliatrices frustrà accessêre catervae,
    Orbisque conspiravit dedecus in suum;
(Nam subruendae pronus architecturae
    Ubique totus orbis erat Gothus)
Aggressus hydram WRENNVS immensam ruit,
    Quanquam tenacis consuetudinis
    Loricâ squammatam adamantinâ.
    Æmula nec partem nodosa triumphi,
    Herculeae ritu, clava sibi vendicat,
    Hic radio totam debili et pusillo
Barbariem sternens, simul omnia monstra subegit
Quotquot saecundo tulit ignorantia partu.

VI.

En multus altis hinc et inde muris
En triumphalis ut resurgat arcus,
Intusque et extra nobiles columnae,
    Artis frequenter olim abortientis
(Ut mos patriciis malus puellis)

Proles adultae matris absoluta!
Hae tandem ingenio columnae
    Hae tandem docto labori
Quamvis Herculo, stataunt nil ultra,———&c.

II. Orthography of the Campanile, or Bell-tower, over the Gate, in the Front and principal Access to the great Quadrangle-court of Christ-church, Oxon, in the Gothick Stile; begun on the old Foundation (laid by Cardinal Wolsey) in June 1681, and finished November 1682.

III. Plan, Elevation, and Section, of the great Library of Trinity College in Cambridge.
Proposals for the Repairs of the Publick-library and Schools at Oxford, with the Drawings annexed; imparted to Dr. Gregory. Now in the Bodleyan Library.

IV. Plan, Orthography, and Section of a circular Library, with a Dome and Lantern, and a Colonade Hexastyle in Front, of the Ionick Order, according to an Intention for Trinity College, not executed. This is a very beautiful and most commodious Model for a large Library.

V. Designs of the Chapel of Emmanuel College in Cambridge.

VI. Plans, Elevation, & Section of a Theatre, or Commencement-house, with a Library annexed, according to an Intention, for the University of Cambridge, about the Year 1678, but not executed.
Designs for the parochial Church at Warwick, after the Fire of the Town in 1694, not executed.
Orthography of the Tower of the parochial Church of St. Mary at Warwick, erected after an unsuccessful Attempt in Execution of a defective prior Design by other Hands.
Orthography of the North Front, (commonly called Solomon's Porch) finished some time before the Surveyor's Decease, in 1723, with the Designs intended for the middle Tower and Spire, & two western Towers, for the collegiate Church of St. Peter in Westminster; contrived in the Gothick Stile, conformable to the old Structure of the Abbey-church and Porch.

PART II. CONCLUSION.

URING the Time of the Surveyor's Employment in the Service of the Publick, and of the Crown, by virtue of Letters-patents, consistent with the Pleasure of six Crowned-heads, under the Great-seals of King Charles the second, King James the second, King William and Queen Mary, Queen Anne, and King George the first, (besides the ordinary Duties of his Office, in the Survey and Care of the Repairs and New-buildings of all the royal Palaces) he began and compleated the cathedral Church of St. Paul, the second greatest Structure in Europe; fifty-one parochial Churches; the great Column called the Monument, and other publick Edifices of London; the two royal Palaces of Hampton-court & Winchester; the royal Hospitals of Chelsea and Greenwich; the North Front, and other Repairs of Westminster-abbey, from the Year 1698 to the Time of his Decease in 1723; the Theatre of Oxford; the Theatre-royal in Drury-lane; the Duke's Theatre in Salisbury-court, sometime since taken down; the magnificent Library of Trinity College in Cambridge; the elegant Chapel of Emmanuel College there; with many other Fabricks of less Note, and private Seats.

"That I take the Boldness (says the learned and ingenious John Evelyn, "Esq.) to adorn this little Work [Account of Architects and Architec-"ture*] with the Name of the Master of the Works, (whose Patronage "alone can give it Reputation) I have no Excuse for, but an Ambition "of publicly declaring the great Esteem I have ever had of his Virtues "and Accomplishments; not only in the Art of Building, but through all "the learned Cycle of the most useful Knowledge, & abstruser Sciences, "as well as of the polite and shining. All which is so justly allowed him, "that he needs no Panegyrick, or other History to eternize them; than "the greatest City of the Universe, which he hath rebuilt & beautified, "and is still improving; witness the Churches, the royal Courts, stately "Halls, Magazines, Palaces, and other publick Structures; besides what "he has built of great and magnificent in both the Universities, at Chel-"sea, and in the Country; and is now advancing of the royal Marine "Hospital at Greenwich, &c. All of them so many Trophies of his Skill "and Industry, and conducted with that Success, that if the whole Art "of Building were lost, it might be recovered, and found again in St. "Paul's, the historical Pillar, and those other Monuments of his happy "Talent and extraordinary Genius."

All these Works form such a Body of civil Architecture, as will appear

*London, 1706. Dedication to Sir Christopher Wren

rather the Production of a whole Century, than the Life and Industry of one Man, of which no parallel Instance can be given.

Anno nono Gulielmi Reg.
In an Act of Parliament in the ninth Year of the Reign of King William, For the Compleating and adorning the cathedral Church of St. Paul, London, a Clause was inserted, To suspend a Moiety of the Surveyor's Salary, until the said Church should be finished; thereby the better to encourage him to finish the same with the utmost Diligence and Expedition.

It was at that Time a common Notion and Misreport, that the Surveyor received a large annual Salary for that Building, and, consequently, it was his Interest to prolong the finishing of the Fabrick, for the Continuance of this supposed Emolument; which, it would seem, occasioned that Clause.

The Surveyor's Salary for building St. Paul's, from the Foundation to the Finishing thereof, (as appears from the publick Accounts) was not more than £200 per Annum. This, in Truth, was his own Choice, but what the rest of the Commissioners, on the Commencement of the Works, judged unreasonably small, considering the extensive Charge; the Pains and Skill in the Contrivance; in preparing Draughts, Models, and Instructions for the Artificers, in their several Stations and Allotments; in almost daily overseeing & directing in Person; in making Estimates and Contracts; in examining and adjusting all Bills and Accounts, &c. Nevertheless, he was content with this small Allowance, nor coveted any additional Profit, always preferring the publick Service to any private Ends.

Anno nono Annae Reg.
Upon the compleating this great Fabrick, a Clause passed in the Act of Parliament of the ninth Year of the Reign of Queen Anne declaring the Church finished, to impower the Commissioners to Pay the Surveyor the Arrears of this Moiety of his Salary.

His Allowance for building all the parochial Churches of the City of London was about £100 per Annum, and the same for the Repairs of Westminster-abbey.

In the Year 1685, Sir Christopher Wren was elected & returned a Burgess for the Borough of Plympton in the County of Devon, and served in that Parliament which began at Westminster, 29 Maii, 1mo. Jacobi II. 1685.

In the Parliament which met at Westminster, 22 January 1689, he was elected and returned a Burgess for the Borough of New-windsor, in the County of Berks, by the Inhabitants paying Scot and Lot; but, upon a Petition, the Resolution of the House was, That the Right of Election was in the Mayor, Bailiffs, and select Number of Burgesses only.

6 *Aug.*

In the Year 1690, 2 do. Gulielmi & Mariæ, R.R. he was elected and returned for the same Borough, by the Mayor, Bailiffs, & select Number

228

of Burgesses only. On Report of the Merits of this Election, the Question being put, " That the House do agree with the Committee, that the Right of Election is in the Mayor, Bailiffs, & select Number of Burgesses only. It passed in the Negative, viz. Yeas 138, Noes 144." 17 *Maii*

In the Year 1700, he was elected and returned a Burgess for the Borough of Weymouth and Melcomb-regis, in the County of Dorset, & served in that Parliament which began at Westminster, 10 Feb. 12mo. Gulielmi R. IIIti.

In the Year 1718, Sir Christopher Wren's Patent for the Office of Surveyor of the royal Works was superseded, in the fourscore and sixth Year of his Age, and after more than fifty Years spent in continued active and laborious Service to the Crown and Publick; at which Time his Merit and Labours were not remembered by some. *Quarto Georgii R. primi*

He then betook himself to a Country Retirement,* saying only with the Stoick,—*Nunc me jubet fortune expeditùs philosophari.*—In which Recess, free from worldly Affairs, he passed the greatest Part of the five last following Years of his Life in Contemplation and Studies, and principally in the Consolation of the holy Scriptures; chearful in Solitude, & as well pleased to die in the Shade as in the Light. ** At Hampton-court*

> " Heroick Souls a nobler Lustre find
> " Even from those Griefs which break a vulgar Mind;
> " That Frost which cracks the brittle common Glass,
> " Makes Crystal into stronger Brightness pass. *Ex MS. D. Sprat*

It was the Observation of a French Virtuoso, in his Panegyrick upon another great Genius of the first Rank in Philosophy, the incomparable Sir Isaac Newton, that he had the extraordinary Fortune to see his own apotheosis:—alluding to the Poet: *Monsieur Fontenelle*

> Scil.—Vivo sublime dedisti
> Nomen, ab obsequiis quod dare, fama, soles. *Ovid*

An Honour, the most worthy very rarely acquire; the Reason is this,—says the Poet:

> Urit enim fulgore suo qui praegravat artes
> Infrà se posites; extinctus ambitur idem.
> *Hor. Ep. L. 2. Ep. 1.*

If therefore, it might be, the Surveyor had not the equal Chánce to be so generally distinguished in his Life-time, by the same Compliment with his Friend, yet was he alike secured of the posthumous Praise——

> Aerias tentasse domos, animoque rotundum
> Percurrisse polum.—— *Hor.*

q 3

And has a just Claim to the peculiar Dignity reserved for those—

Inventas et qui vitam excoluére per artes:
Quique sui memores alios fecêre merendo:
Omnibus his niveâ cinguntur tempora Vittâ.

To these illustrious Astronomers may, most aptly and emphatically, be applied the general Encomium of the Roman Poet—

Felices animae, quibus haec cognoscere primis,
  Inque domos superas scandere cura fuit!
Credibile est illas pariter vitiisque locisque
  Altius humanis exseruisse caput.
Non Venus et vinum sublimia pectora fregit
  Officiumve fori; milit aeve labor.
Non levis ambitio, perfusaque gloria fuco;
  Magnarumve fames sollicitavit opûm.
Admovêre oculis distantia sidera nostris;
  Ætheràque ingenio supposuêre suo.
Sic petitur coelum: ut ferat Ossan Olympus;
  Summaque Peliacus sydera tangat apex.
Nos quoque sub ducibus coelum metabimur illis
  Ponemusque suos ad stata signa dies.
  —*Ovid. Fast.*

" Thrice happy they, who first with Souls refin'd,
" To these Pursuits their generous Care confin'd;
" Who, nobly spurning Earth's impure Abodes,
" Assay'd to climb the Mansions of the Gods.
" Such Breasts sublime, Intemp'rance never broke;
" Such ne'er submitted to Love's shameful Yoke.
" Such fled the wrangling of the noisy Bar,
" The hideous Din of Arms, and painful Toils of War;
" Foes to Ambition, and her idle Lure,
" From Thirst of Fame, from Thirst of Gold, secure,
" Such Souls, examining the distant Skies,
" Unveiled its hidden Lights to mortal Eyes.
" Let huge Olympus lofty Ossa bear;
" Let Pelion tow'r on Ossa high in Air;
" Mountains on Mountains short of Heaven must rise;
" This only Ladder reaches to the Skies.
" Led by these Guides, to measure Heav'n we try,
" And to each Sign its stated Days apply."

Dr. Isaac Barrow, in his Oration at Gresham College, in the Year 1662, gives him this most extraordinary Character: "Certissime constat, ut praecosiores neminem unquam praetulisse spes, ita nec maturiores quenquam fructus protulisse; prodigium olim pueri, nunc miraculum viri, imo daemonium hominis; atque ne mentiri videar, suffecerit nominasse ingeniosissimum et optimum Christophorum Wrennum"(a).

Part of his Thoughts for Discovery of the Longitude at Sea; a Review of some former Tracts in Astronomy and Mathematics, had a Share in the Employment of those Hours he could spare from Meditations and Researches in holy Writ, during his last Retreat, when it appeared, that though Time had enfeebled his Limbs, (which was his chief Ailment) yet had it little Influence on the Vigour of his Mind, which continued, with a Vivacity rarely found at that Age, till within a few Days of his Dissolution; & not till then could cease the continued Aim of his whole Life, to be (in his own Words) *beneficus humano generi;* for his great Humanity appeared to the last, in Benevolence and Complacency, free from all Moroseness in Behaviour or Aspect.

After a short Indisposition, it was the Will of the omnipotent Author and Dispenser of all Beings to release him from this mortal State, and to invest him with Immortality, on the 25th Day of February, in the Year of Grace 1723, and in the ninety-first of his Age.

> Sic benè complevit Nestor sua fata, novemque
> Addiderat lustris, altera lustra novem.
>
> *Ovid. Trist. L. 4.*

Jucundum est, esse secum quàm diutissimè, cum quis se dignum quo frueretur, effecit.   *Sen. Ep. 59.*

As to his bodily Constitution, it was naturally rather delicate than strong, especially in his Youth, which seem'd consumptive; and yet, by a judicious Regularity and Temperance, (having acquir'd good Knowledge in Physick) he continued healthy, with little Intermission, even to this extreme old Age. Further 'tis observable, that he was happily endued with such an Evenness of Temper, a steady Tranquillity of Mind, and christian Fortitude, that no injurious Incidents, or Inquietudes of human Life, could ever ruffle or discompose; and was in Practice a Stoick. Such was Seneca's good Man, "Certus judicii, inconcussus, intrepidus, quem aliqua vis movet, nulla perturbat; quem fortuna, cùm in eum, quod habuit telum nocentissimum, vi maximâ intorsit, pungit, non vulnerat, & hoc rarò. [Ep. 45.] Talis est sapientis animus, qualis mundi status super lunam; semper illic serenum est. [Ep. 60.] In a Word, (as was said on

(a) *J. Ward's 'Lives of Professors of Gresham College,' Appendix, Number X.*

another Occasion by an elegant Writer) " His Knowledge had a right
"Influence on the Temper of his Mind, which had all the Humility,
"graceful Modesty, Goodness, calmness, Strength, and Sincerity of a
" sound and unaffected Philosopher. Lastly, to whose Merits his Coun-
" try is further indebted, than has been yet acknowledg'd." He is interr'd
in the Vaults of the cathedral Church of St. Paul, under the South-aile
of the Quire. Over the Grave is this inscription on a small Table of
Marble:

Subtùs conditur
Hujus Ecclesiae, & Urbis Conditor
C h r i s t o p h o r u s   W r e n,
Qui vixit annos ultrà nonagintà
Non sibi, sed Bono-publico.
Lector, si Monumentum requiris,
Circumspice.

Obiit 25 Feb. Anno 1723. Ætat 91.

[Marmora parva quidem, sed non cessura, viator,
Mausoli saxis Pyramidunque, legis.]
Martial.

[Umbrae dii tenuem dent, & sine pondere terram,
Spirantesque crocos, & in urnà perpetuum ver.]
Juven. Sat. VII.

P. S.
An After-Thought for the Inscription.

H. S. E
C h r i s t o p h o r u s   W r e n,
Hujus Ecclesiae & Urbis Conditor
Qui vixit annos ultrà Nestoreos,
Non sibi, sed Patriae.
Viator, si Tumulum requiris
Despice,
Si Monumentum,
Circumspice.

Obiit 25 Feb. Anno 1723. Ætat. 91.

Blazonry of the Coat of Arms, viz. Argent, a Chevron between three
Lions Heads erased Azure, on a Chief Gules three Cross-croslets Or.
Crest on the Helmet, A Lion's Head erased Azure, transfix'd by a Spear
bloody on the Point.
N.B. The Colours on the Modern Arms differ from the Antient.

232

Suspice & Mirare.

Christophorus Wren Eques Auratus
Totius hujus Fabricae
Magnus Architectus.
Moli huic Immensae,
Sacrae, Eximiae,
Quam Animo Conceperat,
Quam Inchoaverat,
Quam Perfecerat,
Unius Hominis Opus,
Haud Mortali datum.
Bis
Factus Immortalis
De Coelo Invigilat
Mente Permeat, Corpore Sustentat
Quantilli Corpori
Quantus Animus,
Qualis Mens.

Depositum servet Ecclesia
Memor Sui!
Subtus jacet
Fundator, Curator.

Quam Grande Opus!
Quam Perenne Monumentum!
By a St. Paul's Scholar, March 7, 1723.

Sir Christopher Wren being at his Father's House, anno 1651, at Knoyle *Aubrey's Miscel. Cap. v. Pag. 52 ex Ore C.W.*
Wilts, dreamt that he saw a Fight in a great Market-place, which he
knew not, where some were flying, & others pursuing; and among those
that fled, he saw a Kinsman of his, who went into Scotland to the King's
Army. They heard in the Country that the King was come into England,
but whereabout He was they could not tell. The next Night his Kins- *Fought Sep. 3.*
man came to his Father's at Knoyle, and was the first that brought the
News of the Fight at Worcester.

When Sir Christopher Wren was at Paris, about 1665, he was taken ill
and feverish, made but little Water, and had a Pain in his Reins: He sent
for a Physician, who advis'd him to let Blood, thinking he had a Pleurisy;
but Bleeding much disagreeing with his Constitution, he would defer it
a Day longer: That Night he dreamt that he was in a Place where Palm-
trees grew, (suppose Egypt) and that a Woman in a romantick Habit
reach'd him Dates. The next Day he sent for Dates, which cur'd him of
the Pain in his Reins.

By way of Parallel to this, " The Plague raging in the Army of the Em-
" peror Charlemain, he dreamt, that the Decoction of the Root of the
" Dwarf-thistle [a Mountain Plant, since call'd the Caroline-thistle]
" would cure that Disease." See Gerard's Herbal, who tells us this. *N.B.*
" He says the Army was thus deliver'd from the Plague, but mentions
" not the Dream, p. 1158.

     Narrat. Plinius (25 Lib. Cap. 2. Nat. Hist.) Historiam hujusmodi.

" Nuper cujusdam militantis in praetorio mater vidit in quiete, ut radi-
" cem sylvestris rosae (quam Cynorrhodon vocant) blanditam sibi as-
" pectu pridiè in fruteto, mitteret filio bibendam: In Lusitaniâ res gere-
" batur, Hispaniae proximâ parte: Casu accidit, ut milite à morsu canis
" incipiente aquas expavescere, superveniret epistolà orantis ut parêret
" religioni: Servatusque est ex insperato; et posteà quisquis auxilium
" simile tentavit. . . .
" Cùm Ptolomaeus familiaris Alexandri M. in praelio, telo venenato
" ictus esset, eòque vulnere summo cum dolore moreretur, Alexander
" assidens somno est consopitus; tum secundùm quietem visus ei dicitur
" draco is, quem mater Olympias alebat, radiculam ore ferre, et simul
" dicere quò illa nasceretur, ejus autem esse vim tantam, ut Ptolomaeum
" facile sanaret. Cùm Alexander experrectus narrasset amicis somnium
" emisit qui illam radiculam quaererent. Quâ inventâ, et Ptolomaeus sa-
" natus dicitur, et multi milites, qui erant eodem genere teli vulnerati."
[*Cicero de Divinatione, Lib. II.*]—['ΟΝΑΡ 'ΕΚ ΔΙΟΣ ΕΣΤΙ. *Homer. Iliad. A.*

9, Nestor of Athens was not only in his Profession the greatest Man of that
Age, but had given more Proofs of it, than any other Man ever did; yet
for want of that natural Freedom, and Audacity, which is necessary in
Commerce with Men, his personal Modesty overthrew all his publick
Actions. Nestor was in those Days a skilful Architect, and in a manner
the Inventor of the Use of mechanick Powers, which he brought to so
great Perfection, that he knew to an Atom what Foundation could bear
such a Superstructure: And they record of him, that he was so prodigi-
ously exact, that for the Experiment-sake, he built an Edifice of great
Beauty, and seeming Strength, but so contrived as to bear only its own
Weight, and not to admit the Addition of the least Particle. This Building was beheld with much Admiration by all the *Virtuosi* of that Time,
but fell down with no other Pressure but the settling of a Wren upon the
Top of it: Yet Nestor's Modesty was such, that his Art and Skill were
soon disregarded for want of that Manner with which Men of the World
support and assert the Merits of their own Performances. Soon after this
Instance of his Art, Athens was, by the Treachery of its Enemies, burnt
to the Ground. This gave Nestor the greatest Occasion that ever Builder

had to render his Name immortal, and his Person venerable: For, all the new City rose according to his Disposition, and all the Monuments of the Glories & Distresses of that People were erected by that sole Artist; nay, all their Temples, as well as Houses, were the Effects of his Study, and Labour; insomuch that it was said by an old Sage, sure Nestor will now be famous, for the Habitations of the Gods, as well as Men, are built by his Contrivance. But this bashful Quality still put a Damp upon his great Knowledge, which has as fatal an Effect upon Men's Reputations, as Poverty; for, as it was said, *The poor Man by his Wisdom delivered the City; yet no Man remembered that same poor Man: So here we find, The modest Man built the City, & the modest Man's Skill was unknown. But surely Posterity are obliged to allow him that Praise after his Death, which he so industriously declined while he was living.

*Ecclesias-tes, c. ix. v. 15

Aliter,
In Eundem.
[Stylo Martialis.]

Quanta quies placidi est, et quanta scientia Wrenni!
    Sed cohibet vires, ingeniumque pudor,
Ante fores dubitat fortunam admittere stantem;
    Seque piget curae praemia ferre suae.
Laudes ex meritis, magnisque laboribus ortas,
    Ore verecundo noluit esse suas.
Palladiam tenui frontem redimire coronâ
    Contentus, famae nec dare vela suae.
Sed tamen hunc nostri scit temporis esse *Rabirum
    Artis mira suae qui monumenta videt.

*Rabirius Architectus eximius, tem-pore Imp. Damitiani

In eundum, Astronomum et Architectum, Basilicae Divi Pauli, et Urbis Londini Conditorem.

Astra polumque suo concepit pectore Wrennus,
    Paulinam mirâ qui struit arte domum.
Ista manus Triviae templi revocâsset honores;
    Seu Mausolei; seu Babylonis opus.
Grandior ex flammis *Augusta renascitur, artem
    Stantia non poterant tecta probare suam.

*Vetus Lon-dini nomen

De Londino post Incendium Restaurato.

Qualiter Assyrios renovant incendia nidos,
    Una decem quoties saecula vixit avis:
Taliter exuta est veterem †Nova Troja senectam,
    Et sumpsit vultus ‡Principis ipsa sui.

Martial, L. v. Ep. 7 †Vetus lon-dini nomen. ‡Caroli R.

235

APPENDIX.

OF ARCHITECTURE; AND OB-SERVATIONS ON ANTIQUE TEMPLES, &c.

[From some rough Draughts, imperfect.]

TRACT I.

ARCHITECTURE has its political Use; publick Buildings being the Ornament of a Country; it establishes a Nation, draws People and Commerce; makes the People love their native Country, which Passion is the Original of all great Actions in a Common-wealth. The Emulation of the Cities of Greece was the true Cause of their Greatness. The obstinate Valour of the Jews, occasioned by the Love of their Temple, was a Cement that held together that People, for many Ages, through infinite Changes. The Care of publick Decency and Convenience was a great Cause of the Establishment of the Low-countries, and of many Cities in the World. Modern Rome subsists still, by the Ruins and Imitation of the old; as does Jerusalem, by the Temple of the Sepulchre, and other Remains of Helena's Zeal.

Architecture aims at Eternity; and therefore the only Thing uncapable of Modes and Fashions in its Principals, the Orders.

The Orders are not only Roman and Greek, but Phoenician, Hebrew, and Assyrian; therefore being founded upon the Experience of all Ages, promoted by the vast Treasures of all the great Monarchs, and Skill of the greatest Artists and Geometricians, every one emulating each other; and Experiments in this kind being greatly expenceful, and Errors incorrigible, is the Reason that the Principles of Architecture are now rather the Study of Antiquity than Fancy.

Beauty, Firmness, and Convenience, are the Principles; the two first depend upon geometrical Reasons of Opticks and Staticks; the third only makes the Variety.

There are natural Causes of Beauty. Beauty is a Harmony of Objects, begetting Pleasure by the Eye. There are two Causes of Beauty, natural and customary. Natural is from Geometry, consisting in Uniformity (that is Equality) and Proportion. Customary Beauty is begotten by the Use of our Senses to those Objects which are usually pleasing to us for other

236

Causes, as Familiarity or particular Inclination breeds a Love to Things not in themselves lovely. Here lies the great Occasion of Errors; here is tried the Architect's Judgment: but always the true Test is natural or geometrical Beauty.

Geometrical Figures are naturally more beautiful than other irregular; in this all consent as to a Law of Nature. Of geometrical Figures, the Square and the Circle are most beautiful, next, the Parallelogram & the Oval. Strait Lines are more beautiful than curve; next to strait Lines, equal & geometrical Flexures; an Object elevated in the Middle is more beautiful than depressed.

Position is necessary for perfecting Beauty. There are only two beautiful Positions of strait Lines, perpendicular & horizontal: this is from Nature, and consequently Necessity, no other than upright being firm. Oblique Positions are Discord to the Eye, unless answered in Parts, as in the Sides of an equicrural Triangle: therefore Gothick Buttresses are all ill-favoured, and were avoided by the Ancients, and no Roofs almost but Spherick raised to be visible, except in the Front where the Lines answer; in spherick, in all positions, the Ribs answer. Cones & multangular Prisms want neither Beauty or Firmness, but are not ancient.

Views contrary to Beauty are Deformity, or a Defect of Uniformity, and Plainness, which is the Excess of Uniformity; Variety makes the Mean. Variety of Uniformities makes compleat Beauty: Uniformities are best tempered, as Rhimes in Poetry, alternately, or sometimes with more Variety, as in Stanzas.

In Things to be seen at once, much Variety makes Confusion, another Vice of Beauty. In Things that are not seen at once, and have no Respect one to another, great Variety is commendable, provided this Variety transgress not the Rules of Opticks and Geometry.

An Architect ought to be jealous of Novelties, in which Fancy blinds the Judgment; and to think his Judges, as well those that are to live Five Centuries after him, as those of his own Time. That which is commendable now for Novelty, will not be a new Invention to Posterity, when his Works are often imitated, and when it is unknown which was the Original; but the Glory of that which is good of itself is eternal.

The Architect ought, above all Things, to be well skilled in Perspective; for, every thing that appears well in the Orthography, may not be good in the Model, especially where there are many Angles and Projectures; and every thing that is good in Model, may not be so when built; because a Model is seen from other Stations and Distances than the Eye sees the Building: but this will hold universally true, that whatsoever is good in Perspective, and will hold so in all the principal Views, whether direct or Oblique, will be as good in great, if this only Caution be observed, that Regard be had to the Distance of the Eye in the principal Stations.

Things seen near at hand may have small and many Members, be well furnished with Ornaments, and may lie flatter; on the contrary, all this Care is ridiculous at great distances; there bulky Members, and full Projectures casting quick Shadows, are commendable: small Ornaments at too great Distance, serve only to confound the Symmetry, & to take away the Lustre of the Object, by darkening it with many little Shadows.

There are different Reasons for Objects, whose chief View is in Front, and for those whose chief View is sideways.

Fronts ought to be elevated in the Middle, not the Corners; because the Middle is the Place of greatest Dignity, and first arrests the Eye; and rather projecting forward in the Middle, than hollow. For these Reasons, Pavilions at the Corners are naught; because they make both Faults, a hollow and depressed Front. Where Hollows and Solids are mixed, the Hollow is to be in the Middle; for, Hollows are either Niches, Windows, or Doors: The first require the Middle to give the Statue Dignity; the second, that the View from within may be direct; the third, that the Visto may be strait. The Ancients elevated the Middle with a Tympan, and Statue, or a Dome. The Triumphant Arches, which now seem flat, were elevated by the magnificent Figure of the Victor in his Chariot with four Horses abreast, and other Statues accompanying it. No sort of Pinnacle is worthy enough to appear in the Air, but Statue. Pyramids are Gothick; Pots are modern French. Chimnies ought to be hid, if not, to be well adorned. No Roof can have Dignity enough to appear above a Cornice, but the Circular; in private Buildings it is excusable. The Ancients affected Flatness. In Buildings where the View is sideways, as in Streets, it is absolutely required, that the Composition be square, Intercolumnations equal, Projectures not great, the Cornices unbroken, and everything strait, equal, and uniform. Breaks in the Cornice, Projectures of the upright Members, Variety, Inequality in the Parts, various Heights of the Roof, serve only to confound the Perspective, & make it deformed, while the Breaches and Projectures are cast one upon another, and obscure all Symmetry. In this sort of Building there seems no Proportion of Length to the Heighth; for, a Portico the longer the more beautiful in *infinitum:* on the contrary, Fronts require a Proportion of the Breadth to the Heighth; higher than three times the Breadth is indecent, & as ill to be above three times as broad as high. From this Rule I except Obelisks, Pyramids, Columns, such as Trajan's, &c. which seem rather single Things than Compositions: I except also long Porticoes, though seen direct, where the Eye wandering over the same Members infinitely repeated, and not easily finding the Bounds, makes no Comparison of them with the Heighth.

Vitruvius hath led us the true Way to find out the Originals of the Orders. When Men first cohabited in civil Commerce, there was Necessity

238

of Forums & publick Places of Meeting. In cold Countries, People were obliged to shut out the Air, the Cold, & the Rain; but in the hot Countries, where Civility first began, they desired to exclude the Sun only, and admit all possible Air for Coolness and Health: this brought in naturally the Use of Porticoes, or Roofs for Shade, set upon Pillars. A Walk of Trees is more beautiful than the most artificial Portico; but these not being easily preserved in Market-places, they made the more durable Shades of Porticoes; in which we see they imitated Nature, most Trees in their Prime, that are not Saplings, or Dotards, observe near the Proportion of Dorick Pillars in the Length of their Bole, before they part into Branches. This I think the more natural Comparison, than that to the Body of a Man, in which there is little Resemblance of a cylindrical Body. The first Pillars were the very Boles of Trees turned, or cut in Prisms of many Sides. A little Curiosity would induce to lay the Torus at the Top; and the Conjecture is not amiss, to say it was first a Band of Iron, to keep the Clefts, occasioned by the Sun, from opening with the Weight above; and to keep the Weather from piercing those Clefts, it was necessary to cover it with the Plinth, or square Board. The Architrave conjoined all the Pillars in Length, the Couples joined them crossways. I suppose now, that the Ends of the Couples might be hollowed away, as in this Scheme. . . . [*The rest is wanting*].

TRACT II.

MODERN Authors who have treated of Architecture, seem generally to have little more in view, but to set down the Proportions of Columns, Architraves, & Cornices, in the several Orders, as they are distinguished into Dorick, Ionick, Corinthian, and Composite; & in these Proportions finding them in the ancient Fabricks of the Greeks & Romans, (though more arbitrarily used than they care to acknowledge) they have reduced them into Rules, too strict and pedantick, and so as not to to be transgressed, without the Crime of Barbarity; though, in their own Nature, they are but the Modes and Fashions of those Ages wherein they were used; but because they were found in the great Structures, (the Ruins of which we now admire) we think ourselves strictly obliged still to follow the Fashion, though we can never attain to the Grandeur of those Works.

Those who first laboured in the Restoration of Architecture, about three Centuries ago, studied principally what they found in Rome, aboveground, in the Ruins of the Theatres, Baths, Temples, and triumphal Arches; (for among the Greeks little was then remaining) and in these there appeared great Differences; however, they criticised upon them,

239

and endeavoured to reconcile them, as well as they could, with one another, and with what they could meet with in the Italian Cities: and it is to be considered, that what they found standing was built, for the most part, after the Age of Augustus, particularly, the Arches, Amphitheatres, Baths, &c. The Dorick Order they chiefly understood, by examining the Theatre of Marcellus, the Ionick, from the Temple of Fortuna Virilis; the Corinthian, from the Pantheon of Agrippa; the Composite, from the triumphal Arch of Titus, &c. I have seen among the Collections of Inigo Jones, a Pocket-book of Pyrrho Ligorio's, (an excellent Sculptor, and Architect, employed by Pope Paul the third, in the building of the Vatican Church of St. Peter in Rome, about the Year 1540) wherein he seemed to have made it his Business, out of the antique Fragments, to have drawn the many different Capitals, Mouldings of Cornices, & Ornaments of Freezes, &c. purposely to judge of the great Liberties of the ancient Architects, most of which had their Education in Greece.

In further Proof of this, we have now a very remarkable Account of an eminent and learned Critick in Architecture, viz.

Hist.of Amphitheatres, by C. Maffei, Edit. Lond. 1730

" The first Story of the Coliseo at Rome is said to be Dorick, and yet the
" Freeze of it is not plain and smooth. The third Story is Corinthian, but
" without Carving or Ornaments, except in the Capitals. The fourth
" Story is Composite, but with Corinthian Capitals, and like those of the
" third Order, the Corbills in the Freeze shewing them of the Compo-
" site Order. The Pillars of the four Orders, one above the other, do not
" diminish in Dimension, according to Rule, but are all of a Thickness;
" and the Void of the Arches, the Parts, Ornaments, and Measures in the
" different Stories, have not that Diversity of Proportion, which is be-
" lieved to be essential to different Orders. By the Example of this Am-
" phitheatre, (the noblest Remain of ancient Magnificence) as well as by
" many others, it is evident, that in the Rules of the Proportions, & dif-
" ferent Members, &c. of the Orders, there was no certain perpetual and
" universal Law, but the same Orders, Measures, and Manners differed,
" according to the various Kinds of Buildings, the Judgment of the Ar-
" chitect, and the different Circumstances of Things."

But although Architecture contains many excellent Parts, besides the ranging of Pillars, yet Curiosity may lead us to consider whence this Affectation arose originally, so as to judge nothing beautiful, but what was adorned with Columns, even where there was no real Use of them; as when Half-columns are stuck upon the Walls of Temples, or Basilicae; and where they are hung-on, as it were, upon the Outside of triumphal Arches, where they cannot be supposed of any Use, but merely for Ornament; as Seneca observed in the Roman Baths: "Quantum colum-narum est nihil sustinentium, sed in ornamentum positarum, impensae causâ!" It will be to the Purpose, therefore, to examine whence pro-

Epist. 87

ceeded this Affectation of a Mode that hath continued now at least 3000 Years, and the rather, because it may lead us to the Grounds of Architecture, and by what Steps this Humour of Colonades came into Practice in all Ages.

The first Temples were, in all Probability, in the ruder Times, only little *Cellae* to inclose the Idol within, with no other Light than a large Door to discover it to the People, when the Priest saw proper, and when he went in alone to offer Incense, the People paying their Adorations without Doors; for all Sacrifices were performed in the open Air, before the Front of the Temple, but in the southern Climates, a Grove was necessary not only to shade the Devout, but, from the Darkness of the Place, to strike some Terror and Recollection in their Approachers; therefore, Trees being always an adjunct to the *Cellae*, the Israelites were commanded to destroy not only the Idols, but to cut down the Groves which surrounded them: but Trees decaying in Time, or not equally growing, (though planted at first in good Order) or possibly not having Room; when the Temples were brought into Cities, the like Walks were represented with Stone Pillars, supporting the more durable Shade of a Roof, instead of the Arbour of spreading Boughs; and still in the Ornaments of Stone Work was imitated, (as well as the Materials would bear) both in the Capitals, Frizes & Mouldings, a Foliage, or sort of Work composed of Leaves, which remains to this Age.

This, I am apt to think, was the true Original of Colonades environing the Temples in single or double Ailes.

People could not assemble and converse, but under shade in hot Countries; therefore, the Forum of every City was also at first planted round with Walks of Trees—

Lucus in urbe suit mediâ, laetissimus umbrâ.

These Avenues were afterwards, as Cities grew more wealthy, reformed into Porticoes of Marble; but it is probable, at first the Columns were set no nearer than the Trees were before in Distance, and that both Architraves and Roofs were of Timber, because the Inter-columns would certainly have been too large to have had the Architraves made in Stone; but the Architects in After-ages, being ambitious to perform all in Stone, and to load the Architraves also with heavy Cornices of Stone, were necessitated to bring the Pillars nearer together; and from hence arose the Differences of the Eustyle, Sustyle, Diastyle, and Pycnostyle Disposition of Columns, by which Vitruvius and his Followers would make a systematical Science of their Art forming positive Rules, according to the Diameters of their Columns, for the Inter-columns, and the Proportions of the Architrave, Cornice, and all the Members of which they are composed.

Ii   241

But, by the way, it is to be observed, the Diameters of Columns were grosser at first, though Timber Architraves did not require to be borne by a more substantial Pillar, as in the Tuscan Order; but, because in the Groves, the ancient Trees of large Growth (and Antiquity always carries Veneration with it) were used to be of most Esteem. So at first the Columns were six Diameters in Heighth; when the Imitation of Groves was forgot, the Diameters were advanced to seven; then to eight; then to nine, as in the Ionick Order; then at last to ten, as in the Corinthian and Italick Orders: And herein the Architects had Reason, for the great Expence is in raising & carving of the Columns; and slenderer Columns would leave them more Opportunity to shew their Skill in carving and enriching their Works in the Capitals and Mouldings. Thus the Corinthian Order became the most delicate of all others, & though the Column was slenderer, yet bore a greater Weight of entablature than the more ancient Orders.

When the old Statuaries in Greece, such as Phidias, Praxiteles, and their Disciples, began to be celebrated for their Art, and the People grew fond of their Works, it is no wonder (for *honos alit artes*) they fell upon the Corinthian Capital, which in no After-age to this Time has been amended, though the French King, Lewis the fourteenth, proposed Rewards to such Artists as should find out a Gallick Order; therefore Callimachus, the old Architect and Inventor, (according to Vitruvius's Story of the Nurse and Basket) must still retain the Honour of it; for, neither will the Flower-de-luce of the French, nor the Palms of Villalpandus, in his imaginery Scheme of the Temple of Solomon, come up to the Grace of the old Form of the Corinthian Capital.

It seems very unaccountable, that the Generality of our late Architects dwell so much upon this ornamental, and so slightly pass over the geometrical, which is the most essential Part of Architecture. For Instance, can an Arch stand without Butment sufficient? If the Butment be more than enough, 'tis an idle Expence of Materials; if too little, it will fall; and so for any Vaulting: And yet no Author hath given a true & universal Rule for this, nor hath considered all the various Forms of Arches. The Rule given by the Authors for the Butment of Arches, is this: [See Fig. I.] Let A B C be the Arch, of which B is a third Part; extend the Line B C, and make C D equal to C B, and draw the Perpendicular C D F, this determines the Butment G F, (as they say) but wherefore? for add to the Bottom, as K L, the Arch then must certainly press more upon the higher Part than the lower; or if some additional Weight be added above the Arch, that must still press more than before this was added. So this Rule (if it were built upon any sure geometrical Theorem, as it is not) is neither true nor universal; and what is true will be shewn to be only determinable by the Doctrine of finding the Centers of Gravity in the Parts

242

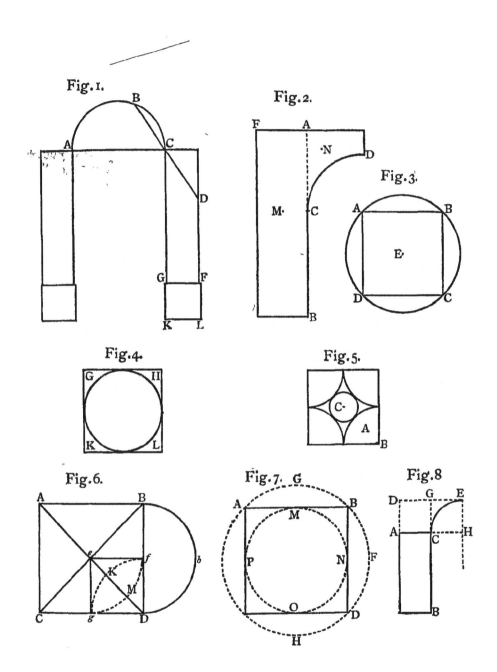

Fig. 1.

Fig. 2.

Fig. 3.

Fig. 4.

Fig. 5.

Fig. 6.

Fig. 7.

Fig. 8

of the proposed Design. In demonstrating this, I will not trouble the
Reader with nice geometrical Speculations, or Calculations, but by easy
Inductions; supposing he hath read Archimedes, or the modern Geometricians, who have purposely treated of Centers of Gravity; or at least,
that he will give Credit to those who have established all the Principles
of this Science by Demonstration unquestionable; so it will not be necessary to dive into the Rudiments.

Let a Stone be cut in this Form, F B a Parallelogram, C D a Semicircle   *Fig.*
added, A B a Perpendicular, M the Center of Gravity of F B, and N of
A C D, now if N be equiponderant to M on each Side the Perpendicular
A B, it is certain the whole Stone will stand immoveable upon the Basis
at B, although it be but half an Arch; add the like Stone on the opposite
Side, till the Horns meet in an entire Arch, so the Whole will stand as
well as the Halves. If any thing be added without M, that alters nothing,
only 'tis an useless Expence; but if any thing be added above N, that alters the Center of Gravity, which therefore must be provided for, by adding more Weight to M; and the same may be shewn in all kinds of Vaulting. So it appears that the Design, where there are Arcades, must be regulated by the Art of Staticks, or Invention of the Centers of Gravity,
and the duly poising all Parts to equiponderate; without which, a fine
Design will fail and prove abortive. Hence I conclude, that all Designs
must, in the first place, be brought to this Test, or rejected. I have examined some celebrated Works, as the Pantheon, and judge there is more
Butment than necessary, though it is flat and low, but I suppose the Architect provided it should stand against Earthquakes, as indeed it hath,
and will. The great Fabrick of St. Peter's if it had been followed as Bramante had designed it, would have been as durable; but the Butment of
the Cupola was not placed with Judgment. however, since it was hooped
with Iron, it is safe at present, and, without an Earthquake, for Ages to
come. Iron, at all Adventures, is a good Caution; but the Architect should
so poise his Work, as if it were not necessary.

The Free-masons were not very solicitous about this, because they used
Buttresses on the Outside of the Wall, which they extended as far as they
guessed would be sufficient; and they had yet a farther Help, by loading
the Buttress with a Pinnacle, to the Height of which they were not confined. The Romans never used Buttresses without, but rather within,
though they cut off a Part of the Arch, but not of the Vaulting that de-
pended on the Arch, as it appears in the Ailes of Dioclesian's Baths, and
in some respects also in the Templum Pacis.

The different Forms of Vaultings are necessary to be considered, either
as they were used by the Ancients, or the Moderns, whether Free-masons,
or Saracens. The Romans, though they sometimes used a Hemisphere,
where the Room was round; or Half-hemispheres, as in the Exedrae of
the Baths, or the Tribunes of Temples & Basilicae, yet generally they used

a plain cylindrical Vaulting, where the Walls were parallel; or Cross-vaulting, where two Cylinders intersect in Diagonals, as in the Templum Pacis; and in all the Theatres in the Passages under the Steps. The Moderns, whose Arches were not circular, but made of Sections of Circles, used commonly another Sort, where the Spandrils resting upon the Pillars, sprang every way round as their Arch rose. It is not easy to give a geometrical Definition, but by calling it a circular inverted Cone (A), resting upon its Apex (B); (C) the Middle, they filled up with Tracery-work, for which this Way gave them great Opportunity of divers Variations, which I need not insist on. Another Way, (which I cannot find used by the Ancients, but in the later eastern Empire, as appears at St. Sophia, and by that Example, in all the Mosques & Cloysters of the Dervises, and every where at present in the East) and of all others the most geometrical, is composed of Hemispheres, and their Sections only: and wheras a Sphere may be cut all manner of Ways, & that still into Circles, it may be accomodated to lie upon all Positions of the Pillars. Let E be a Cupola or Hemisphere, resting upon four Pillars A B C D, from whence arise the four Arches, to which the Sections, being Semicircles, must join on all Sides, whether A B be equal to B C or not. Cut the Hemisphere again horizontally, the Section will be an entire Circle, touching in the Keys of the Arches, and G H K L will be Spandrils resting upon the Pillars, yet still are Parts of the Hemisphere; and if the horizontal Circle be taken away, you may build upon that Circle an upright Wall, which may bear a Cupola again above, as is done at St. Sophia and St. Peter's, and at all the Churches at Rome. I question not but those at Constantinople had it from the Greeks before them, it is so natural, & is yet found in the present Seraglio, which was the episcopal Palace of old; the imperial Palace, whose Ruins still appear, being farther eastward. Now, because I have for just Reasons followed this way in the vaulting of the Church of St. Paul's, I think it proper to shew, that it is the lightest Manner, and requires less Butment than the Cross-vaulting, as well as that it is of an agreeable View; and, at the same time, I shall shew how the Centers of Gravity are to be computed. To shew that it requires less Butment than the diagonal Cross-vaulting, I will compare them both together, without any perplexed Demonstration, as follows—

It is evident that the Spandrils, or loading of the diagonal Cross-arches, where two cylindrical Vaults meet, must be an inverted Pyramid, whose Basis is a Parallelogram, with two Sides strait, and two circular; and wherever it be cut horizontally, it will be cut into like Parallelograms: now, in the other eastern Way of Vaulting by Hemispheres, the Spandrils are the Solids, which are left when a Hemisphere is taken out of a Half-cube; each of these also must be a sort of inverted Pyramid, whose Bases and Sides are circular, and wherever it is cut horizontally, it is cut into Pieces of Circles.

246

What these are that give the Butment of Arcades in the several Forms of Arches may be geometrically determined, for Example in the Roman Way of Cross-arches.

Let A B C D represent the whole Vaulting between four Pillars, then efg Fig. will represent the Quarter of this Vaulting resting upon D. Now, because the solid Half-cylinder C D is cut off by the Half-cylinder B D, it is evident the whole Cross-vault will be equal to one Half-cylinder, whose Diameter is B D, the Heighth f h, and the Length A B; and because D g e f is one fourth Part, this being deducted out of the Cube of f D, the Remainder (supposing it filled up to the Crown) e, is the Body we suppose at D, for the Butment, and the Parts of this circular inverted Pyramid will bear a Proportion with the Ordinates of the Quadrant, being the Radius less the Ordinates squared: so the Ordinates of the Pyramid are known; and by the known Methods the Centers of Gravity will be known of the whole or Part. As for the Gothick Vaulting, turn this Pyramid upon its Axis, and it will be a Conoide in the Whole, and in its Parts as the Circle to the Square circumscribed, and the Center will be given of the Whole and the Parts. Now, the third Way of Vaulting by Fig. Parts of Hemispheres may thus be considered. Let A B C D be four Pillars, and G F H be supposed the whole Hemisphere, before it be cut off by six Arches, and by the two horizontal Sections P O N, then is D O N one of the eight Spandrils; therefore the said Spandril is the Sphere less the Cube divided by 8, or the Hemisphere less half the Cube divided by 4, which is one Spandril, such as O N D. Now, let these several Spandrils in the Roman, the Gothick, or Saracen Way be compared together, (see Fig. VI.) g f D in the Roman, is the Basis of the Square (inverted Pyramid; g K D in the Gothick is but the Quadrant of a Circle inscribed, and g M K D but the Remainder to the Square; which being evidently the least and lightest, and the Center of Gravity nearest to D, I have therefore followed in the Vaultings of St. Paul's, and, with good Reason, preferred it above any other Way used by Architects. But none of these Vaultings are in Buildings thought necessary to be filled up to the Crowns of the Vaultings, but so high as to give Butment to the Arches above the Pillars, which Architects have determined, by Practice, to be a third Part of the Heighth of the Arch. It seems necessary to consider the proper Butment of cylindrical or strait Vaultings upon parallel Walls, or two Pillars only of some Breadth. In order to find this by Steps, we will consider an Arch abstracted from what may be laid upon it, or affixed to it. Let A B be a Body (the Heighth or Thickness doth not enter into this Fig. Consideration) upon the level Top, to lay the Body G E D, the Line G E being a Quadrant, D E a Tangent to it . . . .

[The rest is wanting.]

TRACT III.

THE Tyrian Order was the first Manner, which, in Greece, was refined into the Dorick Order, after the first Temple of that Order was built at Argos. but if we consider well the Dorick Order, we manifestly may trace the same to be but an Imitation in Stone, of what was usually done in Timber, in the long Porticoes they used to build in Cities, by which they tolerated the Heat of the Day, and conversed together: the Roofs of those Porticoes were framed after this Manner.

First, They laid the Timber, called Architrave, to join the Pillars in a Row, upon these they laid the Beams that joined the opposite Rows, then upon these they raised the Rafters, which Vitruvius calls Capreoli, which meeting in a Triangle, made the Roof to cast off Weather; the Rafters were fastened by two Tenons into the very Ends of the Beams, by sawing aslant into the Ends of them, not as we do by Mortises. Upon the Architrave they placed a Plank, the better to join the Ends of these Architraves together upon the Pillars; then the Pins (improperly called Guttæ) driven upwards, would not only fix the Capreoli to the Beams, but stay them from sliding upon the Architraves, and gage the opposite Architraves together, to keep a strait Range in the long Porticoes: & thus may be discerned the Reason of the Triglyphs, & of the whole Dorick Order; and these long Porticoes were the general Method of building Cities in the hot Climates.

When Alexander had determined to build Alexandria, and had settled the Place, he left Dimocrates his Architect to compleat the same, who drew a long Street with Porticoes on both Sides, from the Lake Maeotis to the Sea, and another cross it, that lead to Pelusium, then built Walls and large Towers, each capable to quarter five hundred Men; the noble Ruins of which remain at this Day; (a) then giving great Privileges to Egyptians and Jews, they soon filled the Quarters between the Porticoes with private and publick Buildings. Thus were Cities suddenly raised, and thus was Tadmor built, the Ruins of which shew nothing at present to Travellers, but incredible Numbers of Pillars of the Dorick Order, some yet standing, more broken, which were certainly the Remains of long Porticoes to shade the Streets. Now, how was Tarsus and Anchiala built in a Day? that is, I suppose, the Walls and Gates were set out in a Day, and this Way of setting out the principal Streets by Porticoes, occasioned that hundreds of Pillars, of all sorts, were to be bought at the Quarries ready made, where great Numbers of Artizans wrought for Sale

(a) *Near this City stands a Pillar, erected by one of the Ptolomys, (but vulgarly called Pompey's Pillar) the Shaft of which consists of one solid Stone of Granate 90 Feet high, and 38 in Compass.* [*Le Bruyn's Voyage, p.* 171.]

of what they raised; and this is the Reason why even at Rome the Scantlings are not always found conformable to the Rules, especially in sudden Works; as to instance in the Portico of the Pantheon, where are scarcely two Columns of the same Diameter; some of the Columns being six *Roman Palms and ten Inches [Pollices] in Diameter, others six Palms and five Inches. However, as it is a Coloss-work, and most wonderfully rich, consisting of sixteen huge Columns of the Corinthian Order, each Column being one solid Stone of oriental Granate, the Eye cannot readily discern any Disproportion. And thus in the great Pillar of London, the Heighth exceeding the due Proportion of the Order, one Module is imperceptible to the Eye.

See Monsieur Desgodetz

*The Roman Palm is nine inches English Measure

Pliny the younger, proposing to repair and enlarge, by the Addition of a Portico, an old Temple of Ceres, that stood upon his Estate in Tuscany, directs his Architect immediately to buy four Marble Columns, of any sort he pleased. By this Method of purchasing, at any time, Columns of all Orders and Proportions, ready formed at the Quarries, as Goods in a Shop, or Warehouse, the Ancients had an Advantage of erecting Porticoes (the stately Pride of the Roman Architecture) of any Grandeur, or Extent, in a very short Time, and without being over scrupulous in the Exactness of the Dimensions.

Plinii Epist. Lib. 9

TRACT IV.

AN Example of Tyrian Architecture we may collect from the Theatre, by the Fall of which, Sampson made so vast a Slaughter of the Philistines, by one Stretch of his wonderful Strength. In considering what this Fabrick must be, that could at one Pull be demolished, I conceive it an oval Amphitheatre, the Scene in the Middle, where a vast Roof of Cedarbeams resting round upon the Walls, centered all upon one short Architrave, that united two Cedar Pillars in the Middle; one Pillar would not be sufficient to unite the Ends of at least one hundred Beams that tended to the Center; therefore, I say, there must be a short Architrave resting upon two Pillars, upon which all the Beams tending to the Center of the Amphitheatre might be supported. Now, if Sampson, by his miraculous Strength pressing upon one of these Pillars, moved it from its Basis, the whole Roof must of necessity fall.

The most observable Monument of the Tyrian Style, and of great Antiquity, still remaining, is the Sepulchre of Absalom*: the Body of this Structure is square, faced on every Side with Pillars, which bear up an hemispherical Tholus solid; a large Architrave, Freeze, and Cornice lie upon the Pillars, which are larger in proportion to their Heighth, than what we now allow to the Tuscan Order; so likewise is the Entablature larger.

*Over against Jerusalem eastward in the Valley of Jehosaphat

249

This whole Composition, though above 30 Feet high, is all of one Stone, both Basis, Pillars, and Tholus, cut as it stood out of the adjacent Cliff of white Marble.

It is to be wished, some skilful Artist would give us the exact Dimensions to Inches, by which we might have a true Idea of the ancient Tyrian Manner; for, 'tis most probable Solomon employed the Tyrian Architects in his Temple, from his Correspondency with King Hiram; and from these Phoenicians I derive, as well the Arts, as the Letters of the Grecians, though it may be the Tyrians were Imitators of the Babylonians, and they of the Ægyptians.

Great Monarchs are ambitious to leave great Monuments behind them, and this occasions great Inventions in mechanick Arts.

What the Architecture was that Solomon used, we know but little of, though holy Writ hath given us the general Dimensions of the Temple, by which we may, in some measure, collect the Plan, but not of all the Courts.

Villalpandus hath made a fine romantick Piece, after the Corinthian Order, which, in that Age, was not used by any Nation; for the early Age used much grosser Pillars than the Dorick: in after Times, they began to refine from the Dorick, as in the Temple of Diana at Ephesus, (the united Work of all Asia) and at length improved into a slenderer Pillar, & leafy Capital of various Inventions, which was called Corinthian; so that if we run back to the Age of Solomon, we may with Reason believe they used the Tyrian Manner, as gross at least, if not more, than the Dorick, and that the Corinthian Manner of Villalpandus is mere Fancy.

Of the Temple of Diana at Ephesus, according to the Account of Pliny.

THE Temple of Diana at Ephesus, a most surprizing Example of the Grecian Magnificence, introduced the Ionick Order: it was two hundred and twenty Years in building, at the joint Expence of all the States of Asia, each Government contributing a Pillar. In this Structure the Capitals were first formed with Voluta's, and the Proportions changed from the Dorick to a slenderer Pillar. The Description in Pliny is short, and what no Authors, ancient or modern, seem sufficiently to explain. The Account, therefore, of this prodigious Fabrick, the first Instance of the Use of the Ionick Order, requires to be as fully and clearly illustrated, as the most authentick Aid we can have from Antiquity will allow.

The Length of the whole Temple was 425 Feet, the Breadth 220 Feet. The Pillars were in Number 127, each 60 Feet high. To make out this Number of Pillars, the Disposition must be Decastyle-dipteron, and the Columns thus reckoned; 40 in the Fronts, fore and aft, and 60 in the

Plan of the Temple of Diana at Ephesus with the Shrine.

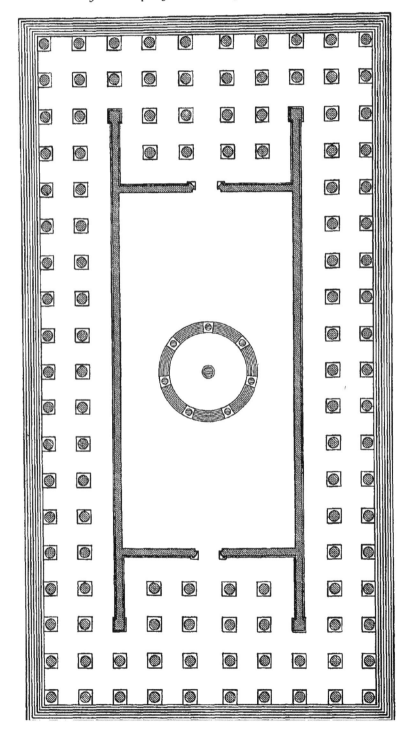

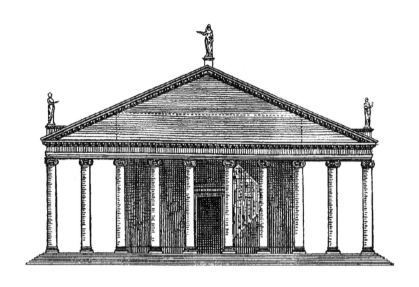

Front of the Temple of Diana at Ephesus.

The Shrine in the Temple.

The Ground Plan.

Ailes; so this Peribole makes just 100; besides these, are 16 in the Pronavi, & the 4 Antae, making in all 120. The Colonade affords no more, but the Tabernacle, or Shrine situated in the Middle of the Cella, wherein stood the Coloss Image of Diana Multimammea, contains seven, and answers the Number in Pliny.

This strange Idol, (which is represented in the Coins of Ephesus, & other Asiatick Cities) of as odd a Figure as any Indian Pagod, (the Remains of very ancient Superstition, before the Ionick Migration, which, it seems, the Greeks would still preserve, believing it fell out of Heaven, and sent by Jupiter) was made of Cedar; & the Cella had a flat Roofing of Cedar; for vaulted it could not well be, for want of Butment, being 115 Feet broad, and near as high, & 230 feet long. Thus was the Huntress placed, as it were, in a Grove of Marble Pillars.

All the ancient Idols were encircled with Groves; and this seems to be the Reason of the perpetual Adherence of all Architecture to this Form, and no other, of Colonades about Temples; meaning to represent the original Groves, as the Capitals, and all the Ornaments carry still the Figures of Leaves.

Diana Artemis was the Moon, her Solemnities were by Night: the nineteen Pillars in the Ailes represented her Period; the seven Pillars of the Chapel in the Middle of the Cella, the quarter of her menstrual Course. This, I suppose, was the ΝΑΪΣΚΟΣ we translate the Shrine of Diana; the Representation of which, 'tis supposed, and not of the whole Structure, the Silversmiths of Ephesus formed in Models for Sale to Strangers, "which brought no small Gain to the Craftsmen." In like manner, at this Day, small Models of Wood, garnished with Mother of Pearl, of the holy Sepulchre at Jerusalem, are usually made for Sale to Pilgrims and Foreigners. *Acts of the Apostles, c. xix. v. 24*

The Columns being 60 Feet high, the Diameter, according to Rule, must be 6 Feet 8 Inches, that is, a ninth Part; thus every Column would contain at least 110 Tun of Marble, besides Base and Capital, and the vast Stones of the Entablature, but more especially of the middle Intercolumn, which being wider than the rest, to open more Way for the Entrance, as usual in the Greek Temples, was about 22 Feet, and could not bear its own Weight, unless the Architrave and Freeze were both of one Stone, which together would be above 150 Tun; the setting of which (for it seems the Architect despaired) was miraculously attributed to the Goddess herself, as beyond the Reach of human Skill.

Thirty-six of the Columns were carved by Scopas, a famous Statuary of the School of Praxiteles; & the outward Walls of the Cella were adorned with Pictures, about the Time of Apelles.

Modern Travellers tell us, there are great Heaps of Ruins at this Day, & large Vaults, which probably were the Substructions of the Colonades.

I imagine the Ascent to it was easy, and not with many Steps, that the 'ΑΠΗ'ΝΗ 'ΙΕΡΑ', *Thensa Sacra*, might commodiously pass: this was a covered Wagon, drawn by two Mules, in which the Idol was placed, and carried through the Streets to the Circus, upon grand Solemnities.

[We often see this Temple represented upon Medals, with the Figure of Diana; but the Frontispiece, because of the small Room left in these sort of Monuments, is never to be seen there charged with more than eight Pillars, sometimes with six, with four, or only with two.]

Observations on the Temple of Peace, built by the Emperor Vespasian

*300 *Feet long,* 200 *Feet broad* †228 *Feet long,* 66 *Feet broad*

1. THE Greatness of this *Temple, the most magnificent of old Rome, is prodigious; it is longer than our †Westminster-hall, and the middle Nave only, besides the Ailes, is more than a seventh Part broader; in Heighth it exceeds the highest Cathedral now in the World.

2. The Walls are thin, where the Roof presses not; but admirably secured where the Weight lies, first, by the Piles behind the Pillars, which are of that Thickness backward, that they are sufficient Butment to the Arch of the Ailes: (this not being observed in the Gothick Cathedrals, the Vault of the Ailes resting against the Middle of the Pillars of the Nave, bend them inward; & therefore, in Westminster-abbey, they are cramped, in some Places, cross the Aile to the outward Wall, with vast Irons, to secure the Vault of the Aile from spreading.) Secondly, the Weight of the Roof above hath a mighty Butment from the slope Walls between the Windows, which answer to the Half-frontispieces of the Ailes; from whence the flying Buttresses of the Gothick Fabricks seem to have have taken their Original.

3. This Temple ascends to its vast Heighth each Way, by three Degrees; the mighty Nave is butted by the Ailes, and the Ailes by the Tribunals, and little Rooms without; which we may well suppose to be those Archives, wherein the Sibyll's Books, the Spoils of the Jewish Temple, and the Records of Rome, the most sacred for Antiquity, were kept.

4. Thus it rises to be equal in Heighth to half the whole Breadth between the side Tribunals; and a Line drawn from the Key of the Vault of the Nave, to the Key of the Arch of the Aile, determines the Breadth of the Aile: so that in the farthest Part you see always half the Vault of the Nave; which makes it seem free and spacious, containing more than an Acre of Ground in its Pavement, & might well contain an Assembly of 20,000 Persons; the common Use of it being a Hall of Justice, and for that Reason it was made very lightsome; whereas the consecrated Temples were generally very obscure.

252

5. I have admired the Greatness and Firmness of this Pile, but I cannot commend the Architect's Judgment for obscuring the majestick Stature of it with an humble Portico, & low Wings, which cause the visual Ray to cut off very much of the Height; so that in Perspective the Front will look exceeding broad and flat, and, to those that approach the Entrance, will seem as it were grafted upon the low Portico; though the Grace in the double Frontispiece and Acroteria, doth something make amends, distinguishing the mighty Breadth into several Parts.

6. But shall I accuse Antiquity for want of Skill in Opticks, of which every where it shews such admirable Proofs? since particularly here the Architect hath given great Testimony of it in the Contrivance of his Cornice, wherein he hath left out the Corona, or Hanging-square, by an unusual Example. The Corona seems an essential Part in all Cornices, as that which gives Denomination to the whole, and is necessary to the Beauty of a Cornice; because, by its Projecture, it shadows all the lower Members, receiving upon its plane Surface a terse Light from above; this gives the Eminence and distinct Appearance which we see in the Parts of a Cornice at distance; but the Artist here ingeniously apprehending that his Lights in this Fabrick stood Level with his Cornice, and therefore it would want the Effect for which it is used, and that the Hanging-face of it would be fore-shortened to nothing, to the Eye which beholds it from beneath, wisely left out this Member, which, if these optical Reasons did not prevail, would never have been used, since, of all Members, this is that which most loads the Cornice, and makes us, for want of Stones of such Vastness, & Money to move them, despair, in these Days, of coming near the Greatness of such a Pillar and Entablement as is here used, where the Projecture of the Cornice is near 5 Feet.

7. It was not therefore Unskilfulness in the Architect that made him chuse this flat kind of Aspect for his Temple, it was his Wit and Judgment. Each Deity had a peculiar Gesture, Face, and Dress hieroglyphically proper to it; as their Stories were but Morals involved: and not only their Altars and Sacrifices were mystical, but the very Forms of their Temples. No Language, no Poetry can so describe Peace, & the Effects of it in Men's Minds, as the Design of this Temple naturally paints it, without any Affectation of the Allegory. It is easy of Access, and open, carries an humble Front, but embraces wide, is luminous and pleasant, and content with an internal Greatness, despises an invidious Appearance of all that Heighth it might otherwise justly boast of, but rather fortifying itself on every Side, rests secure on a square and ample Basis.

8. I know very well the Criticks in Architecture will scarce allow this Temple to be accurate, doubting a Decay of the Art in the Time of Vespasian, who finished this Temple, but it was Claudius who began it, when we need not suspect Corruption. Nor need we scruple that the En-

tablement of the Columns is not continued, but that the Arches of the Ailes break higher than the Architraves; for these Arches resemble so many Tribunals, which are usually made in the Form of Niches, with the vaulted Head, adorned with a reticulate Work, but are not frequently

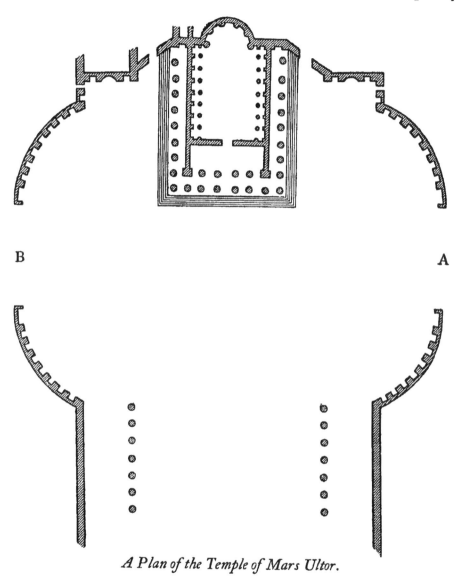

A Plan of the Temple of Mars Ultor.

set upon any Imposts, like the Arches of a Gate: but in the Inside of the best Works, the whole Entablement is seldom precisely kept; sometimes the Architrave is not expressed, as within the Portico of the Temple of Vesta at Tivoli; most frequently is the Freeze omitted, and always in the

254

Inside of the Porticoes of Temples is the Cornice omitted, unless you will call the Mouldings of the Listels a Cornice. Within the Portico of the Pantheon, over the Capitals, runs a compound Moulding of Architrave and Cornice combined in one, yet all together make not the due Bigness of the Cornice : in the open Air it is as well the Protection from Weather as the Crown of the Pile, and therefore not to be interrupted nor broken forward, without just Reason; within, where it is an Impediment, 'tis often omitted, as in this Case, by its great Projection, it would have obscured the Descent of the Light. The same Order of Arches without Imposts is observed throughout, in the Portico before the Temple, in the Windows of the Fronts, in the Passages through the Tribunals, in the Niches; & though we have not extant more Examples of the like, yet I am apt to believe the Basilicae, which were vaulted with Stone, followed this kind of Fabrick; and as it is vast, and well poised, so it is true, well proportioned, and beautiful, & was deservedly esteemed by the Romans themselves, as one of the most considerable Structures of Rome.

Observations on the Temple of Mars Ultor, built by Augustus; the Ruins of which are seen near the Torre de Conti, at Rome.

Templa feres, et me victore, vocaberis Ultor.

Ovid. Fast, L. 5.

I.

As studiously as the Aspect of the Temple of Peace was contrived in Allusion to Peace & its Attributes, so is this Temple of Mars appropriated to War: a strong and stately Temple shews itself forward ; and, that it might not lose any of its Bulk, a vast Wall of near 100 Feet high is placed behind it; (because as Vitruvius notes, Things appear less in the open Air) and though it be a single Wall, erected chiefly to add Glory to the Fabrick, and to muster up at once a terrible Front of Trophies & Statues, which stand here in double Ranks, yet an ingenious Use is made of it, to obscure two irregular Entrances, which come from a bending Street: and to accommodate itself as well to the Situation, as to give Firmness to the Wall but 5 Feet thick, it is built in various Flexures, (because a strait Wall is easier ruined by Tempests) : these Flexures give Opportunity to form two other Frontispieces, in which are seen Niches much greater than ordinary, and may be supposed to contain the Trophies.—Thus stands the Temple like the Phalanx, while the Walls represent the Wings of a Battalia.

Prospicit armipotens operis fastigia summi,
Et probat invictos summa tenere Deos.

255

Prospicit in foribus diversae tela figurae,
    Armaque terrarum milite victa suo.
Hinc videt Ænean oneratum pondere sacro,
    Et tot Iuleae nobilitatis avos.
Hinc videt Iliaden humeris ducis arma ferentem,
    Claraque dispositis acta subesse viris.
Spectat et Augusto praetextum nomine templum,
    Et visum, lecto Caesare, majus opus.
Digna gigantèis haec sunt delubra trophaeis, &c.

Ovid. Fast. L. 5.

II.

In this Court we have an Example of circular Walls; and certainly no Enclosure looks so gracefully as the circular: 'tis the Circle that equally bounds the Eye, and is every where uniform to itself; but being of itself perfect, is not easily joined to any other Area, and therefore seldom can be used. a Semicircle joining to an Oblong, as in the Tribunal at the End of this Temple, is a graceful Composition.

III.

If I might divine in Architecture, I would say, that the two Porticoes that made up the Court were directly opposite to the two Side-frontis-pieces, and that the Walls of the Court might continue on the other Side of a Street, leaving open the Passages A B ; and this might be the Reason that Palladio sought no farther for them, finding Foundations to end at A and B. By this means, those that walk in either Portico, will have the Prospect of a Side-frontispiece before them; those that walk in the Ante-temple, will have that goodly Tour of Statues diffused about them; and those that enter the Court, have an excellent Perspective of the Whole; those that come down from the Temple, will have the View of the Temple of Neptune, which, Palladio says, stood over-against it. The Romans guided themselves by Perspective in all their Fabricks; and why should not Perspective lead us back again to what was Roman ? If I presumed, 'twas Tully that animated me, who assures us, that Reason is the best Art of Divination.

I cannot omit commending the Fronts of the Porticoes: the Listels are invented to make Roofs, too narrow for a Vault, rise airy and light; the Ornaments between, consisting of a Trayle of Fillets continuing in square Angles, seem to me to have been borrowed from Beds of Gardens, and very properly would suit to that End.

IV.

The Cornice of the Wall advises us what Cornice to use in plainer Works; and gracefully is the Basis of the Columns made a continued Basis to the

256

whole Temple. But the Pillar with the Capital of Horses-heads, (supposed by Palladio to be one of the inward Ornaments) belongs not to this, but the other neighbouring Temple of Neptune; for, 'twas Neptune who was called Dominator Equorum. This, and the Temple of Peace, and the Pantheon, are those which Pliny particularly mentions among the most remarkable Works of Rome.

V.

The Squares in the Wall of the Cella opposite to the Inter-columnations, tell us how extremely the Ancients were addicted to square and geometrical Figures, the only natural Foundation of Beauty.

VI.

We find the most adorned Temples of the Corinthian Order have the Walls of the Cella channelled; so much they affected the Ostentation of great Stones, that where there were Joints, they would not seem to obscure them, that the Shafts of the Pillars might the better appear entire, and to give a darker Field behind them: the right Proportion of them is double in Length to their Breadth: the Appearance is best where there is much together.

Of the Sepulchre of Mausolus King of Caria.

THE Sepulchre of Mausolus is so well described by Pliny, that I have attempted to design it accordingly, and also very open, conformable to the Description in Martial.

Aere vacuo Pendentia Mausolèa.

And yet it wanted not the Solidity of the Dorick Order, which I rather call the Tyrian, as used in that Age.
The Skill of four famous Artists, Scopas, Briaxes, Timotheus, and Leochares, all of the School of Praxiteles, occasioned this Monument to be esteemed one of the seven Wonders of the World. These Architects living before the Time of Alexander, & before the Beginning of the Temple of Diana at Ephesus, (for Mausolus died, according to Pliny, in the second Year of the *hundredth Olympiad, which was before the Ionick *Aliter 106
Order was first in Use) I conclude this Work must be the exactest Form of the Dorick. It appeared from the City Halicarnassus to the Sea, that is, North and South, 64 Feet, and so much every way; for, each Artificer took his Side: and being hexastyle, contained in all 36 Pillars; that is to say, 20 for the four fronts, and 16 within, which supported the Pteron, (as Pliny calls it) in the Manner expressed in the Plan.

Pteron is an unusual Term, and not, I think, to be found in the Authors we have. Harduin, in his Notes on Pliny, and others consider the Word, as in the plural Number, Ptera, (ΠΤΕΡΑ') Alae, and think it imports the same Meaning as Pteromata in Vitruvius: *Muri duo in altitudinem consurgentes alarum instar.* But if we take it, as it is, in the singular Number, it cannot bear here that Signification; but may relate, as I conclude, to what we now call an Attick Order, and what rose above the Cornice, to have been called by this Term, in Greek Authors of Architecture, now lost.

This Pteron was here raised as high again as the Order below, to bear the triumphal Chariot of King Mausolus. The like the Romans did in their triumphal Arches; but in this, it is raised so high, because it stands upon a second Range of Columns within, and that the Chariot might be seen at Sea, for such was the Situation of Caria, where all the Ships that doubled this South-west Cape of Asia must keep the usual Tract to Rhodes. Supposing then in the Order, which Vitruvius calls Systyle, (where the Inter-column is double to the Diameter of the Column) if the Column is 4 Feet Diameter, and the Inter-column 8 Feet, the whole Façade will be 64 Feet. The Heighth of the Columns of $7\frac{1}{2}$ Diameter will be 30 Feet, and with the Dorick Entablature of a fourth Part of the Column, will make $37\frac{1}{2}$ Feet, which is just 25 Cubits; as Pliny makes the Heighth of the first Story · above the Cyma of the Cornice must be a Zocle of $2\frac{1}{2}$ Feet, for fixing the Statues, which will make in all 40 feet from the Floor. Upon the 16 inward Columns rose the Pteron, (the ancient Greek Term, as I have noted, for whatever was erected above the Cornice, which we now call an Attick Story) the Pilasters whereof, that they might be visible, were supported on a Substructure, or Pedestal, of 20 Feet, so elevated to be seen above the Statues of 7 Feet, & being 14 Feet behind the Cyma of the outward Columns, could not well be lower. The Pilasters then of the Pteron being 24 Feet, made with their Cornice 30 Feet more; and upon this the Stone Covering rising 24 Feet more, *in metae cacumen,* (as Pliny phrases it) made the whole Pteron 74 Feet. Now, if round about the lower Colonade is added an Ascent in Steps of 10 Feet, (the third of the Pillar) there will be to the Platform on the Top 124 Feet, upon which stood the triumphal Chariot of Mausolus, in Marble, 16 Feet high; so the whole Heighth will be 140 Feet, as by Pliny. The whole Circumference I have computed 416 Feet, which exceeds Pliny's by 5 Feet. The Bottom and Façade, Pliny reported as he was informed by Greek Measure, I have computed by just Proportions, which indeed are very fine. First, the Ascent in Heighth is a third Part of the Pillar; then the Column with the Architrave being 32, will be half the Façade 64, and the Face of the Pteron and Pedestal, will have the Appearance of being as high as broad over the Heads of the Statues. The Ascent of Steps up to the Platform is only the proper Stone Covering, the Stones being 12 Inches high, and 6 Inches saile. The Breadth at the lower Steps to the whole Heighth, is as 3 to 4, which is the Sides of Pythagorick rectangular Triangles. The Ordinance of the Whole falls out so wonderfully, and the Artists being contemporary with the School of Plato, I know not but they might have something to practise from thence, in this harmonick Disposition. I have joined the 16 inward Pillars into four Solids, and continued the same to the Top; opening also the middle Inter-column of the Pteron, that Solid may be upon Solid, and Void upon Void; so all is firm, yet airy. I have omitted Triglyphs in the Freeze, which I take to be the only Place for the Inscription, and Monuments were never without. I believe Triglyphs are proper for Porticoes chiefly, as in Imitation of Timber Entablatures. There might be round upon the first Order 20 Statues; 16 more below upon the Solids in Niches; and 12 in Niches of the Pteron, in all 48, each Statuary taking 12. Pythis, a fifth Artist, (says Pliny) made the Coloss Figure of Mausolus, in a Chariot drawn by four Horses.

The Plate of the above is omitted, on account of the Drawing being Imperfect.

FINIS.

HERE ENDS THE LIFE OF SIR CHRISTOPHER WREN, FIRST PUBLISHED IN 1750 AND NOW REPRINTED AT THE ESSEX HOUSE PRESS, CAMPDEN, GLOUCESTER-SHIRE, IN THE YEAR 1903. THE WORK HAS BEEN EDITED FROM THE ORIGINAL EDITION BY ERNEST J. ENTHOVEN AND CARRIED OUT UNDER THE SUPERVISION OF C. R. ASHBEE. THE TWENTY DRAWINGS OF WREN'S CHURCHES ARE BY E. H. NEW, & THE OTHER DESIGNS ARE REPRODUCED FROM THE 1750 EDITION.

ESSEX HOUSE, CAMPDEN, GLOS'

INDEX.

s 3

i

vii

Published in England by Edward Arnold,
37 Bedford Street, Strand; and in America
by Samuel Buckley & Co., 100 William
Street, New York.
250 copies.   This is No. 86

CPSIA information can be obtained at www.ICGtesting.com
Printed in the USA
BVOW09s1103260215

389469BV00010B/156/P